Indigenous in the City

Indigenous in the City

Contemporary Identities and Cultural Innovation

Edited by
Evelyn Peters and Chris Andersen

UBCPress · Vancouver · Toronto

21 20 19   5

Printed in Canada on FSC-certified ancient-forest-free paper
(100% post-consumer recycled) that is processed chlorine- and acid-free.

Library and Archives Canada Cataloguing in Publication

Indigenous in the city: contemporary identities and cultural innovation / edited by Evelyn Peters and Chris Andersen.

Includes bibliographical references and index.
Also issued in electronic format.
ISBN 978-0-7748-2464-4 (bound). – ISBN 978-0-7748-2465-1 (pbk.)

1. Indigenous peoples – Urban residence. 2. Native peoples – Urban residence – Canada. 3. Indigenous peoples – Ethnic identity. 4. Native peoples – Canada – Ethnic identity. I. Peters, Evelyn J. (Evelyn Joy). II. Andersen, Chris.

| E98.U72I54 2013 | 305.897 | C2013-900492-0 |

Canadä

UBC Press gratefully acknowledges the financial support for our publishing program of the Government of Canada (through the Canada Book Fund), the Canada Council for the Arts, and the British Columbia Arts Council.

This book has been published with the help of a grant from the Canadian Federation for the Humanities and Social Sciences, through the Awards to Scholarly Publications Program, using funds provided by the Social Sciences and Humanities Research Council of Canada.

UBC Press
The University of British Columbia
2029 West Mall
Vancouver, BC V6T 1Z2
www.ubcpress.ca

Contents

Acknowledgments

We are indebted to a number of individuals and institutions for their help in bringing *Indigenous in the City* into being. The book's foundation was laid at a 2009 workshop in Saskatoon, Saskatchewan, entitled "Indigenous Urbanization Internationally." Funding for the workshop from the Social Sciences and Humanities Research Council of Canada's Aid to Research Workshops Program is gratefully acknowledged, as is the assistance of several graduate students from the departments of geography and Native studies at the University of Saskatchewan, including Pamela Ouart, Tyler Fetch, and Nicholas Fraser. We are grateful to the participants of this workshop for working with us in producing the various chapters.

Darcy Cullen, acquisitions editor at UBC Press, skillfully guided us through the editorial stage. Holly Keller, production editor, was extremely helpful as she assisted in finalizing the volume. We appreciate the support and advice of the anonymous reviewers and the UBC Press Publications Board. Kristen Chew's copy-editing skills were invaluable, and we appreciate her patience with seemingly endless formatting challenges. The Department of Indian Affairs and the Office of the Federal Interlocutor for Métis and Non-Status Indians, Canada, also provided assistance with publications costs, and we thank them as well.

Indigenous in the City

Introduction

EVELYN PETERS AND CHRIS ANDERSEN

The historic development of discourses that defined Indigenous peoples and their cultures as incongruous with modern urban life means that urban areas exert particular influences on struggles over the meaning of Indigenous identities.[1] The association of "authentic" Indigenous identities with non-urban locations positions urban Indigenous cultures and lifeways as inauthentic and less legitimate. Cultural innovations in cities are often not viewed as central to the production of contemporary Indigeneity, and individuals who do not have ties to non-urban Indigenous communities can face challenges in defining and asserting Indigenous identities. While scholars have provided alternative frames for thinking about contemporary Indigenous identities, issues of continuity in the context of diversity and change remain especially fraught in cities.

Issues related to the nature of urban Indigenous identities are especially important in the context of growing numbers of Indigenous people living in urban areas. In 2007, for example, the United Nations Permanent Forum on Indigenous Issues, acknowledging the growing number and proportion of Indigenous people living in cities, devoted a half day to the discussion of urban Indigenous peoples and migration. At the same time, it called for the special rapporteur on the situation of human rights and fundamental freedoms of Indigenous peoples to undertake a study of the social and economic rights of Indigenous peoples living in cities. In many developed countries, most Indigenous people live in urban areas, yet relatively few researchers work in this area and little is known about Indigenous urbanization patterns and experiences. Indeed, contemporary perspectives on Indigenous realities rarely focus on life in major metropolitan centres; instead, scholarship tends to focus on Indigenous lifeways in rural/remote locations.

Despite the dominant scholarly emphasis on Indigenous cultures and communities in rural or remote areas, some research is beginning to position urban areas as spaces of Indigenous resilience and cultural innovation. Urban Indigenous peoples have resisted expectations of assimilation by building communities in and beyond urban areas and by reformulating Western institutions and practices to support their particular Indigenous identities. Indigeneity survives, adapts, and innovates in modern cities.

The focus of this volume is Indigenous negotiations of identity in urban areas. This introduction provides a context for the chapters that follow by summarizing the development of colonial discourses of difference, which defined Indigenous peoples, and their contemporary implications in urban areas. Following from this, we briefly summarize alternative perspectives for thinking about Indigenous urbanization and the continuing challenges regarding ways of thinking about urban Indigenous identities. Contributors to this volume provide new ways of thinking about urban Indigenous identities, and, more specifically, they collectively emphasize both the overarching issues and concerns common to urban Aboriginal residents *and* their distinctive (and, in many cases, city- and region-specific) histories. By way of conclusion, we summarize the contributions of individual chapters.

Colonial Discourses of Difference and Their Contemporary Implications

Racialization has been a powerful tool in European cultural processes. Scholarly explanations of the work racialization does argue that it legitimized the sense of superiority felt by imperial and White settler groups (Anderson 2000). But, in order to understand particular discursive formulations of social groups in European thought, it is important to go beyond the general accounts of how the racialization of social groups supported imperial processes. A collective emphasis on certain markers of difference is key to shaping the relationships and experiences of particular racialized groups. Different groups have been defined differently under varying circumstances and on the basis of different signifiers of difference (Brah 1992; Mawani 2009). People's negotiation and contestation of these definitions also produce varied results. There is a need to look at specific accounts in order to understand the effects of colonizing and counter-colonial discourses on different peoples (Thomas 1994).

The evolution of colonial discourses about Indigenous identities and urban space are significant in the production of difference in European thought. The massive migration of people in the late twentieth and early twenty-first centuries makes it less and less possible for cultural identities to be tied to particular places, assuming they ever really were (Appadurai 1988; Clifford 1988). The spread of media means that even people who stay in familiar and ancestral locations find that familiar links between places and identities have changed (Gupta and Ferguson 1992). Despite these ruptures, however, dominant interpretations maintain a stubborn association of "authentic" Indigenous identities with non-urban spaces, far from the metropolitan centres of society in distance and/or history. Feminist scholar Anne McClintock (1995, 40) describes mainstream perceptions of Indigenous cultures as existing in "anachronistic space ... prehistoric, atavistic and irrational, inherently out of place in the historical time of modernity." In the introduction to their recent edited collection *Indigenous Experience Today*, anthropologists Orin Starn and Marisol de la Cadena (2007, 7) note that, despite the attempts of a variety of scholars, politicians, and common people to influence representations of Indigenous peoples, this activism "did not undo the opposition between the 'primitive' and the 'civilized,' which remained pivotal in indigeneity's field of meaning, practices, and politics."

Mappings of space and identity that increasingly represented cities as areas in which Indigenous peoples and cultures were "out of place" emerged in Europe in the 1700s. Beginning in the late seventeenth century, European societies began to draw distinct boundaries between the human and the non-human. Humanness was associated with the (supposedly) distinctive capacity to alter nature (Anderson 2003). Contact with Aboriginal people, many of whom did not appear to Europeans to engage in nature-altering activities, positioned them close to the nature side of the culture/nature divide that emerged in Europe at that time and defined them as being at the "ground-zero of the human, sitting at its extreme and limit" (Anderson 2003, 427).

Economist Robert Meek (1976) argues that, beginning in the 1750s, European thinkers accepted the idea that all human societies naturally progressed through four stages, each associated with a distinct mode of subsistence (hunting, pastorage, agriculture, and commerce) and with particular values, behaviours, laws, government, and conceptions of property. By the 1780s, these ideas were an integral part of Enlightenment social thought.

Characterized as existing primarily within a subsistence animal-harvesting economy (evidence of agriculture among some groups was dismissed as random and not significant), and perceived as not possessing systems of property, commerce, or government, Indigenous peoples of the Americas provided a "plausible working hypothesis about the *first* stage" (67 [emphasis in original]). Geographer Kay Anderson (2000, 302) provides an additional context for colonial discourses that positioned Indigenous peoples in terms of their "proximity to 'nature,' infantility, eroticism, and absence of civilised manners."

As towns began to emerge during the settlement processes of Canada, the United States, Australia, and New Zealand, dichotomies such as primitivism/civilization and nature/culture were translated into distinct practices and spatial arrangements. Historian David Hamer's (1990, 11-12) review of the perceptions of contemporaries during the emergence of nineteenth-century frontier towns in these countries shows that, "although towns played a major role in policies of subjecting and controlling indigenous peoples[,] ... the Maori, the aborigines, and the North American Indians were increasingly treated as not 'belonging' in this European form of community." Established on sites used by Indigenous peoples, many early settlements originally had large Indigenous populations, continuously or seasonally. However, contemporary Europeans viewed towns as replacing one way of life (characterized by savagery and the wilderness) with another (characterized by progress and civilization). Consequently, Indigenous people were viewed as part of the wild nature of the wilderness, and their presence in urban centres soon came to be viewed as incongruous. Frequent removal of Indigenous residents from towns was rationalized in terms of the supposedly "corrupting and demoralizing effect on indigenous peoples of a civilization with which, as people at a more 'primitive' level of social development, they were not fitted to cope" (217).

A detailed history of the mechanisms through which Indigenous people in different countries were excluded from urban spaces has yet to be written. In Canada, these practices included the enforcement of private property regulations; relocation of reserves when cities grew around them; illegal surrenders of reserve lands near city boundaries; the pass system, which confined First Nations people to reserves on the Prairies; and the intense hostility many Aboriginal people faced when they visited urban areas (Blomley 2004; Stanger-Ross 2008; Wilson and Peters 2005). Scholars have documented similar processes in other countries (e.g., Edmonds 2010; Jacobs 1996). According to Hamer (1990, 12), fewer and fewer Indigenous people lived in towns, and "their presence in towns became more and more ghostly." The conceptual and physical removal of Indigenous people from urban spaces that accompanied colonial urbanization reinforced perceptions about the incompatibility of urban and Indigenous identities.

These ideas have retained much of their currency. In *The White Man's Indian*, an exploration of the history of US images of American Indians, historian Robert Berkhoffer (1979, 29-30) notes the lack of options for Indigenous people in the United States who were not living traditional subsistence lifestyles. He argues that, from non-Indigenous perspectives, American Indians who were neither assimilated nor "noble or wildly savage" were seen as "imperfect creatures, the degraded or reservation Indian." Postcolonial theorist Terry Goldie's (1989) survey of images of Indigenous peoples in the white literature of Canada, Australia, and New Zealand found that Indigenous cultures were presented as authentic only when they were practised in isolated areas, far from the metropolitan centres of society. Native studies scholar Renya Ramirez's (2007) summary of scholarship on American Indian urbanization finds that many writers consider movement to cities to be synonymous with assimilation. Historical anthropologist Nicholas Thomas (1994) notes that the celebration of primitivized Indigenous cultures marginalized urbanized members of these populations. Anderson (2000) argues that the contemporary identification of Indigenous people with "wild" nature, in opposition to significations of "the city" as the hallmark of "civilization," underlay the contrast between savagery and civilization that characterized protests against the establishment of Redfern, an Aboriginal housing development in central Sydney, Australia.

Alternative Views of Contemporary Indigenous Cultures

Many scholars and activists, Indigenous and non-Indigenous alike, have challenged the implications of the strand of early European thought that assumed that it was impossible for Indigenous peoples to participate in the modern world without abandoning their Indigenous cultures and identities (Starn and de la Cadena 2007). Sahlins's work in particular puts forward a powerful argument that points out that all societies need to construct their existence in relation to external circumstances, natural or social, that they cannot control. He argues that, for all societies, the "more or less self-conscious fabrication of culture in response to impervious outside 'pressures' is a normal process" (Sahlins 2000, 489), and he asks how people can respond to external circumstances other than by "devising on their own heritage, acting according to their own categories, logics, understandings?" As a result, "cultural continuity thus appears in and as the mode of cultural change. The innovations follow logically ... from the people's own principles of existence" (494). Recognizing the "terror that Western imperialism has inflicted," he nevertheless points out that Indigenous people create cultural coherence and continuity by assimilating influences from other cultures into a logic of their own (Sahlins 1999, iii). Sahlins also argues that Indigenous peoples worldwide engage with international commodities and relations in order to develop their own cultural orders and to create their own spaces in the world cultural order, a process that he terms the "indigenization of modernity" (x). Morgan (2005) makes a similar point in a context more specific to those we explore here, emphasizing that urban Indigenous Australian communities never merely mimic those of pre-existing non-Indigenous communities but, rather, "attach" themselves to these locales in ways powerfully embedded in their own traditions and histories while still producing novel and enduring social relations specific to the urban contexts in which they live.

Continuing Challenges in Defining Urban Indigenous Identities

Despite the useful interventions of Sahlins and other scholars and activists, contemporary formulations of what it means to be Indigenous continue to complicate interpretations of *urban* Indigenous experiences and identities. Indigenous people in UN forums have often challenged the need for a general definition of identity, arguing that seeking one "right" definition is both counterproductive and damaging (Niezen 2003, 19; United Nations General Assembly 2007). However, academics and policy makers have frequently found it necessary to produce definitions of the populations with which they are concerned. Despite apparent agreement that there are variations in how individuals and groups define themselves as Indigenous peoples, in these definitions a relationship or attachment to ancestral territories appears again and again as a marker of Indigenous peoples' identities.[2] Arguably, this emphasis affects contemporary interpretations of urban Indigenous experiences and identities.

For example, in a reflection on lessons learned in twentieth-century anthropology, Sahlins (1999, i) emphasizes that contemporary Indigenous peoples belie the "theoretical oppositions between tradition and change, Indigenous culture and modernity, townsmen and tribesmen." Challenging assumptions that urbanization resulted in detribalization, he refers to studies that show the complementarities and interdependence of Indigenous homelands and metropolitan "homes abroad" (xvii). Sahlins argues that these connections also hold for Indigenous people living in cities away from their traditional territories within national territories. Further, even though they live in cities, urban Indigenous people are "symbolically focussed on the homeland, whence its members derive their identity and their destiny" (xix). Sahlins notes that linkages of kinship take on new functions in the city as community and tribal affiliations organize migration patterns, the care of dependents, and the organization of urban housing and employment. In other words, the characteristics of urban Indigenous identities and communities continue to be shaped by connections to traditional territories and communities through circular migration or other linkages. What this looks like in practice is, of course, a matter of empirical investigation, which several of our contributors undertake.

Clifford's (2007) recent formulation resembles Sahlins's in its emphasis on a connection to an Indigenous homeland.[3] Arguing that a "feeling of connectedness to a homeland and to kin, a feeling of grounded people-hood" (205) is central to Indigenous peoples' identities, he recognizes that many Indigenous people, including those in cities, are not living in their ancestral territories. According to Clifford, the characteristics of tribal origins are reproduced in new locations for people living away from their tribal homelands: "The tribal home – its animals, plants, social gatherings, shared foods, ancestors, and spiritual powers – is not imagined from a distance. It is activated, 'practiced' ... made meaningful in a range of sites by seasoned rituals, social gatherings, visits, and subsistence activities" (213). Clifford recognizes that circular migration is not characteristic of all urban Indigenous residents: "Urban populations may or may not return to rural places for family gatherings, ceremonial events, dance festivals, subsistence activities, pow wows, and so forth. For some it is a matter of frequent visits; others go once a year, for summer or midwinter social activities; some return rarely or never" (205). However, the source of Indigenous identities, cultures, and social networks in the city, according to Clifford, is still the non-urban homeland.

It is noteworthy that Sahlins's and Clifford's formulations rest on a particular geography that itself assumes the dichotomy of Indigenous homelands and urban sites. They fail to recognize that most cities are located on sites traditionally used by Indigenous peoples, including settlements equivalent in size and complexity of organization to that of European cities at the time. The creation of Indigenous "homelands" outside of cities is in itself a

colonial invention. Moreover, for many Indigenous peoples, ancestral homelands are not contained by the small parcels of land found in reserves, reservations, and rural Māori and rural Australian Aboriginal settlements; rather,
they are the larger territories that include contemporary urban settlements.

The lived reality of many Indigenous people includes significant connections to ancestral homelands, close by or distant. For many this connection
includes frequent returns or circular migration. Moreover, an emphasis on
this relationship has supported Indigenous struggles for territory, resources, economic development, and recognition as distinct peoples. However, a
connection to Indigenous homelands as the primary marker of Indigenous
identities creates particular challenges for urban Indigenous communities
and identities. It also impedes the development of a scholarship that highlights the ways in which urban Indigenous people are reformulating Western
institutions and practices to support Indigenous cultures and identities so
that Indigenous people can continue to survive as distinct people(s) in contemporary societies.

Privileging a connection to ancestral homelands as a marker of Indigenous
identity reinforces dominant visions of Indigenous peoples as authentic
only if they live in remote areas and engage in "traditional" lifestyles or, conversely, only if we assume that these homelands are located exclusively in
such areas. When the source of Indigenous identities and the focus of lifeways is located outside the urban milieu, innovations that emerge from
interactions with non-Indigenous society are positioned as less central or
even as less "authentic" than transplanted tribal traditions. Different Indigenous relationships to ancestral lands are homogenized, and people who
may not possess these connections are excluded. In particular, an emphasis
on a connection to land and ancestral territories (as dominantly conflated
with rural or remote areas) generates questions about the identities of urban
Indigenous dwellers whose connection to tribal homelands may be sporadic, may not continue to exist, or may never have existed. It poses particular barriers for individuals with Indigenous and non-Indigenous ancestry
who may not have had a strong connection to traditional, rural Indigenous
communities (e.g., Lawrence 2004; Proulx 2006), and for many third- and
fourth-generation urban residents (e.g., Jackson 2001).

A focus on (non-urban) tribal homelands as the source of urban
Indigenous identities also ignores the ways many urban Indigenous people
have created organizations and communities across cultural and tribal
groupings. Clearly, participation in urban organizations that represent
Indigenous interests across tribal origins and participation in the life of

non-urban tribal communities are not mutually exclusive. Many urban Indigenous people have memberships in multiple social and political communities. However, the assumption that tribal societies organize and animate the social, economic, and political life of urban Indigenous people creates urban Indigenous groups and interests as necessarily fragmented and often in conflict with each other.

Viewing non-urban tribal communities as the primary influence on Indigenous peoples' lives in cities misses the complex ways in and through which Indigenous peoples selectively interact with urban societies to create meaningful lives in cities. Anthropologist Francesca Merlan's (2007) recent critique of the emphasis on an Aboriginal attachment to land as defining Aboriginal identities in Australia is relevant here. While she recognizes the achievements that have come about because of this emphasis, she also argues that this focus has "delayed recognition of the ways in which, now that Indigenous people are no longer chiefly dependent on land for their daily subsistence, their relations are recontextualized and revitalized to other aspects of their lives" (143). In other words, the preoccupation with an Indigenous relationship to land has deflected attention away from an understanding of the ways that many contemporary Indigenous people express their identities in contemporary urban settlements. Heather Howard and Craig Proulx (2011, 4-6) describe how urban Indigenous people who are unable to use expected identity markers, such as a traditional attachment to Aboriginal lands, choose from a variety of other resources to construct identities, including pan-Aboriginal cultures and activities in urban areas.

Scope of This Volume

Throughout the twentieth century, urban locales have been understood in the academy and more broadly as places where Indigenous culture goes to die. In contrast, this book demonstrates the resilience, creativity, and complexity of the urban Indigenous presence, both in Canada and internationally.

Indigenous in the City explores how Indigenous peoples in cities produce ways of living that move beyond marginalization and the everyday realities produced by the legacy of colonial dispossession. It is impossible to deny the reality of socio-economic and cultural challenges that many urban Indigenous people face in their everyday lives. They are overrepresented in statistics on poverty, unemployment, poor health, and low levels of formal education. Although initiatives to restore or preserve Indigenous languages have often emerged in cities, statistics show that urban Indigenous peoples are less likely to have an Indigenous language as their mother tongue than are rural residents (e.g., Norris 2011). Continued attention to these facets of Indigenous urbanization provides an important context for program and policy initiatives. However, the comparison of characteristics of Indigenous marginalization is not our focus.

While an analysis of the relationship between neoliberalism/globalization and Indigeneity in cities would produce some important insights into emerging forms of cultural identity, this is also beyond the scope of this book. Comaroff and Comaroff (2009) provide a critical analysis of the emerging characteristics of a relatively new emphasis on expressing cultural identity through the incorporation of ethnic groups and the commodification of cultural resources (social and natural). They argue that these forms of cultural identity emerge in the context of the neoliberal creation of entrepreneurial subjects, the increasing hegemony of intellectual property regimes, the globalization of the desire to express identity through consumption, and an increasing reliance on legal regulation through copyrights and patents. As Comaroff and Comaroff suggest, urban Indigenous peoples are largely excluded from these developments because of their lack of territory and their heterogeneity (12). An exploration of the connections between new forms of Indigenous identities in cities and the economic, political, and legal processes in contemporary societies would make an important contribution to our understanding, but we argue that, because the characteristics of urban Indignity are still poorly understood, such an analysis is premature. The focus in this book is on how cities create challenges and opportunities for the creation of new forms of Indigenous identities that can provide a baseline for further research.

We cannot begin to claim comprehensiveness in covering the diversity of Indigenous experiences across different geographies or for different social groups. Our focus is on four developed settler nations – Canada, the United States, Australia, and New Zealand. While there are historical differences in the relationships between settlers and Indigenous peoples in these countries, there are also commonalities rooted in histories of colonial dispossession and definitions of the relationship between urban and Indigenous identities. It is these commonalities that make this choice interesting. It remains for other researchers to explore similarities and differences in processes of urban Indigenous identity making in other countries. Even within the four settler nations that are the focus of *Indigenous in the City*, we cannot possibly cover all variations of city size, location, and cultural diversity. For example, most of the chapters focus on large cities (Auckland, Brisbane, Denver, Sydney). In Canada, however, the emphasis is on Prairie cities, which contain the largest urban Aboriginal populations. We recognize the diversity of Indigenous populations reflected in cultural differences and varied histories and relationships to the state; a single volume cannot hope to address all of these variations, especially over four separate countries. Urban experiences also differ according to social characteristics such as gender, age, and socio-economic status. Our focus is not on describing and comparing similarities and differences in the urban experiences of all of these groupings; instead, we hope to identify important themes and insights that have broader application and that generate new research and understanding.[4]

Indigenous in the City explores the complexity of urban Indigeneity in Canada and abroad and, more specifically, the co-constitutive influence of urban locales on the production of Indigenous identities. While government policy has long attempted to deal with the Indigenous presence in urban locales, scholarly research has generally positioned it as incompatible with authentic Indigeneity (which was to be found in rural/non-urban locales). Indeed, "urban" and "Indigenous" are still largely seen as incompatible. We position urban Indigenous identities not as incomplete or diminished vestiges of more authentic Indigenous locales (like those of rural areas) but, rather, as complex, highly vernacular engines of Indigenous cultural power. This book explores the various geographical and temporal contexts within which urban Indigeneity not only exists but also continues to evolve, in all its complexity – sometimes in concert with the broader and non-Indigenous urban community, sometimes in direct and even deliberate tension with it.

Chapter Summaries

The authors of the chapters in this volume pay close attention to the ways Indigenous people create their identities in the urban milieu and to how, in so doing, they "indigenize modernity." The chapters are grouped into four parts, each of which is organized by country: Canada, the United States, Australia, and New Zealand, respectively. Each part begins with an introduction to the institutional and policy context of Indigenous urbanization in the country under discussion, and the first chapter of each part provides a demographic overview of Indigenous identities and urbanization. The chapters that follow explore different aspects of urban Indigenous identities.

While the demographic overview chapters provide an overview of urbanization processes in each country, most of the subsequent chapters in each
section focus on particular cities.

In Chapter 1, Mary Jane Norris, Stewart Clatworthy, and Evelyn Peters
use census data to explore Aboriginal urbanization in Canada between 1951
and 2006. While migration to urban centres appeared to fuel the increased
proportion of the Aboriginal population living in cities in earlier decades, by
1986, migration to cities ceased to be the source of population increases;
instead, the main sources of increasing urbanization became changes in
self-identification. These data suggest that, in contrast to earlier expectations about the inevitability of Aboriginal assimilation in cities, Aboriginal
identities continue to be important in urban areas.

In Chapter 2, arguing that the experiences and characteristics of Aboriginal people in Canadian cities make their identities distinct from the
aggregate identity categories of Indian, Métis, and Inuit (as presented in the
Canadian census), Chris Andersen identifies elements that distinguish
urban Aboriginal identities from those found in northern, rural, and reserve
Aboriginal communities. Differences include Aboriginal social and economic marginalization in the urban population, a growing middle class,
and population diversity in terms of cultural origins and legal status. Because
of this, Andersen argues that programs and services often feel the need to be
"status blind." Despite a fragmented and ad hoc policy environment and
struggles over which Aboriginal political body represents them, urban Aboriginal institutions have emerged to provide community and services to
urban Aboriginal peoples. Informal networks and women's services play
important organizing roles in urban Aboriginal communities. They are beginning to frame some of the ways in which people can define their Aboriginality in urban contexts.

In Chapter 3, Yale Belanger's focus is on the 2002 Federal Court decision
in *Canada v. Misquadis*, which determined that urban Aboriginal political
organizations can represent urban Aboriginal interests. In handing down
this decision, the court defined off-reserve Aboriginal people as a group
of self-organized, self-determining, and distinct communities. The ruling
upset a number of commonly held assumptions about urban Aboriginal
populations, such as the notion that migrants to cities were leaving their
Aboriginal cultures; that Aboriginal identities were tied to rural communities; and that, as a result, urban Aboriginal communities were politically
fragmented. *Misquadis* recognizes the ability of urban Aboriginal peoples

to come together in an urban environment to create Indigenous political communities that are distinctive from Indigenous political communities on reserves and settlements.

In Chapter 4, Evelyn Peters and Carol Lafond explore First Nations peoples' innovations in creating inclusive urban spaces where First Nations cultures and identities can be practised and adapted to the demands of city life. In-depth interviews with First Nations people living in Saskatoon, Saskatchewan, highlight the challenges many First Nations residents face in appropriating urban spaces. These challenges include perceptions that traditional ceremonies are more appropriate in rural areas as well as every-day discrimination in the public spaces of streets, stores, and other institutions. First Nations resilience is apparent in the construction of spaces of cultural safety within the urban milieu, including the affirmation of First Nations cultures and identities in private home spaces, urban social networks, and the micro-spaces of shared language use.

In Chapter 5, Ron Laliberte describes some of the complex ways Métis identities are formulated in the Canadian Prairie city of Saskatoon, Saskatchewan. In western Canada, the Métis emerged as a distinct cultural and political Indigenous people during the middle and latter part of the nineteenth century. In other areas of Canada, though, the past century of legislative colonialism has meant that some individuals with European and First Nations ancestry have also begun to identify as Métis. Laliberte finds that both sources of self-identification are present in Saskatoon but that individuals from diverse backgrounds and locations formed a collective identity around the history and cultural traditions of the historic Métis. The emergence of a pan-Métis community in Saskatoon may provide a cultural home to Indigenous individuals who do not have strong ties to reserve or rural Métis communities and histories. In this way, urban Métis identities are dynamically constructed in response to the challenges and opportunities of urban life.

In Chapter 6, Pamela Ouart and the Saskatoon Indian and Métis Friendship Centre examine the changing focus in the design and delivery of programs and services at the Saskatoon Indian and Métis Friendship Centre (SIMFC) between 1968 and 1982. Created in an environment that assumed that Aboriginal cultures were irrelevant and even detrimental to successful Aboriginal adjustment to cities, friendship centres were initially expected to play a role only in referring migrants to mainstream services. Because of its assumed irrelevance, Aboriginal cultural heterogeneity was expected to disappear. Over the two and one-half decades described in this chapter, the SIMFC was able to play a part in designing and delivering programs and services, and it played an important role in creating in the city an Aboriginal community that recognized and accommodated cultural diversity.

In Chapter 7, Ryan Walker focuses on how urban Aboriginal identities are recognized in urban planning and policy making in two Canadian cities: Winnipeg and Saskatoon. He describes two examples of the failure to engage Aboriginal community perspectives in planning and policy making and two examples in which Aboriginal people helped to co-produce, with government officials, urban services and design. Walker argues that, by adding depth to local civic identities, recognizing and including Aboriginal cultures and viewpoints contributes to the construction of a postcolonial city. Aboriginal participation in decision making also recognizes self-government, a central characteristic of Aboriginal identities.

Moving to a US context, in Chapter 8, Matthew Snipp reminds us that contemporary American Indian urbanization processes reflect earlier *de*-urbanization, which involved removing American Indians from urban areas and resettling them in rural areas. Snipp highlights the complexity of urban identities that emerge in cities, in part because of the increasing number of multiracial American Indian and Native Alaskan residents. Multiracial origins are linked to heterogeneity in socio-economic status; individuals with American Indian/Native Alaskan and non-Indigenous ancestry tend to have higher socio-economic status than those who report only American Indian/Native Alaskan ancestry. All of these elements support the idea that American Indians and Native Alaskans are challenged to find new ways of being Indigenous in the city.

In Chapter 9, in her in-depth interviews with four generations of five American Indian families in Denver, Colorado, Nancy Lucero finds that there is a growing divergence in the conceptualization of Indian identities across the generations. Some of these differences are associated with the integration of biculturality into urban identities and with changing relationships with reservation communities. Lucero's research supports the idea that living in urban areas shapes the context of Indian identity creation but that urbanization is not synonymous with assimilation. Instead, dynamic and distinctly urban Indian identities emerge as younger generations in particular spend a large amount of time and mental and emotional energy reflecting on, maintaining, and defining their own American Indian cultural identities.

In Chapter 10, Jay Johnson makes a broadly allied argument in that he emphasizes the important role of the powwow in expressing a Native North

American identity in urban space. Johnson describes how tribally specific dance styles, regalia, face painting, and dance techniques help to connect urban Natives to distant tribal homelands. However, powwows have also developed intertribal dances as dancers borrow from each other and new dance styles evolve. He argues that, through tribally specific and intertribal dances, clothing, and techniques, the powwow creates "togetherness" from different segments of Native society. The urban powwow allows urban Natives to create temporary bounded Native places that help to preserve culture, community, and identity. And, again, they do so according to contexts and social relations that are often city-specific.

In Chapter 11, in an Australian context, John Taylor identifies three main factors contributing to Aboriginal urbanization: migration, natural increase, and increasing self-identification. Most of the recent growth of Australian urban Aboriginal populations reflects increases in the enumeration of already urban-based Aboriginal residents; migration to urban areas was not a major component of growth after 1976. Rather than breaking ties with communities of origin, Aboriginal people in Australia are building broader communities of association based on commonalities in Aboriginal life in both urban and rural locations. Taylor argues that, contrary to expectations, processes of urbanization have reinforced Aboriginal identities, as evidenced by the steady rise in Aboriginal urban numbers based on self-identification.

In Chapter 12, Kelly Greenop and Paul Memmott's case studies of Australian Indigenous peoples in Brisbane show, in rich, concrete detail, how Indigenous peoples are weaving together Indigenous and non-Indigenous cultures and traditions and shaping Indigenous identities in urban life. Greenop and Memmott focus on the evolution of contemporary identities through kinship relationships, socio-spatial behaviours, song and dance, and a variety of classical symbols used in place making within the intercultural space of urban Brisbane. In contrast to prevailing narratives about the cultural loss that is concomitant with urbanization, Greenop and Memmott describe new Indigenous identities and expressions that have roots in the past but that also reflect Indigenous peoples' interactions with non-Indigenous urban society. They see the city as a site for the production of varied and complex Indigenous identities.

In Chapter 13, George Morgan explores how four young Aboriginal men in Redfern, Sydney, define their Indigenous identities in relation to employment strategies based on narrowly constructed notions of cultural entrepreneurship. His analysis highlights the complexity of these urban identities, the ways they are refracted in and through individual histories, and how they are intertwined with other axes of identity such as gender, gang culture, class, and education. The resistant identities developed by these young men suggest that it will be difficult for them to take advantage of niche employment/small enterprise opportunities available to people from culturally diverse and, particularly, Aboriginal backgrounds.

In Chapter 14, Tahu Kukutai's examination of Māori urbanization patterns introduces the New Zealand-focused chapters. Kukutai questions whether binaries such as urban/rural and urban/tribal are relevant for understanding contemporary urban Māori realities. She suggests that spatial differences do exist with regard to age structure, socio-economic status, Māori language use, and *iwi* (tribal) identification. However, these variations are outweighed by differences within cities and across regions. While qualitative sources associate "authentic" Māori identities with rural areas and iwi affiliations, Kukutai cautions against the use of urban/rural or urban/tribal binaries and points to the need to use more nuanced frameworks if urban Māori structures and the richness of urban Māori realities are to be fully understood.

In Chapter 15, Brad Coombes looks at urban Māori identities through the lens of environmental justice research. Coombes's focus is the pollution of Otara Creek, a culturally important fishing resource for the pan-Māori community in Otara, South Auckland. The Māori community positioned its requests for assistance to rehabilitate the creek within the context of their treaty rights to and authority over resources. Environmental agencies have been ambivalent towards these efforts. Rejecting an explanation based on overt biases towards marginalized groups, Coombes argues that this response seems to reflect the view that these urban Māori are "out-of-place" migrants, whose treaty rights to resources are weaker than those held by Māori who remain in rural areas.

In Chapter 16, Brendan Hokowhitu addresses the constructed nature of Māori Indigeneity. When state urbanization programs failed to absorb urban Māori into dominant, Pākehā (white) culture, new cultural forms were produced. Coming into contact with resistance, civil rights, and decolonizing discourses from other places, urban Māori produced new radical Indigenous subjectivities that drastically complicated New Zealand's political landscape. According to Hokowhitu, the threat to the nation-state posed by radical urban Indigeneity overdetermines urban Māori subjects as a corrupt aberration. Through a series of legal decisions that excised urban Māori collectives from treaty claims, urban Māori subjectivities were increasingly defined as inauthentic forms of Indigeneity that, in turn, have been positioned in terms of a necro- (rather than bio-) political imperative. This has affected the forms of governance through which urban Māori are recognized collectively and has shaped their ability to operate within such confines.

Conclusion

The international focus of *Indigenous in the City*, its emphasis on urban Indigenous issues, and the participation of Indigenous scholars in writing about Indigenous urbanization means that it fills a unique niche. More than half of the authors are Indigenous, and the majority are leaders in their fields. While most researchers who focus on cultural groups in urban areas emphasize ethnic groups and immigrants, these authors and their research interests ensure that urban Indigenous peoples are not conflated with ethnic groups. While the difference of Indigenous peoples' from a white normativity means that, bureaucratically, they are often treated similarly to other ethnic groups, their histories, identities, rights, and entitlements, both nationally and internationally, differ from those of the latter (for additional discussion, see Andersen forthcoming; Sawchuk 1998[5]). A focus on urban Indigenous peoples adds an important and original dimension to theoretical frameworks for understanding urban cultural groups, increasing our understanding of the social, economic, and political dynamics of cities. While there are a few books on contemporary urban Indigenous communities and identities, most focus on one city, and there is no work available that addresses urban Indigenous identities in four countries. The interdisciplinary nature of this book provides readers with varying lenses through which to view Indigenous cultures and identities in urban areas. Together, these chapters make a unique contribution to our understanding of contemporary Indigenous identities in cities.

Notes

1 We capitalize the terms "Indigenous," "Native," and "Aboriginal," in keeping with the capitalization of words such as "European" and "American" when referring to specific peoples.
2 A survey of contemporary definitions of Indigenous identities is beyond the scope of this chapter, but a number of frequently referenced examples are listed here to support this point. The report to the UN Economic and Social Council of the Special Rapporteur, Mr. José Martinéz Cobo, notes that Indigenous people "are determined

to preserve, develop and transmit to future generations their ancestral territories and their ethnic identity" (Martinéz Cobo 1987, 29). The United Nations Permanent Forum on Indigenous Issues emphasizes that Indigenous peoples around the world have sought recognition of their identities, their ways of life, and their right to traditional lands, territories, and natural resources (United Nations Permanent Forum on Indigenous Issues n.d.). One of the characteristics of Indigenous peoples recognized by the World Bank (2005) is "collective attachment to geographically distinct habitats or ancestral territories in the project area and to the natural resources in these habitats and territories." On the basis of an overview of a variety of definitions of Indigenous peoples, Coates (2004, 14) suggests that some commonalities are "small size, attachment to the land, value system and culture rooted in the environment, commitment to a sustainable lifestyle, mobility, and cultural conservatism."

3 The situation of urban Indigenous peoples is not Clifford's or Sahlins's main focus, nor do they elaborate on this issue in other writing. However, despite their valuable critiques of dominant discourses about the inevitable disappearance of cultures in the modern world (see, for example, Clifford 1988), they reproduce assumptions about the relationship between Indigenous people and the city that impedes a fuller understanding of the ways contemporary Indigenous peoples are managing their relationships with urban places.

4 Some suggestions for additional reading on the four countries that are the focus of this book follow, with the caveat that many urban Indigenous experiences in these countries remain to be explored. Readers interested in urban Inuit identities in Canada are referred to Tomiak and Patrick (2010) and Patrick and Tomiak (2008). Ramirez (2007) provides an ethnographic account of urban Indigenous experiences in the US Silicon Valley and other US cities. Cowlishaw (2010) provides another perspective on Aboriginal people in Sydney, Australia. Marek's (2010) thesis explores aspects of Māori identity-making in Auckland.

5 Sawchuk (1998, 26-27) argues that, although "Canadian" Native leaders legitimately balk at the idea of being understood as "simply part of an ethnic group," the processes of identity reformation that have occurred in the last four decades constitute a specific instance of larger processes of ethnic identity negotiation. Thus, he coins the term "ethno-Aboriginality" to capture both the distinctiveness of Aboriginality and its conceptual links to the larger processes that shape ethnicity temporally.

References

Andersen, C. Forthcoming. Ethnic or categorical mobility: Challenging conventional demographic explanations of population growth. In *Aboriginal populations: social, demographic, and epidemiological dimensions*, ed. Frank Trovato and Anatole Romaniuc. Toronto: University of Toronto Press.

Anderson, K. 2000. "The beast within": Race, humanity, and animality. *Environment and Planning D: Society and Space* 18: 301-20.

−. 2003. White natures: Sydney's Royal Agricultural Show in post-humanist perspective. *Transactions of the Institute of British Geographers* 28: 422-41.

Appadurai, A. 1988. Place and voice in anthropological theory. *Cultural Anthropology* 3(1): 16-20.

Berkhoffer, R.F. 1979. *The white man's Indian: Images of the American Indian from Columbus to the present.* New York: Vintage.

Blomley, N. 2004. *Unsettling the city: Urban land and the politics of property.* New York: Routledge.

Brah, A. 1992. Difference, diversity and differentiation. In *"Race," culture and difference*, ed. James Donald and Ali Rattansi, 126-45. London: Sage.

Clifford, J. 1988. *The predicament of culture: Twentieth-century ethnography, literature, and art.* Cambridge, MA: Harvard University Press.

–. 2007. Variety of Indigenous experience: Diasporas, homelands, sovereignties. In *Indigenous experience today*, ed. O Starn and M. de la Cadena, 197-224. New York: Berg.

Coates, K.S. 2004. *A global history of Indigenous peoples: Struggle and survival.* New York: Palgrave Macmillan.

Comaroff, J.L., and J. Comaroff. 2009. *Ethnicity, Inc.* Chicago: University of Chicago Press.

Cowlishaw, G. 2010 *The city's outback.* Sydney: University of New South Wales Press.

Edmonds, P. 2010. *Urbanizing frontiers: Indigenous peoples and settlers in 19th-century Pacific Rim cities.* Vancouver: UBC Press.

Goldie, T. 1989. *Fear and temptation: The image of the Indigene in Canadian, Australian, and New Zealand literatures.* Montreal and Kingston: McGill-Queen's University Press.

Gupta, A., and J. Ferguson. 1992. Beyond "culture": Space, identity, and the politics of difference. *Cultural Anthropology* 7(1): 6-23.

Hamer, D. 1990. *New towns in the New World: Images and perceptions of the nineteenth-century urban frontier.* New York: Columbia University Press.

Howard, H.A., and C. Proulx, eds. 2011. *Aboriginal peoples in Canadian cities: Transformations and continuities.* Waterloo: Wilfrid Laurier University Press.

Jackson, D.D. 2001. "This hole in our heart": The urban-raised generation and the legacy of silence. In *American Indians and the urban experience*, ed. S. Lobo and K. Peters, 189-206. New York: Altimira.

Jacobs, J.M. 1996. *Edge of empire: Postcolonialism and the city.* New York: Routledge.

Lawrence, B. 2004. *"Real" Indians and others: Mixed-blood urban Native peoples and Indigenous nationhood.* Lincoln: University of Nebraska Press.

Marek, S.A. 2010. Māori geographies of Whakamanatanga. PhD diss., University of Hawai'i, Mānoa.

Martinéz Cobo, J.R. 1987. *Study of the problem of discrimination against Indigenous populations.* Vol. 5: *Conclusions, proposals and recommendations.* New York: United Nations.

Mawani, R. 2009. *Colonial proximities: Crossracial encounters and juridical truths in British Columbia, 1871-1921.* Vancouver: UBC Press.

McClintock, A. 1985. *Imperial Leather: Race, Gender and Sexuality in the Colonial Contest.* New York: Routledge.

Meek, R.L. 1976. *Social science and the ignoble savage.* Cambridge: Cambridge University Press.

Merlan, F. 2007. Indigeneity as relational identity: The construction of Australian land rights. In *Indigenous experience today*, ed. O. Starn, and M. de la Cadena, 125-50. New York: Berg.

Morgan, G. 2008. Aboriginal migration to Sydney since World War II. *Sydney Journal* 1(3): 75-82.

Neizen, R. 2003. *The origins of Indigenism: Human rights and the politics of identity.* Berkeley and Los Angeles: University of California Press.

Norris, M.J. 2011. Aboriginal languages in urban Canada: A decade in review, 1996-2006. *Aboriginal Policy Studies* 1(2): 4-67.

Patrick, D., and J. Tomiak. 2008. Language, culture and community among urban Inuit in Ottawa. *Études/Inuit/Studies* 32(1): 55-72.

Proulx, C. 2006. Aboriginal identification in North American cities. *Canadian Journal of Native Studies* 26(2): 405-39.

Ramirez, R.K. 2007. *Native hubs: Culture, community and belonging in Silicon Valley and beyond.* Durham, NC: Duke University Press.

Sahlins, M. 1999. What is anthropological enlightenment? Some lessons of the twentieth century. *Annual Review of Anthropology* 28: i-xxiii.

–. 2000. *Culture in practice: Selected essays.* New York: Zone.

Sawchuk, J. 1998. *The dynamics of Native politics: The Alberta Metis experience.* Saskatoon: Purich.

Stanger-Ross, J. 2008. Municipal colonialism in Vancouver: City planning and the conflict over Indian reserves, 1928-1950s. *Canadian Historical Review* 89(4): 543-80.

Starn, O., and M. de la Cadena, eds. 2007. *Indigenous experience today.* Berg: New York.

Thomas, N. 1994. *Colonialism's culture: Anthropology, travel and government.* Princeton, NJ: Princeton University Press.

Tomiak, J., and Patrick, D. 2010. Transnational migration and Indigeneity in Canada: A case study of urban Inuit. In *Indigenous cosmopolitans: Transnational and transcultural Indigeneity in the twenty-first century*, ed. M.C. Forte, 127-44. New York: Peter Lang Publishing.

United Nations General Assembly. 2007. *United Nations Declaration on the Rights of Indigenous Peoples.* A/RES/61/295, 13 September. http://www.un.org/.

United Nations Permanent Forum on Indigenous Issues. 2007. Report on the sixth session (14-25 May). Economic and Social Council. Official Records Supplement No. 23. E/2007/43. E/C.19/2007/12. http://daccess-ddsny.un.org/.

–. N.d. About UNPFII/History. http://www.un.org/.

Wilson, K., and E.J. Peters. 2005. "You can make a place for it": Remapping urban First Nations spaces of identity. *Society and Space* 23: 395-413.

World Bank. 2005. Operational manual, operational policies: Indigenous peoples, O.P. 4.10. http://wbln0018.worldbank.org/.

PART 1

Aboriginal Urbanization in Canada: Background

"ABORIGINAL," THE COLLECTIVE TERM most often used to refer to Indigenous peoples in Canada, obscures tremendous cultural, historical, and legal complexity. A basic dimension of this complexity has to do with the distinctive histories of the three groups defined by the Constitution Act, 1982: the North American Indians (often called "First Nations" in Canada); the Métis, who are descendents of Europeans and First Nations people, and who established a unique cultural and political regime in western Canada; and the northern Inuit peoples. Within these larger groupings there are many distinct cultures. Using linguistic groupings as one measure of cultural differences, there are more than fifty distinct language groups among First Nations peoples, there are several Inuktitut dialects among the Inuit, and the Métis speak a variety of First Nations languages as well as Michif, which evolved out of their First Nations and European ancestry (Royal Commission on Aboriginal Peoples 2006, 11).

In contrast to the views of First Nations people, who saw treaties as establishing mutually beneficial relationships between different nations, settler governments in Canada, like those of the United States and New Zealand, saw treaties as extinguishing land claims and other First Nations rights. While treaties were signed with many First Nations in Canada, large territories were omitted. Contemporary land claims have been negotiated in some of these areas; in other areas, settlements have not yet been achieved. Over six hundred reserves, areas set aside for First Nations communities, were established across Canada, some pursuant to treaties and others pursuant to provincial and federal policies in the absence of treaties. Most reserves were intentionally established away from urban areas, ostensibly to reduce contact between settlers and First Nations peoples but also to ensure that prime land was not under the control of First Nations governments. Under the Constitution Act, 1867, section 9(24), jurisdiction over "Indians and Lands reserved for Indians" is assigned exclusively to the federal government. This assignment of jurisdiction meant that the federal government provided services to First Nations people living on reserves through the Indian Affairs Branch. A variety of strategies for reducing reserve lands and the systematic underdevelopment of reserve economies over the decades have contributed to the poverty that accompanies many First Nations migrants to urban centres. Nevertheless, many reserves are valued by their members as familiar communities where First Nations cultures can be lived away from the racism that characterizes interaction in many cities. The Canadian federal government maintains that its responsibility for First Nations only affects reserve residents and that First Nations people in cities, for the most part, have no rights to special programs or services.

While there is some record of communities comprised of descendents of First Nations and Europeans in the Maritimes, Ontario, and Quebec, the most common emphasis in Métis history is on the development of the distinct Métis community, culture, and political organization that emerged in the Red River Settlement, in what is now the City of Winnipeg in Manitoba, between about 1810 and 1870. With the establishment of the Dominion of Canada in 1867, the people of the Red River Settlement negotiated the Manitoba Act, 1870, to clarify their rights and position in the new Canadian politics, establishing a self-governing Métis community. Within a decade, as settlers flooded into the settlement, most positions of political influence passed to newcomers. Facing settler hostility, and with Canada's failure to protect Métis land rights, much of the original Métis population dispersed to territories west. The Canadian government's strategy of addressing Métis land rights with scrip – certificates that entitled Métis people to claim money or land – was subject to widespread fraud and maladministration. As a result, most Métis people were dispossessed of their lands. While the Métis were identified as Aboriginal people in Canada's Constitution Act, 1982, both federal and provincial governments refuse to acknowledge responsibility for Métis people, and their Aboriginal rights are largely undefined.

No treaties were signed with Inuit populations, who can be found in the far North, in Labrador, northern Quebec, the Northwest Territories, and Yukon. The Canadian Supreme Court ruled in 1939 that the federal government had constitutional responsibility for the Inuit (Royal Commission on Aboriginal Peoples 1996, 454-59). In the absence of a demand for northern lands for settlement, no reserves were established and the government's policy was to encourage Inuit to remain on the land as self-sufficient hunters. By the 1950s the federal government had begun to define a program of socio-economic development that emphasized relocation to southern areas. At present, though, almost all Inuit live in the North, and only about 10 percent live in southern areas. Since 1975, a series of comprehensive claims negotiated between Inuit nations and the federal government has provided the basis for Inuit social and economic development.

In 1901, the Canadian census showed that only 5.1 percent of Aboriginal people lived in urban areas, and that percentage had increased only to 6.7 percent by 1951 (Kalbach 1987, 102). Urbanization began to increase in 1950 and climbed sharply in the 1970s and 1980s. Since then, the proportion of Aboriginal people living in cities has grown steadily. According to the 2006 census, 53.2 percent of Aboriginal people lived in urban areas (Peters 2010). The differing histories and legal status of these Aboriginal peoples means that their urbanization patterns vary. In 2006, approximately 45 percent of the 698,025 First Nations people counted in the census lived in urban areas. Of the 389,780 Métis individuals, approximately 70 percent lived in cities. The Inuit were the least urbanized, with about one-third of their population classified as urban dwellers. What these groups have in common, though, is the fact that their contemporary urbanization occurred in the context of their historic removal from urban settlements. While Aboriginal people were found in most early urban settlements, they were increasingly defined as out of place (Hamer 1990). A variety of mechanisms, ranging from individual Indian agent actions; police cooperation; and federal, provincial, and municipal policies and practices worked to confine First Nations peoples to reserves and to remove them from urban areas (Peters forthcoming). While there is relatively little documentation of Métis people and cities, available research suggests that Métis people were also unwelcome in urban space and were forced to settle on road allowances and fringe settlements outside the boundaries of urban areas (Campbell 1973; Davis 1965; Lagassé 1958).

The reasons behind urbanization processes are complex and vary to some extent between First Nations, Métis, and Inuit. As with American Indians, the experiences of First Nations and Métis veterans made them more prepared to participate in urban economy and society (Dosman 1972). The extension of provincial standards in health, social assistance, and education to reserves and rural areas in the mid-1900s supported population growth, increased contact with urban society, and generated higher expectations. As the poor conditions on reserves and in rural Métis communities came to public attention, policy makers looked to urbanization for at least a partial solution. The Hawthorne Report (1966-67), commissioned by the federal government to investigate and make recommendations concerning the conditions of First Nations peoples, viewed urbanization as a solution to poor socio-economic conditions in rural reserves. Following the US model, the Canadian Department of Indian Affairs organized a relocation program designed to assist First Nations to move to urban areas (Peters 2002). Legislation introduced in 1985 allowed women who had lost Indian status by marrying non-status men, and their children, to regain their status. Because most of these women chose or were forced to live off the reserve, the resulting increase in First Nations populations was concentrated in cities. Even without public policy intervention, rapid population growth on reserves and rural Métis communities made out-migration seem inevitable. The intense hostility Aboriginal migrants appear to have faced in small towns probably influenced a migration pattern that favoured larger cities (Peters 2002).

While Métis people were not identified separately in the 1951, 1961, and 1971 censuses, the available evidence suggests that a higher proportion of Métis than other Aboriginal groups lived in cities even in the 1940s and 1950s (Lagassé 1958). Very few Inuit took up permanent residence in government-established towns and villages until the 1950s, when a series of famines and epidemics throughout the Arctic made the Inuit more dependent on the government and church resources provided there. By 1961, 95 percent of the Inuit population lived in approximately fifty permanent villages, but the small size of many of these settlements meant that they did not meet the criteria of "urban" as defined in the Canadian census (Damas 2002). As a result, the Inuit have the lowest urbanization rates (about 38 percent) of Aboriginal groups in Canada. Land claims settlements and the resulting creation of employment in government administration and politics has had a significant effect on Inuit settlement in larger urban areas in the North (Searles 2010). In recent decades, urbanization (defined as the proportion of a group living in urban areas) has been fuelled more by changing responses to census categories than by migration to urban areas. Métis populations have been particularly affected by this process, leading to relatively high growth in urban Métis populations (Guimond, Robitaille, and Senécal 2009).

One feature of contemporary Canadian Aboriginal life in urban areas is the growing number of and role played by urban Aboriginal organizations. In larger cities, urban Aboriginal organizations are now found in a wide variety of policy sectors, including economic development; child, youth, family, and senior services; education; and justice; as well as in cultural fields (e.g., language, dance, theatre, music, and media). The failure of any level of government to claim responsibility for urban Aboriginal people contributes to a situation in which organizations rely on unstable and fragmented funding (Graham and Peters 2002). Similar to the emergence of "pan-tribal" urban organizations in US cities (Straus and Valentino 2001), small numbers and the nature of federal policies meant that early organizations in Canadian cities were "pan-Aboriginal"; in other words, they did not distinguish according to legal status or different Aboriginal cultures. As urban Aboriginal populations grew in many cities, the emphasis increasingly shifted away from pan-Aboriginal approaches to particular cultures and histories. Because many urban Aboriginal people desire to practise their particular cultures, pan-Aboriginal organizations often attempt to involve elders and representatives from a variety of nations in their programs and services. Nevertheless, urban Aboriginal people who live in cities in which their culture of origin is a minority often find that, in order to gain access to culturally specific services, they need to visit or return to their communities of origin (Wilson and Peters 2005).

While there are variations between cities, a comparison of socio-economic indicators for Aboriginal and non-Aboriginal people in Canada's largest cities suggests that urban Aboriginal people are economically marginalized in comparison to non-Aboriginal people (Peters 2010). Silver's (2006) interviews with twenty-six urban Aboriginal community leaders identified a number of factors affecting Aboriginal people's economic situation in urban areas, including the failure of both residential and non-residential schools to provide them with the skills required in urban employment and the often daily experience of racism, with the resulting destruction of self-esteem and identity. As with the American Indians described in LaGrand's (2002) study, the urbanization of Aboriginal people in Canada occurred at a time when urban economies increasingly required education and skill levels that relatively few Aboriginal people possessed. Nevertheless, there are some signs of an emerging urban Aboriginal middle class that further contributes to the diversity of urban Aboriginal communities (Silver 2006; Wotherspoon 2003).

There are some concerns among Canadian Aboriginal people about the possibility of maintaining "authentic" Aboriginal identities in urban areas (Searles 2010; Urban Aboriginal Task Force 2007). However, Newhouse (2000) maintains that urban Aboriginal people are reformulating Western institutions and practices to support Aboriginal cultures and identities so that they can survive as distinct people in contemporary urban areas. Andersen and Denis (2003, 385) argue that "we need to start thinking about urban [Native] communities as legitimate communities ... [I]t is long past the time when we can make the mistake of perceiving them as vestiges or missives of some more legitimate land-based community ... They are the source of new forms of culture, association and self-perception – both individual and collective – about what it means to be Aboriginal" (see also Howard and Proulx 2011).

References

Andersen, C., and C. Denis. 2003. Urban Natives and the nation: Before and after the Royal Commission on Aboriginal Peoples. *Canadian Review of Sociology and Anthropology* 40(4): 373-90.

Campbell, M. 1973. *Halfbreed.* Toronto: McClelland and Stewart.

Damas, D. 2002. *Arctic migrants/Arctic villagers.* Montreal and Kingston: McGill-Queen's University Press.

Davis, A.K. 1965. *Edging into mainstream: Urban Indians in Saskatchewan.* Bellingham: Western Washington State College.

Dosman, E.J. 1972. *Indians: The urban dilemma.* Toronto: McClelland and Stewart.

Graham, K.H., and E.J. Peters. 2002. *Aboriginal communities and urban sustainability*. CPRN Discussion Paper No F/27. Ottawa: Canadian Policy Research Networks.

Guimond E., N. Robitaille, and S. Senécal, 2009. Aboriginal people in Canadian cities: Why are they growing so fast? *Canadian Issues* Winter: 11-17.

Hamer, D. 1990. *New towns in the New World: Images and perceptions of the nineteenth-century urban frontier.* New York: Columbia University Press.

Hawthorn, H.B., ed. 1966-67. *A survey of the contemporary Indians of Canada: A report of economic, political and educational needs and policies.* Ottawa: Queen's Printer.

Howard, H.A., and C. Proulx, eds. 2011. *Aboriginal peoples in Canadian cities: Transformations and continuities.* Waterloo: Wilfrid Laurier University Press.

Kalbach, W.E. 1987. Growth and distribution of Canada's ethnic populations, 1871-1981. In *Ethnic Canada: Identities and inequalities,* ed. Leo Dreidger, 82-110. Toronto: Copp Clark Pitman.

Lagassé, J.H. 1958. *People of Indian ancestry: A social and economic study.* Winnipeg: Department of Agriculture and Immigration.

LaGrand, J.B. 2002. *Indian metropolis: Native Americans in Chicago, 1945-75.* Urbana: University of Indiana Press.

Newhouse, D.R. 2000. From the tribal to the modern: The development of modern Aboriginal societies. In *Expressions in Canadian Native studies,* ed. R.F. Laliberte et al., 395-409. Saskatoon: University of Saskatchewan Extension Press.

Peters, E.J. 2002. "Our city Indians": Negotiating the meaning of First Nations urbanization in Canada, 1945-1975. *Historical Geography* 30: 75-92.

–. 2010. Aboriginal people in Canadian cities. In *Canadian cities in transition: New directions in the twenty-first century,* ed. T. Bunting, P. Filion, and R. Walker, 4th ed., 375-90. Don Mills, ON: Oxford University Press.

Royal Commission on Aboriginal Peoples. 1996. *Looking forward, looking back.* Vol. 1. Ottawa: Minister of Supply and Services.

Searles, E. 2010. Placing identity: Town, land, and authenticity in Nunavut, Canada. *Acta Borealia* 27(2): 151-66.

Silver, J. 2006. *In their own voices: Building urban Aboriginal communities.* Halifax: Fernwood.

Straus, T., and D. Valentino. 2001. Retribalization in urban Indian communities. In *American Indians and the urban experience,* ed. S. Lobo and K. Peters, 5-94. Walnut Creek, CA: Alta Mira.

Urban Aboriginal Task Force. 2007. *Urban Aboriginal Task Force: Final report.* Toronto: Urban Aboriginal Task Force.

Wilson, K., and E.J. Peters. 2005. "You can make a place for it": Remapping urban First Nations spaces of identity. *Society and Space* 23: 395-413.

Wotherspoon, T. 2003. Prospects for a new middle class among urban Aboriginal peoples. In *Not strangers in these parts: Urban Aboriginal peoples,* ed. D. Newhouse and E.J. Peters, 147-66. Ottawa: Policy Research Initiative.

1

The Urbanization of Aboriginal Populations in Canada

A Half Century in Review

MARY JANE NORRIS, STEWART CLATWORTHY, AND EVELYN PETERS

As with Indigenous populations in other countries discussed in this volume, the available literature, as of 2011, suggests that Aboriginal migration to urban areas in Canada is a relatively recent phenomenon. Statistics indicate that, in 1901, only 5.1 percent of Aboriginal people lived in urban areas and that that percentage had increased to only 6.7 percent by 1951 (Kalbach 1987, 102). According to the 1951 census, few Aboriginal people resided in urban areas, and most cities had Aboriginal populations that numbered only in the hundreds. This situation had changed significantly by 2006, when the latest Canadian census indicated that slightly over half of Aboriginal people lived in cities.

There is a long historical tradition in Western thought that holds urban and Aboriginal cultures to be incompatible. The urbanization of the Aboriginal population in Canada has occurred despite these assumptions, and Aboriginal people in cities have continued to emphasize the import-ance of strong Aboriginal identities in urban life. This emphasis is reflected in contemporary demographic processes contributing to the growth in urban Aboriginal populations. In particular, census data demonstrate that, while the migration of Aboriginal people to cities may have fuelled the urbaniza-tion of Aboriginal populations at the outset of the study period, changing patterns of Aboriginal self-identification have come into play in more recent decades. The significance of various factors affecting Aboriginal population growth varies between different cities and for different subgroups of the Canadian Aboriginal population.

In this chapter, we use population and migration data from Canadian censuses to explore trends in Aboriginal urbanization and migration from 1951 to 2006, with a major focus on identifying the contributions of different factors, such as migration, natural increase, and changes in patterns of self-identification, in contributing to Aboriginal population growth. This approach provides a basis for evaluating earlier assumptions about the implications of urbanization for maintenance of Aboriginal identities.

Aboriginal Identities in Urban Areas

Ideas about the incompatibility of urban and Aboriginal cultures and identities, and how this affects Aboriginal success in urban life, are reflected in early academic work and policy making concerning Aboriginal urbanization in Canada (Anderson 1998; Berkhoffer 1979; Goldie 1989; see also Belanger, this volume). The decision by Aboriginal people to migrate to cities was interpreted by scholars and policy makers to mean that they had rejected their traditional cultures and wished to assimilate. In fact, a common theme in the literature on Aboriginal urbanization, even in the 1970s, was that Aboriginal culture presented a major barrier to successful adjustment to urban society (Nagler 1973). As a result, government organizations with a mandate to address the situation of urban Aboriginal residents emphasized integration (Peters 2002).

Some of these ideas continue to circulate. For example, Newhouse and Peters (2003, 247) argue that writing about Aboriginal people in Canada most often associates the idea of Aboriginal community with rural and reserve Aboriginal settlements. Presenters to the Royal Commission on Aboriginal Peoples' Round Table on Aboriginal Urban Issues talked about the challenges Aboriginal people face in urban areas because cities represented "an environment that is usually indifferent and often hostile to Aboriginal cultures" (Royal Commission on Aboriginal Peoples 1993, 2; see also Walker, this volume).

Increasingly, though, various researchers have challenged prevailing stereotypes that represent Aboriginal cultures and identities as out of place in urban environments. The Canadian Royal Commission on Aboriginal Peoples (1993) was important in refocusing these well-worn discourses. In a report summarizing the hearings the commission conducted with Aboriginal people in different parts of the country, we read:

> Crossing the city limits does not transform Aboriginal people into non-Aboriginal people; they go on being the particular kind of person they have always been – Cree, Dene, Mohawk, Haida. The intention of Aboriginal people to go on expressing their Aboriginal identity and to pass it on to their children was a consistent theme in presentations by urban Aboriginal people at the round table and in hearings across the country. (3)

In its final report, the commission argued that strong cultural identities were an important element of Aboriginal people's success in cities.

In his overview of contemporary Aboriginal issues in Canada, Wayne Warry (2007, 111) writes: "Perhaps the greatest myth about Aboriginal people is that when they move to the city, they abandon their culture." The Ontario Urban Aboriginal Task Force's (Urban Aboriginal Strategy 2007) interviews with almost two thousand Aboriginal people in Thunder Bay, Ottawa, Barrie-Midland-Orillia, Sudbury, and Kenora found that most participants (73 percent) stressed the importance of traditional Aboriginal cultures and that 80 percent participated in Aboriginal cultural activities. David Newhouse (2003, 251) argues that the rapid growth in recent decades of urban Aboriginal organizations reflects the "presence of urban Aboriginal people who are interested in creating and participating in healthy vibrant communities and who see the city as an opportunity and renewal rather than a place of cultural erosion" (see also Ouart, this volume). The 2010 Environics Institute's polling of more than two thousand Aboriginal people in Canada's major cities found that 88 percent were very proud to be First Nations, Métis, or Inuk and that an additional 13 percent were somewhat proud (Environics Institute 2010, 48).

Demographic factors affecting Aboriginal urbanization provide another lens through which to view the role of Aboriginal cultures and identities in contemporary urban environments.

Methods

This chapter summarizes patterns of Aboriginal urbanization in Canada between 1951 and 2006. An analysis of migration patterns in different periods demonstrates that movement from reserves and rural areas to cities played different roles in Aboriginal urbanization in different time periods.[1] Four mutually exclusive and exhaustive geographic areas were used to explore Aboriginal migration: Indian reserves and settlements, rural areas, large cities (urban census metropolitan areas [CMAs]), and small urban areas (non-census metropolitan areas [non-CMAs]). Large cities, or CMAs, are defined as urban areas with a minimum core population of 100,000. In 1951 and 1961, large urban areas were called census subdivisions (CSDs). Small cities, or non-CMAs, include all other urban areas. According to Statistics Canada (2010, 231), an urban area "has a population of at least 1,000 and no fewer than 400 persons per square kilometre." Rural areas comprise all remaining areas, including the undeveloped fringes of urban areas but excluding lands defined as Indian reserves and settlements. An analysis of the components of growth (natural increase, migration, and change in self-identification) for the 1996-2001 period helps to highlight the role of self-identification and the continuing importance of Aboriginal identities in urban areas.

An exploration of Aboriginal population data for ten large cities with Aboriginal populations of more than ten thousand in 2006 shows that urbanization processes varied in different cities. These cities include: Winnipeg, Edmonton, Vancouver, Calgary, Toronto, Saskatoon, Ottawa/Gatineau, Montreal, Regina, and Thunder Bay. While there are some smaller cities (e.g., Prince Albert, Saskatchewan) with Aboriginal populations of over ten thousand, census data are not available for earlier time periods so these cities were not part of the more detailed analysis. Comparing aspects of urbanization for First Nations and Métis populations highlights differences for different Aboriginal groups in different parts of the country. The focus is on First Nations and Métis people because Inuit populations are very small in most large cities.

A number of factors affect the comparability of data in different time periods. A major consideration is the fact that census definitions of Aboriginal populations vary for different censuses. The exclusion of the Métis in the 1951, 1961, and 1971 censuses affects estimates of Aboriginal population growth for these time periods. Aboriginal population counts from 1951 to 1981 are based on questions that asked individuals to identify their ethnic origins or ancestry. The 1981 census introduced the possibility of multiple ethnic origin responses and, as a result, estimates of growth for the 1971-81 period may be overstated. Concepts of Aboriginal based on multiple ethnic origins or ancestry continued to form the basis for Aboriginal population counts for the 1986 and 1991 censuses. New data based on whether individuals identified with an Aboriginal group were made available beginning in 1996. This "identity population" (i.e., those who identified as a North American Indian, Métis, or Inuit person) was considered to more accurately capture the meaning of what had been termed an Aboriginal "core population" (Goldmann and Siggner 1995, 20). Understandings of the meaning and significance of population categories also change over time (Andersen 2008). From one census to the next, boundaries for reserves, cities, and CMAs can change, as can their rural/urban classifications, including the definitions of urbanization. In fact, changes in the urbanization of Aboriginal people from one census to the next could be affected by the fact that areas previously classified as rural are classified as urban in the next census (Jette and Snider 2009). All of these elements mean that time series data are not directly comparable. Nevertheless, census data provide the best records available for exploring general trends and patterns.

Urbanization Patterns, 1951 to 2006

The proportion of the total Aboriginal population residing in urban areas in Canada has increased steadily from just 6.7 percent in 1951 to slightly more than 53 percent in 2006. By 2006, more than one-quarter (25.7 percent) of the Aboriginal population lived in the ten large cities that are the focus of more in-depth analysis (see Table 1.1).

Average annual growth rates of the urban Aboriginal populations are considerably higher than the average annual growth rates of the total Aboriginal

TABLE 1.1

Total Aboriginal population residing in all urban areas and in ten large cities, Canada, 1951-2006

Year	All urban areas		Ten large cities	
	Number	% of total Aboriginal population	Number	% of total Aboriginal population
1951	11,015	6.7	2,524	1.5
1961	28,382	12.9	5,571	2.5
1971	90,705	30.7	43,320	19.5
1981	192,680	40.0	90,325	18.8
1996	394,710	49.4	199,680	25.0
2001	494,010	50.6	244,500	25.0
2006	623,925	53.2	301,095	25.7

Sources: Peters (2002); Siggner and Costa (2005); Statistics Canada (2008).

TABLE 1.2
Average annual growth rate of total population and urban Aboriginal
population, Canada, 1951-2006

Period	Total population	Urban Aboriginal population	Aboriginal population in ten large cities
1951-61 (10-year average)	2.7	8.8	7.5
1961-71 (10-year average)	2.9	10.5	15.4
1971-81 (10-year average)	3.6	7.2	7.0
1981-96 (15-year average)	2.8	4.6	7.5
1996-2001 (5-year average)	3.0	4.5	4.0
2001-2006 (5-year average)	3.6	4.6	4.5

Sources: Peters (2002); Siggner and Costa (2005); Statistics Canada (2008).

population for each period (see Table 1.2). Growth rates of urban Aboriginal populations are relatively high at the beginning of these time periods, when urban Aboriginal populations are relatively small. The 1961 to 1971 period shows the greatest differences between the growth of urban Aboriginal populations and the growth of the total Aboriginal population, with differences decreasing after 1981. Growth rates in the ten large cities were very similar to those of the urban Aboriginal population overall. These comparisons indicate that the growth in urban Aboriginal populations is not a result of higher fertility rates in cities but, rather, represents other demographic forces.

The considerable growth of Aboriginal populations observed over the past half century in both urban areas in general and individual cities in particular brings us to the subject of the extent to which migration has contributed to urban growth. Migration data are not available for the entire Aboriginal population before 1986. Data for Registered Indians are available from 1966 to 1971, and from 1976 to 1981, and they provide some insights into the dynamics of urban growth for this population (Clatworthy and Norris 2007). For the periods 1966 to 1971 and 1976 to 1981, rural areas and smaller cities experienced a negative net outflow (i.e., more out-migrants than in-migrants) of Registered Indians. Large cities experienced a large positive inflow between 1966 and 1971 but a small negative outflow between 1976 and 1981. Net migration to reserves was positive for both of these periods. In other words, migration contributed to the growth of urban Registered Indian populations in the 1966 to 1971 period.

There are no data available that document migration patterns for other Aboriginal groups before 1986, and the absence of census counts for Métis people between 1951 and 1971 makes it difficult to pinpoint the dynamics of this population with any degree of accuracy. However, various documents from the 1950s and 1960s suggest that observers saw substantial increases in migration of both First Nations and Métis people for the first few decades following 1951. The emergence of friendship centres to assist with migrant adaptation to urban life and attempts by provincial governments to make the federal government responsible for programming for urban Aboriginal populations indicates growing numbers, with consequent growing demands on the public purse (Bostrom 1984; Peters 2002).

While migration appears to have been a major factor at the beginning of the period of Aboriginal urbanization, its impact on urbanization clearly diminished over later periods, with large urban areas experiencing either small net inflows or net outflows of migrants. Table 1.3 describes Aboriginal net migration levels (i.e., differences between in-migration and out-migration) by location of residence from 1986 to 2006. These data show that migration does not appear to be a major contributor to Aboriginal urbanization after 1986. Between 1986 and 2006, small cities consistently lost more migrants than they gained. Although there was a net inflow of migrants to large cities during the 1986-91 period (+5,540), it accounted for just 7 percent of the observed Aboriginal population growth (75,295) in urban areas between 1986 and 1991. Between 2001 and 2006, the net migration of +3,570 Aboriginal people to large cities represents only 4 percent of the observed growth (86,290) of the urban Aboriginal population in these cities.

An analysis of factors affecting population growth in the ten large cities with significant Aboriginal populations underscores the fact that migration is not a significant factor affecting contemporary Aboriginal urbanization in

TABLE 1.3

Net migration of the Aboriginal population by location, Canada, 1986-2006

Location	1986-91	1991-96	1996-2001	2001-6
Large cities	+5,540	−6,150	−430	+3,570
Small cities	−8,405	−6,270	−4,095	−135
Rural areas	−6,675	+205	−6,430	−13,350
Reserves	+9,504	+12,215	+10,995	+10,995

Source: Norris and Clatworthy (2011).

Canada. Population change can be attributed to three main components: natural increase (i.e., the excess of births over deaths), net migration (in-migrants minus out-migrants), and changes in patterns of self-identification. Guimond (2008, 2003) terms the latter "ethnic mobility," and it refers to changes in self-reporting of identity from one census to another.

Analyses of components of growth for the 2001-06 period have not been undertaken at the time of writing, but data available for the 1996-2001 period for the ten large cities show that natural increase accounted for one-third (33 percent) of the growth in the Aboriginal populations of the ten large cities and that net migration accounted for less than 1 percent (0.2 percent) of population growth. The largest factor influencing population growth was ethnic mobility. Some of this growth may be related to the fact that legislation passed in 1985 allowed for the reinstatement of First Nations people who, through a variety of processes, had lost their status. The reinstatement process has been stretched out over time. However, a large part of the increase comes from individuals who did not identify as Aboriginal in previous census years and who were now choosing to do so. Researchers have documented a similar phenomenon in the United States, identifying US ethnic politics that embraced ethnic pride and Indian activism (Nagel 1995) as contributing factors in that choice. Siggner (2003a) suggests that shifting attitudes towards Aboriginal peoples in Canada were important in changing patterns of self-identification during this time. US researchers suggest that urban residents were more likely to reclaim their Indian identities and that similar processes may be occurring in Canadian cities.

Demographic data, then, offer a unique perspective on earlier assumptions about the desirability and inevitability of the assimilation of Aboriginal populations into mainstream urban cultures. While these data do not provide information about ways that individuals and communities express these identities (see, for example, Lucero; Johnson; Greenop and Memmott; and Morgan, this volume), they do indicate that urban Aboriginal people continue to view Aboriginal identities as important facets of how they describe themselves in the census.

Differences by Urban Areas

The histories and components of growth vary significantly for different cities over the past fifty years. Table 1.4 shows the 1951 and 2006 Aboriginal population estimates for the ten urban areas with large Aboriginal populations in 2006, and it lists cities in order of their 2006 Aboriginal population

TABLE 1.4

Aboriginal population in ten cities, Canada, 1951 and 2006

City	1951	2006	% of urban population, 2006
Winnipeg	210	68,385	10.0
Edmonton	616	52,100	5.1
Vancouver	239	40,310	1.9
Calgary	62	26,575	2.5
Toronto	805	26,575	0.5
Saskatoon	48	21,535	9.3
Ottawa-Gatineau (Hull)	70	20,590	1.8
Montreal	296	18,865	0.5
Regina	160	17,105	8.9
Thunder Bay	n/a	10,055	8.2
Total	2,506	301,095	

Sources: Statistics Canada (1974, 2008).

size (this order is retained in subsequent tables). The 2006 Aboriginal populations of these urban areas range in size from slightly more than ten thousand for Thunder Bay to 68,400 for Winnipeg. Aboriginal urbanization has resulted in relatively large urban Aboriginal communities in three cities – Winnipeg, Edmonton, and Vancouver. In four cities – Winnipeg, Saskatoon, Regina, and Thunder Bay – urban Aboriginal populations comprise almost one-tenth of city populations, making them the single largest cultural group in many of those urban areas. The total Aboriginal population of these ten urban areas has increased dramatically, up over a hundredfold from just 2,506 in 1951 to some 301,000 by 2006.

Table 1.5 describes average annual growth rates for ten large cities with Aboriginal populations greater than ten thousand in 2006. All cities experienced high levels of growth between 1961 and 1971, the period of greatest growth for most cities. Two distinct patterns of growth can be seen in this comparison. The Prairie cities of Winnipeg, Calgary, Saskatoon, and Regina experienced high levels of growth (between 9.1 and 21.1 percent) for every time period from 1951 to 1981. Aboriginal populations continued to grow after 1981 but at smaller annual rates. Edmonton's and Vancouver's patterns are similar except for their lower growth rate in the 1951-61 periods. The other main pattern is exhibited by the large cities of Montreal, Ottawa, and Toronto, where growth rates are generally low compared to other cities but

TABLE 1.5
Average annual growth rates for ten large cities, Canada, 1951-2006

City	1951-61	1961-71	1971-81	1981-96	1996-2001	2001-6
Winnipeg	17.8	16.4	9.7	7.2	4.0	4.2
Edmonton	4.9	15.7	10.2	6.1	4.5	4.9
Vancouver	8.3	18.9	8.3	4.8	3.4	1.8
Calgary	18.3	21.1	12.4	5.3	7.6	3.9
Toronto	4.0	9.6	7.5	1.4	4.7	5.5
Saskatoon	15.7	17.9	14.7	9.4	4.6	1.2
Ottawa-Gatineau (Hull)	9.9	13.6	11.9	7.4	3.0	8.8
Montreal	5.5	20.3	4.7	1.6	2.2	10.0
Regina	12.9	18.2	9.1	5.2	2.9	1.7
Thunder Bay	n/a	10.4	11.8	6.1	2.3	4.2
Average	10.8	16.2	10.0	5.5	3.9	4.6

Source: Norris and Clatworthy (2011).

with increases in the 2001-06 period. Thunder Bay's growth rates peaked in the 1971-81 period and then declined, but they increased again in the period between 2001 and 2006.

Table 1.6 shows the components of urban Aboriginal population growth (natural increase, net migration, and change in self-identification) for each of the ten cities between 1996 and 2001. These statistics show that the significance of different components in explaining the growth of urban Aboriginal populations varies widely from city to city. While change in self-identification is an important factor for some cities, natural increase appears to be a relatively major contributor to Aboriginal population growth in other cities. Migration made the largest contribution to Aboriginal population growth in Thunder Bay, making up 24.8 percent of the Aboriginal population increase between 1996 and 2001. Natural increase accounted for the largest share of growth in the Prairie cities of Winnipeg (47 percent), Saskatoon (55 percent), and (notably) Regina (80 percent) as well as in the Ontario city of Thunder Bay (63 percent). In Vancouver, Toronto, and Montreal, almost all of the population increase between 1991 and 2006 came from changes in patterns of self-identification. Even in cities where natural increase was the most important component of population growth, changes in self-identification were significant. Only in Thunder Bay did changes in

TABLE 1.6

Components of Aboriginal population growth, large cities, Canada, 1996-2001

City	Natural increase (%)	Net migration (%)	Change in identification (%)
Winnipeg	46.6	5.6	47.8
Edmonton	30.1	11.8	58.1
Vancouver	22.8	-14.2	91.4
Calgary	25.1	13.2	61.7
Toronto	23.6	-28.3	104.7
Saskatoon	54.4	9.9	35.6
Ottawa-Hull	14.8	6.3	78.9
Montreal	20.4	-5.8	85.4
Regina	80.0	-31.7	51.7
Thunder Bay	62.6	24.8	12.6

Source: Norris and Clatworthy (2011).

self-identification account for less than one-third (12.6 percent) of the population increase during this period.

This analysis suggests that not only has urban Aboriginal population growth occurred at varying rates among the highlighted urban areas but also that growth among these urban areas has resulted from different processes.

There is almost no material available that focuses individually on different cities in Canada and their unique histories of Aboriginal urbanization. However, patterns appear to vary considerably, with the implication that urban Aboriginal communities in different cities will have dissimilar characteristics, needs, and capacities. Cities with high rates of migration in early time periods covered in this chapter might have more second- or third-generation residents, with implications for how they express and practise their urban identities (see Lucrero, this volume). Where these urban Aboriginal populations are large, it is likely that there would be greater "institutional completeness" (Breton 1964), with organizations that address a large number of policy areas. Cities where in-migration still contributes significantly to urban Aboriginal population growth will continue to require services that were created historically to assist migrants to adapt to urban life.

Where changes in self-identification contribute significantly to urban growth, the needs of urban Aboriginal populations may be configured differently. Available data suggest that the populations that began to identify as

Aboriginal in recent censuses are more likely to have higher education (Siggner 2003b). In other words, this population may have a higher socio-economic status than the rest of the urban Aboriginal population. While very little research is available on the urban Aboriginal middle class, focus groups with middle-class Toronto Aboriginal residents indicated that they did not make use of Aboriginal organizations because these were mostly service organizations focusing on a variety of social problems. Instead, they emphasized the need for Aboriginal language and cultural programs that addressed their aspirations (Urban Aboriginal Strategy 2005). Urban areas where Aboriginal population growth is largely attributed to changing patterns of self-identification may have needs that are not captured by programs and services designed to meet the needs of the migrating population represented during earlier periods of Aboriginal urbanization.

Differences between Urban First Nations and Métis Urbanization

Patterns and components of urbanization are also different for First Nations and Métis populations. The 2006 census shows that Métis people are more highly urbanized than First Nations people, with 69.4 percent of the Métis population living in cities, compared to 44.7 percent of First Nations people. Scattered studies in the western provinces suggest that, historically, Métis may have been more likely to live in or near urban settlements than First Nations people (Davis 1965; Lagassé 1958). The failure to identify Métis in the 1951, 1961, and 1971 censuses means that it is difficult to reconstruct early patterns of Métis urbanization.

Table 1.7 describes recent urbanization patterns for these two populations. While the size of both populations increased substantially, Métis populations grew much more rapidly than First Nations populations, almost doubling in the decade between 1996 and 2001. A components of growth analysis is not available for First Nations and Métis populations, but Table 1.7 suggests that migration was not a major contributor to population shifts. Analysis by Guimond, Robitaille, and Sénecal (2009) suggests that changes in patterns of self-identification have contributed substantially to the growth of urban Aboriginal populations and that these processes have been particularly significant for urban Métis:

Estimates produced for the 1986-2001 period show that nearly 42,000 Indians living off-reserve in 2001 did not self-report as Indian in 1986, or one off-reserve Indian in eight (13%), and over 101,000 Métis in 2001 did

TABLE 1.7

First Nations and Métis urbanization, Canada, 1996-2006

	Population size		% increase 1996-2006	Net migration 1996-2006
	1996	2006		
First Nations	211,615	312,020	47.4	160
Métis	136,960	270,510	97.5	-2110

Sources: Clatworthy and Norris (2007; forthcoming, 2013); Norris and Clatworthy (2011).

TABLE 1.8

First Nations and Métis population growth in large cities, Canada, 1996-2006

City	% of total Aboriginal population, 1996		Absolute population increase, 1996-2006	% of total Aboriginal population, 2006	
	First Nations	Métis	First Nations: Métis	First Nations	Métis
Winnipeg	44.2	53.1	1:2.9	38.5	61.0
Edmonton	46.6	49.3	1:1.6	44.2	54.6
Vancouver	68.3	26.2	1:2.4	60.6	38.9
Calgary	49.0	45.6	1:2.2	42.0	57.0
Toronto	77.1	16.7	1:0.9	68.6	30.1
Saskatoon	57.1	39.6	1:1.3	54.3	44.6
Ottawa-Gatineau (Hull)	61.0	29.1	1:1.2	55.3	41.0
Montreal	56.2	33.2	1:0.6	57.4	34.1
Regina	60.8	34.1	1:1.9	56.8	43.0
Thunder Bay	78.2	16.0	1:0.7	73.8	23.6

Source: Statistics Canadá (2008).

not report as Métis in 1986, which amounts to four Métis in ten enumerated in 2001 (Guimond 2009). Moreover analysis reveals that over 90 percent of ethnic transfers took place in urban areas (15-16).

These patterns are not uniform across large cities, and patterns of First Nations and Métis population growth have some interesting implications for local Aboriginal politics. Table 1.8 shows that, in 1996, First Nations comprised the majority of the Aboriginal population in seven out of ten cities. In eastern cities (i.e., Thunder Bay, Toronto, Montreal, and Ottawa) and in Vancouver, the First Nations majority was substantial (between 61 and 78.2 percent). In Calgary, the two populations comprised about equal proportions of the urban Aboriginal community. Métis were in the majority only in the historic fur trade cities of Edmonton and Winnipeg.

Métis population increases between 1996 and 2006 outstripped First Nations population increases in seven of the ten cities under discussion. In Vancouver, Calgary, and Regina, the increase in Métis populations was almost double or more than those of First Nations; and, in Winnipeg, Métis population growth was almost three times that of First Nations population growth. In Toronto, population increases were about the same for First Nations and Métis people; in Montreal and Thunder Bay, First Nations increases were quite a bit larger than Métis increases.

By 2006, as a result of these changes, Métis populations represented a much more significant proportion of urban Aboriginal populations, particularly in the Prairie provinces, the traditional homeland of the Métis Nation. In Winnipeg, Edmonton, and Calgary, Métis comprised the majority of the urban Aboriginal population, while they represented over 40 percent of the population in Regina and Saskatoon. Vancouver, Ottawa, Toronto, and Thunder Bay also saw a substantial increase in the proportion of urban populations that were Métis, although Métis populations were still the minority in these cities. Proportions remained similar despite population increases only in Montreal. The implications of these shifts include a greater demand for Métis-specific services and organizations, and increased capacity within the urban Métis population to provide programs and services.

Conclusion

Like indigenous people in the United States, Australia, and New Zealand, the majority of Aboriginal people in Canada live in cities (see Snipp; Taylor; and Kukutai, this volume). Despite earlier expectations of assimilation, urban Aboriginal people in Canada did not disappear into mainstream society, and recent censuses suggest that processes of reclaiming Aboriginal identities have been the main factor leading to the growth of Aboriginal populations in recent decades. The implications of these processes remain to be fully explored. Historically, government policies and programs assumed that the appropriate focus involved facilitating migrant adaptation to urban life. If migration is not the main driver of Aboriginal urbanization, what should be the emphasis of policies and programs in urban areas?

Clearly, the marginality of many urban Aboriginal people demonstrates the importance of initiatives to facilitate success in education and employment. However, initiatives that support strong cultural identities and communities may also be important. As Lawrence (2004, 159) notes: "The nature of urban life – where most work and home environments are organized in ways that ignore the demands of family or community, and where there are few all-Native spaces – encourages a growing individualism that only concerted struggle can challenge." The Ontario Urban Aboriginal Task Force notes that urban Aboriginal organizations were at the forefront of developing ways of expressing Aboriginal identities in urban areas. It argues:

> If alternative positive representations of being Aboriginal and new forms of Aboriginal cultural expressions along with institutions to support those expressions (such as cultural centres) are not available for this group to maintain their identity, they may feel marginalized and not participate in the Aboriginal community within the urban centre. (Urban Aboriginal Task Force 2007, 74)

Support for the creation of Aboriginal places, which can serve as a basis for the maintenance and redefinition of Aboriginal cultures in urban areas, may represent an appropriate response to emerging patterns of urban Aboriginal self-identification.

At the same time, it is important to recognize the dynamics of different cities and different subgroups within the Aboriginal population. These diversities have had relatively little academic attention and require additional research.

Note

This chapter builds on research (Norris and Clatworthy 2011) that was supported by the Office of the Federal Interlocutor (OFI), Indian and Northern Affairs Canada (INAC), in 2010, arising from the "Indigenous Urbanization in International Perspective" workshop.

1 Apart from the analysis of migration patterns, reserves within individual CMAs were not excluded from calculations of urban Aboriginal populations. The exception is Montreal, where the reserve of Kahnawake was excluded from the 1981 census count for comparability with later censuses, given the incomplete enumeration of the reserve in all censuses since 1981. Most reserves are located outside of urban areas.

References

Andersen, C. 2008. From nation to population: The racialization of "Métis" in the Canadian census. *Nations and Nationalism* 14: 347-68.

Anderson, K. 1998. Science and the savage: The Linnean society of New South Wales, 1874-1900. *Ecumene* 5: 125-43.

Berkhoffer, R.F. 1979. *The white man's Indian: Images of the American Indian from Columbus to the present.* New York: Vintage.

Bostrom, H. 1984. Recent evolution of Canada's Indian policy. In *The dynamics of government programs for urban Indians in the Prairie provinces,* ed. R. Breton and G. Grant, 519-44. Montreal: Institute for Research on Public Policy.

Breton, R. 1964. Institutional completeness of ethnic communities and the personal relations of immigrants. *American Journal of Sociology* 70: 193-205.

Clatworthy, S.J., and M.J. Norris. 2007. Aboriginal mobility and migration in Canada: Trends, recent patterns and implications, 1971 to 2001. In *Aboriginal policy research: Moving forward, making a difference,* ed. J.P. White, S. Wingert, D. Beavon, and P. Maxim, 4:207-34. Toronto: Thompson Educational.

–. Forthcoming, 2013. Aboriginal mobility and migration in Canada: Trends, patterns and implications, 1971 to 2006. In *Aboriginal populations: Social, demographic, and epidemiological dimensions,* ed. F. Trovato and A. Romaniuk. Edmonton: University of Alberta Press.

Davis, A.K. 1965. *Edging into mainstream: Urban Indians in Saskatchewan.* Bellingham: Western Washington State College.

Environics Institute. 2010. *Urban Aboriginal peoples study.* Main Report. http://uaps.ca/.

Goldie, T. 1989. *Fear and temptation: The image of the Indigene in Canadian, Australian, and New Zealand literatures.* Montreal and Kingston: McGill-Queen's University Press.

Goldmann, G., and A.J. Siggner. 1995. Statistical concepts of Aboriginal people and factors affecting the counts in the Census and the Aboriginal Peoples Survey. Paper presented to the 1995 Symposium of the Federation of Canadian Demographers, Ottawa, October.

Guimond, E. 2003. Fuzzy definitions and population explosion: Changing identities of Aboriginal groups in Canada. In *Not strangers in these parts: Aboriginal people in cities,* ed. D. Newhouse and E.J. Peters, 35-50. Ottawa: Policy Research Initiative.

Guimond E., N. Robitaille, and S. Senécal. 2009. Aboriginal people in Canadian cities: Why are they growing so fast? *Canadian Issues* Winter: 11-17.

Jette, D., and M. Snider. 2009. Affiliation of First Nation communities with urban zones: Analysis of census data 1996-2006. Paper presented at the Aboriginal Policy Research Conference, 10 March 2009, Strategic Research and Analysis Directorate, Indian and Northern Affairs Canada.

Kalbach W.E. 1987. Growth and distribution of Canada's ethnic populations, 1871-1981. In *Ethnic Canada: Identities and inequalities,* ed. L. Dreidger, 82-110. Toronto: Copp Clark Pitman.

Lagassé, J.H. 1958. *People of Indian ancestry: A social and economic study.* Winnipeg: Department of Agriculture and Immigration.

Lawrence, B. 2004. *"Real" Indians and others: Mixed-blood urban Native peoples and indigenous nationhood.* Vancouver: UBC Press.

Nagel, J. 1995. American Indian ethnic renewal: Politics and the resurgence of identity. *American Sociological Review* 60: 947-65.

Nagler, M. 1973. *Indians in the city: A study of the urbanization of Indians in Toronto.* Ottawa: Saint Paul University, Canadian Research Centre for Anthropology.

Newhouse, D. 2003. The invisible infrastructure: Urban Aboriginal institutions and organizations. In *Not strangers in these parts: Aboriginal people in cities,* ed. D. Newhouse and E.J. Peters, 243-54. Ottawa: Policy Research Initiative.

Newhouse, D., and E.J. Peters. 2003. Introduction. In *Not strangers in these parts: Aboriginal people in cities,* ed. D. Newhouse and E.J. Peters, 5-13. Ottawa: Policy Research Initiative.

Norris, M.J., and S.J. Clatworthy. 2011. Urbanization and migration patterns of Aboriginal populations in Canada: A half century in review (1951 to 2006). *Aboriginal Policy Studies* 1, 1: 13-77. http://ejournals.library.ualberta.ca/.

Peters, E.J. 2002. "Our city Indians": Negotiating the meaning of First Nations urbanization in Canada, 1945-1975. *Historical Geography* 30: 75-92.

Royal Commission on Aboriginal Peoples, Canada. 1993. *Aboriginal Peoples in urban centres.* Ottawa: Minister of Supply and Services.

Siggner, A.J. 2003a. The challenge of measuring the demographic and socio-economic condition of the urban Aboriginal population. In *Not strangers in these parts: Aboriginal people in cities,* ed. D. Newhouse and E.J. Peters, 119-30. Ottawa: Policy Research Initiative.

–. 2003b. Impact of "ethnic mobility" on socio-economic conditions of Aboriginal peoples. *Canadian Studies in Population* 30: 137-58.

Siggner, A.J., and R. Costa. 2005. *Aboriginal conditions in Census metropolitan areas, 1981-2001.* Catalogue no. 89-613-MIE-No. 008. Ottawa: Statistics Canada.

Statistics Canada. 1974. *Perspective Canada: A compendium of social statistics.* Catalogue no. 11-507E. Ottawa: Statistics Canada.

–. 2008. *Aboriginal population profile, 2006 Census.* Catalogue no. 92-594-XWE. Ottawa: Statistics Canada. http://www12.statcan.ca/.

–. 2010. *2006 Census dictionary.* Catalogue no. 92-566-X. Ottawa: Statistics Canada.

Urban Aboriginal Strategy. 2005. *Urban Aboriginal Task Force progress report 1.* http://www.servicecanada.gc.ca/.

Urban Aboriginal Task Force. 2007. *Urban Aboriginal Task Force final report.* Toronto: Ontario Federation of Indian Friendship Centres.

Warry, W. 2007. *Ending denial: Understanding Aboriginal issues.* Peterborough, ON: Broadview.

2

Urban Aboriginality as a Distinctive Identity, in Twelve Parts

CHRIS ANDERSEN

> *Crossing the city limits does not transform Aboriginal people
> into non-Aboriginal people; they go on being the particular
> kind of person they have always been – Cree, Dene, Mohawk,
> Haida.* (Royal Commission on Aboriginal Peoples 1993, 3)

> *We need to situate the debates about identity within all those
> historically specific developments and practices which have
> disturbed the relatively "settled" character of many populations
> and cultures ... which I would argue are coterminous with
> modernity.* (Hall 1996, 4)

At one level, making the claim that urban Aboriginal identities are distinctive is hardly earth shattering. Given that most recent theorizing on identities position it as situated, contextual, and multiple, it might seem obvious to expect the density of experiences particular to urban landscapes to produce and nest distinctive *urban Aboriginal* identities. A recent Environics report (2010) reveals that 30 percent of all urban Aboriginal residents are second and third generation, meaning that they have never lived any place but in a city. Likewise, those who are first generation (i.e., those who moved to the city from someplace else) have lived in that city for a significant portion of their lives, often longer than a decade (Environics Research 2010, 30). These findings would seem to suggest long-standing Aboriginal attachments to urban centres. However, no matter how reasonable it may be to posit a distinctive urban identity, well-documented Canadian jurisdictional peccadilloes around federal government interpretations of section 91(24) of the British North America Act (see Graham and Peters 2002) have effectively precluded official *recognition* of urban Aboriginality as a distinctive identity. This remains the case despite the half million of us who have lived and continue to live in Canada's cities, and the decades-long legacy of urban Aboriginal community-building in often inhospitable terrain.

Currently, the Canadian state measures Aboriginal "identities" primarily through the census. Statistics Canada has undertaken a census every decade since 1871, and of its many questions (sixty-one in total, as of the 2006 census's main long-form questionnaire), four currently inquire into elements of Aboriginality: ancestry/ethnicity, self-identification (according to three categories), First Nation band membership, and Registered Indian/ treaty status. The cross-tabulation of these variables with numerous linguistic and socio-economic classifications effectively constitutes the backbone of "evidence-based" Aboriginal policy making in Canada. Though Statistics Canada proffers statistical summaries of an "Aboriginal identity" population, however, one might ask what these categories actually measure – that is to say, what makes it an "identity" population?

This is an important question, not least because literature on censuses and identity make starkly clear the sometimes yawning chasm between state-imposed classifications (such as Statistics Canada's) and the complex self-identifications of pre-state Indigenous collectivities (see, generally, Anderson 1991; Appadurai 1993; Curtis 2001). In this conceptual space, I trace out a justification for an additional category of Aboriginality – *urban Aboriginal* – as a distinctive and equally legitimate form of Aboriginal identity in addition to those already present in the long-form questionnaire. I undertake this in two broad parts. Part one draws on contextual understandings of identity to trace out a conceptual argument for *urban Aboriginality* that, though every bit as "real" as competing figurations, exists in contexts different from those fixed in census classification categories. Part two then puts forward an argument for the legitimacy of an urban Aboriginality identity largely distinct from those of northern, rural, or reserve Aboriginal communities, and I present twelve contextual elements that specifically shape its distinctiveness. I conclude with a discussion of the implications of recognizing the distinctiveness of urban Aboriginality in the census, and I offer an option for producing more robust, "evidence-based" understandings of its dimensions.

Identity, Dialogically Framed

In its explanation of "Aboriginal identity," Statistics Canada spends little time discussing the implications of the fact that its so-called self-identification question (i.e., "Is this person an Aboriginal person?") is accompanied only with choices it deems relevant. The question's second part reads: "that is, North American Indian, Métis, or Inuit (Eskimo)?" From this, we can take away the idea that, for Statistics Canada, individual Indigenous self-identification is not in itself a useful tool for governance; rather, respondents must self-identify as North American Indian/First Nations, Métis, and/or Inuit, and these three only. The issue here, then, is not that, as Aboriginal respondents, we cannot "see" (parts of) our selves in such administrative categories; rather, the problem is that, despite the limited response options provided in census taxonomies and despite the tremendous legitimacy that Statistics Canada and the Canadian state more generally bring to bear on these categories, this is not the *only* way we see ourselves, nor is it a way of viewing ourselves that holds any great fidelity to our "livedness" in (of particular relevance here) urban locales. Thus, while Statistics Canada categories can certainly be said to measure elements of Aboriginal identification, they do so only according to the information required for policy intervention. Moreover, these categories are by definition synoptic, required to produce the geographic administrative equivalence (i.e., a response of "North American Indian" in Vancouver, British Columbia, must mean the same thing, administratively, as the same response in Goose Bay, Newfoundland-Labrador) crucial to this policy intervention.[1] Classifications are instruments that necessarily measure only what they can see, and the federal government's gaze (and whose categories largely comprise the basis of data collection taxonomies) has not, until recently, directed its lens towards urban Aboriginal communities.

In his discussion of cultural identities in the face of the numerous diasporas complicating the conceptual and material landscape of modernity's last two centuries, cultural studies scholar Stuart Hall posits two overlapping/competing senses of identity that are useful for thinking through the relationship between urban and non-urban contexts of Aboriginal identity. In the first, Hall argues that identity can be positioned as an "essence," an underlying, authentic presence that binds a people together. He writes that, in these and similar perceptions, "cultural identities reflect the common historical experiences and shared cultural codes which provide us, as 'one people,' with stable, unchanging and continuous frames of reference and meaning, beneath the shifting divisions and vicissitudes of our actual history" (Hall 1993, 223). This "oneness" acts as a touchstone that may be used to define the authentic experiences of an ethnic (or, in this case, an Aboriginal) collectivity. In an Aboriginal context, we might think about such essences as being tied to tropes about an Aboriginal connection to land and territory with its attendant spiritual significance. Indeed, though not immediately apparent, successive iterations of Canadian government positioned such historical life modalities as of sufficient difference (along with perceived mixed ancestry and lifestyles) to produce policy silos that, over time, have produced real and enduring policy differences between these categories (see Peters 2010 for a summary of these policy differences).

Hall also positions identity in a second sense. If the construction of identity just canvassed is premised on an essence that requires excavation or uncovering – that is, decolonization as a reaffirmation/recovery of what we *are* – identity can also be understood in terms of what we may *become*. In this guise, it does not uncover the past but retells it given the materials and resources available in the contexts within which we live: "Far from being eternally fixed in some essentialised past, [identities] are subject to the continuous 'play' of history, culture and power" (Hall 1993, 225). These new identities paradoxically offer a form of commonality of difference in the face of these centuries-long projects of dislocation, but they also offer the possibility of envisioning new boundaries and homelands over time and space. Hall's argument is neither that identity is a timeless essence or fixed point of origin *nor* that it is best characterized by fragmentation and discontinuity. Instead (and more sophisticatedly), his point is that diasporic/ethnic/minority identities exist in the interstices and gravitational pull of *both* impulses (225-27). Identity as *being,* essence, or sameness offers a sense of community and a point of solidarity, while offering the dignity of historical grounding. Conversely, identity as the process of *becoming* acknowledges the discontinuities and fragmentations marking our colonial experiences. This linkage is not an "either/or" choice but, rather, "its complexity exceeds this binary structure of representation. At different places, times, in relation to different questions, the boundaries are re-sited" (228). Thus, "vectors" of similarity and continuity *and* difference and rupture always characterize the framing of modern identities (226).

Hall's argument is useful in its analytical attention to context and agency. In his fidelity to context and to the raw materials of power and history, Hall (1995, 649 [emphasis in original]) tells us that "everywhere, cultural identities are emerging which are not fixed, but poised, in *transition*, between different positions; which draw on different cultural traditions at the same time; and which are the product of those complicated cross-overs and cultural mixes which are increasingly common in a globalized world." These social contexts are, he explains, marked by a diaspora "composed of people who have been *dispersed* forever from their homelands" (629 [emphasis in original]) and who, although possibly retaining links with those homelands, nevertheless forge new identities with new forms of affinity and commonality not entirely separate from but not reducible to those of their forebears.[2] For example, using Hall, Proulx (2006, 408) points out how the specific configurations of discursive and material space in urban locales (including the impacts of residential schools, adoption, and colonial legislation) distinctively shape the processes that tether individual subjectivity to Aboriginal identification.

Historically, anthropologists – and those engaging in anthropologically based ethnography – have conducted the most complex analyses of urban Aboriginal identities (e.g., Howard and Proulx 2011; Lawrence 2004; Proulx 2006, 2003). However, such research has also looked at the central role of women in creating and maintaining community (Howard-Bobiwash 2003) and, more specifically, at the various ways in which such community was communicated through events like powwows (Buddle 2004), Native-centred institutions (Howard 2011; Newhouse 2003; Sanderson and Howard-Bobbiwash 1997) and, in certain instances, radio (Buddle 2005). US-based scholars have explored similar issues in a more complex, city-specific context than we have in Canada (a point to which I return in conclusion) but, nonetheless, have highlighted the distinctive dynamics of Aboriginal identity creation and maintenance in urban spaces (see Darnell 2010; Darnell, Munguia, and Cristina 2005; Jackson 2002; LaGrand 2002).

Though exploring distinctive trajectories of identity specific to their research spaces, such research bears out Hall's broader discussion about the (dis)continuities between urban and non-urban Aboriginal communities/ life. If (to quote Hall again) urban identities offer new(er) and distinctive forms of "complicated cross-overs and cultural mixes" missing in earlier policy constructions of Aboriginal taxonomies (themselves rooted in earlier modes of Aboriginal life), the three constitutional/census categories through which the Canadian state intervenes in Aboriginal collectivities cannot possibly be thought (or made) to accurately characterize the "livedness" of urban Aboriginal identities. Indeed, in juxtaposing urban Aboriginal communities with First Nations, Hanselmann and Gibbins (2003, 14) suggest that, while First Nations are homogenous, land-based, and constitutionally recognized, urban Aboriginal communities are characterized by legal and cultural heterogeneity, a lack of territoriality, variable and complex identifications, socio-economic diversity, hypermobility, and a greater range of attachment (or lack thereof) to "the urban community," both culturally and politically. In the conclusion to this chapter, I offer some suggestions as to why we might want to do a better job of capturing the distinctiveness of urban Aboriginality and how we might do so, but first I lay out twelve elements of urban Aboriginality that make it distinctive.

Making the Case for a Distinctive Urban Aboriginality

I would like to disaggregate, analytically, elements I consider crucial to talking about the distinctiveness of urban Aboriginal communities and life – a life that encompasses the suturing of urban space, time, and context to pre-existing tendrils of Aboriginal identity (see Proulx 2006, 410). Such analysis bears the weight of two dangers: first, it runs the risk of allowing us to assume that these elements can be examined in isolation from the others; second, more often than not, it relies on existing statistics, rather than on less synoptic, more reflexive investigative techniques, to substantiate the distinctiveness. Having said this, I still believe that, taken together, these twelve elements mark urban life in ways that make it qualitatively different from that experienced in other locales. We begin, in no particular order of importance, with economic marginalization.

(1) Economic Marginalization
Peters (2007) states that, though the relationship between Aboriginal poverty levels and urban location are complex and vary from city to city, urban Aboriginal residents are likely to be poorer than their non-Aboriginal neighbours. She argues that "a larger proportion of First Nations and Métis people are poor, a smaller proportion earn good incomes, unemployment rates are much higher even though participation rates are similar, and a smaller proportion are in managerial, supervisory and professional occupations" (9). She explains, however, that, while the gap between Aboriginal

and non-Aboriginal urban residents is not worsening, neither is it improving. More broadly, Silver et al. (2008, 16-17) state that economic marginalization produces a spectrum of effects on related elements of lifestyle, forcing: higher unemployment, higher rates of single parenthood, higher rates of domestic violence, lower education levels, higher proportion of income spent on rent, higher mobility rates both within and between cities as well as between cities and non-urban communities, higher rates of household crowding, and higher rates of homelessness. While the poverty experienced by urban Aboriginal residents differs little from that experienced by similarly located non-urban Aboriginals, the social context of this marginalization produces different experiences and shapes the courses of action available and – equally important – those *perceived* as available to address it. Though economic marginalization does not represent the experiences of all urban Aboriginals, it nonetheless constitutes an important element for understanding the urban Aboriginal experience.

(2) Growing Professional/Middle Class

While urban Aboriginality has become synonymous with socio-economic deprivation, existing evidence suggests that, although for complex reasons, urban Aboriginality may also be characterized by a growing middle class (Lawrence 2004; Newhouse and Peters 2003; UATF 2007; Wotherspoon 2003). The Ontario Urban Aboriginal Task Force's final report, for example, found that one-quarter of its respondents made more than $40,000 per year. Likewise, the National Association of Friendship Centres' report on Aboriginals with disabilities noted the presence of an Aboriginal middle class in Regina, the result of the presence of the First Nations University of Canada and a large provincial and federal government bureaucracy (Durst 2006, 29). Whether viewing it favourably, as Wotherspoon (2003) does, or as a threat to the continuation of "tradition" in urban settings, as Lawrence (2004) does, it nonetheless appears to be gaining traction as part of the density of urban Aboriginal experiences.

Interestingly, Ontario's Urban Aboriginal Task Force (UATF) found that the developmental-based flavour of urban Aboriginal institutions produced feelings of alienation among middle-class respondents, who felt disconnected from the kinds of activities it emphasized and who were most likely to report experiencing racism from other Aboriginal residents, who called them "apples" (UATF 2007, 171). Likewise, the UATF found that, although middle-class respondents were most likely to have the means to visit home communities, their increasing disconnection from their urban Aboriginal community at large could lead, over generations, to their understanding their Aboriginality in terms of ancestral curiosity rather than as a self-identified connection to their city's urban Aboriginal community (193).

(3) Racism/Social Exclusion

Despite some signs of a growing middle class of urban Aboriginals, the now intergenerational literature on urban Aboriginality has, until recently, focused on the social exclusion of urban Aboriginals from the broader cityscapes in which they live, and for good reason. Peters (1996, 2000) contends that such arguments are fundamentally predicated on the notion that Aboriginal people do not belong in the city – *real* Aboriginality, as such, belongs in rural areas or on-reserve – and she provides examples of the ways in which municipalities work in concert with other levels of government to ensure the continued separation of dominant "whitestream" (see Denis 1997) from Indigenous spaces (see also Razack 2000). Silver et al. (2008, 29-30) go so far as to say not only that this racism is fundamental to the urban Aboriginal experience but also that it distinguishes urban Aboriginal experiences of poverty from non-Aboriginal experiences (see also Jackson 2002).

Social exclusion or racism can take various forms, one of which is economic marginalization and its already mentioned effects. However, racism is also a daily reminder of the *symbolic* exclusion of urban Aboriginals from the cities in which they reside. For example, the final report of Ontario's UATF (2007, 20) suggests that 78 percent of Aboriginal respondents indicated racism as a significant problem in contexts such as: when searching for affordable housing, in first-encounter job interviews, in public spaces such as shopping malls and schools, and even in encounters with urban Aboriginal residents. Moreover, the sometimes "intense hostility" (Peters 2002) displayed by policing forces and the justice system has come to light in western cities, most notoriously through the murder of Neil Stonechild and the subsequent Stonechild Inquiry into the so-called Starlight Tours in Saskatoon (see Green 2006), and the murder of Saulteaux woman Pamela George in Regina (see Razack 2000). These are contemporary examples of the larger processes of "othering" that anchor(ed) the diverse projects of Canadian colonialism from the nineteenth century onward and that have produced enduring stereotypes through which urban Aboriginals are perceived and (in some cases, officially) acted upon.

(4) Cultural Diversity

Though its extent varies by city, a necessary consequence of large-scale Aboriginal urbanization over the past half century, and particularly since the 1970s, is that urban Aboriginal populations are highly intra-multicultural. Urban Aboriginal residents arrive, or have parents or grandparents who arrived, from a wide range of Aboriginal communities, whether First Nations reserves, smaller cities and towns, or rural communities. This has affected urban Aboriginal residents' understandings and feelings of attachment to the kinds of "groups" comprised by census classifications. Peters (2007, 26, Table 6) notes that a 2003 survey of six hundred Aboriginal people reveals that urban Aboriginal people (i.e., First Nations and Métis) felt as much attachment to other Aboriginal people in their city of residence as they did to those in their own cultural group. Though the data are provisional and based on a small sample size, they nonetheless raise the possibility that official statistical categories like "First Nations," "Inuit," and "Métis," with their associated socio-demographic cross-tabulations, may not, from an identity standpoint, be as relevant as is the distinctiveness of urban locale for understanding the forms of identity produced between urban Aboriginal residents.

This diversity is not always presented as a positive feature. Nearly two decades ago, the Royal Commission on Aboriginal Peoples Round Table on Aboriginal Urban Issues suggested, for example, that "the diversity of origins and cultures of Aboriginal people living in a particular city often poses difficulties in establishing a sense of community, even for those whose ties with their homelands and original communities have weakened over time" (RCAP 1993, 4). More recently, Norris and Jantzen (2003, 113) argue that "significant diversity of Aboriginal cultures may also create barriers to social cohesion, community development, and cultural retention; [and it may] limit opportunities for institutional and political development." However, others consider this diversity to be a source of power that urban Aboriginal communities can use to develop and strengthen themselves: "there are no quick or easy solutions for Aboriginal people in Winnipeg's inner city, or in other similar urban centres. But a unique path to a better future is being built here, and creative urban Aboriginal people are both the engineers and the builders" (Silver et al. 2008, 38-39). Below, I outline how such cultural diversity manifests itself in a major institutional interface between urban Aboriginal residents and government: service delivery organizations. Whether viewed positively or negatively, this cultural diversity affects urban

Aboriginal experiences in ways not exportable to non-urban locales. As I explain next, this diversity is not just cultural but legal.

(5) Legal Diversity

Peters (2005) argues that historical federal interpretations of the state's legal responsibilities towards "Indians" (a term that, by the end of the nineteenth century, was notoriously porous), which were anchored in assumptions about where "real Indians" belonged, effectively produced a policy coordination vacuum in Canada's cities. However, other legal categorizations produced in the wake of these assumptions continue to exert an impact on Aboriginal communities, particularly in an urban context. While Canadian Aboriginal legal categorization was (and largely remains) a spatial designation in that those designated as status Indians are able to live on, and expect benefits from, reserve communities while those not so designated tend to live off-reserve (and, disproportionately, in Canada's cities), urban milieus reflect a complex mix of status Indians, non-status Indians, Métis, Inuit, Registered Indians who belong to Indian bands, Registered Indians who do not belong to Indian bands, treaty Indians, non-treaty Indians, and numerous cultural groups that are the product of the effects of "out-marriage." This has led to distinctive kinds of struggles in urban centres. For example, the UATF (2007, 21) found that various kinds of discrimination between urban Aboriginals were rooted in internal hierarchies tied to investment in legal distinctions: "Respondents recounted experiences of internal racism on the basis of whether one has Status or not ... and/or whether one has links to a First Nation community. Internal racism can also intersect with gender to discriminate against Aboriginal women on the basis of their 'Bill C-31' Status" (see Lawrence 2004 for the lengthiest discussion of these issues in an urban context).

Perhaps equally important from an identity standpoint, these legal distinctions (which, over five or so generations, have solidified into entrenched cultural distinctions) continue to exert a powerful role in the urban identity landscape. As one colleague asked after hearing my project explanation: "Why aren't you just differentiating between urban First Nations, urban Métis, and urban Inuit?" If urban Aboriginality can be said to exist at all, it does so not in place of the more venerable legal categories like those enshrined in the Constitution but, rather, alongside them and as a specific effect of their differential recognition by various levels of Canadian government. Said (1993) argues that one of colonialism's most powerful effects is rooted in the idea that, in colonial nation-states, "the other" (in this case, Aboriginal people) can only be one thing. My point here is thus that urban Aboriginality is beginning to jostle, as a form of allegiance or affinity, with longer-standing and seemingly more natural categories. This has, in turn, produced discussions around the appropriate constituencies of service-delivery institutions.

(6) Status Blindness

The UATF suggests that legal diversity in an urban setting is problematic because it produces internal struggles between urban Aboriginal residents invested in one or more of the various hierarchically organized Canadian legal categories. Silver et al.'s (2008, 12) excellent discussion of the urban Aboriginal community in Winnipeg suggests that distinctions between First Nations, Métis, and Inuit can be problematic not so much in the context of situated constructions of identity but, more mundanely, in the context of the jurisdictional quagmire through which federal, provincial, and municipal officials seek to avoid administrative responsibility for urban Aboriginals. They argue further that, in this policy climate:

> Urban Aboriginal people have been forced back upon their own creativity to build an organizational infrastructure – usually "status-blind," i.e., available to all Aboriginal people regardless of their legal status or particular Aboriginal ancestry – to meet urban Aboriginal needs. The critical nature of this work has increased with the process of urbanization and constitutes an important part of a holistic and culturally rooted form of urban Aboriginal community development. (13)

Interestingly, while Silver et al. seem to suggest a "melting pot" approach, other discussions of urban Aboriginal service delivery take a different approach. While the Royal Commission on Aboriginal Peoples recommends that "services to Aboriginal people in urban areas generally be delivered without regard to legal or treaty status" (4.7.9), others hedge this recommendation by suggesting that status blindness is not akin to cultural homogeneity. For example, Calvin Hanselmann's (2003, 11) series of reports on urban Aboriginal policies and practices recommends that status-blind programming be "respectful of cultural distinctions among Aboriginal people while being available to all urban Aboriginal people." Likewise, Loxley and Wein (2003, 227) suggest that the Aboriginal Council of Winnipeg supports urban, status-blind institutions "but at the same time ... does not believe in a melting pot approach to urbanization. Rather, it respects the diversity of the different groups and believes in the portability of treaty rights." Clearly, different viewpoints on these issues, evidence of the various modes of identification that are in competition in the urban milieu, will continue to shape future debate. What it is important to take from the notion of status blindness, however, is that it may signal a willingness to move beyond traditional jurisdictional barriers with regard to thinking about what urban Aboriginal communities will and do mean in Canada. This does not necessarily signal a move from a less to a more enlightened government, but it does open up new nodes of struggle between competing identities, the very resources of "power, culture, and history" to which Hall refers (see above).

(7) Urban Aboriginal Institutions

Both the legal diversity and the ensuing status-blindness debates are perhaps most poignantly brought home in the work carried out under the auspices of the numerous urban Aboriginal service-delivery institutions that shape what Peters (2007, 29) terms the "institutional life" of urban Aboriginal communities (see also Howard 2011; Newhouse 2003). Peters (2007, 27) argues, in fact, that institutions like those in the service-delivery industry have emerged as central components in the production of urban Aboriginal collective identity and, perhaps equally important, offer a mechanism through which urban self-government might take root. Moreover, her findings from a project examining selected social service delivery institutions suggest that they are growing in number, size, and range of policy sectors and that they service a significant proportion of the urban Aboriginal population.

Additionally, findings from the UATF (2007, chap. 5) suggest that urban Aboriginal institutions like friendship centres play a powerful role in emphasizing certain elements of traditional or "cultural" practices while managing the tensions created between ensuring the integrity of specific cultural practices and the necessarily "pan-Indian" approaches that characterize such a broad cultural mix in the urban milieu. Having said that, respondents in the UATF Report who self-describe as middle class found that service-delivery organizations focused too closely on the delivery of policy and not enough on meeting their needs, specifically around the maintenance of their cultural identities in urban areas (87). Perhaps the larger point here is that urban Aboriginal institutions are forced to manage a diversity of cultural identification forms that are simply not present in First Nations reserve communities, in Métis settlements, or in many rural communities and, for this reason, represent a distinctive element of the urban Aboriginal identity landscape (see Sanderson and Howard-Bobiwash 1997).

(8) Distinctiveness of Urban Aboriginal Policy Ethos

Canada's urban Aboriginal institutions are ensconced in a policy delivery landscape marked by a complex mélange consisting of a historically rooted *policy coordination vacuum* and attempts by various provinces and municipalities to "fill in the gaps" on an ad hoc basis premised on urban Aboriginal residents' status as members of a larger disadvantaged group (or simply as provincial citizens). We have already noted the impact of federal geographically circumscribed interpretations of the state's responsibilities towards those designated as status Indians. This has had an additional impact on the policy milieu in urban centres. Hanselmann and Gibbins (2003), borrowing from RCAP's discussion, argue that long-standing interpretations resulted in a policy vacuum in which urban Aboriginal residents did not receive the same level of service delivery as did First Nations-based Aboriginal people; did not receive levels of service delivery in keeping with their non-Aboriginal counterparts; and did not receive culturally appropriate service delivery (RCAP 1996, 538, cited in Hanselmann and Gibbins 2003, 26).

Urban service delivery mechanisms stepped in to fill this gap. And, while we may take Hanselmann's (2002) point about the inconsistency and ad hoc nature of much of the policy and programming that tends to occur in a policy vacuum, urban Aboriginal institutions are nonetheless operating as a primary identification mechanism for urban Aboriginal communities. To put it another way, urban Aboriginality is strongly tethered to development-based notions of "community" – to the extent that such service delivery mechanisms seek to do their part in "closing the gap" between Aboriginal clients and their non-Aboriginal counterparts. Hanselmann and Gibbins's (2003, 1 [emphasis added]) somewhat gloomy (though realistic) assessment of urban Aboriginal policy in Canada suggests that it

> has been characterized by a lack of jurisdictional clarity and as much by policy avoidance as by intergovernmental collaboration. It is also a policy area that inevitably must engage not just the federal and provincial governments but all three conventional orders of government – federal, provincial and municipal. There is, moreover, a legitimate debate over the extent to which urban policy should explicitly recognize Aboriginality; whether there should be programming, for example, for the Aboriginal homeless as opposed to the homeless in general. *Needless to say, this is not a debate that*

complicates public policy design and implementation in First Nation communities. (See also Andersen and Strachan 2012.)

(9) The Character of Informal Networks

Informal networks – and here I am thinking about networks of support that exist outside of formal policy or service-delivery silos – can play a powerful role in the more general quality of life to which urban Aboriginal residents have access. This is not necessarily surprising, as much of the massive literature on "community" stresses the importance of social networks in the production and legitimation of the very idea of community among those who feel allegiance to it. That is to say, to the extent that "community" is linked to feelings and practices of attachment, social networks operate as the paths through which attachments are produced and maintained. Literature on social capital (see Studdert 2005; Puttman 1995, 2000) stresses the importance of networks as binding agents.

In their study on "hidden homelessness" (which includes staying with family and friends rather than "on the street"), Peters and Robillard (2007) argue that informal networks play a crucial role for Aboriginal people in preventing the move from "hidden" to "absolute" homelessness, especially for those moving from First Nations reserves into cities. Likewise, Baskin et al. (2009, 2) suggest that the social isolation for young Aboriginal mothers who move to cities can exert an enormous impact on their food security: "as many Aboriginal peoples are being displaced from their home communities and moving into urban centres, there is a higher chance that there are less familiar bonds and supports to assist young single mothers living in cities." Unlike on First Nations reserves, where social networks might be comprised largely of extended family, informal urban networks are less likely to contain family and more likely to contain friends. And yet, despite the presence of second- and even third-generation urban Aboriginal residents, family – especially extended family – continues to play a role in meaningful social attachments for urban Aboriginal residents. As I discuss next, this is evidence of the continued connections between urban and non-urban locales.

(10) Attachment to Non-Urban Communities

In the previous section, I noted Hall's (1995) discussion about the situated, contextual character of identities. Recall his specific emphasis on how the large-scale displacements and diasporas of an increasingly globalizing world produce new forms of identification as we cross the seemingly natural frontiers of our homelands and move into new locales. While his point is more broadly conceived, Aboriginal diasporas operate according to a similar logic. As such, we may understand the ways in which movement into new communities, with their distinctive material forms and circulation of meanings, produce identification contexts that are distinct from those of old locales while yet remaining wedded to them.

Scholars have noted the fact that conceptually separating urban and non-urban geographical and social spaces often misses an important part of what it means to be Aboriginal in a contemporary context. Peters and Robillard (2007), for example, note that Aboriginal homelessness literature often conceptualizes the problems at a scale that fails to account for movement back and forth between the city and the reserve. Likewise, Hull (1984) and Norris and Clatworthy (2003) note the so-called hypermobility of Aboriginal populations, more recently understood in migration patterns between cities but also in migration patterns between the city and the reserve – a pattern Norris and Clatworthy refer to as "churn."

Peters (2005) explains that the reasons for this are part of a series of complex "push/pull" factors and are at least partly due to the difficulty experienced by recent Aboriginal migrants to the city. She also suggests that earlier literature tends to view continued urban Aboriginal residence as evidence of integration, to be juxtaposed with movement back to "home" communities. However, a continued connection to long-standing cultural communities is also important to urban Aboriginal residents' feelings of well-being and to their overall sense of identity. Viewed in light of the larger literature on migration, Peters suggests that such movements can legitimately be interpreted in the context of attachments to land or, more generally, as part of a revitalization of political and economic ties to other locales. Evidence from the UATF (2007, 65) final report reveals that, of those who responded to the question, 86 percent stated that they maintained links to their home communities for a variety of reasons (see also Environics 2010). These continued ties, though valuable for a number of reasons, have become strongly linked to more recent struggles over political representation: Who represents urban Aboriginals?

(11) Struggles over the Political Representation of Urban Aboriginals
If Aboriginal migration to urban areas has been under way for more than a century, this movement has not been matched by equally vigorous changes in the constituencies of political representation. While the Assembly of First Nations, the Métis National Council and its provincial affiliates, and the Inuit Tapiriit Kanatami all purport to represent their constituents in all parts

of Canada, so too does the Congress of Aboriginal Peoples and numerous additional regional, provincial, and municipal organizations (Hanselmann 2003, 172). Such claims notwithstanding, Hanselmann argues that the lack of an effective, unified political voice is rooted, in part, in an urban Aboriginal heterogeneity comprised of long-standing legal and cultural distinctions, which in turn have produced difficulties for official policy makers who are attempting to operate in this milieu.

Todd (2003, 257) explains National Association Friendship Centre research regarding which of three models of urban Aboriginal governance is most palatable to urban Aboriginal residents. Given the choices of government by nation, by territory, or by local community, respondents chose governance by the urban Aboriginal community as a whole. This is in keeping with RCAP's recommendation of a "community-of-interest" model of governance in urban areas. Indeed, such findings are manifesting themselves more concretely in cities that are producing complex amalgams of competing political representative bodies to produce locally useful representative organizations based on local expertise (see Newhouse 2003, 250). The Aboriginal Council of Winnipeg, for example, includes the Winnipeg Council of Treaty and Status Indians (representing Status Indians) and the Urban Indian Association (representing Status Indians, non-Status Indians, and Métis) (Loxley and Wein 2003, 224). Likewise in the City of Vancouver, the BC Association of Friendship Centres and the United Native Nations established the Aboriginal People's Council, and several cities include municipally based integrative organizations. The Urban Aboriginal Strategy, housed in the Office of the Federal Interlocutor for Métis and Non-Status Indians, has also played a role in producing (previously absent) spaces for dialogue in urban contexts. What is perhaps most interesting about these struggles, however, is not simply that they cut across more established categories or classifications but, rather, that Aboriginal women played such a prominent formal role in the process. It is to this that I now turn.

(12) Place(s) of Aboriginal Women in Urban Aboriginal Social Relations

Urbanization appears to be more a female than a male phenomenon, in that about 10 percent more Aboriginal women than men live in urban areas (54 percent of the total Aboriginal women's population versus 49.5 percent of the men's). Peters (2008) suggests that, though the factors behind this slight sex imbalance are complex and not fully known, they are probably the result of a number of different elements, including differential employment opportunities; access to social services delivery; and the patriarchal imposition of Indian Act rules and regulations that have devalued the traditional roles of Aboriginal women and forced them out of their First Nations communities and into Canada's cities (349). And, the growing middle class notwithstanding, the disproportionate number of urban Aboriginal women likely means that they suffer a disproportionate amount of the endemic poverty and associated effects that characterize many urban Aboriginal communities (see Jaccoud and Brassard 2003).

Despite their being among the most vulnerable of the city's urban Aboriginal population, Aboriginal women, according to some literature, are far more likely than are Aboriginal men to be involved as decision makers in the institutions of urban Aboriginal community development. The UATF (2007, 165) suggests that women were more likely to be involved in executive directorship or social service staffing than men, and Loxley and Wein (2003, 228) argue that, at least in Winnipeg, "Aboriginal women have been very active in establishing institutions ... that provide housing, child care, cultural facilities, shelters for women and children, health care facilities, and training institutions." Silver et al. (2006, 2) echo this statement, suggesting that their research informants indicated that, to a large extent, community development work was undertaken by women, both in its conceptualization and implementation stages. This may be compared to the far lower rates of women's political power on First Nations reserves (see also Howard-Bobiwash 2003; Krouse and Howard 2009).[3]

Likewise, however, urban Aboriginal women have borne the brunt of some of the most negative effects of urban Aboriginal/non-Aboriginal relations. Perhaps most starkly demonstrated in the now infamous Robert Pickton trial, a major aspect of these negative relations includes the sexualization of Aboriginal women in urban locales. This reflects not only the broad stereotypes of Aboriginal women (i.e., "sexually easy") but also the disproportionate number of young Aboriginal women who end up as sex trade workers on the streets of Canada's cities (see Oxman-Martinez, Lacrois, and Hanley 2005) and the (related) number of missing and murdered Aboriginal women – many in transit from rural to urban locales (see Amnesty International 2004).

While this list of twelve elements is certainly not exhaustive, while the choices can be debated, while laundry lists do little to explain the affiliations crucial to the construction of collective identity, and while much of the evidence marshalled here is anecdotal and requires further research, I nonetheless believe that it sketches out what is distinctive about urban Aboriginal identity. In the conclusion, I explain why I think exploring the complex dimensions of urban Aboriginal identity is so important, and I offer a suggestion as to how they can most efficiently be used for policy purposes.

Conclusion

Governments – all governments – officially gather information pertaining to specific categories for one main purpose: to facilitate administrative policy intervention in population segments of interest. This information, gathered primarily through the census, is utilized in a wide variety of policy contexts, and, as urban issues increasingly come under the federal gaze, effective policy intervention will require effective data. Such data do not currently exist. The reason this is so important in an urban context is that, like that for First Nations in general, existing urban Aboriginal scholarship tells us that community characteristics vary greatly according to city. Thus, data that capture this nuance and specificity will prove crucial to providing effective (i.e., responsive and accurate) and cost-efficient policy. At the very least, we might be in a better position to answer questions about why the Urban Aboriginal Strategy, the federal government's main attempt to treat urban Aboriginality as a distinctive identity, works so well in certain cities and so poorly in others. This is no doubt partly the result of city-specific conditions (like general demographic make-up) or relations between the urban Aboriginal community and municipal and provincial officials. But I would suggest that it also demonstrates a poor source of evidence for policy intervention. Indeed, if demographic models cannot contextually situate on-the-ground realities, how can we expect anything different?

Yet, Statistics Canada's administrative knowledge of Aboriginality has, in recent decades, expanded beyond cross-tabulations of socio-economic indicators with main long-form indicators of Aboriginality through the addition of a number of Aboriginal peoples surveys. For example, in 1991, for the first time, Statistics Canada delivered the Aboriginal Peoples Survey as a means of gaining more detailed information on the social and economic conditions of Aboriginal people in Canada. Three specific supplements currently exist that can be delivered in one of at least eighteen different Aboriginal languages: a "Child and Youth Supplement" (youths aged 6-14); an "Arctic Supplement"; and a "Métis Supplement." These supplements each ask a variety of in-depth questions relating to education, language, labour activity, income, health, community technology, mobility, and housing. In addition, each survey asks a series of questions specific to that supplement (see APS 2006a, 2006b, 2006c). In all, the surveys inquire, with an almost Orwellian level of detail, about the lives of the questionnaire respondents, providing an avalanche of usable data for those populations.

In this context, what would an urban supplement look like?[4] Although I would not presume to present detailed questions to make up an urban supplement at this point, we might nonetheless think about its final formulation through one or both of the two consultation processes already utilized by Statistics Canada to formulate the Aboriginal Peoples Survey and the Aboriginal Children's Survey. The Aboriginal Peoples Survey included extensive consultations with five of the six national Aboriginal organizations (i.e., Métis National Council, Inuit Tapiriit Kanatami, Native Women's Association of Canada, National Association of Friendship Centres, and Congress of Aboriginal Peoples) as well as with regional partners. The Aboriginal Children's Survey, in contrast, was constructed through a technical advisory group comprised of experts on various subjects and whose guidance assisted in formulating the eventual questions used to collect policy-relevant information. With a couple of small exceptions, most participants in the process (from the national Aboriginal organizations and the various government ministries) were happy with the survey process and outcomes.

Urban Aboriginality is a distinctive identity, and urban Aboriginal residents – whether they identify with a particular First Nation or cultural group, as Métis, as Inuit, or as none of these – are *living in urban communities* that, though bearing similarities to more familiar Aboriginal communities, are in no way reducible to them. Given their distinctiveness, and given the federal government's elevated interest in urban Aboriginality as a distinctive arena of policy interest (and thus intervention), it only makes sense to produce a stronger, more nuanced evidence base from which to undertake such intervention. An Aboriginal Peoples Survey-based urban supplement represents a useful way to strengthen the existing knowledge base.

Notes

1 My point here is not that identity can never really be measured as such; rather, it is that existing Statistics Canada categories do a poor job of measuring it in ways that facilitate complex or contextual self-understandings, particularly those specific to urban spaces. Nor is this their purpose.
2 The analytical costs of buying Hall's argument wholesale about contextual identity are high in that they tend to presuppose that, in "the homelands," one finds a purity that never existed. Likewise, his argument is politically fraught in that it effectively bites at the ankles of longer-standing forms of political representation.

3 This should not, however, be pushed too far: Aboriginal women's social and political power cannot be fully appreciated simply in the context of its public manifestation. On the other hand, there is no reason to believe that urban Aboriginal women's increased public presence belies a weakened private state.
4 Although the Aboriginal Peoples Survey is essentially an urban-based statistical survey (since it only interviews respondents living off-reserve), it does not ask city- or even region-specific questions.

References

Amnesty International. 2004. *Stolen sisters: A human rights response to discrimination and violence against Indigenous women in Canada.* http://www.amnesty.ca/.

Andersen, C., and J. Strachan. 2012. Urban Aboriginal policy in a coordination vacuum: The Alberta (dis)advantage. In *Fields of governance 2: Making urban Aboriginal policy in Canadian municipalities,* ed. E. Peters, 127-59. Montreal: McGill-Queen's University Press.

Anderson, B. 1991. *Imagined communities: Reflections on the origin and spread of nationalism.* London: Verso.

Appadurai, A. 1993. Numbers in the colonial imagination. In *Orientalism and the postcolonial predicament,* ed. C.A. Breckenridge and P. van der Veer, 314-39. Philadelphia: University of Pennsylvania Press.

APS (Aboriginal Peoples Survey). 2006a. *Aboriginal Peoples Survey.* Ottawa: Statistics Canada.

–. 2006b. *Aboriginal Peoples Survey: Arctic Supplement.* Ottawa: Statistics Canada.

–. 2006c. *Aboriginal Peoples Survey: Métis Supplement.* Ottawa: Statistics Canada.

Baskin, C., B. Guarisco, R. Koleszar-Green, N. Melanson, and C. Osawamick. 2009. Struggles, strengths and solutions: Exploring food security with young urban Aboriginal moms. *Esurio: Journal of Hunger and Poverty* 1(1): 1-20.

Buddle, K. 2004 Media, markets and powwows: Matrices of Aboriginal cultural mediation in Canada. *Cultural Dynamics* 16(1): 29-60.

–. 2005. Aboriginal cultural capital creation and radio production in urban Ontario. *Canadian Journal of Communication* 30(1): 7-40

Curtis, B. 2001. *The politics of population: State formation, statistics, and the census of Canada.* Toronto: University of Toronto Press.

Darnell, R. 2010. Nomadic legacies and contemporary decision-making strategies between reserve and city. In *Aboriginal peoples in Canadian cities: Transformations and continuities,* ed. H.A. Howard and C. Proulx, 39-68. Waterloo: Wilfrid Laurier University Press.

Darnell, R., M. Munguia, and M. Cristina. 2005. "Nomadic legacies an urban Algonquin residence." In *Papers of the Thirty-Sixth Algonquian Conference,* ed. H.C. Wolfart, 173-86. Winnipeg: University of Manitoba.

Durst, D. 2006. *Urban Aboriginal families of children with disabilities: Social inclusion or exclusion?* Ottawa: National Association of Friendship Centres.

Environics Research, Inc. 2010. *Urban Aboriginal peoples study.* Toronto: Environics Research Groups Limited.

Graham, K., and E. Peters. 2002. Aboriginal communities and urban sustainability. *Discussion Paper F/27: Family Matters*. Canadian Policy Research Networks Inc.

Green, J. 2007. From *Stonechild* to social cohesion: Anti-racist challenges for Saskatchewan. *Canadian Journal of Political Science* 39(3): 507-27.

Hall, S. 1993. Cultural identity and diaspora. In *Colonial discourse and postcolonial theory: A reader*, ed. P. Williams and L. Chrisman, 222-37. New York: Harvester Whaeatsheaf.

–. 1995. The question of cultural identity. In *Modernity: An introduction to modern societies*, ed. S. Hall, D. Held, D. Hubert, and K. Thompson, 595-634. London, UK: Polity.

–. 1996. Introduction: Who needs identity? In *Questions of cultural identity*, ed. S. Hall and P. du Gay, 1-17. London: Sage.

Hanselmann, C. 2002. *Uncommon sense: Promising practices in urban Aboriginal policy-making and programming*. Calgary: Canada West Foundation.

–. 2003. Shared responsibility: Final report and recommendations of the *Urban Aboriginal Initiative*. Calgary: Canada West Foundation.

Hanselmann, C., and R. Gibbins. 2003. *Another voice is needed: Intergovernmentalism in the urban Aboriginal context*. Calgary: Canada West Foundation.

Howard, H.A. 2011. The Friendship Centre: Native people and the organization of community in cities. In *Aboriginal peoples in Canadian cities: Transformations and continuities*, ed. H.A. Howard and C. Proulx, 87-108. Waterloo: Wilfrid Laurier University Press.

Howard, H.A., and C. Proulx, eds. 2011. *Aboriginal peoples in Canadian cities: Transformations and continuities*. Waterloo: Wilfrid Laurier University Press.

Howard-Bobiwash, H. 2003. "Women's class strategies as activism in Native community building in Toronto." *American Indian Quarterly* 27(3-4): 566-82.

Hull, J. 1984. 1981 census coverage of the Native population in Manitoba and Saskatchewan. *Canadian Journal of Native Studies* 4(1): 147-56.

Jaccoud, M., and R. Brassard. 2003. The marginalization of Aboriginal women in Montréal. In *Not strangers in these parts: Urban Aboriginal peoples*, ed. D. Newhouse and E. Peters, 131-45. Ottawa: Policy Research Initiative.

Jackson, D.D. 2002. *Our elders lived it: American Indian identity in the city*. DeKalb: Northern Illinois University Press.

Krouse, S., and H. Howard, eds. 2009. *Keeping the campfires going: Native women's activism in urban communities*. Omaha: University of Nebraska Press.

LaGrand, J.B. 2002. *Indian metropolis: Native Americans in Chicago, 1945-75*. Urbana: University of Illinois Press.

Lawrence, B. 2004. *"Real" Indians and others: Mixed-blood urban native peoples and Indigenous nationhood*. Vancouver: UBC Press.

Loxley, J., and F. Wein. 2003. Urban Aboriginal development. In *Not strangers in these parts: Urban Aboriginal peoples*, ed. D. Newhouse and E. Peters, 217-42. Ottawa: Policy Research Initiative.

Newhouse, D. 2003. The invisible infrastructure: Urban Aboriginal institutions and organizations. In *Not strangers in these parts: Urban Aboriginal peoples*, ed. D. Newhouse and E. Peters, 243-53. Ottawa: Policy Research Initiative.

Newhouse, D., and E. Peters. 2003. Conclusion: The way forward. In *Not strangers in these parts: Urban Aboriginal peoples*, ed. D. Newhouse and E. Peters, 281-84. Ottawa: Policy Research Initiative.

Norris, M.J., and S. Clatworthy. 2003. Aboriginal mobility and migration within urban Canada: Outcomes, factors and implications. In *Not strangers in these parts: Urban Aboriginal peoples*, ed. D. Newhouse and E. Peters, 51-78. Ottawa: Policy Research Initiative.

Norris, M.J., and L. Jantzen. Aboriginal languages in Canada's urban areas: Characteristics, considerations and implications. In *Not strangers in these parts: Urban Aboriginal peoples*, ed. D. Newhouse and E. Peters, 93-118. Ottawa: Policy Research Initiative.

Oxman-Martinez, J., M. Lacroix, and J. Hanley. 2005. *Victims of trafficking in persons: Perspectives from the Canadian community sector*. Ottawa: Department of Justice Canada.

Peters, E. 1996. "Urban" and "Aboriginal": An impossible contradiction?, In *City lives and city forms: Critical research and Canadian urbanism*, ed. J. Caulfield and L. Peake, 47-62. Toronto: University of Toronto Press.

–. 2002. Urban Aboriginal peoples. In *Urban affairs: Back on policy agenda?*, ed. C. Andrew, K. Graham, and S. Phillips, 45-70. Montreal and Kingston: McGill-Queen's University Press.

–. 2005. Indigeneity and marginalisation: Planning for and with urban Aboriginal communities in Canada. *Progress in Planning* 63: 327-404.

–. 2007. First Nations and Métis people and diversity in Canadian cities. In *Belonging? Diversity, recognition and shared citizenship in Canada*, ed. K. Banding, T.J. Courchene, and F. Seidle, 207-46. Ottawa: Institute for Research on Public Policy.

–. 2010. Emerging themes in academic research in urban Aboriginal identities in Canada, 1996-2010. *Aboriginal Policy Studies* 1(1): 78-105.

Peters, E., and V. Robillard. 2006. Aboriginal identification in North American cities. *Canadian Journal of Native Studies* 26(2): 405-39.

–. 2007. Urban hidden homelessness and reserve housing. In *Aboriginal Policy Research*, ed. J.P. White, P. Maxim, and D. Beavon, 4:189-206. Toronto: Thompson.

Putnam, R. 1995. Bowling alone: America's declining social capital. *Journal of Democracy* 6(1): 65-78.

–. 2000. *Bowling alone: The collapse and revival of the American community*. New York: Simon and Schuster.

Razack, S. 2000. Gendered racial violence and spatialized justice: The murder of Pamela George. *Canadian Journal of Law and Society* 15(2): 91-130.

Royal Commission on Aboriginal Peoples (RCAP). 1993. *Aboriginal peoples in urban centres*. Report of the National Round Table on Aboriginal Urban Issues. Ottawa: Minister of Supply and Services.

Said, E. 1993. *Culture and imperialism*. New York: Verso.

Sanderson, F., and H. Howard-Bobiwash, eds. 1997. *The meeting place: Aboriginal life in Toronto – In celebration of the Native Canadian Centre of Toronto's 35th anniversary*. Toronto: Native Canadian Centre.

Silver, J., J. Hay, D. Klyne, P. Ghorayshi, P. Gorzen, C. Keeper, M. MacKenzie, and F. Simard. 2008. *In their own voices: Building urban Aboriginal communities.* Halifax: Fernwood.

Studdert, D. 2005. *Conceptualizing community: Beyond the state and individual.* Hampshire, UK: Palgrave Macmillan.

Todd, R. 2003. Urban Aboriginal governance: Developments and issues. In *Not strangers in these parts: Urban Aboriginal peoples*, ed. D. Newhouse and E. Peters, 255-65. Ottawa: Policy Research Initiative.

UATF. 2007. *Urban Aboriginal task force: Final report.* The Ontario Federation of Indian Friendship Centres, the Ontario Métis Aboriginal Association, and the Ontario Native Women's Association.

Wotherspoon, T. 2003. Prospects for a new middle class among urban Aboriginal people. In *Not strangers in these parts: Urban Aboriginal peoples*, ed. D. Newhouse and E. Peters, 147-66. Ottawa: Policy Research Initiative.

3

Breaching Reserve Boundaries

Canada v. Misquadis and the Legal Creation of the Urban Aboriginal Community

YALE D. BELANGER

In 2002, the Federal Court in *Canada v. Misquadis* ruled that Human Resources and Skills Development Canada (HRSDC) had discriminated against the urban Aboriginal community, a decision upheld on appeal (*Ardoch Algonquin First Nation v. Canada (Attorney General)* 2003). The court determined that Aboriginal political organizations can represent urban Aboriginal interests and that the HRSDC must provide funding for the infrastructure required to deliver services and establish representative governance. In doing so, the court defined off-reserve Aboriginal people as a group of self-organized, self-determining, and distinct communities, analogous to a reserve community. While reinforcing the political connection between on- and off-reserve Aboriginal people, the court more importantly created an Aboriginal community separate from the reserve. This chapter revisits *Misquadis* and explores the underlying assumptions about urban Aboriginal communities upset by this ruling.

Overview

Writing in 2005, Thomas Biolsi (240-41) concluded that the nation-state "structures both political realities and subversive political imaginaries," leading to sovereignty being zoned accordingly, "so as to benefit some citizens systematically and, just as systematically, to disempower or otherwise harm other citizens." Historically, Canada embraced a similar approach, resulting in the materialization of a socially accepted systemic dichotomy that physically and ideologically situated those groups of individuals whom officials categorized as uncultured Indigenous populations in relation to progressive colonials. No consideration was given to those individuals moving to the cities in lieu of remaining on reserves, and urban migrants suffered from a lack of resources needed either to ease their transition or to promote their permanency. By the 1950s, political infighting had blossomed over where the precise responsibility for urban Indian populations actually lay. To the dismay of later urban Aboriginal peoples, federal policy makers came to consider reserve populations as Canada's authentic Indian communities under the Indian Act, making them solely entitled to federal programming dollars and rendering all Aboriginal peoples more manageable. First Nations, for example, remained dependent on federal funding and vulnerable to bureaucratic whims, whereas urban Aboriginal peoples were compelled to battle federal officials for legal recognition, hoping to secure the attendant funding arrangement (for a parallel discussion examining the New Zealand-Māori experience, see Hokowhitu, this volume). In this milieu, urban Aboriginal peoples were regarded as both a homogeneous grouping *and* a heterogeneous cultural jumble of reserve ex-patriots who had willingly abandoned their home First Nations. The assumed goal of federal policy, I would argue, was to have Indigenous peoples translate their upward mobility into private landowning capitalism and to develop a coincident acceptance of assimilation that federal authorities deemed to equal a budding intolerance for reserve relations and past living conditions. This assumed goal led to what Groves and Morse (2004, 267) classify as the "stunted development in the political recognition of [Aboriginal] collective identities": a problematic development for any community "whose capacity or willingness to achieve an autonomous existence was palpably absent."

A 2002 Federal Court decision put federal officials on notice that a shift away from entrenched attitudes was inevitable. That year, *Canada v. Misquadis* defined off-reserve Aboriginal people as a group of self-organized, self-determining, and distinct communities, analogous to First Nations (i.e., reserve communities). Ruling that HRSDC had discriminated against the urban Aboriginal community, the court also concluded that Aboriginal political organizations could represent urban Aboriginal interests. *Misquadis* reinforced the Supreme Court of Canada's *Corbière v. Canada* (1999) decision, which highlights the issue of "Aboriginality-residence" and its potential to discriminate against Aboriginal individuals living off-reserve. Each majority decision reasoned that living outside the reserve community did not silence an individual's voice in reserve politics, effectively eliminating the political lines that had previously distinguished reserve from urban residency (see also *Canada v. Esquega* 2008). With *Misquadis*, however, the urban Aboriginal community was legally recognized as a political community unique and separate from the reserve.

Several underlying assumptions held by the government and bureaucrats about urban Aboriginal communities were upset by the *Miquadis* decision, particularly the one previously accepted as fact: that people who foreswore reserve life for the city were progressives who wanted nothing more to do with their home First Nations. Related to this belief, which suggests an Aboriginal identity innately tied to the land – or, more accurately, to reserve communities – is a second assumption: that it is impossible for urban Aboriginal peoples to establish a sense of political community in cities (see Johnson, this volume). The reliance on stereotypes suggesting the existence of historic political animosities and cultural cleavages permitted bureaucrats to hold the popular belief that it was not possible to engender accord among celebrated enemies living in close urban proximity, something the *Misquadis* court nullified. The third and final assumption upset by *Miquadis* was that urban Aboriginal peoples, as city dwellers, had no legal rights, that leaving their reserves was a willing abdication of any and all claims to existing or future Aboriginal rights, and, more specifically, that their departures were an abdication of the rights accorded status Indians. The Māori of New Zealand confronted similar forces (see Kukutai, this volume). Suffice it to say, urban Aboriginal populations in Canada were afforded limited status by policies that failed to articulate either their rights or the attendant government responsibilities.

Misquadis fails to articulate specifically what an urban Aboriginal political community looks like, how it should operate, or what this conferral of community status means to First Nations and urban Aboriginal peoples. A lack of legal clarity notwithstanding, *Misquadis* has forced a re-examination of how popular stereotypes influence societal perceptions of urban Aboriginal communities, specifically, as occupying a foreign space, and how urban Aboriginal leaders are strategically positioning their populations as political communities to challenge Canada's continued reliance on a narrow band of identity markers for policy development. Arguably, the *Misquadis* court followed suit by articulating the belief that organized urban Aboriginal peoples are, indeed, political communities and that they collectively represent communities of rights. The purpose of this chapter is to expand upon this description to convey how the courts, to date, have portrayed what it means to be an urban Aboriginal community.

Stereotypical Conceptions of "Aboriginal Community"

Aboriginal people live on reserves. Until recently this was a Canadian certainty, and in many ways it is one that still enjoys substantial political currency. Canada's historiography is replete with references to reserve communities, and social science scholars during the twentieth century focused almost exclusively on reserve communities. Even the most comprehensive study probing the nature of Aboriginal difficulties, the highly acclaimed report by the Royal Commission on Aboriginal Peoples (RCAP) published in 1996, embraced a conceptual framework that focused decidedly on reserve/traditional lands, much to the detriment of urban Aboriginal issues. As defined by the Indian Act, Indians were considered a homogeneous grouping of individuals administered by Indian and Northern Affairs Canada (INAC) according to the act's provisions, and it was generally understood that they would remain on reserves until they chose to renounce their heritage. Individuals leaving the reserves were supposed to follow one of two paths: they would become farmers tending a private parcel of land or they would abandon the reserve and move to a nearby non-Aboriginal community. Upon relocating, they would cease to be federal responsibilities and become provincial citizens. And, in the process, they would become entitled to provincial programming. Inadequate bureaucratic attention was paid to Aboriginal people who chose to leave their home communities yet maintained their cultural affiliations. This lack of attention occurred because, from a federal perspective, they were no longer legally Indians.

From a policy standpoint, reserve residents were Canada's authentic Indigenous peoples according to the Indian Act and, thus, remained a federal responsibility. This meant that the government provided annual funding for community programming and band government operations. Urban Aboriginal peoples, however, were ignored as policy concerns. More important, federal policy established a reserve-urban binary by recognizing First Nations as political communities while making no provisions for urban Aboriginal peoples. This inflexible dichotomy between reserve and urban populations fuelled a process whereby the state determined Indian authenticity, which, in turn, informed federal funding formulas that rendered "invisible the complexity of historical interactions and the diversity of social groups" (Furniss 1999, 18). However, as Lucero (this volume) points out, the lived environment is an infinitely complex setting consisting of intersecting identities, which combine to formulate new identifies ad infinitum. Policy makers ignore these processes when conceptualizing monolithic urban Aboriginal communities (see Andersen, this volume).

The Supreme Court of Canada has acknowledged that all Aboriginal peoples "have been affected by the legacy of stereotyping" (*Corbiere v. Canada* 1999). A failure to distinguish urban Aboriginal policy concerns from reserve concerns continues to influence popular attitudes towards Aboriginal people, despite the fact that recent statistics confirm that permanent urban residency has displaced the reserve as the primary residence for the majority of Aboriginal people nationally. Yet, in the wake of escalating urbanization, Aboriginal people are still considered foreign visitors occupying an alien environment, an incommensurability that obliges limited municipal, provincial, or federal consideration (Peters 1996). Peters concludes that this is not surprising, considering the historically accepted incongruity between Aboriginal peoples and urban life. My current research into the not-in-my-backyard (NIMBY) phenomenon in southern Alberta and nationally suggests that urban architects have exploited this tension to discourage urban Aboriginal settlement, thereby enabling city founders across Canada to develop communities of like-minded individuals who crafted inclusive citizenship criteria that exclude Aboriginal participation. Consequently, Aboriginal individuals are expected to embrace accepted political models (i.e., municipal council, provincial legislative, and federal parliamentary) and collective municipal citizenship.

The key conclusions driving Indian policy development before *Misquadis*, and ultimately resulting in the failure to see urban Aboriginal peoples as policy concerns, hinge specifically on their predictable failure as organized political communities due to their displacement from their traditional territories and their historic governing and social processes. The resultant lack of guiding political principles compels cultural integration, which, inevitably, is followed by individuals' embracing accepted political models and collective municipal citizenship. This conceptualization is further grounded by a national multicultural policy that promotes a cultural plurality designed to assist the participation of ethnic groups (e.g., Indians) within Canadian society. Stereotypes stressing the simultaneous homogeneity and heterogeneity of urban Aboriginal peoples, regrettably, enable federal officials to distance themselves from this newly established collective of municipal individuals and enable the provinces to withhold appropriate programming from Indians who are still federally a section 91(24) responsibility.

Misquadis v. Canada

When Roger Misquadis sought access to the Aboriginal Human Resources
Development Strategy (AHRDS) in the 1990s, Human Resources Development Canada (HRDC) informed him that he would have to apply to his
biological mother's band on Manitoulin Island for funding in order to gain
access to the five-year, $1.6 billion program. A life-long Toronto resident,
Misquadis had little connection to Manitoulin Island, even if INAC considered it to be his "home" by virtue of his Indian registration. Intended to
improve Aboriginal employment skills, the AHRDS provided labour market
development programs to be delivered by Aboriginal organizations responsible for human resources development in order to enable Aboriginal communities to meet their own labour market needs. HRDC entered into
agreements with provincial and regional affiliates of the Assembly of First
Nations, the Métis National Council, and the Inuit Tapiriit Kanatami to
promote the importance of Aboriginal management and control over local
decision making in order to counter earlier programmatic failings. The
HRDC refused to consider establishing agreements with off-reserve Aboriginal communities and rural First Nations communities lacking reserves,
although, when pressed, it later responded by establishing an urban component of the AHRDS to provide urban and off-reserve access to services.

Misquadis and a coterie of off-reserve Aboriginal people claimed that
HRDC programming favoured First Nations, Métis, and Inuit peoples and
denied the urban Aboriginal population equal benefits. Federal officials
countered that the "local community control" concept was not intended to
suggest that every Aboriginal community could gain control over the design
and development of training and development programs; rather, the issue
was to ensure that intended beneficiaries (read: reserve communities) had
access to resources. The Federal Court (Trial Division) and the Federal
Court of Appeal disagreed with the HRDC's reasoning, concluding that
the AHRDS demeaned the petitioners' human dignity by restricting federal
programming to reserve residents. Unlike First Nations, which could exercise community control through representative political and legal bodies,
urban Aboriginal peoples were deprived of a similar opportunity, thus
leading to differential treatment. The court ruled that living off-reserve did
not specifically hinder the opportunity for local control of their human resources programming; rather, the root cause was Aboriginality-residence.
First articulated in *Corbiere*, the distinction between reserve and urban
Aboriginal communities was assumed to suggest that those living off-
reserve were individuals who had willingly chosen to be assimilated by

mainstream society. The court determined that the choice to live off-reserve is profound, that it is often compelled rather than voluntary, and that Aboriginality-residence led to numerous negative policy outcomes. In sum, the court maintained that urban Aboriginal communities should not be disadvantaged by virtue of their urban members' residency.

Since the AHRDS was an ameliorative program available to all Aboriginal peoples regardless of residency, the court held that the failure to recognize "that the respondents lived in communities which were functioning Aboriginal communities as worthy of recognition as reserve-based communities" was discriminatory (para. 36) as they were unique and separate political communities. This reflects the *Corbiere* (1999) decision, which rendered invalid the Indian Act's voting provisions on the basis that they violated section 15(1) of the Canadian Charter of Rights and Freedoms. As such, urban Aboriginal residency, defined by the court as "Aboriginality-residence," was considered an analogous ground of discrimination. Justices McLachlan and Bastarache determined at the time that "the complete denial to off-reserve members of the right to vote and participate in band governance treats them as less worthy and entitled, not on the merits of their situation, but simply because they live off-reserve" (*Corbiere v. Canada* 1999, 221). The court's determination that disenfranchisement by virtue of urban residency was discriminatory extended the First Nations franchise to band members living outside the community. And, with the franchise, they received a say in the community's daily governance.

In a similar 2007 decision, the Federal Court determined that chiefs and councillors do not have to live on reserves to be considered for political office, a decision upheld on appeal (*Canada v. Esquega* 2008). The latter case was in response to the Governor in Council's decision to set aside the election of all nine councillors selected in the November 2004 Gull Bay First Nation election because three candidates did not reside on reserve for the purposes of subsection 75(1) of the Indian Act. Consequently, only band members who resided on the reserve, located near Thunder Bay, Ontario, were deemed worthy of consideration for political office. Relying on the *Corbiere* decision as precedent, the court supported the principle that an urban community of Aboriginal peoples may aspire to maintain ties with its home First Nation. The central issues concerned the potential impact of such alliances upon reserve politics and program administration, and whether band funds would, with time, be dedicated to urban social and political issues. *Misquadis*, while similarly acknowledging political connections with First Nations, specifically identifies the urban Aboriginal community as a unique political community analogous to, yet distinct from, First Nations.

From the HRDC's perspective, exploiting the urban/reserve dichotomy was a suitable tactic, echoing Grammond's (2009, 40) contention that federal policies are developed with the intention of ensuring that those individuals who lack a legitimate membership claim are not "tempted to avail themselves of a portion" of federal resources allocated to status Indians living on reserve. HRDC officials argued that the diffuse nature of Aboriginal communities demanded an "economy-of-scale" approach to ensure that participating organizations and communities had the established infrastructure in place to ensure uniform service delivery. They also expressed fears about community fragmentation as a reason for withholding funding (*Canada v. Misquadis* 2002, paras. 148, 149). Fragmentation, in this instance, better describes an absence of a centralized governing authority related to program administration than it does community divisiveness and social disintegration. The court found "no clear evidence the applicants' communities are fragmented as to who represents them in labour training matters, HRDC did not realistically try to find out and it ignored the very organizations which operated successfully under Pathways" (para. 150).[1]

The *Misquadis* court expressed its confidence in the urban Aboriginal communities' ability to organize and to ascertain and implement coherent strategies on a case-by-case basis, enabling the development of plausible remedies (*Canada v. Misquadis* 2002, para. 155). Consequently, the issue now confronting contemporary Aboriginal and Canadian leaders is in many ways the amorphous definition of community, which lacks specific parameters. For example, Justice Lemieux, in his decision, did not consider the complex systems or the intricate web of connections characteristic of what constitutes a community, nor did he identify the contours of local social and political organization. The court also did not provide a discussion regarding social norms or, on a more basic level, what the community in question sought to achieve outside of local resources control. The *Misquadis* court did state that the "key to making the program work successfully" rested on "local decision-making by representative groups mandated by the applicants' communities" (para. 148). The specific form of that control remains undefined, along with questions of jurisdiction. The court did, however, leave it to the HRDC to consult with urban Aboriginal leaders to best determine how to fashion inclusion (para. 40).

By relying on the HRDC to consult with urban Aboriginal leaders, the *Misquadis* court anticipated that the government would abide by the court's order. However, since the court's determination was "more closely akin to a declaration of unconstitutionality coupled with an order directing the government to remedy the infringement of the respondents' rights," and since no public officer can be ordered to carry out a legal duty, the decision lacked teeth (para. 42). Furthermore, the Appeals Court recognized the potential difficulty in remedying the AHRDS, which expired 31 March 2004 without further alteration. The Appeals Court did conclude that the lower court's remedy should "guide any relevant negotiations under any new program that may succeed the current Strategy" (*Ardoch Algonquin First Nation v. Canada (Attorney General)* 2003, para. 51). Neither court spoke to the issue of government funding, yet their respective decisions unintentionally pitted urban Aboriginal communities against First Nations, all of which were theoretically now competing for a limited pool of resources. The lack of concrete discussion related to program execution was disturbing, as was the failure to highlight a clear and coherent policy vision delineating government responsibilities. Accordingly, these and like issues will become fodder for future litigation and negotiations, initiating what will likely become a long and drawn-out course of action resulting in marginal gains for the parties involved.

Legal Recognition of the Urban Aboriginal Community

Misquadis acknowledges something many Aboriginal people in Canada, along with an emerging collective of scholars (see the essays in Howard and Proulx 2011; and Newhouse and Peters 2003), have long suggested: that the existence of an organized urban Aboriginal political community should come as no surprise. Although *Misquadis* fails to articulate what role historic political processes and ideas played in this evolution, the court did challenge the implicit policy principle that First Nations are authentic while urban Aboriginal communities are non-authentic. According to this line of thought, First Nations have retained a modicum of historic governing structures while residing on the remaining parcels of their traditional homelands, whereas urban Aboriginal peoples are removed from this environment – physically, socially, and politically. Therefore, it is felt, they lack the historic orientation needed to secure political and cultural stability, and this lack of cultural and political mooring means that urban Aboriginal peoples are destined to fail as organized political communities. A reflection upon the urban Aboriginal community's evolution makes such attitudes appear somewhat brash, even if it is apparent that this stereotype continues to inform a collective societal understanding of what the urban Aboriginal community represents.

The HRDC's program model, for example, expresses little confidence that urban Aboriginal peoples could politically organize, and it bases that lack of confidence in part on cultural variances and diminished social capital within urban Aboriginal communities. The HRDC responded to the complaints made by Misquadis by describing in its factum HRDC officials' fears about urban Aboriginal political and cultural fragmentation, which led to the decision to deny programming to the urban Aboriginal community. A cadre of academics and policy makers further confirmed Aboriginal peoples to be in the throes of urbanization rather than settled urban residents, a state of flux that denied the possibility of administrative capacity. Federal policy provides little clarity for it specifies that a First Nation individual's home cannot be sited in multiple centres, even if these sites fall within previously utilized precolonial homelands (see Borrows 2000). Newhouse (2003), for one, is critical of this reductionist perspective and writes about what he describes as a largely overlooked infrastructure of Aboriginal organizations led by friendship centres that, in turn, led to amplified urban Aboriginal political visibility, beginning in the 1970s (see also Belanger, Fitzmaurice, and Newhouse 2008). What he and others alluded to is that this foundation and increased visibility, dating from the 1970s, resulted in the urban Aboriginal community's becoming fully established by the 1990s, a fact confirmed by the *Misquadis* court. The court takes it one step further, however, and identifies what policy makers and the RCAP commonly term a community of interest to be a political community possessing restricted administrative abilities.

The court's confirmation that a new Indigenous community is operating in a traditional Indigenous territory is a provocative decision. Historically, however, precontact Indigenous political systems embraced fluid citizenship models that promoted ease of movement among communities – models that attained international political standing when European Crowns negotiated treaties or instituted diplomatic relationships with First Nations (Barsh 1986; Henderson 2003, 2008). Accordingly, groups of individuals could "break away" from the larger collective to establish new political communities while still retaining membership in the larger nation. For instance, small family-oriented communities were common in the Plains region as individuals would break away from larger communities to establish their own with supportive followers. Informed by the ethic of non-interference that dictates individuals should refrain from telling others what to do (e.g.,

Brant 1990), those breakaway communities, frequently family-oriented, were common features of the precontact North American Indigenous environment. The ethic of reciprocity also meant that multiple memberships were customary features of this environment. In an effort to maintain regional balance, social contacts extended to various communities, resulting in the creation of reciprocal obligations of kinship and solidarity (see Little Bear 1996). *Misquadis* has, in a similar fashion, disabused us of the notion that to leave the First Nation is to abandon one's Indigeneity. Now, residency is no longer the issue. Instead, concern is being displayed over the political capacity to administer local programming, something the federal government acknowledges as a component of Aboriginal self-government.

As in historic times, economic and social pressures today have propelled individuals to relocate and to create new communities located in cities that happen to reside within traditional Indigenous territories. Such processes reflect a spirit of self-determination historically advocated by Indigenous leaders and that reinforces ties to traditional lands, even those covered in concrete. Canadian policy has yet to catch up to this way of thinking, and federal officials have yet to reconcile themselves to the notion of urban Aboriginal self-determination or, in this instance, the right of Aboriginals to self-administer appropriate programs in the city. The United Nations (2008, 4) has provided clarity by concluding that Indigenous peoples have the right as self-determining peoples to full and effective participation in all matters that concern them, according to the principle of free, prior, and informed consent, and to avoid "violation of their laws, traditions, and customs." It should be noted that self-determination as an internationally acknowledged right is not restricted to remote or rural areas. A close reading of the UN's self-determination criteria suggests that it applies also to urban Aboriginal communities (Belanger 2010). The intersection of various forces is apparent. The *Misquadis* court, in pronouncing the urban Aboriginal community a political community with the attendant right to self-administer, resonates with the historic Indigenous choice to establish an independent community in a traditional territory while retaining participatory rights in regional political processes, which the UN identifies as self-determination.

Detractors may erroneously argue that urban Aboriginal peoples are promoting separation from First Nations community and culture or, for that matter, from Canadian society. But, in fact, any demands made by urban Aboriginal groups reflect a wish to fulfil community desires for partnerships with both non-Aboriginal communities and governments that were guided by the spirit of treaty relationships, constitutional arrangements, and continuing group rights (e.g., Henderson 2006; Macklem 2001). Several First Nations in Canada, like the Federation of Saskatchewan Indians (FSI), known today as the Federation of Saskatchewan Indian Nations, have formally articulated what they believe these rights represent. Intending to establish the principles of Indigenous self-determination, the FSI produced a position paper in 1977 entitled *Indian Government*, which affirmed the inherent Aboriginal right to self-government. This paper briefly informed the federal government's approach to defining and negotiating self-government with First Nations and communities with a land base. However, in the early 1980s, Canada formally appropriated the self-government concept and tapered its scope (Belanger and Newhouse 2008).

First Nations and Aboriginal leaders continue to promote their "right to maintain their distinctiveness and to collectively determine their future development," which undermines attempts to limit our understanding of self-government for the purposes of reclaiming lost lands or to improve localized economic development to strengthen cultural saliency (Niezen 2003, 130). Additional evidence of the First Nations desire for self-determination is encapsulated in Indigenous claims that Canada failed to consult their leaders prior to facilitating their reluctant incorporation into the state (Tully 2000). From a federal perspective, however, urban Aboriginal peoples are provincial citizens, and officials portray the choice to move from the reserve as the repudiation of the reserve in lieu of seeking out improved urban living conditions. Assimilation is deemed to occur when an individual takes up urban residency, and no official thought is given to the fact that urban community building is occurring. This undermines historic Aboriginal citizenship regimes, which promote fluidity of citizenship, the need to acknowledge that historical and ideological continuity promotes multiple memberships, and the need to establish new communities in response to shifting economic, social, and political contexts (e.g., Henderson 2003; Slattery 2007). The UN (2007) provides a detailed definition of self-determination in its recently tabled Declaration on the Rights of Indigenous Peoples, to which Canada recently granted its assent. Article 2 of the declaration, for instance, expressly states that "Indigenous peoples and individuals are free and equal to all other peoples and individuals and have the right to be free from any kind of discrimination, in the exercise of their rights, in particular that based on their indigenous origin or identity." Expanding on this, Article 3 indicates that "Indigenous peoples have the right to self-determination. By virtue of that right they freely determine their political status and freely pursue their economic, social and cultural development."

Misquadis implicitly recognizes both of these articles in suggesting that urban Aboriginal communities possess a limited right to self-determination and, specifically, a right to deliver services. The court debunks the popular notion that urban residents are in some way less Aboriginal than reserve residents by highlighting the appellants' disadvantage at the hands of HRDC administrators, who perpetuated a stereotype by treating this group as "less worthy of recognition, and viewed [it] as being disorganized and less accountable than other [read: reserve] Aboriginal peoples" (para. 126). Justice Lemieux concluded that urban Aboriginal peoples "have the right to be free from any kind of discrimination, in the exercise of their rights," which in this case involved the right to deliver programs "based on their indigenous ... identity," which was tied to the city. The evidence presented demonstrating the urban Aboriginal community's organizational structure also impressed the justice, although he failed to identify a specific organizational model. He ruled that they had the right to federal funding aid in order to design, implement, and fund training programs to meet the needs of the appellants' urban communities (paras. 155, 158). Justice Lemieux dismissed concerns surrounding possible urban political fragmentation, the existence of which would question the possibility of urban Aboriginal political stability, although he did not detail his reasoning with specific discussion.

The Urban Aboriginal Community and Policy Implications

The significance of the *Misquadis* decision for both off-reserve and non-status Indians is easily apparent as it provides legal recognition of "Aboriginal communities outside the constructs of bands and reserves under the Indian Act, and affirms the rights of individuals in these communities to be given equal respect and consideration in application of the law" (Jamal 2005, 130). With this formal recognition, we are reminded of a number of important issues that continue to present significant policy concerns. For example, as a policy community, urban Aboriginal peoples continue to be vastly underrepresented in terms of federal programming and funding opportunities. Second, as discussed above, government officials previously assumed that Aboriginal people lose political and cultural coherence with urban permanency. Finally, reliance upon the Indian Act's rigid identity markers to define what constitutes an Indian or an Indian community, according to federal criteria, remains, at best, problematic.

The desire by First Nations to establish appropriate urban programs has been hampered by federal offloading of Indian programming, a situation that has been further aggravated by the complex matrix of Indian legislation and the various acts and policies that assign responsibility for First Nations development to a range of public agencies and individual band and tribal councils exploited by the HRDC. Justice Lemieux, however, did not accept arguments suggesting that Canada was entitled to abandon responsibility for urban Aboriginal peoples due to the constitutional complexity that federal officials insisted made successful political interaction difficult. The court, thus, put Canada on notice that improved financial support for urban service delivery is needed both to assist with individual transition to the urban environment and to encourage ongoing political structuring. Interestingly, and without specifically identifying the policy process being advocated, Justice Lemieux urged HRDC administrators to engage in what Walker (this volume) describes as co-production, or the generation and implementation of policies by state actors and community forces, in turn ensuring place making based on the full participation of urban Aboriginal peoples in policy, planning, and programming in the built environment (see also Ouart, this volume; Belanger and Walker 2009).

Promoting Aboriginal service delivery would also promote a sense of community, and funding is needed to generate this momentum. In recent years, various strategies have been offered to facilitate augmented funding arrangements that range from formally recognizing the urban Aboriginal community as a policy community – specifically delineating various agencies responsibility for Aboriginal peoples – to expanding the Aboriginal rights dialogue and, perhaps, to utilizing litigation. In the last case, advocates have been pressuring federal officials to accept health care as an Aboriginal right. If this becomes reality, urban Aboriginal peoples would have a recognized Aboriginal right to health care that would not be negatively affected by spending already committed by the government to status Indians confined to reserve communities. In such instances, suing the government to ensure its continued fiduciary obligation towards "Indians, and lands reserved for the Indians" has been proposed (MacDonald and Attaran 2007, 321).

Some people may consider the *Misquadis* decision to be only a slight victory, due to the fact that the court's decision identifying the urban Aboriginal right to administer operating funds more accurately reflects Canada's ongoing fascination with delegating authority to administer federal transfer payments than with any desire to embrace the spirit of Aboriginal self-determination. That the court determined the scope of jurisdiction and authority may also irritate some as it gives the impression of an inability, on the parts of both the courts and governments, to consider Aboriginal issues beyond a historic policy orientation stressing protection, assimilation, and civilization (e.g., Ladner and Orsini 2005). Also, as suggested above, formal recognition of the urban Aboriginal community could lead to increased tensions between First Nations and urban Aboriginal communities as they compete for a fixed revenue pool. The possibility of increased polarization is ameliorable, however, through augmented Indian affairs funding attributable to Canada's fiduciary duty as accepted in 1867 (e.g., Reynolds 2005). The *Misquadis* decision, as a benchmark, is important for discussion purposes and for expanding what is arguably a stale discourse on the topic of Aboriginal self-determination. It also highlights, as Hokowhitu (this volume) does in his examination of the emergence of a fourth space of Māori sovereignty, an important policy implication based on the fact that urban Aboriginal peoples in Canada are afforded fewer rights than are their neighbouring tribally based First Nations.

Planning must also take place in most cities that are home today to multiple Aboriginal peoples on what was historically the land of only one, or a few, First Nations, as with Vancouver's Aboriginal community. Prior to European contact, British Columbia boasted more than fifty-two languages and multiple First Nations. The land on which Vancouver is today was, historically, part of Coast Salish territory; at the start of the twenty-first century, on any given day, you are likely to find any of the province's multitude of First Nations (e.g., Squamish, Nisga'a, Tsimshian) in the city (see Norris, Clatworthy, and Peters, this volume; for similar American trends, see Snipp, this volume). Vancouver has also become an important political and economic centre for band councils with satellite offices as well as for a growing urban Aboriginal populace. Each of these groups, from its own perspective, is a unique cultural entity that endeavours, to the best of its members' abilities, to live closely to one another. There is a need to respect these historic and contemporary relationships, something that current policies have failed to identify. Urban Aboriginal leaders would be advised to take the lead in establishing relationships with political actors in their immediate orbit, a process that would both improve their visibility and institute a formal sense of community.

Granted, this is a difficult chore for, even with political evolution taking place, the Indian Act will continue to acknowledge First Nations only as political entities entitled to governance and program funding. In this regard, the Indian Act is, for good reason, duly criticized for its failure to respond to urban concerns. On the issue of economic development, for example, little thought was given to First Nations economic development prior to the creation of the Indian Economic Development Fund in the early 1970s and the Native Economic Development Program in 1983. Until 1951, the Indian Act contained fewer economic development provisions than there were rules in place to punish First Nations leaders for failing to cooperate with government demands for access to reserve lands for mineral exploration, for rights-of-way for highways and railways, and for leasing land to local farmers and ranchers (Treaty 7 Elders et al. 1996, 217). Reliance on legislation that is the root of interjurisdictional disputes and lacklustre community development practices should not be considered an appropriate course. Justice Lemieux's conclusion that urban Aboriginal communities have a nascent right to self-determination further challenges this legislative dependency, suggesting that our continued reliance upon identity models that assume a fixed identity tied to a specific geographical location (i.e., reserves) is problematic. A dearth of studies handicaps our analysis, but it is logical to suggest that the regular movement of individuals to and from the reserve results in interpersonal contact that influences urban Aboriginal political development since "political communities are organic and not fixed in time." In particular, "over the past several decades they have not only persisted among Aboriginal peoples in rural and reserve environments but also taken on urban identities specific to the city as a home-place, whether singly or intertwined with reserve/rural communities elsewhere" (Belanger and Walker 2009, 121).

As the Harvard Project on American Indian Economic Development reports, current Indian policies are developed according to a one-size-fits-all model, which relies on minimal input from Aboriginal people (e.g., Cornell and Kalt 2010). This approach neglects cultural and regional variance in favour of streamlining bureaucratic attempts at policy creation and implementation. Formal recognition of the urban Aboriginal community in Canada as a political community presents an opportunity to break away from static bureaucratic models by integrating community-based strategies into federal policy development. In addition to informing urban Aboriginal policy creation, the policies, once established, would reflect the diversity of cultures and unique circumstances characteristic of urban lifestyles. Input from the community as reflected in official policy would legitimize the process, thereby leading to acceptance and the belief that the Aboriginal voice is informing policy creation and implementation. Finally, assessing this performance is vital, and it demands the creation of comprehensive comparative indictors as well as provisions for monitoring and performance measurement to ensure urban Aboriginal social, political, and economic growth.

Conclusion

Canada v. Misquadis proclaims urban Aboriginal communities to be political communities and, in the process, establishes a legal framework to guide urban and First Nations community leaders, Canadian policy makers, and federal, provincial, territorial, and municipal officials to better determine what an urban Aboriginal community is and what it represents to the various agencies drawn into its orbit. I would argue that these are not absolute conventions; rather, they are part of an evolutionary process that began decades back – and one that continues to offer perspectives that assist in defining "urban Aboriginal community" within complex socio-political and socio-economic matrices. This important step in an emergent dialogue will, in all likelihood, guide urban Aboriginal leaders' community development strategies, although we must remain aware that urban Aboriginal populations have long envisioned acting on their own behalf, something the *Misquadis* court acknowledges to be an aspect of Indigenous self-determination. I would also concur with Greenop and Memmott's proposal (this volume, 257) that the fluidity of Aboriginal identity development be considered "part of the normal cultural dynamics that occur, rather than [being] fram[ed] ... within a viewpoint of assimilation and loss, as has occurred in the past." The logical outcome based on the above analysis would be modifications to service delivery protocol, thereby ensuring greater and more equal program representation (Peach 2004). As Tomiak (2009, 1) states, "a major challenge for Indigenous people who reside in urban areas is the lack of clarity with regard to the roles and responsibilities of different levels of government, Aboriginal governments, and local institutions." *Canada v. Misquadis* provides a road map to help further clarify these roles.

Notes

The author thanks Gabrielle Weasel Head for her fine research assistance. Any errors in fact and/or interpretation are the author's sole responsibility.
1 In August 2003 the City of Winnipeg released *First Steps: Municipal Aboriginal Pathways*. The city's principal long-range policy and decision-making document, *Plan Winnipeg 2020 Vision*, includes a policy statement to "Promote Self-Reliant Aboriginal Communities."

References

Ardoch Algonquin First Nation v. Canada (Attorney General). 2003. FCA 473.

Barsh, R.L. 1986. The nature and spirit of North American political systems. *American Indian Quarterly* 19(3): 181-98.

Belanger, Y.D. 2010. *The United Nations Declaration on the Rights of Indigenous Peoples (UNDRIP) and Urban Aboriginal Self-Determination in Canada.* Ottawa: National Association of Friendship Centres.

Belanger, Y.D., K. Fitzmaurice, and D.R. Newhouse. 2008. Creating a seat at the table: A retrospective study of Aboriginal programming at Canadian Heritage. *Canadian Journal of Native Studies* 28(1): 33-70.

Belanger, Y.D., and D.R. Newhouse. 2008. Reconciling solitudes: A critical analysis of the self-government ideal. In *Aboriginal self-government in Canada: Current trends and issues,* 3rd ed., ed. Y.D. Belanger, 1-19. Saskatoon: Purich.

Belanger, Y.D., and R. Walker. 2009. Interest convergence and co-production of plans: An examination of Winnipeg's "Aboriginal Pathways." *Canadian Journal of Urban Research* 18(1): 118-39.

Biolsi, T. 2005. Imagined geographies: Sovereignty, Indigenous space, and American Indian struggle. *American Ethnologist* 32(2): 239-59.

Borrows, J. 2000. "Landed" citizenship: Narratives of Aboriginal political participation. In *Citizenship in diverse societies,* ed. W. Kymlicka and W. Norman, 326-44. Toronto: Oxford University Press.

Brant, C. 1990. Native ethics and rules of behaviour. *Canadian Journal of Psychiatry* 35: 534-39.

Canada (Attorney General) v. Esquega. 2008. FCA 182.

Canada (Attorney General) v. Misquadis. 2003. FCA 370.

Corbiere v. Canada (Minister of Indian and Northern Affairs). 1999. 2 SCR 203.

Cornell, S., and J.P. Kalt. 2010. American Indian self-determination: The political economy of a successful policy. Working paper. The Harvard Project on American Indian Economic Development.

Furniss, E. 1999. *The burden of history: Colonialism and the frontier myth.* Vancouver: UBC Press.

Grammond, S. 2009. *Identity captured by law: Membership in Canada's Indigenous peoples and linguistic minorities.* Montreal and Kingston: McGill-Queen's University Press.

Groves, R.K., and B.W. Morse. 2004. Constituting Aboriginal collectivities: Avoiding new peoples "in between." *Saskatchewan Law Review* 67(1): 263-305.

Henderson, J. (Sakej) Youngblood. 2003. *Sui generis* and treaty citizenship. *Citizenship Studies* 6(4): 415-40.

–. 2006. *First Nations jurisprudence and Aboriginal rights: Defining the just society.* Saskatoon: Native Law Centre.

–. 2008. Treaty governance. In *Aboriginal self-government in Canada: Current trends and issues.* 3rd ed., ed. Y.D. Belanger, 20-38. Saskatoon: Purich.

Howard, H.A., and C. Proulx, eds. 2011. *Aboriginal peoples in Canadian cities: Transformations and continuities.* Waterloo: Wilfrid Laurier University Press.

Jamal, M. 2005. The *Misquadis* case. In *Legal aspects of Aboriginal business development*, ed. J.E. Magnet and D.A. Dorey, 123-36. Toronto: Butterworths.

Ladner, K., and M. Orsini. 2005. The persistence of paradigm paralysis: The First Nations Governance Act as the continuation of colonial policy. In *Canada: The state of the federation 2003*, ed. M. Murphy, 185-206. Kingston: Institute of Intergovernmental Relations.

Little Bear, L. 1996. Relationship of Aboriginal people to the land and the Aboriginal perspective on Aboriginal title. In *For seven generations: An information legacy of the Royal Commission on Aboriginal Peoples* [CD-ROM] (Ottawa: Canada Communications Group), cited in Royal Commission on Aboriginal Peoples, *Treaty making in the spirit of co-existence: An alternative to extinguishment.* Ottawa: Canada Communications Group, 1994.

MacDonald, N., and A. Attaran. 2007. Jordan's principle, government's paralysis. *Canadian Medical Association Journal* 177(4): 321.

Macklem, P. 2001. *Indigenous difference and the Constitution of Canada.* Toronto: University of Toronto Press.

Newhouse, D.R. 2003. The invisible infrastructure: Urban Aboriginal institutions and organizations. In *Not strangers in these parts: Urban Aboriginal peoples*, ed. D.R. Newhouse and E.J. Peters, 243-54. Ottawa: Policy Research Initiative.

Newhouse, D.R., and E.J. Peters, eds. 2003. *Not strangers in these parts: Urban Aboriginal peoples.* Ottawa: Policy Research Initiative.

Niezen, R. 2003. *The origins of indigenism: Human rights and the politics of identity.* Berkeley: University of California Press.

Peach, I. 2004. *The Charter of Rights and off-reserve First Nations people: A way to fill the public policy vacuum.* Saskatchewan Institute of Public Policy, Public Policy Paper No. 24. Regina: Saskatchewan Institute of Public Policy.

Peters, E. 1996. "Urban" and "Aboriginal": An impossible contradiction?" In *City lives and city forms: Critical research and Canadian urbanism*, ed. J. Caulfield, and L. Peake, 47-62. Toronto: University of Toronto Press.

Reynolds, J.I. 2005. *A breach of duty: Fiduciary obligations and Aboriginal peoples.* Saskatoon: Purich.

Slattery, B. 2007. A taxonomy of Aboriginal rights. In *Let right be done: Aboriginal title, the* Calder *case and the future of Indigenous rights*, ed. H. Foster, H. Raven, and J. Webber, 111-28. Vancouver: UBC Press.

Tomiak, J. 2009. *Urban Aboriginal self-governance in Ottawa, Winnipeg and Vancouver: Trends, problems and perspectives.* Ottawa: Institute on Governance.

Treaty 7 Elders and Tribal Council with W. Hildebrant, S. Carter, and D. First Rider. 1996. *The true spirit and intent of Treaty 7.* Montreal and Kingston: McGill-Queen's University Press.

Tully, J. 2000. The struggles of Indigenous peoples for and of freedom. In *Political theory and the rights of Indigenous peoples*, ed. D. Ivison, P. Patton, and W. Sanders, 36-59. Cambridge: Cambridge University Press.

United Nations. 2008. United Nations Declaration on the Rights of Indigenous Peoples. New York: United Nations.

4

"I Basically Mostly Stick with My Own Kind"

First Nations Appropriation of Urban Space
in Saskatoon, Saskatchewan

EVELYN PETERS AND CAROL LAFOND

*So there is that process within the urbans that I see, there's like a transition
you could almost say. That people are going back and looking at their culture
and saying, "You know what? We always had these principles of good living,
good life, education. Understanding what our roles are. We're not asking
people to go back to an old way, to go live in a teepee and stuff like that."
We're saying, "Those principles were there. Let's apply them today in our
society." (#19, adult male)*

In the quotation above, a First Nations man in Saskatoon, Saskatchewan,
summarizes the process of cultural innovation characterizing First Nations
peoples' use of the principles underlying First Nations cultural traditions to
fashion life in an urban setting. Cities are central sites for the development
of urban social movements, where groups with different interests, cultures,
and access to resources struggle to redefine their place (Isin 1999; Sandercock
1998). Holston (1998, 50) writes that these movements are "especially the
product of the compaction and its reterritorialization in cities of so many
new residents with histories, cultures, and demands that disrupt the normative and assumed categories of social life." In writing about these urban
social movements, many researchers turn to Lefebvre's (1996) writing on
the "right to the city" in order to understand the extent to which new residents have access to city spaces in ways that support their interests and

identities. According to Purcell (2003, 576-77), in Lefebvre's conceptualization, the right to the city is based on *inhabitance*; it is earned by living in
the city. The right to the city is the right of all city dwellers to "full and complete usage" of urban space in their everyday lives (Lefebvre 1996, 179, quoted in Purcell 2003, 577). It includes the right to appropriate urban space "to
live in, play in, work, in, represent, characterize, and occupy" so that it meets
the needs of inhabitants (Purcell 2003, 577-78).

As noted in the introduction to this volume (Peters and Andersen), the
history of colonial representations means that urban Indigenous people
face particular challenges in appropriating urban spaces in ways that support urban Indigenous identities. Decades of activism have failed to unseat
the association between Indigeneity and primitiveness in contrast to urbanism and civilization. As a result, Indigenous people living in cities face constant reminders that they and their cultures are viewed as "out of place" in
urban space. This chapter explores spaces of exclusion and inclusion experienced by First Nations people in Saskatoon. Their perspectives highlight the
challenges they faced in appropriating urban space to support their identities and cultures as well as the resilience with which they constructed spaces
of cultural safety within the urban milieu.

First Nations People and Urban Space

A number of studies address the ways that colonial histories affected First
Nations people's identities in cities (Peters 2011). They document the mechanisms though which First Nations peoples and communities were physically removed from growing urban spaces and the ways First Nations cultures
were defined as being incompatible with urban life (Wilson and Peters
2005). Presenters to the Round Table on Aboriginal Urban Issues for the
Canadian Royal Commission on Aboriginal Peoples (1993, 2) note the resulting challenges Aboriginal people face in urban areas because cities
represent "an environment that is usually indifferent and often hostile to
Aboriginal cultures." The association of "authentic" First Nations identities
with spaces outside the city means that in urban areas they are viewed as
"inauthentic" or degraded (Berkhoffer 1979, 30; Goldie 1989; Howard and
Proulx 2011).

This labelling of urban First Nations identities forms the basis of settler
racism, which affects First Nations lives on a daily basis. In its 1993 Round
Table on Aboriginal Urban Issues, the Royal Commission on Aboriginal

Peoples (1993, 45) reports that "Aboriginal people face racial discrimination every day, in every urban centre, on the streets, at work, and sometimes at home." Based on her analysis of the court case following the murder of a First Nations woman by two non-Aboriginal men in Regina, Saskatchewan, Razack (2002) concludes that stereotypes about urban Aboriginal people expose them to violence that is not controlled by the dominant justice system.

Another challenge for urban First Nations people comes from their cultural diversity. Clatworthy's (2000, xiii) study of the composition of urban First Nations populations in Winnipeg demonstrates their diverse cultural origins and legal status, and it concludes that these characteristics create a "barrier to social cohesion, culture and language retention and the development of a shared sense of community." Proulx (2003) notes the continuing tension in the face of diversity and limited resources that characterize the Aboriginal community in Toronto, Ontario.

In contrast, some sources view cities as places of opportunity for dynamic and emergent Aboriginal identities. From the public hearings it conducted across the country, the Royal Commission on Aboriginal Peoples (1993, 3) reports:

> Crossing the city limits does not transform Aboriginal people into non-Aboriginal people; they go on being the particular kind of person they have always been – Cree, Dene, Mohawk, Haida. The intention of Aboriginal people to go on expressing their Aboriginal identity and to pass it on to their children was a consistent theme in presentations by urban Aboriginal people at the round table and in hearings across the country.

In interviews with twenty-six Winnipeg inner-city Aboriginal community leaders, Silver (2006, 26) found that adult education for Aboriginal people, Aboriginal organizations based on Aboriginal culture, and parenting and involvement in school contributed to rebuilding "the pride in being Aboriginal and an understanding of the process and consequences of colonization." Respondents cited by the Ontario Urban Aboriginal Task Force (2007) list a number of factors that support urban Aboriginal identities: these include being with other members of the urban Aboriginal community; the values of caring, family, food, and daily acts of sharing; traditional teachings, ceremonies, and elders; languages; and cultural events. Based on their interviews with twenty Winnipeg Aboriginal youths, Belanger et al. (2003) found that they associated Aboriginal cultural identities with traditional activities (smudging, dancing, and powwows) and with events that aided in identity construction in the urban setting (such as university courses and programs for Aboriginal youth). Newhouse (2000, 404) highlights the effort required to support Aboriginal cultures in urban environments: "it does mean that one will need to take extraordinary steps to ensure the survival of Aboriginal cultures, including languages and spirituality."

Following a short description of the methods used in this study, we explore how First Nations participants were able to appropriate Saskatoon's urban spaces in ways that supported their identities as First Nations people. While participants experienced vulnerability, racism, and exclusion in many public places, they were also able to create public and private places where their cultures and identities were nurtured and safe.

Methods of Data Collection and Analysis

This chapter draws from a collaborative research project that focuses on urban Aboriginal identities in Saskatoon. Collaborators include the Saskatoon Tribal Council (STC) and researchers in geography and Native studies at the University of Saskatchewan. Saskatoon is a Canadian Prairie city with a population of 21,535 First Nations and Métis people, representing 9.3 percent of Saskatoon's population in 2006. In 2006, slightly more than half of the Saskatoon Aboriginal population (54.3 percent) identified as First Nations (Statistics Canada 2008). A protocol governing the research and writing process was negotiated with the STC before the grant application was submitted.

In a two-day seminar, the researchers (faculty and graduate students, a majority of whom identified as First Nations or Métis) working on the project created an interview guide. They drew on their own experiences and the results of previous work on urban First Nations and Métis identities in Canadian cities. Questionnaires were open-ended, inviting participants to share their stories and experiences and the sense they made of various events. The interviewers asked participants to describe activities and situations that helped support their cultural identities while they lived in the city and to give examples of places or experiences in the city in which their cultural identities were challenged or seen as being out of place.

The STC recruited participants by disseminating information about the study and by referring individuals. It also provided a room for interviews at its Saskatoon offices. Our focus is adult (twenty-six or older) First Nations men and women. Many of the participants worked at the STC. The purpose of this study is not to obtain a representative sample but to gain some under-standing of the structure of individuals' appropriation of urban spaces. Interviewers were First Nations students, and the interviews took place between 1 June 2007 and 31 August 2007. Interviews were taped and inter-view times varied from forty-five minutes to one and a half hours. After the interview, participants were offered an honorarium in recognition of their contribution. Tapes were transcribed and Atlas ti, a software coding program, was used to explore themes in the responses. These themes are represented below by a series of quotations from the interviews. The quo-tations have been edited to take out repetition and expressions that are not key to our analysis (e.g., "eh," "like," "you know"). In some earlier projects we found that participants were embarrassed by literal transcriptions that preserved every hesitation and repetition, so we have edited them out. Keeping every pause and word can also take attention away from what the participants are communicating. We recognize that in some types of textual analysis all of these elements are important, but that is not the case here.

Table 4.1 summarizes some basic characteristics of the participants. While average ages are similar for men and women, education and employ-ment levels were higher for women than for men. Women's employment and education rates were substantially higher than the average in the 2006 census for Saskatoon's First Nations female population (Statistics Canada 2008). Men's postsecondary education rates were higher than the census average, but the data for percent with less than Grade 12 education and for percent employed were close to the First Nations male average in Saskatoon. In aggregate then, participants represent a relatively more highly educated and employed population than is found in the larger Saskatoon First Nations population. A few participants lived on a reserve close to Saskatoon and commuted to the city for work. Most had grown up on a reserve, although a number attended boarding schools and lived on reserve only in the summers.

TABLE 4.1
Description of participants

	Women (*n* = 14)	Men (*n* = 12)
% with post-secondary education	64.3	38.5
% with less than Grade 12	21.5	61.5
Average age	39.1	41.2
% employed	85.6	50.0
% with connections to a reserve	71.4	83.3

Comparison data for this characteristic are not available from the census. Most participants would be able to compare reserve and urban opportunities and circumstances. It is important to emphasize, though, that this is not a representative sample; these data are provided primarily as context for the analysis that follows.

Exclusionary Public and Institutional Spaces

There are six main themes in participants' descriptions of the barriers to their ability to use and produce urban spaces in ways that support their cultures and identities. The responses of ten participants suggest that the city is not conducive to the creation of ceremonial spaces. Seven participants detail their or their children's vulnerability on the streets because of police treatment. Seven describe shopping stores as places in which their Aboriginal identities are associated either with theft or with not having money to purchase consumer goods. Participants also describe negative experiences in places of employment, housing, and health care institutions. The following paragraphs provide some details about First Nations experiences of exclusionary public and institutional spaces in Saskatoon.

Ceremonial and Celebratory Spaces

For almost half of the participants, cities are not places where their need for First Nations cultural and traditional ceremonies and celebrations could be adequately or appropriately met. Two participants detail why city spaces are difficult to adapt to these purposes:

> *A lot of First Nations people, they're forced to live in areas of the city that create more challenges for them to be able to maintain their own space the way that you need to, to carry on your own culture and traditions. Like in our family, where you keep sacred objects and things like that, they have to be protected and that's difficult a lot of times. People think that you can put a sweat for nothing, and now we have to pay for rocks and firewood. If you live in the country or on reserve then you have access to those things for free. (#7, adult female)*

> *It would make more sense to do [ceremonies and feasts] out on the reserve than to do [them] in the city here. When you're done with your feasts, you're putting away the fabric and the tobacco and you*

have to take it out of the city to put your stuff away. Out in the
country everything you need is right there. There's no laws, it doesn't
get noticed, and you don't need to make new things. You don't have
to worry about explaining what you're doing. Here people want to
know things, and some things are so traditional that it's hard for
you to tell them that it's something that they can't speak of. So it's
just easier when you're back home where everybody understands
what's happening. (#12, adult male)

These participants identify the cost of materials and the lack of understanding of other city residents. In the city these activities would "get noticed," presumably because many city residents would associate them with non-urban people and cultures. This lack of understanding or acceptance also means that it is difficult to keep sacred objects and traditions safe in the urban environment. Another participant indicates: "I feel safer doing my cultural activities at home than here in the city" (#8, adult female). Others simply note that participation in First Nations ceremonies and celebrations is an important element of their cultural identities, but they speak about it as taking place on the reserve. In these cases, the barriers to appropriating urban space for these cultural traditions are implicit rather than explicit.

I'm going back to [the reserve] next month to do a cultural event for
the weekend. It's a rain dance so I thought I'd take my family over
there and give back what I can. When we do our [ceremonies] it's
all in our language too, otherwise the Creator won't hear us 'cause
the language he gave us we're supposed to use to send upwards.
(#20, adult male)

Our family has regular cultural events, sweats, and we do our part
as far as powwows. We've got our home communities and attend
those as a family. It's very accessible to us because my wife's reserve
is only forty-five minutes from here and mine's an hour and fifteen
minutes so that's what we do. (#5, adult male)

For some First Nations people, then, the urban environment is perceived as unwelcoming to First Nations cultural practices. Other authors in this volume note the continuing ties many Indigenous people have with rural communities of origin (see Norris, Clatworthy, and Peters; Taylor; and Kukutai).

It may be that ideas about appropriate places for conducting traditional ceremonies underlie part of these attachments.

Vulnerability on the Streets

Stories about mistreatment by police highlight, especially, young men's vulnerability on the streets. Participants were not explicitly asked about their experiences with police, yet more than a third had stories about how they or members of their family had been picked up and accused of crimes they had not committed. These stories illustrate the difficulty many First Nations people have in appropriating urban space in the conduct of their everyday lives simply because they are visibly First Nations (see Comack and Silver 2008 for similar stories in Winnipeg). Two stories follow:

> *My son told me they were driving and they were stopped and they [police] were going to interrogate them. They said, "Come on you guys, you guys stole that, you know." My son said, "Just because we're brown, Dad, they wanted us to confess right there that we did that." And then I told him, "If you get into a situation, tell 'em you wanna talk to your dad." I said, "And tell them that your dad is a lawyer or something." So he's done that in that one instance.* (#19, adult male)

> *On the day before, on Christmas Eve, my son and his friend got picked up by the city police waiting [at] a bus stop on 33rd. They picked him up about 7 o'clock in the evening and they kept him in jail. They took away what change he had, took away his I.D. and his I-pod and they released him at 5 o'clock in the morning and he asked them for a ride home and they said they couldn't. They were accusing them of being gang members and they're not, and they accused them of a break and enter about two blocks from our house. They took them to that house and even the son and the father said, "No. Those weren't the boys that took the stuff that was stolen." But they still took them back downtown and they didn't allow the boys to phone home. Meanwhile me and [my husband] were driving around the city looking for them.* (#4, adult female)

First Nations women are also vulnerable in public places, with people signalling that they are prostitutes:

*Growing up and having to deal with racial discrimination, you
know, walking down the street and being called a "little Indian ho"
or something and for no reason. You know that really pisses a
person off. (#21, adult female)*

For many First Nations people then, the public areas of the streets are not
safe. On the basis of their appearance they are assigned, to use Goffman's
(1963) term, a "spoiled identity." In Goffman's theory, "spoiled identities" are
assigned through stigmatization, which attributes deviant characteristics,
behaviour, or reputation to particular groups, thus justifying discriminatory
behaviour towards them. First Nations people on the streets can be assigned
criminal identities. As a result, public space is not something that they can
safely appropriate for everyday activities without the threat of police harassment. This, of course, reminds them that their right to use these spaces is
under the control of the dominant society.

Discrimination in Stores and Other Situations
First Nations participants' experiences in retail and grocery stores demonstrate that they are stigmatized in these spaces as well as on the streets.
More than one-third of participants recounted experiences in which the
attitudes of store personnel communicated to them that they did not belong
in these establishments. Two types of interactions were reported: the first
is that First Nations people are ignored, and the second is that salespeople
make it clear that they would prefer not to serve them. The following example describes a First Nations man who is attempting to purchase clothing
for his children:

*I'd go shopping and there's a specific store in Saskatoon where they
kept ignoring me, and I would be walking [towards them] and
they'd turn around and take off the other way. I basically showed
him my cash and my wallet and said, "You know I have money. I
wasn't here wasting time and you missed out." And I walked out of
the store, and I knew it was because they thought I was probably
just killing time. (#5, adult male)*

In this and other examples, visibly First Nations people are viewed as "out
of place" because salespeople assume they are simply "killing time" rather
than engaging in appropriate shopping behaviour. In other cases, First

Nations people received excessive attention because they were assumed to be shoplifters:

> *I won't go to [that grocery store] anymore because they kicked*
> *[my son] out at winter time. It was minus forty degrees. They said,*
> *"You look like somebody that stole from him." He didn't even have a*
> *chance to say anything, they just kicked him out, so he snuck in the*
> *store to come and find me and he was crying and I said "That's it.*
> *I'm not coming back here again."* (#20, adult female)

> *Some businesses right away they watch you and they have people*
> *walking behind you, those floor walkers, and they automatically*
> *assume because you're walking with a school bag or with a diaper*
> *bag or with other bags from other stores that you're gonna boost*
> *[steal] and that's really frustrating.* (#4, adult female)

In other venues, First Nations people experience attitudes that define them as inappropriate workers, renters, and patients. Participants were aware of the perceptions of potential employers:

> *I don't sound Anishinabe over the phone, and there's many a time*
> *when I've gotten that interview and then they see me and that's*
> *when I know in my gut I'm not gonna be hired because of what they*
> *see.* (#17, adult female)

> *It's disappointing when a Native man has the same qualifications*
> *as the white man but they pick a white man first. They think that*
> *a Native man won't get up in the morning or show up for work.*
> (#46, adult male)

Participants also knew that many landlords perceived First Nations people as problematic renters:

> *We needed a bigger place and I phoned and phoned, and they would*
> *ask me what I did and I said I was attending the First Nations*
> *University. They assumed that I was probably First Nations and*
> *they asked how many children I have, and we have five children,*
> *and right away almost nobody could have any kids. And I had to*

call more than ten places. Then we looked at two other houses and
right in front of us the landlord, who was a male Caucasian, gave it
away to other [non-Aboriginal] people. (#2, adult female)

A number of participants also faced challenges obtaining health care because their symptoms were quickly attributed to drug or alcohol addictions. One of the participants left nursing school because staff prejudices were too upsetting for her:

In the hospitals you hear staff talking in the staff cafeteria about,
"Oh, this Indian came in this morning drunker than a skunk and
he was trying to get some pills," and then it turned out that person
wasn't even drunk. They were a diabetic whose sugar was high and
their condition had worsened to the point that they weren't even
able to carry themselves right or walk right. And that's why I gave
up on health care. I wanted to make a difference when I was taking
my nursing but I couldn't go through with it because it was just
bothering me too much. (#4, adult female)

These experiences took a strong emotional toll. Almost every participant talked about the emotional costs of moving about in public space. One woman talked about the need to build up confidence because everywhere she went she encountered signals that told her she was not "worthy":

People need to know how to build up confidence in a person, because
you're gonna run into different people all the time no matter whether
you're going to shop for groceries or going to Wal-Mart, you're
always gonna run into other people and you just gotta learn how
to have that confidence about yourself that when you go into some
place you're not gonna let anybody make you feel you're not worthy.
(#2, adult female)

Another woman indicated that the ways she was treated made her question where she fit in and caused depression:

A lot of times I get very, very, very depressed. I'm just wondering
where do I come from like, what group do I actually really fit in
with. But then I'll phone my mom and after I got done talking with
her I was okay. (#35, adult female)

A First Nations man who initially insisted that he experienced no challenges being identified as First Nations in the city subsequently broke
down when he talked about non-Aboriginal perceptions of First Nations
peoples:

> *Being identified as First Nations it's never been a problem [for me]*
> *... It's just the people that see us and put labels on us and they're the*
> *ones that are afraid of us. For a city this size, there's a lot of racism,*
> *and the way they look at us, there's this stigma ... This is really hard*
> *for me ... I figured that I had everything under control but it just*
> *awakened some hostilities that I thought I had laid to rest.*
> (#33, adult male)

On a daily basis, many First Nations people must prepare themselves for
discomfort and lack of safety when they participate in the ordinary institutions of the city. They do not have a "right to the city" in the sense of being able
to freely appropriate urban public space for their own needs and desires.

Inclusive Urban Spaces of Work, Aboriginal Events, and University

Against these spaces of vulnerability and stigmatization, First Nations
participants created some inclusive places in Aboriginal organizations, in
Aboriginal cultural events, and in Native studies at university. Half of
the participants described Aboriginal organizations as creating supportive
places; some of these individuals worked for the STC, some worked elsewhere. Half of the participants also described attending various celebrations and ceremonies organized through a number of organizations. Finally,
a number of participants indicated that taking university classes helped
them regain pride in being First Nations.

For some participants, working in an Aboriginal organization is positive
because it provides them with access to Aboriginal ceremonies:

> *Working here I still get to the smudging ceremonies and the*
> *powwows. If you need time off to attend one of those ceremonies you*
> *can usually get it pretty easy. They have no problem with a guy*
> *taking off in the afternoon to go to a sweat, so that's pretty good.*
> (#30, adult male)

Others emphasized the comfort of feeling like they belonged:

*With our working relationship here ... I find a sense of family,
belonging ... I find I'm very close with everybody here and I'm quite
happy about that.* (#28, adult female)

*I feel more at home when I'm in a First Nations organization or
meeting.* (#6, adult female)

Finally, some participants noted that seeing Aboriginal organizations in-
stilled pride. One participant explicitly mentioned that, when Aboriginal
people are seen working in business organizations, it sent a message that
Aboriginal people belonged to the community:

*I like the idea when I go into a store or even a fast food place and
you see Aboriginal people in there, you think, "Okay, well now
people are starting to recognize that these people are part of the
community too."* (#6, adult female)

While about half of the participants saw reserve and rural space as more
appropriate for First Nations celebrations and ceremonies, about half identified attending First Nations events put on by various organizations as one
way they supported their cultural identities in cities. According to participants, these events created positive spaces for the expression of urban First
Nations identities (see a similar argument in Johnson, this volume):

*The whole Treaty Day thing. And a few years ago my grandfather
celebrated his ninety-fifth birthday at White Buffalo. I had the
opportunity to be the M.C. and it was a good experience.*
(#16, adult male)

*When there's powwows or something here I'll take [my kids] there,
let them know who they are. They've been invited to go to sweat
lodges and things like that to learn about how it was ... We have
to know where we come from.* (#20, adult female)

I love going to powwows. (#32, adult female)

One individual detailed how a group he was involved with found appropriate ways of creating ceremonial spaces within the city. What is particularly
interesting about his discussion is the involvement of different cultural

groups in ceremonies. The heterogeneity of urban First Nations peoples means that particular First Nations practices and protocols are not readily available, particularly to First Nations groups who are in a minority in the urban First Nations community. Other researchers have found that this is one reason that First Nations people will go back to their reserves of origin to participate in activities appropriate to their particular culture (Wilson and Peters 2005). The group of First Nations referred to by this participant engaged in each other's ceremonies, creating shared First Nations cultural space within the city:

> *There's a group of us, a cross-section of people. There's like the Saulteaux, Cree, and different people. Within our group, we have people that do ceremony, that do sweats, for example. We have different types of ceremonies that are available to us, where elders are brought in, so we go and interact at that level. And we have the powwows. I dance, by the way. I'm a traditional dancer. So we do the powwows. (#19, adult male)*

While this is different than the "pan-Métis" strategy Laliberte (this volume) documents, it is a way of accommodating different traditional practices and adapting them to the urban milieu.

Participants' reflections about these events provided a stark contrast to exclusionary spaces in which First Nations identities are perceived as "spoiled identities." One participant reframed the perception of urban First Nations peoples by pointing out that the city was located in First Nations territory, that the city's name was based on a First Nations word for a local berry, and that First Nations were not leaving. She insisted that First Nations people contributed positively to the richness of the city's cultural environment:

> *I think we add a richness to [Saskatoon] that reflects where it's located [in Treaty Six space]. I think there's more of an awareness because we're here and we're not leaving. There's more to us than poverty and diabetes. There's a richness to our language, to our customs, to our heritage, and the very name [of the city] itself [Saskatoon] is the berry ... that's what it's named for. (#10, adult female)*

For another participant, these public events were ways of showing the rest of the population that First Nations were "good people" who helped to spread positive attitudes:

*When they have these powwows and they allow the people to come
in and watch they're showing people that they are good people. If
a family of people comes [to] watch a powwow, they talk to their
friends about this, and it sparks their interest and they wanna check
it out. So that's how it spreads. It's very contagious. Happiness is
contagious. That's what happens at powwows. It spreads happiness.
Positive attitudes in the end.* (#22, adult male)

Participants viewed these spaces of resistance as having the potential to challenge stereotypes of urban First Nations people that limit their access to urban public space.

Some participants were able to find a safe space in university classes that focused on Aboriginal subject matter. One participant related how, because of his Native studies class, he began to ask his father about his cultural background. As a result, his father, who had not previously shared details about his cultural traditions, began to teach him:

*I started university and I remember talking with my father and
asking about these cultural questions, so he asked me, "Where are
you learning this from? Who is teaching you this?" I said, "I'm going
to university, Dad, and we have this white professor that's teaching
us Indian studies." So he started laughing at me. He said, "You know
that's a sad day when a white man has to teach you your culture."
And I said, "Well what do I need to do then to find out about my
culture?" So that's when he started teaching me protocol. And
because of that I think I became a better person and a stronger
person. He was raised within the culture, by the old people. My dad
had a lot of knowledge and I was never aware of that because when
he married my mother he became a Roman Catholic as well and
practised that. And then in his older years he started taking his
pipe back out and he said, "Yeah, this is what I used to do."*
(#19, adult male)

Another participant described how, initially, the university was an intimidating space because the majority of students were non-Aboriginal. With other students in his cohort, he created a "Native space" within the university. Upon reaching his graduation, he felt that he was challenging negative stereotypes of First Nations people:

> *When I was going to university it was very intimidating to walk in*
> *there ... nothing but white students all over the place. And we were*
> *fortunate that we had our own lounge over at the ITEP [Indian*
> *Teacher Education Program] Lounge. We had our own place there.*
> *What helped me feel really, really good as a Native person was*
> *walking across that stage to go pick up my degree back in '87. And*
> *hearing my kids hollering "Yeah dad!" And looking at the majority*
> *white crowd I remember thinking that, "Hey, I'm a Native person.*
> *Look at me." You know, I've shown these people that Native people*
> *can graduate just as good as they. (#50, adult male)*

In the context of exclusionary urban public space, First Nations participants were able to carve out some spaces of pride, comfort, belonging, and
contribution.

Inclusive Private Spaces

Many First Nations participants experienced the private spaces of home and
First Nations family and community as the safest and most comfortable
places in which to practise their cultures and traditions. Almost half (elev-
en) mentioned their largely First Nations social networks positively (on the
importance of First Nations social networks, see Andersen, this volume; and
Greenop and Memmott, this volume). Eleven respondents described their
experiences within the home, and five identified the micro-spaces created
when they spoke their First Nations language in culturally supportive spaces.

Urban Social Networks
One participant detailed how Aboriginal social networks formed when she
was a university student in Saskatoon in the 1980s. She indicated that
Aboriginal people in the university identified each other through their appearance and that urban Aboriginal organizations facilitated the building of
urban Aboriginal community (see also Ouart, this volume). In another section of her interview, she noted that her social networks and the presence of
other family members in the city made her urban experience a positive one:

> *I was in university and our network of Aboriginal people, we'd all*
> *just kind of bumped into one another. Like we knew who everybody*
> *was on campus pretty much if they had a darker face. So invariably*
> *we'd end up either at parties or other social functions. Where the*

*Cultural Centre is located now used be a business centre ... called
SINCO, and they used to have this hall where they'd have dances,
so you'd meet up with the people that were not from the university
because the SINCO Centre was part of the FSI [Federation of
Saskatchewan Indians]. You had your politicians and your support
people who worked for the FSI and then you had us as students.
The Friendship Centre used to have dances. If you got a good band
that's where everybody was, so you had an expanded network of
Aboriginal people.* (#10, adult female)

Many other participants noted that most of their socializing occurred within the urban Aboriginal community:

*There's a lot of Saulteaux people, my relatives live here in the city.
They're the people I talk to most when I'm in the city. People that
I know.* (#12, adult male)

I'm generally around Native people. (#28, adult female)

*I basically mostly stick with my own kind, with First Nations. I
don't really have too much to do with white people any more unless
I'm applying for work or something.* (#33, adult male)

*There is the whole sense of community, like at my mother's place,
for instance, we still practise a lot of the visiting every day and so
there's always those reminders [of cultural identity]. I have a lot of
family that lives here in the city too.* (#16, adult female)

Two elements are noteworthy in the above quotes. First, some participants seem to intentionally limit their interaction to the Aboriginal community, and this behaviour is almost certainly influenced by the discrimination they experience in urban public space. Second, cultural practices of "visiting" likely absorb people's time for socializing and help to consolidate their identities as First Nations people within the city.

Home
In her article entitled "Homeplace: A Site of Resistance," bell hooks (1992, 2) writes about black homes as spaces "where black people could affirm one another and by so doing heal many of the wounds inflicted by racist

domination." First Nations participants presented their home environments in a similar way – as places where they passed on cultural identities and practised private First Nations cultural traditions.

A number of participants described how they taught their children who they were as First Nations people and attempted to instill in them a sense of pride in their identity:

> *When you're looking at your genealogy chart and where you come from and there's a long line of respected people there ... I try and teach my children. I have a son and a daughter and I tried to teach them who they were and to be proud of who they were. I learnt that from my mom and dad.* (#11, adult female)

Another participant emphasized the importance of teaching her children pride in their identities because it helped to prepare them for the negative stereotypes they would inevitably face outside the home:

> *The biggest thing is just being a mother, knowing that I have to be there for my children and protect them and teach them. I think if you feel confident in yourself, you can do anything and go anywhere. And it's harder for people to belittle you or put you down because you already feel comfortable with yourself. So if anybody was to say anything, like make a racial comment, I think you'd be able to handle it better.* (#2, adult female)

The home was also a site for teaching children appropriate First Nations behaviours and protocols so that they would know how to act in First Nations settings and not embarrass their parents:

> *My kids know what to do at feasts or at sweats or ceremonies. It's just natural for them to understand. We teach them the basics that they have to know. I guess the easiest way is to say ... if anybody met my kids they'd know that they have an identity, that they learnt respect. And when they see an older person coming into the house, they'll get up off that chair that they're sitting in.* (#4, adult male)

Another participant felt that, because his children had been brought up with pride in their identities, they would be able to combine First Nations trad-itions and societal influences in order to create alternative urban futures:

*All of them, all of my kids identify [as First Nations]. We raised our
children within the culture and they compete [in dancing] at that
level. They're proud of who they are. I think this generation is gonna
make a difference. We have warriors that have knowledge within
the urban people. We have what we call contemporary warriors
who are able to be influenced not only by traditional [ways] but
[by] the [contemporary] society, and [what they] take from there
they make it their own. They bring that within their culture and
they make it strong, and I see these young people, like my son and
them, they're contemporary warriors.* (#19, adult male)

Participants also mentioned private cultural practices conducted in their
homes:

*We got our smudge stuff. We got our stuff hanging on our walls that
we need, too, and it's always there. I'm pretty private though. I don't
go around preaching to everybody how I practise my culture.*
(#5, adult male)

*This is my own personal thing. I follow traditional path. Practise pray-
er in the morning, using smudging of sweet grass.* (#19, adult male)

Micro-Spaces of Language and Cultural Interaction

Finally, some participants talked about the micro spaces of cultural inclusion created when they spoke their language with other people. The ability
to do this clearly gave them pleasure and put them "at ease":

*But I try teach [my kids] Saulteaux, what this and this means, and
when they pronounce it, it's pretty, it's enjoyable. It makes me proud
that I know that information for them and just being around the
people from my reserve and them not being shy to ask me what
words mean.* (#41, adult male)

*A lot of the times I'll identify myself from my language. So somebody
comes up to me and starts talking Cree, I'll respond in Cree. A lot of
times the elders will say something to me in Cree, then I'll respond
in Cree and that kind of puts me at ease. Then they can talk to me.*
(#40, adult male)

Conclusion

First Nations people's daily experiences in public spaces, spaces of work, and other institutions interfere with their "right to the city," their right to use urban spaces in ways that support their goals, aspirations, and needs. Assumptions of inappropriateness, criminality, laziness, and irresponsibility associated with being visibly First Nations means they are not free to act like ordinary inhabitants of the city and so must create an exclusionary urban space. Many participants were uncomfortable engaging in larger ceremonial gatherings in the city, were vulnerable to police harassment or worse on the streets, and faced discriminatory attitudes in stores, in their search for housing, and in the health care system. However, First Nations residents were also able to appropriate some urban spaces in ways that were supportive of their cultures and identities. Aboriginal-run organizations and businesses provided comfortable environments, allowed workers to participate in cultural events, and were seen as communicating a positive message about belonging to the larger urban populations. Aboriginal content in university and First Nations events sponsored by a variety of organizations supported the expression of First Nations cultural identities. It was in the private spaces of home and First Nations social networks that First Nations participants were able to regroup and to develop strategies for coping with public discrimination and stereotypes. In these spaces, participants passed on pride in, and knowledge about, First Nations cultures to their children and engaged in practices that expressed their spirituality. They enjoyed sharing their languages with other First Nations speakers and socializing with other First Nations people.

Living in the city means living in an environment that is often hostile to First Nations cultures and identities. Participants in this study explained how they appropriated urban spaces to ensure cultural survival. In the words of one of the participants, they are "warriors," adapting to the conditions of urban life by using principles and practices taken from First Nations traditions.

Note

The research assistance of Jim Tailfeathers is gratefully acknowledged. The research was funded by a SSHRC Strategic Research Grant entitled Urban First Nations and Métis Identities.

References

Belanger, Y., L. Barron, C. McKay-Turnbull, and M. Mills. 2003. *Urban Aboriginal youth in Winnipeg: Culture and identity formation in cities.* Report prepared for Canadian Heritage, Winnipeg, Manitoba.

Berkhoffer, R.F. 1979. *The White man's Indian: Images of the American Indian from Columbus to the present.* New York: Vintage.

Clatworthy, S. 2000. *First Nation affiliation among registered Indians residing in select urban areas.* Winnipeg: Four Directions Project Consultants.

Comack, E., and J. Silver. 2008. "A Canadian exception to the punitive turn? Community responses to policing practices in Winnipeg's inner city." *Canadian Journal of Sociology* 33(4): 815-84.

Goffman, E. 1963. *Stigma: Notes on the management of a spoiled identity.* Englewood Cliffs, NJ: Prentice Hall.

Goldie, T. 1989. *Fear and temptation: The image of the Indigene in Canadian, Australian, and New Zealand literatures.* Montreal and Kingston: McGill-Queen's University Press.

Holsten, J. 1998. Spaces of insurgent citizenship. In *Making the invisible visible: A multicultural planning history,* ed. L. Sandercock, 37-56. Berkeley: University of California Press.

hooks, b. 1992. Homeplace: A site of resistance. In *Yearning: Race, Gender and Cultural Politics,* ed. b. hooks, 1-50. Toronto: Between-the-Lines Press.

Howard, H.A., and C. Proulx, eds. 2011. *Aboriginal peoples in Canadian cities: Transformations and continuities.* Waterloo: Wilfrid Laurier Press.

Isin, E.F. 1999. Cities and citizenship. *Citizenship Studies* 3(2): 165-72.

Lefebvre, H. 1996. *Writings on cities.* Malden, MA: Blackwell.

Newhouse, D. 2000. From the tribal to the modern: The development of modern Aboriginal societies. In *Expressions in Canadian Native studies,* ed. R. Laliberte, P. Settee, J.B. Waldram, R. Innes, B. Macdougall, L. McBain, and F.L. Barron, 395-409. Saskatoon, SK: University of Saskatchewan Extension Press.

Peters, E.J. 2011. Emerging themes in academic research in urban Aboriginal identities in Canada, 1996-2010. *Aboriginal Policy Studies* 1(1): 78-105.

Proulx, C. 2003. *Reclaiming Aboriginal justice, identity and community.* Saskatoon: Purich.

Purcell, M. 2003. Citizenship and the right to the global city: Reimagining the capitalist world order. *International Journal of Urban and Regional Research* 27(3): 564-90.

Razack, S.H. 2002. Gendered racial violence and spatialized justice: The murder of Pamela George. In *Race, space and the law: Unmapping a white settler society,* ed. S.H. Razack, 131-56. Toronto: Between the Lines Press.

Royal Commission on Aboriginal Peoples. 1993. *Aboriginal peoples in urban centres.* Report of the National Round Table on Aboriginal Urban Issues. Ottawa: Minister of Supply and Services.

Sandercock, L. 1998. *Making invisible the visible: A multicultural planning history.* Berkeley: University of California Press.

Silver, J. 2006. *In their own voices: Building urban Aboriginal communities.* Halifax: Fernwood.

Statistics Canada. 2008. Labour force activity (8), highest certificate, diploma or degree (13), attendance at school (3), Aboriginal identity (8), age groups (12A) and sex (3) for the population 15 years and over of Canada, provinces, territories, census metropolitan areas and census agglomerations, 2006 Census – 20 percent sample data. Catalogue no: 97-559-XCB2006027. 28 October.

Urban Aboriginal Task Force. 2007. *Urban Aboriginal Task Force. Final report.* Toronto: Ontario Federation of Indian Friendship Centres.

Wilson, K., and E.J. Peters. 2005. "You can make a place for it": Remapping urban First Nations spaces of identity. *Society and Space* 23: 395-413.

5

Being Métis

Exploring the Construction, Retention,
and Maintenance of Urban Métis Identity

RONALD F. LALIBERTE

The definition of Métis identity has long been a source of controversy. In 1982, the recognition of the Métis as one of three Canadian Aboriginal groups (i.e., Indian, Inuit, and Métis) was reinforced with their inclusion in section 35 (2) of Canada's Constitution Act. Métis political organizations view Métis people as members of a culturally distinct group with its own history, language, tradition, and government. The national political organization of the Métis, the Métis National Council (MNC), states: "Métis means a person who self-identifies as Métis, is of historic Métis nation ancestry, is distinct from other Aboriginal peoples and is accepted by the Métis nation" (Gionet 2009). The MNC defines the Métis nation homeland as "an area in west central North America." Others have put forward a broader definition of "Métis." For example, Frideres (1998, 38) argues that there is "no one exclusive Métis people in Canada," noting that the eastern Canadian Métis are seen as different from those of the historic Métis homeland centred in western Canada. The 2006 Canadian census definition of the term "Métis" reflects this broader definition: "Métis refers to people who identify as Métis on the Census" (Gionet 2009). In effect, the census definition allows people to decide for themselves whether they are Métis and does not connect Métis identity to an association with the historic Métis nation. Andersen (2008) argues that census criteria displace the idea of a Métis identity based on Indigenous nationhood and introduce an identity based on race – that is, of "mixed" European and Indigenous ancestry.

In essence, then, there are two seemingly opposing dynamics of Métis identity: one that is based on European and Indigenous ancestry and one that is rooted in the ability to trace descent back to the historic Métis nation emerging in western Canada. Such diversity of identities and realities among those who identify as Métis not only reinforces the complexity, ambiguity, and fluidity of Métis identity formation but also creates tension and dissention around who qualifies as Métis.

Yet, Métis identity has never been stronger and it shows no signs of weakening. Nowhere is this more evident than in the recent dramatic increase in the number of people who identify as Métis in answer to census questions. In 2001, census data found the Métis population totalled 292,310 people representing a 43 percent population increase from five years previously (Statistics Canada 2001). This was the highest population increase among the Aboriginal groups in Canada. In subsequent years, this trend continued as the census in 2006 reported that the number of those who identified as Métis rose to 389,785 people, nearly doubling the size of the Métis population since 1996 (Statistics Canada 2006). Most Métis, approximately seven out of ten, or 69 percent of the Métis population, lived in an urban area, especially in large cities in western Canada, making them the most urbanized of the Aboriginal groups (Statistics Canada 2006).

Despite the high percentage of Canada's Métis population residing in cities, there is almost no literature that discusses urban Métis identity. This chapter begins to address this gap in the literature by exploring how Métis people speak about their Métis identity in the city. The following section briefly reviews some available literature on dimensions of urban Indigenous or Aboriginal identities. Then I provide a summary of the emergence of a Métis culture and nationalism, particularly in central North America. After a short methodology section, I explore the main elements of urban Métis identity found in interviews with Métis in Saskatoon, Saskatchewan. By way of conclusion, I discuss some of the political ramifications of these results.

Literature on Urban Indigenous/Aboriginal Identity

To understand urban Aboriginal identity, it helps to take into consideration the fact that many Aboriginal people have resided in the urban setting for over five decades and that their lives are as diverse and complex as are those of any other urban group. During the 1960s and 1970s, much of the literature on urban Aboriginal people characterized their lives as consisting of abject poverty as a result of racial discrimination, lack of employment, and poor housing, which, in turn, caused their marginalization (Nagler 1970; Brody 1971; Dosman 1972; Krotz 1980). Recent literature, however, provides deeper insights into the existence and reality of urban Aboriginal people, including: urban Aboriginal people have a high mobility rate compared to that of non-Aboriginal people (Norris and Clatworthy 2003); there is a diversity of Aboriginal languages spoken in the urban areas (Norris and Jantzen 2003); an increasing segment of the urban Aboriginal population is moving towards positions within what Wotherspoon (2003) calls "the new middle class"; and, although urban Aboriginal people are victims of social exclusion, they are increasingly becoming more engaged in a process of decolonization aimed at healing and revitalizing their traditional cultural values (Silver et al. 2006). In short, recent literature indicates that urban Aboriginal people are becoming more integrated into the economic and social fabric of urban life. Furthermore, it suggests that, as Aboriginal people continue to become immersed in, and adapt to, the urban setting, this process inevitably affects and shapes their identity.

Although some literature exists on Aboriginal urbanization, there is very little on urban Aboriginal identities (but see Howard and Proulx 2011; Proulx 2006). As Peters, Maaka, and Laliberte (2009, 1) point out, identification as an Aboriginal person in Canada has important implications since the state often provides social and economic benefits based on Aboriginal rights and population size. Healey (2006, 4) defines identity as:

> a sense of belonging that derives from shared origins or characteristics. Shared origins include having the same parents or being born in the same geographical area. Shared characteristics include a common language or livelihood, elements that are frequently (though not always) a function of origin. According to this understanding, someone that identifies or is identified as belonging to a group must share origins and characteristics, or elements of both, with other members of the group.

However, as Peters, Maaka, and Laliberte (2009, 1) point out:

> Increasingly views have moved away from the essentialist perspective on identity which defines it as a recognition of common origin or shared characteristics with another person or group, leading to a natural allegiance, with a "stable core of the self" which does not change over time or place. Identities are now viewed as socially constructed. From this viewpoint,

rather than representing a pre-existing "essential self," identities exist only as they are constructed to differentiate between "self" and "other."

As such, Indigenous identities are not understood as historical and unchanging reflections of Indigenous cultures of the past; instead, Indigenous people draw on the Indigenous past and on their struggles with colonialism to create a new future – one that defines a historical trajectory of their own as opposed to that of their colonizers (Peters, Maaka, and Laliberte 2009, 3). As Peters, Maaka, and Laliberte assert: "This perspective shifts the focus from a debate about the sources of Aboriginal identities to a discussion of how Aboriginal people draw on their cultural heritage and their experience of colonialism to make sense of their place in contemporary society" (ibid.)

Bronwyn Fredericks (2004, 3), a Murri woman from South East Queensland, Australia, reinforces Peter, Maaka, and Laliberte's (2009) perspective on identity formation. She states:

> There is no single urban Aboriginal experience or identity. The experiences are as diverse as the population and include a diversity of experience, need, prospects shaped by gender, education, religion, age and level of human security. Culture cannot stay the same, it is dynamic and there are many cultural configurations. Aboriginal people live in the contemporary world and weave in and out of two, three and even more cultural domains. We are part of colonization, just as it is part of us. Aboriginal culture has needed to adapt, adjust and modify itself in order to survive within the contemporary world.

Furthermore, says Fredericks (2004, 31), "Urban Aboriginal people are not 'hybrids' or alienated from the Aboriginal experience. Aboriginal culture is dynamic and new Aboriginal identities have developed in response to urban life. Urban identities will keep developing and adapting as they did in the past and as they do in the present. This is about our survival."

Kinship ties have been articulated as a primary defining feature of Indigenous identity and social organization (Yamanouchi 2009; Maaka and Fleras 2005; Strauss 1943). Kinship refers to one's relatives by both blood and marriage and was an integral part of traditional Indigenous cultures. Macdougall's (2006, 433) study of the Métis of northwestern Saskatchewan during the fur trade points out that kinship ties were important for the retention and transfer of Métis cultural identity: "Familial relationships or the concept of relatedness was an idealized social value by which Métis people attempted to order their society." Macdougall goes on to argue that the Métis style of life based on familial relationships was transmitted intergeneration-ally through the extended family (434). Troupe's (2009) study of early Métis organizing in Saskatoon finds that, although women were not often in a public leadership role, relationships between families were usually based on women's kinship ties, and women played essential supporting roles behind the scenes for Métis political and social activities.

In many cities, the urban Aboriginal population is diverse and made up of Aboriginal people who may not share the same cultural background or speak the same Aboriginal language (Norris and Jantzen 2003). Consequently, this makes it difficult for some to establish social relations with other urban Aboriginal people based on kinship ties (Yamanouchi 2010, 1). Nevertheless, urban Aboriginal organizations provide a venue for bringing together Ab-original people who are not related through kinship. In doing so, urban Aboriginal organizations reinforce the links between different Aboriginal people by promoting the commonality of their traditional values and beliefs. As a result, Aboriginal organizations have been conducive to the develop-ment of "pan-Aboriginality," which promotes unity and treats Aboriginal people as "one homogenous group" regardless of tribal or band differences (Frideres 1998, 286-88). Although some fear that pan-Aboriginality under-mines tribal identities and knowledge, others view it as important for pro-moting unity among urban Aboriginal communities and for the persistence of urban Aboriginal cultural identities (Proulx 2003).

Urban Aboriginal organizations also help those who cannot establish kinship ties but want to re-identify as Aboriginal. In such instances, urban Aboriginal identity can be defined through a combination of ancestry, ap-pearance, cultural knowledge, and Aboriginal community participation. Yamanouchi (2010, 4) describes this process as being "fluid": for example, although someone does not appear Aboriginal and cannot verify Aboriginal kinship ties, she or he may be accepted through participating in, and con-tributing to, the community and through demonstrating a good grasp of Aboriginal cultural knowledge.

While kinship ties are still an important element for the identity of Aboriginal people, the social construction of Aboriginal identity in the urban environment is complex. In particular, Yamanouchi (2010, 4) argues that the rise in the number of urban Aboriginal people whose kinship ties are not recognized by dominant organizations, and claims to be Aboriginal by people who were not raised in an Aboriginal community, causes urban

Aboriginal identity to be "ambiguous." As a result, some urban Aboriginal individuals are accused of being "inauthentic" or are characterized as "wannabees" (i.e., individuals with no Aboriginal blood but who "want-to-be" Aboriginal). Lawrence (2004) documents the challenges urban mixed-ancestry Aboriginal people face in defining their identities in the city. Because they have for the most part not grown up in an Indigenous community, do not speak an Indigenous language, and often cannot identify with either their European or their Aboriginal heritage, many of them feel that others do not view them as truly Aboriginal. I now turn to how these issues affect Métis living in Saskatoon.

A Brief Historical Overview of Métis Identity

The history of the Métis as a distinct Aboriginal group is relatively short. While communities of individuals with Aboriginal and non-Aboriginal ancestry came into being in many areas of Canada, the term "Métis" is most often used to refer to those who can trace their ancestry back to the historic Métis of the settlements in the Red River area, which is now part of southern Manitoba. Descendants of European men and First Nations women, the Métis played a particular role in the fur trade in what would later become the Prairie provinces. During the 1800s, the Métis population increased and the Red River area became the centre of Métis cultural identity. In 1821, the North West Company and the Hudson's Bay Company (HBC) amalgamated under the name of the Hudson's Bay Company. The newly reformed company shut down nearly half of its trading posts throughout the northwest, causing many Métis employees and their families to relocate to the Red River Settlement. Before long the Métis comprised the majority of the settlement's population.

By the mid-1800s, the cultural identity of the Métis was well established throughout the northwest. The strength of Métis identity was bolstered by the important economic roles they filled as fur trade employees, agriculturalists, and hunters and trappers (Sealey and Lussier 1975, 14). The Métis also dominated the buffalo hunts, which provided hides and meat for pemmican, a commodity in great demand by the HBC. The necessity for organization and discipline on the buffalo hunts played a significant role in shaping Métis political organization and cohesiveness (Barkwell 1991, 14-17). Other hallmarks of Métis cultural identity at the time included: a land tenure system consisting of river lots, where people cultivated small gardens and raised a few livestock; the blending of the material culture of their forefathers with that of their maternal ancestry to create a unique style of dress (Sealey and Lussier 1975, 13-18); the blending of the Cree and French languages to create their own language, called "Michif" (Crawford 1985, 231-40); a distinct form of floral art (Brasser 1985, 221-28); and the blending of the dance steps of the Plains First Nations with the reels and square dances of their Scottish fathers to create a dance called the Red River Jig (Sealey and Lussier 1975, 18-19).

In the late 1800s, however, two events severely undermined the Métis sense of nationalism. In 1869, as settlers poured into the Red River area, the HBC negotiated to transfer its territory to the newly formed Dominion of Canada. As a result of not being consulted on the transfer, the Métis at Red River seized power and demanded their rights be negotiated before they would join Canada. Under the leadership of Louis Riel, the Métis formed a provisional government and negotiated with Canada the Manitoba Act, 1870, which stipulated that the Métis would receive land grants in recognition of their rights. In time the Canadian government made numerous changes to the Manitoba Act that, in effect, dispossessed the Métis of their land allotments (Sprague 1980). Because of the hostility of the settlers and the inability to secure land rights in Manitoba, the majority of the Métis population dispersed, with many Métis people moving deeper into the northwest.

In the early 1880s, the Métis located around the south branch of the Saskatchewan River in the Northwest Territories and centred in the St. Laurent/Batoche areas petitioned the Canadian government to secure their land rights. When the government failed to respond, Riel, who was exiled to the United States following the Métis resistance in 1869-70, was called back to champion the rights of the Métis. In response, the government sent the militia to the northwest to suppress the unrest among the Métis and defeated them in the "Battle of Batoche." Following 1885, the government sent scrip (certificates that entitled the holder to homestead land) commissions to the northwest to deal with the Métis land claims. However, the overwhelming majority of Métis scrip ended up in the hands of land speculators, who bought them at prices well below face value (Hatt 1986). Landless, defeated, demoralized, and ostracized by non-Aboriginal society, many Métis became impoverished and were relegated to the fringes of settlements, where they lived in shacks and did odd jobs to survive (Giraud 1956).

In the early 1900s, the strength of Métis identity was likely at its lowest point in the history of the Métis as a people. As a result of the racial discrimination from all levels of non-Aboriginal society, "they suppressed their Métis identity" (Dobbin 1984, 186-87). Moreover, their living and health conditions were deplorable (Pocklington 1991; Barron 1990). Yet, in spite of their condition, provincial Métis organizations began to emerge in the 1930s to agitate for Métis rights. As Pocklington (1991, 21) states, "a remarkable resurgence occurred in which a formidable Métis organization was created almost overnight and a government forced once again to address the issue of land for the Métis." The resurgence of the Métis under such oppressive conditions was not only an indication of the resilience of their identity but also of their strength of character, as reflected in the determination to pursue the measures necessary for redress of their grievances. Many of these organizations involved both Métis and First Nations people (then called "non-status Indians") who had, for various reasons, lost their official status with the government. The political alliance reflected the fact that both groups experienced similar problems, such as poverty and a lack of recognition from the federal government (Sawchuk 1985, 141).

During the 1960s, the civil rights movement of the blacks in the United States created fertile ground for the Métis to once again assert their identity and press the government to address their grievances. In addition, outspoken Métis leaders, such as Howard Adams, were instrumental in reigniting a sense of Métis nationalism (Purich, 1988, 160-63). The identification of the Métis as one of three Aboriginal peoples in the 1982 Canadian Constitution raised the profile of Métis people and provided additional grounds for pursuing the recognition of Métis Aboriginal rights. The Constitution also drove a wedge between non-status First Nations and Métis people, and, because of the need to clearly identify their members (who might benefit from any rights or privileges granted to Métis people), Métis political organizations began to restrict their membership to Métis (see Métis Nation Saskatchewan at http://www.mn-s.ca). This history provides a context for the expressions of Métis identities for urban Métis residents.

Methodology

Saskatoon is a Prairie city in Saskatchewan in western Canada, and in 2006 it had a population of 230,855 people, of whom 9,610 were Métis and 11,510 were First Nations (Statistics Canada 2006). It is situated a relatively short distance from a number of small Métis communities and First Nations reserves. In the summer of 2007, interviews were conducted with individuals who resided in the urban environment and identified as Métis people. The interviews were conducted for a collaborative research study that focused on urban Aboriginal identities. The research partners in the study included the Saskatoon Indian and Métis Friendship Centre (SIMFC) and faculty members in the geography and Native studies departments at the University of Saskatchewan. My analysis draws on the data collected from forty-two semi-structured in-depth qualitative interviews that were conducted for this project. Informants were contacted through the SIMFC, through posters, and through the snowball technique. Informant consent was gained verbally or by a signed consent form. In keeping with Aboriginal tradition, an honorarium was offered to informants for sharing their knowledge. The interviews were on average one hour in length and were tape-recorded for accuracy.

The informants were divided into cohorts. The largest cohort consisted of 34 adult Métis, 25 years of age and older, with 19 being female and 15 being male. The average age of the adult females was 48 and of the adult males was 43. The other cohort consisted of 8 young Métis, 18 to 24 years of age, with 6 being female and 2 being male. The average age of the young females was 22 and of the young males was 21. Of the Métis females, 56 percent of the adult females had postsecondary education compared to 50 percent of the young females. Of the Métis males, 67 percent of the adult Métis had postsecondary education compared to none of the young Métis. Also, among the Métis females, 56 percent of the adult females were employed compared to 33 percent of the young females. Among the Métis males, 47 percent of the adult males were employed compared to none of the young males.

Most of the interview questions were open-ended, and reviewers prodded participants to elaborate on their answers in order to obtain rich descriptions. The questions upon which I focus were designed to elicit participants' views of their Métis identity. For example, participants were asked to describe their cultural identity, how they maintained their Métis identity, and what reinforced their identity in the urban environment. The data were then analyzed for emerging themes. Extensive quotes are reproduced in this chapter in order to present Métis perspectives using the subjects' own words. Although the research project was not designed to generate a representative sample, the absence of published material on this topic means that these results could serve as a foundation for subsequent analysis.

Exploring Urban Métis Identity

In their descriptions of their cultural identities, 88 percent of the informants linked their Métis identity to family members or ancestors. Along with family connections, 71 percent of the informants linked their Métis identity to their communities of origin. This suggests that a connection to a specific place and to land outside of the urban setting has particular relevance in defining the identity of many urban Métis people. Some of the comments related to kinship and place of origin are as follows:

> *I'm originally from St. Laurent, Saskatchewan. It's a farming community about sixty miles northeast of Saskatoon ... and right beside the South Saskatchewan River ... It is I believe the only parcels of land that are described as river lots in Saskatchewan dating back to, to early years ... It's about five miles from Batoche ... My ancestors are [of] Scottish descent as well as French and Aboriginal.* (Métis male, 54)

> *I'm from a place called Ile a la Crosse ... and I'm Métis. My grandma was full-blooded Cree and my grandfather was English so that makes me a half-breed and I speak my language very fluently and I understand the language. So ... in regards to cultural identity I identify myself as a Métis.* (Métis male, 48)

> *I grew up in a small Métis town ... about 550 kilometres northwest of Saskatoon and it's called Ile a la Crosse ... [I was] really fortunate to grow in a community where a lot of people there were Métis and the culture is pretty strong and there was never an identity issue because ... my mom was [Métis], my dad was and so were my grandparents ... and my siblings. Also [in] school ... we were taught about our history so ... I learned from an early age about Métis history in Saskatchewan and in Canada. So I think that's really quite unique and really built a strong identity. And that's where I grew up and then I moved to Saskatoon when I was nineteen and I've been here since.* (Métis female, 34)

> *My mom was a Lavallee and my dad was Bourassa. And I married a Gardepy. That's a full-blown Métis ... Just growing up there was so many Métis that we didn't even know the difference I don't think. Like the Henrys and the Fiddlers and all that, you know, Bissetts and the Barrettes and the Parenteaus and, you know, we didn't know the difference. 'Cause we grew up with the whole bunch.* (Métis female, 76)

I was originally born in Turtleford just outside Thunderchild First
Nation. I then moved to Meadow Lake and been there for ... three-
quarters of my life prior to moving to Saskatoon ... I'm a Métis guy.
I still have scrip land passed on to me through my ... kōhkom
[grandmother] who was born and raised right in Batoche. My scrip
land is still in Batoche ... My dad was Norwegian, my mom was
Métis. (Métis male, 44)

My father was from Lac La Biche, Alberta, and my mother was
from Ile a la Crosse ... I'm proud of my heritage. I'm proud of my
culture and the traditions and I don't have a problem, you know,
making that known ... I am Aboriginal and I am Métis and I'm
proud of my culture. (Métis female, 60)

These quotations highlight the importance of growing up in a Prairie Métis community when structuring contemporary urban Métis identities. The first quotation refers to river lots, which characterized early Métis settlements in Red River, giving every family access to the river. Two quotes refer to Ile a la Cross, a well known northern Métis community. The seventy-six-year-old Métis woman quoted next lists a number of Métis family names and indicates that she grew up surrounded by so many Métis that she "didn't know the difference." The next quotation mentions scrip – certificates for land issued by the federal government to deal with Métis land claims, and Batoche, an important Métis historical site. The last participant identifies two Métis communities as part of the source of her identity. Reserves have been identified as important sites for the cultural identities of First Nations peoples (Cardinal 1969), and it appears from these quotations that historic Métis communities played a similar role. All of the communities referenced by these participants are located in the historic Métis homeland. And this raises a question about whether mixed-ancestry communities in other parts of Canada gave rise to similar community identities. While some participants note their mixed ancestry, suggesting that they recognize this as an important component of Métis identities, this was not the main marker of their Métis identities.

Another subset of participants also link Métis identity to mixed ancestry, but in these cases, Métis appears to be an identity they adopted because they could not, or chose not, to be First Nations. In other words, this identity appears almost as a "default," a "non-First Nations" identity, in contrast to the rich cultural communities that supported other participants' Métis identities:

> *My mother is Ojibwa and my father is white.* (Métis male, 41)

> *My dad's Treaty ... and my mom was white.* (Métis male, 40)

> *My dad is an immigrant from Ireland ... I could probably be Treaty ... but it's just too much work ... My mom's full-blooded Native ... It's ... a lot of research that I just don't have the time to do.* (Métis female, 19)

> *If someone questions my heritage or my ethnic background I identify myself as a Métis man. Currently I'm non-status, but I'm going through to get my status ... My mom gave up her status when she married my dad because he's white ... but she's re-applying for her status as well.* (Métis male, 43)

> *[I'm] Migmah [Micmac], Acadian Scottish ... my father's from New Brunswick ... his grandfather came to New Brunswick from Gaspe from a reserve ... and his mother was born ... on a reserve on Gaspe across from Hamilton. And in the political context in eastern Canada if you are of mixed descent, which means Acadian and Migmah, that's considered Métis.* (Métis female, 26)

> *My family in Alberta, they're all Treaty and I chose to be Métis because my family didn't register me as a Native when I was born ... I didn't know how to go about it and I know I have Aboriginal background so I registered myself as Métis.* (Métis male, 28)

Claiming Métis identity primarily on the basis of mixed ancestry demonstrates variations in understandings of what it is that generates Métis identities. It may be that, unlike the Toronto mixed-ancestry individuals who experienced difficulty claiming an Aboriginal identity, Aboriginal mixed-ancestry individuals in Saskatoon, in the heart of the historic Métis homeland, find that associating with the Métis provides them with a way of expressing the Aboriginal part of their background. The co-existence of these different sources of Métis identity means that the Métis community in Saskatoon is diverse.

According to participants, it is mainly through parents that the cultural identity of urban Métis people is learned, internalized, and maintained. More specifically, Métis identity is transmitted intergenerationally mainly through Métis female parents and grandparents, indicating that Métis women play a significant role in the retention, maintenance, and persistence of urban Métis identity. When one seventy-one-year-old Métis woman was asked how she maintained her identity, she stated:

> *We have taught them [i.e., her children] what I was taught through my parents; you should always be proud of who you are and where you come from. With my children, I am very happy that they're that way. It's a great way to be.*

Another Métis woman, age fifty-four, was asked how she passed on Métis identity to her granddaughter, and she stated:

> *We talk ... a lot about it. We brought books home from the library that specifically talk about the Michif language and Gabriel Dumont ... and the whole revolution and stuff ... We read to her.*

In urban areas, participants maintain and express their Métis identities through a variety of cultural traditions and practices. These include food, language, commemorative events, dancing and music, and dress. There is also mention of maintaining relationships with other Métis, especially through kinship networks:

> *I attended ... some of the cultural events ... like the Red River Jig and the fiddling ... which is all ... part of our culture and so I try to attend as many as I can ... in our community ... When I was growing up, one of the things that I noticed so much was the hospitality given to ... basically anyone that ... would come around, whether it be at lunch time, supper time, or just the gatherings and just sittin' around telling stories or the old house dances ... I think some of the Métis people still ... do that in the city, and it's the gatherings and it's being able to ... discuss a lot of this stuff that is not work related ... It's the family close-ness that really has a big impact on Métis peoples.* (Métis male, 54)

> *I continue today ... to keep my language, that's what makes part of my identity is language, which I still have. I haven't lost ... my*

language, my tongue. I can still speak it and understand it and also I still practise some of the ... history, like the jigging part of it and the fiddle music. (Métis male, 48)

When we have Louis Riel Day ... I'm always proud on that day that I'm Métis but I'm proud any time. (Métis female, 60)

I'm excited to tell people I'm Métis, that I can speak my Michif language ... I'm proud of it, proud of where I come from because ... we're the second oldest settlement in Saskatchewan. (Métis male, 48)

Batoche Days ... that's our cultural identity ... John Arcand Fiddlefest is one of the biggest ... When I got married we jumped over a broomstick and we did all that stuff, the traditional Métis [way] ... We did ... our jigging ... and ... [wore] our sashes ... and all that kind of stuff so [it was] pretty neat. (Métis male, 44)

My daughter ... she's married to ... a Métis and the younger girls are Métis ... I try to teach them ... what the sash is and get them involved with things at the Friendship Centre and ... I'm trying to make my grandson jig. (Métis female, 52)

We ... wear a Métis sash ... I always instill in my grandchildren ... to be proud that they are Métis ... I teach them about the sash, what it means, and different ... foods that we have like bullets (boiled meat balls) and bannock and [that] sort of thing. (Métis female, 56)

Made sure they [his children] learned their language and their culture, dance jig, most of them play guitars ... I jigged practically all my life ... I danced for the Queen in Regina once. (Métis male, 52)

Basically, I keep in touch with my family, that's pretty much the only way I can [maintain my Métis identity]. My parents, my aunties, the elders, and I make sure my children get in touch with them ... and I think it's learned ... like from generation to generation, it's passed down. (Métis male, 28)

These practices are characteristics of the Métis culture that emerged in the historic Métis homeland. Urban Aboriginal organizations build on these practices to help to create a Métis presence in the city and to shape a shared and larger collective Métis cultural identity in the urban setting. Participants indicate that urban Aboriginal organizations play a significant role in the maintenance of Métis identity (see Ouart and Kukutai, this volume, concerning the important role of urban Indigenous organizations). Organizations such as the SIMFC, Wanuskewin (park and museum), the Gabriel Dumont Institute (education and research organization), the White Buffalo Youth Lodge (youth activity and recreation centre) as well as Oskayak (high school) and Saskatchewan Native Theatre are mentioned as places where Métis people frequently visit one another. However, the organization mentioned most frequently is the Central Urban Métis Federation Inc., (CUMFI), Local 165 of the Métis Nation-Saskatchewan. Between 15 and 36 percent of the informants stated they were members of CUMFI. CUMFI provides a means of establishing social relations among urban Métis people who come from diverse backgrounds and various regions. Here are some examples of participant statements about local urban Aboriginal organizations:

I belong to a really strong Métis Local. We have all kinds of different cultural activities. Also being at the Friendship Centre we have a lot of Métis celebrations and promote the Métis culture in the area of music and artefacts. (Métis female, 56)

Keep in touch with your local and ... participate with your locals ... the activities and stuff. Being with the Métis, the CUMFI local ... a lot of my family members are in there. (Métis female, 25)

CUMFI [is a] prime example ... Central Urban Métis Federation has a very strong presence and identity in Saskatoon. (Métis male, 44)

I'm Local 165 – CUMFI ... I go to all their functions and I donate my time ... whenever they need me. (Métis female, 76)

Well, being involved [with] our local CUMFI, being involved at [the] Friendship Centre, just getting involved with [these] programs. (Métis female, 52)

I do participate in ... pretty well all of the functions that are going on at the Friendship Centre and through CUMFI, which is the Local. (Métis female, 71)

Urban organizations such as CUMFI are instrumental in promoting a collective identity among urban Métis people based on the traditions and practices of the Métis culture that emerged in central North America. Even though the Métis in Saskatoon come from different backgrounds and areas of the country, many find a collective cultural community and identity in the activities of urban Aboriginal organizations.

Several participants whose own families consist of a First Nations and a Métis parent emphasize the importance of teaching their children both cultures:

> *My kids are half Saulteaux [First Nations] and half Métis so ...*
> *we have to teach them both sides of the cultural aspects of our ...*
> *identities so [my wife] can teach them First Nations culture ... the*
> *traditions ... and I teach 'em the Métis part of it, [the] Métis history*
> *part of ... my identity and culture.* (Métis male, 48)

> *My husband he's First Nations ... but I'm not ... [There are] Red*
> *River Jig classes which I'm gonna be bringing my daughter to in the*
> *spring when they start up again. I'm gonna ... teach her how to*
> *dance. Like she's part of both ... She doesn't have to think that she's*
> *only Treaty to dance this way or Métis to dance this way ... I*
> *brought my son in here for drum lessons when they had their*
> *powwow drumming lessons.* (Métis female, 33).

Of interest here is the fact that, while children are being taught aspects of both cultures, these cultures are clearly seen as different, and children are being instructed in these differences. As other authors have noted, in the city there are more opportunities for families to be comprised of partners from different cultures (e.g., see, this volume, Lucero; Snipp; Taylor). While it is not possible to generalize from the limited examples in this study, the participants' understanding of the uniqueness of First Nations and Métis cultures resulted in their attempting to communicate a bicultural identity to children rather than a pan-Aboriginal culture that did not identify the different cultural sources of particular practices.

The majority of Métis people interviewed for this study felt that urban Métis people were not being recognized in the city to the same extent as were First Nations people. These comments indicate a consciousness that, as Aboriginal people, Métis people should have a position similar to that of First Nations peoples with respect to government programs and services:

They [non-Aboriginal people] tend to always think of only First Nations ... I've been to a few workshops [where] I've had to set them straight and say ... "We have to be included too," because ... when you apply for funding it says Indian and Métis ... I make a balance of First Nations stuff and Métis stuff and when I'm in a group I ... usually stress that I'm Métis and to please include the Métis when they speak about Aboriginal groups, First Nations, and Métis. (Métis female, 60)

After 120 years ... we don't have any rights at all ... we're still struggling to get health, education, and housing paid for ... Everything that we have is paid by ourselves, housing, health, education, so it's a struggle for our people ... to identify ourselves as Métis in comparison to the First Nations people ... We don't have any rights, our rights, and I feel that the identity is still there even though we don't have these things ... We're still [able] to identify ourselves as Métis people. (Métis male, 48)

They're [the Métis] recognized in the Constitution as being one of the three Aboriginal peoples ... But as far as [rights and services for] Métis specific[ally,] they still haven't [taken responsibility], probably because ... the federal government ... says, "Well, no, you're [a] provincial [responsibility]." (Métis male, 44)

Native [i.e., First Nations] people have all of their own stuff, powwow ... Wanuskewin ... They got stuff going on like that all the time. There they are teaching dances at Mount Royal [high school], teaching them about powwow ... [For] Métis people I don't see anything ... happening in the city at all ... Métis really get into those old songs and jigging and stuff, but you don't see jigging lessons or anything. ... It's a lot easier being Native than it is Métis ... But Métis ... it's hard to keep your culture identity. (Métis male, 44)

The Saskatchewan Indian Federation, and the Saskatoon Tribal Council, they got ... so much traditional stuff, parenting classes. I don't understand it, I'm Métis ... What they need is more programs for Métis people to be able to understand themselves ... understand their ways of life. (Métis male, 48)

I find it unfair, because a lot of what First Nations people have today, Métis people fought and struggled for those rights and I don't feel that they get a fair share of them. I think they get left out a lot. I think they should have a lot more rights covering our medical, and basically a lot more rights covering every area. (Métis male, 38)

Generally, participants felt that Métis people were being left out of economic development and cultural initiatives for urban Aboriginal groups. Comments by Métis informants suggest that the lack of funding for these initiatives creates difficulties for the retention and maintenance of urban Métis identity. Some participants pointed out that, despite this lack of support, Métis identities survive in urban areas.

Summary and Implications

This chapter discusses themes linked to being Métis in Saskatoon. Origins in historic Métis communities and family or kinship ties are seen as important sources of an urban Métis identity. However, some participants identify as Métis mainly because of their mixed ancestry and their inability or lack of desire to gain First Nations status. Urban Métis people learn their cultural identity and what it means to be Métis from their parents, and informants identify Métis women as playing the most significant role in the persistence of urban Métis identity through maintaining Métis cultural traditions and values and transmitting them to family members. In Saskatoon, Métis individuals from diverse backgrounds and locations form a collective identity around the history and cultural traditions of the historic Métis in central North America. Urban Aboriginal organizations use these markers of identity to create a shared Métis identity. Participants feel that, in comparison to urban First Nations people, urban Métis people are excluded from economic development and cultural initiatives. While it is beyond the scope of this study to further verify this assertion, comments by Métis informants suggest that such economic disparity negatively affects urban Métis identity. Nevertheless, this study finds that most urban Métis people possess a strong Métis cultural identity.

When these factors are considered together, they strongly suggest that a pan-Métis identity exists in the urban environment. Other researchers identify a pan-Indian or a pan-Aboriginal identity emerging in some cities as individuals from different Aboriginal origins create community and share

practices. What is unique in Saskatoon is evidence of the emergence of a
Métis identity based on the cultural markers of the Red River Métis but
shared by individuals whose origins are within this community. Clearly,
these results cannot be generalized, and additional research is needed to
explore the nature of this process. It is also not clear whether this development is unique to Saskatoon. Troupe (2009) documents a long history of
Métis organizations in Saskatoon, and it may be that pan-Métis identities
with these characteristics are most likely to develop in cities with strong
urban Métis organizations. The creation of a pan-Métis identity represents
one way that urban Aboriginal people are creating new responses and communities, drawing on historic traditions. Urban Métis identities are dynamically constructed in response to the challenges and opportunities of urban
life (see Greenop and Memmott, this volume, for a similar argument concerning urban Aboriginal people in Australia).

The presence in Saskatoon of participants who identify as Métis, but who
come from different backgrounds and locations throughout Canada, suggests that many urban Métis will not meet the criteria established by Métis
political organizations for membership. This is especially true when these
organizations require members to be able to trace their ancestry back to the
historic Métis homeland. This has the potential to lead to political conflict
between those in the urban environment who identify as being Métis based
on criteria established by Métis political organizations and those who self-
identify as Métis based mainly on mixed ancestry. There may be two implications. The first has to do with the cultural dislocation of individuals who
know about their Aboriginal ancestry but who have no ties to an Aboriginal
community. In the Toronto context, Proulx (2006, 423) writes:

> Aboriginal peoples who are not connected to culturally specific identity
> relations must use whatever resources at their disposal to create or claim
> Aboriginal identities thereby filling the holes in their hearts. How individ-
> uals choose to identify and the resources they choose to use in this process
> must be understood as flexibly inventive reacting to both internal and ex-
> ternal personal and cultural change.

The emergence of a pan-Métis community in Saskatoon may provide a cultural home to such individuals. Furthermore, individuals unable to gain
membership in Métis political organizations might organize themselves into
an urban Métis political group and press the government for funding to address such issues in their communities as housing, employment, education,

and gangs. While the potential for conflict among those who identify as Métis in the urban setting could be avoided if Métis political organizations devised membership criteria that were more inclusive, this is highly unlikely as long as governments demand that Métis political organizations clearly identify their members before any rights or privileges are granted to Métis people.

While it is difficult to envision how this issue is going to be resolved, one thing is certain: urban Métis identity is evolving as Métis people adapt and change to the realities of their urban experiences and existences. Whether this will lead to a new and distinct urban Aboriginal identity is uncertain. In pondering such issues, Belise's (2006, 105) assertion that one of the strongest traits of the Métis is "their ability to resist definition and adjust to changing historical, political, and racial contexts" should be kept in mind.

Note

The research assistance of Jim Tailfeathers, Tyler Fetch, and Michelle Hogan is gratefully acknowledged. The research was funded by a SSHRC Strategic Research Grant entitled Urban First Nations and Métis Identities.

References

Andersen, C. 2008. From nation to population: The racialisation of Métis in the Canadian census. *Nations and Nationalism* 14(2): 347-68.

Barkwell, L. 1991. Early law and social control among the Métis. In *Struggle for recognition: Canadian justice and the Metis nation*, ed. W. Corrigan and L.J. Barkwell, 7-37. Winnipeg: Pemmican.

Barron, L. 1990. The CCF and the development of Métis colonies in southern Saskatchewan during the premiership of T.C. Douglas, 1944-1961. *Canadian Journal of Native Studies* 10(2): 243-70.

Belisle, D. 2006. Finding home on the way: Naming the Métis. *Prairie Forum* 31(1): 105-20.

Brasser, T.J. 1985. In search of Métis art. In *The new peoples: Being and becoming Métis in North America*, ed. J. Peterson and J. Brown, 221-29. Winnipeg: University of Manitoba Press.

Brody, H. 1971. *Indians on skid row*. Ottawa: Northern Science Research Group, Department of Indian Affairs and Northern Development, Information Canada.

Cardinal, H. 1969. *The unjust society: The tragedy of Canada's Indians*. Edmonton: M.G. Hurtig.

Crawford, J. 1985. What is Michif? Language in the Métis tradition. In *The new peoples: Being and becoming Métis in North America*, ed. J. Peterson and J. Brown, 231-51. Winnipeg: University of Manitoba Press.

Dobbin, M. 1984. The Métis in Western Canada since 1945. In *The making of the modern West: Western Canada since 1945*, ed. A.W. Rasporich, 183-93. Calgary: University of Calgary Press.

Dosman, E.J. 1972. *Indians: The urban dilemma*. Toronto: McClelland and Stewart.

Fredericks, B. 2004. Urban identity. *Eureka Street: A Magazine of Public Affairs, the Arts and Theology* 14(10): 30-31.

Frideres, J.S. 1998. *Aboriginal peoples in Canada: Contemporary conflicts*. 5th ed. Scarborough: Prentice Hall, Allyn and Bacon.

Gionet, L. 2009. Canadian social trends: Métis in Canada: Selected findings of the 2006 census. http://www.statcan.gc.ca/.

Giraud, M. 1956. The western Metis after the insurrection. *Saskatchewan History* 9(1): 1-15.

Hatt, K. 1986. The North-West Rebellion Scrip Commissions, 1885-1889. In *1885 and after: Native society in transition*, ed. F.L. Barron and J.B. Waldram, 152-65. Regina: Canadian Plains Research Centre.

Healey, S. 2006. Cultural resilience, identity and the restructuring of political power in Bolivia. Paper submitted to the 11th Biennial Conference of the International Association for the Study of Common Property, Bali, Indonesia, 19-23 June.

Howard, H.A., and C. Proulx, eds. 2011. *Aboriginal peoples in Canadian cities: Transformations and continuities*. Waterloo: Wilfrid Laurier University Press.

Krotz, L. 1980. *Urban Indians: The strangers in Canada's cities*. Edmonton: Hurtig.

Lawrence, B. 2004. *"Real" Indians and others: Mixed-blood urban Native peoples and Indigenous nationhood*. Lincoln: University of Nebraska Press.

Maaka, R., and A. Fleris. 2005. *The politics of Indigeneity: Challenging the state in Canada and New Zealand*. Dunedin: University of Otago Press.

Macdougall, B. 2006. Wahkootowin: Family and culture identity in northwestern Saskatchewan Métis communities. *Canadian Historical Review* 87(3): 431-62.

Nagler, M. 1970. *Indians in the city*. Canadian Research Centre for Anthropology, St. Paul University, Ottawa.

Norris, M.J., and S. Clatworthy. 2003. Aboriginal mobility and migration within urban Canada: Outcomes, factors and implications. In *Not strangers in these parts: Urban aboriginal peoples*, ed. D. Newhouse and E.J. Peters, 51-78. Ottawa: Policy Research Initiative.

Norris, M.J., and L. Jantzen. 2003. Aboriginal languages in Canada's urban areas: Characteristics, considerations and implications. In *Not strangers in these parts: Urban Aboriginal peoples*, 93-118. Ottawa: Policy Research Initiative.

Peters, E.J., R. Maaka, and R. Laliberte. 2009. "I'm sweating with Cree culture not Saulteaux culture and there goes the beginning of Pan Indianism": Census categories and urban Aboriginal cultural identities. Invited presentation, Aboriginal Demography Workshop, University of Alberta, October 17.

Pocklington, T. 1991. Prelude to the formation of the Alberta Métis settlements. In *The government and politics of the Alberta Métis settlements*, 1-23. Regina: Canadian Plains Research Center, University of Regina.

Proulx, C. 2003. *Reclaiming Aboriginal justice, identity and community*. Saskatoon: Purich.

–. 2006. Aboriginal identification in North American cities. *Canadian Journal of Native Studies* 26(2): 405-39.

Purich, D. 1988. *The Métis*. Toronto: Lorimer.

Sealey, D.B., and A.S. Lussier. 1975. *The Métis: Canada's forgotten people*. Winnipeg: Manitoba Métis Federation.

Sawchuk, J. 1985. The Metis, non-status Indians and the new Aboriginality: Government influence on Native political alliances and identities. *Canadian Ethnic Studies* 17(2): 135-46.

Silver, J. 2006. *In their own voices: Aboriginal community development in Winnipeg's inner city*. Winnipeg: Canadian Centre for Policy Alternatives.

Sprague, D. 1980. The Manitoba land question, 1870-1882. *Journal of Canadian Studies* 15(3): 74-84.

Statistics Canada. 2001. Aboriginal peoples of Canada: A demographic profile. http://www12.statcan.ca/.

–. 2006. Aboriginal peoples of Canada in 2006: Inuit, Métis and First Nations, 2006 census. http://www.statcan.gc.ca/.

Strauss, C.L. 1943. The social use of kinship terms among Brazilian Indians. *American Anthropologist* (n.s.) 45(3): 398-409.

Troupe, C.L. 2009. Métis women: Social structure, urbanization and political activism, 1850-1980. MA thesis, University of Saskatchewan.

Wotherspoon, T. 2003. Prospects for a new middle class among urban Aboriginal people. In *Not strangers in these parts: Urban Aboriginal people*, ed. D. Newhouse and E.J. Peters, 147-66. Ottawa: Policy Research Initiative.

Yamanouchi, Y. 2009. Exploring ambiguity: Aboriginal identity negotiation in southwestern Sydney. In *Environment and Planning A 2010* 42: 285-99.

6

Laying the Groundwork for Co-Production

The Saskatoon Indian and Métis Friendship Centre, 1968-82

PAMELA OUART AND THE SASKATOON INDIAN
AND MÉTIS FRIENDSHIP CENTRE

As Aboriginal people relocated to urban areas in Canada in the 1950s and 1960s, they often found that the services they were offered did not suit their needs. To address this issue, Aboriginal people began advocating for organizations that would provide culturally appropriate services. Early attempts at organizing immediately faced challenges because of mainstream ideas about what Aboriginal identities were in urban areas, including the notions that Aboriginal migration to urban areas meant that Aboriginal people were discarding their cultures and wishing to assimilate. Early observers homogenized distinctive urban Aboriginal identities and defined urban Aboriginal people primarily as recipients of mainstream services.

By the start of the twenty-first century, academic scholarship recognized the important role of urban Aboriginal organizations in maintaining and redefining Aboriginal identities in cities. Newhouse (2000) notes that urban Aboriginal identities are consciously and systemically reconstructed in cities and that Aboriginal organizations play an important role in this process. Similarly, the Ontario Urban Aboriginal Task Force's (2007, 74) study of Aboriginal communities in major cities in that province notes that urban Aboriginal organizations are at the forefront of developing Aboriginal communities in urban areas. Interviews by Silver et al. (2006) with twenty-six Winnipeg inner-city Aboriginal community leaders show that Aboriginal organizations based on Aboriginal cultures helped these leaders to overcome barriers linked to racism and colonial histories, and to empower themselves. The authors note that Aboriginal organizations led by Aboriginal leadership contributed to rebuilding "the pride in being Aboriginal and an understanding of the process and consequences of colonization" (26).

While there is a considerable body of literature on the development of urban Aboriginal communities in US cities (e.g., LaGrand 2002; Weibel-Orlando 1999), there appears to be less material on this topic in Canadian urban areas (but see Proulx 2003; Hall 2009; Sanderson and Howard-Bobiwash 1997). The Saskatoon Indian and Métis Friendship Centre (hereafter the Friendship Centre) was the first Aboriginal service organization in Saskatoon. An examination of its early years provides insight into how Aboriginal people engaged with prevailing assumptions about their identities and their role in the city in the early years of organizing. Using material from the co-production literature, which examines citizen participation in the delivery of services, this chapter explores the Friendship Centre's engagement with mainstream attitudes as it attempts to define a role for itself and the Aboriginal community in the urban milieu.

Co-Production

The literature on co-production provides a useful framework for exploring the challenges facing the Friendship Centre in its early years. Scholars of public administration became more interested in co-production, or citizen involvement in the provision of public services, in the 1970s and the 1980s (see Parks et al. 1981 for a good review). The co-production of services provided an alternative to the traditional model, by which public servants design and provide services to citizens who demand and consume them. In 1983, Brudney and England (1983, 59) defined co-production as follows: "Co-production is an emerging conception of the service delivery process which envisions direct citizen involvement in the design and delivery of city services with professional service agents." Rationales for citizen involvement in service delivery include the heightened effectiveness of the public sector and the improvement of democratic governance (Cooper and Kathi 2005, 43).

Bovaird (2007) provides a useful conceptual framework for analyzing the roles for professional services providers and members of the community in co-production. He argues that the full range of co-production activities includes service planning, design, commissioning, managing, delivering, monitoring, and evaluation. In the application of this framework, he reduces these key areas to two main activities – service planning and service delivery. Bovaird presents a matrix of possible relationships between professionals and community members, with extremes ranging from professionals as sole service deliverers and planners to community members as sole service deliverers and planners, with different forms of interaction in between (e.g., community delivery of professionally designed services or full co-planning and community delivery) (848). He argues that the value of the typology is that it opens up the range of ways that professionals and community members could interact in the co-production of services.

Co-production has been seen as an attractive approach to service delivery for urban Aboriginal populations. Aboriginal-controlled social services generally have greater scope in delivering programs that incorporate Aboriginal principles, beliefs, and traditions; create important employment opportunities for urban Aboriginal residents; and result in significant economic benefits for Aboriginal communities (Hylton 1999, 85-86). Walker, Moore, and Linkater (2009) argue that policy and programming relating to Aboriginal people needs to be coproduced with Aboriginal people and organizations because having a voice in policy and programming is in line with Aboriginal communities' goals of self-government. The Indigenous right to self-determination is an important component of Aboriginal identities, and Aboriginal people, as a result, distinguish themselves from other minority cultural groups, rejecting approaches based on multiculturalism (Johnson 2008; Walker 2008). The Royal Commission on Aboriginal Peoples (1996, 584) suggests that the development of urban Aboriginal organizations creates meaningful levels of control over some of the issues that affect urban Aboriginal residents' everyday lives. Co-production, which involves a significant role for Aboriginal organizations in planning service delivery, would best represent aspirations for self-government.

However, during the time period addressed in this chapter, urban Aboriginal organizations faced considerable barriers from different levels of government preventing them from engaging in co-production of any sort. These barriers emerged from the assumption that Aboriginal cultures were incompatible with success in city life. Anthropologist Mark Nagler (1970), for example, when writing about Aboriginal migrants to Toronto, reproduced common stereotypes of Aboriginal people in suggesting that Aboriginal migrants to cities did not value wealth and consumer goods because they did not have the motivation to work hard. According to Nagler, these attitudes, in combination with Aboriginal migrants' lack of adherence to European conceptions of time, meant that they would have difficulty succeeding economically in urban areas. The social support provided by Aboriginal cultures in urban areas was viewed as useful only as a stopgap measure while Aboriginal people became accustomed to the cultural mainstream (Peters 2002). These assumptions affected government expectations concerning the roles that early urban Aboriginal organizations could play.

Government officials viewed integration as the main goal for urban Aboriginal migrants, and they saw urban Aboriginal organizations as being key for their integration and assimilation (Dosman 1972). According to federal and provincial governments, the appropriate goal for urban Aboriginal organizations was to help Aboriginal people in urban areas become familiar with urban life and to assimilate into mainstream society, which was to be achieved through referrals to mainstream organizations. Governments assumed, consequently, that there was no need to support culturally specific programming because the need for this programming would only be temporary at best. Because Aboriginal cultures were seen as antagonistic to successful assimilation, government officials assumed that Aboriginal people did not have the capacity to contribute to what governments defined as successful initiatives in the city. Governments viewed urban Aboriginal people as homogenous, with similar objectives, needs, and concerns. This idea was also associated with the assumption of inevitable assimilation because "Nativeness" was seen as an initial stage in the process of assimilation (see also Belanger, this volume). Nuances of different cultures and rights were not viewed as significant for the process of adapting to the city; instead, all Aboriginal people were seen as requiring the same programs and services, which stressed adaptation and referral to mainstream organizations.

The small number of Aboriginal people in cities during the early stages of urbanization also created challenges. Small numbers meant that different Aboriginal cultures needed to find services from the same organization. Organizations felt they had a responsibility to serve all Aboriginal people in the city, and often those Aboriginal individuals who became involved in working to create Aboriginal organizations were from diverse cultural backgrounds themselves (Price 1975; Dosman 1972). Although this was not seen as ideal by community organizers, Silver (2006, 13) points out that Aboriginal people were forced to become creative in serving their communities. This often meant that organizations were "pan-Aboriginal," meaning that services and programs served all Aboriginal people and did not follow only the cultural protocols of individual Aboriginal cultures.

Government assumptions about the relationship between Aboriginal cultures and identities and Aboriginal peoples' ability to succeed in urban centres implied that there was no role for co-production of services for urban Aboriginal people: this was to be left to non-Aboriginal organizations and government professionals. The analysis of the challenges and success of the Friendship Centre demonstrates how this organization addressed and reshaped these assumptions about its appropriate roles in the city.

Methods

The Friendship Centre was incorporated in 1968 in Saskatoon, and this study follows it over its first fifteen years. It is important to explore the experiences of the Friendship Centre during its early years in order to understand the source of its policies and programming. It is also important to document how the urban Aboriginal community struggled to create an organization that suited its needs.

Data were collected through a number of archives, interviews, and personal collections. In total, twelve interviews and one focus group were conducted with individuals who were identified as important both in the documents and by Friendship Centre personnel. A snowball method was used to gain participants for interviews. Tobacco and tea were presented to elders at the beginning of the interview as a way to show respect for the knowledge that they were about to share. All participants signed a consent form approved by the University of Saskatchewan Ethics Review Board.

It was extremely difficult to find data documenting the early days of the Friendship Centre. The Friendship Centre itself saved almost no documents, and other sources were quite thin. Due to the historical time frame of this research, many participants were not able to pinpoint dates or identify people and programs. However, there was enough information available to sketch out the general dates, programming intentions, and the nature of challenges the Friendship Centre faced during the establishment process.

An adapted form of grounded theory and thematic analysis was used to analyze the interviews and documents. I say an "adapted" form of grounded theory because, as Dey (2004, 80) argues, the split in two forms of grounded theory means that we cannot use grounded theory as a "single, unified methodology, tightly defined and clearly specified." Therefore, we used many relevant parts of grounded theory as they worked for this case study. We used ATLAS/ti to assist in the coding process, which allowed for easy organization and retrieval of data, which, in turn, allowed for a clearer picture of the structure of the data to emerge for interpretation and theory building (Schillerup 2008).

Development of the Friendship Centre

When Aboriginal people began migrating to urban areas in Canada, there were no programs in urban areas directed specifically with their needs in mind. In the late 1950s, the Canadian Citizenship Branch began to develop policies and programs for Aboriginal people in urban areas and expected that its experience in helping immigrants adapt to Canadian life could be applied to urban Aboriginal migrants (Peters 2002).

As Satzewich and Wotherspoon (1993, 241-43) describe the history and characteristics of federal involvement in the "Friendship Centre Movement," the Citizenship Branch, beginning in 1959 with a "pilot project" in Winnipeg, had, by the mid-1960s, provided federal funding for friendship centres in a number of cities. In 1962, it had developed a program that reimbursed provincial governments for half of the costs of core funding for friendship centres. Following a review of friendship centres in the early 1970s, the Citizenship Branch adopted its Migrating Native Peoples Program, which set out regulations for providing core funding for friendship centres in cooperation with provincial governments. For federal and provincial governments, the main purpose of friendship centres during the early period of their existence was to integrate Aboriginal people into urban support systems. This was a period in Canadian history during which many of the Aboriginal political organizations in existence today had their genesis (Abele and Graham 2012). Federal and provincial government funding for friendship centres emphasized that their purpose was to provide referrals and to help with integration, and they were anxious that friendship centres should not take on a political role. Dosman (1972, 124) confirms that this was the context for the development of the Friendship Centre:

> The IAB [federal Indian Affairs Branch] and the IMB [provincial Indian Métis Branch] limit their support to functional or non-profit associations such as sewing clubs and Indian and Metis organizations that serve as social brokerage groups for the government. None of these are meant to have an independent power base; they are to serve as adjuncts to bureaucratic and service-oriented programs.

As a result, the role of the Friendship Centre developed during a time of extremely constrained expectations for that role.

The Developmental Years of the Friendship Centre, 1966-71
Although the federal government had a friendship centre program available, it was up to the community to advocate for a centre in its city. Discussions about the creation of a friendship centre in Saskatoon started in 1966,
and the organization, supported by a mixed Aboriginal and non-Aboriginal
board, opened an office in 1967 (Dosman 1972, 165). A lack of organizational capacity and leadership, and the perception among Aboriginal supporters
of too much influence by non-Aboriginal members, meant that the organization was unable to obtain either core or program funding from any level of
government. As a result, the office closed by the end of 1969.

A new, primarily First Nations board was able to obtain interim funding
from the Saskatoon City Council in late 1969, and provincial funding under
the federal-provincial cost-sharing arrangements began in 1970 (Dosman
1972, 208; Saskatchewan Archives Board 1979). The Friendship Centre's
1970 application to the Saskatoon City Council for funding used careful language to demonstrate its familiarity with the role it was expected to play in
referral and integration, emphasizing that solutions to Aboriginal "problems" were to be found in the expertise of non-Aboriginal organizations.

> The Friendship Centre is a community concept, and it will function and
> operate upon that basis. It will not be exclusive but rather it will be a centre
> through which Indian & Metis and the rest of Saskatoon could meet to make
> the Indian and Metis part of Canadian Society ... At all times in our individ-
> ual services we stress the referral aspect of helping the individual to find the
> means to a solution for his problem. (City of Saskatoon Clerk's Office 1970)

In 1970, the Friendship Centre was re-opened in new premises, and by the
end of 1971 it had achieved stability in terms of its funding from various
levels of government, receiving regular grants from provincial and municipal governments.

In the description of its activities and the financial statement accompanying the Friendship Centre's 1971 request for support from the City of
Saskatoon, it is possible to understand the role the centre played at that
point in time (City of Saskatoon Clerk's Office 1971). The Friendship Centre
served as a meeting space for a number of organizations, including an
Alcoholics Anonymous group, the Chimo Ladies (an Aboriginal arts and
crafts women's group), the Native Youth Movement, Native Sons hockey
and baseball clubs, and the Saskatoon Urban Indian Association. It hosted a
Native fastball tournament, a powwow, the Indian Princess Pageant, and a

number of meetings with federal and provincial heads of departments. The Friendship Centre also had a partnership with the University of Saskatchewan Extension Division, allowing Cree classes to be taught there. The amount in the budget for wages suggests that the SIMFC had only one employee, who was probably acting in an executive director's role.

This description indicates that the Friendship Centre acted primarily as a meeting place during the early period of its formation. While it received government funding for the costs of renting and administering a meeting place, it received no funding to develop or deliver programming. Nevertheless, the Friendship Centre was able to generate a small amount of funding (about $3,500 out of a total budget of about $16,700) through donations. This money allowed it to provide some support to the Aboriginal organizations that met in its space and to run activities that supported Aboriginal cultural activities in the city. These activities were also supported by volunteers who extended the Friendship Centre's influence by offering their services for free ("Friendship Centre Opens," *Star Phoenix*, 28 September 1979). The volunteer spirit within the Friendship Centre in Saskatoon, along with high levels of volunteerism, showed how much the Aboriginal community supported the Friendship Centre. These were necessary for the centre's success, and they showed that community members wanted to make it a place where they felt comfortable and that would benefit other Aboriginal people in, or migrating to, the city (Trotchie 1972).

Referring back to Bovaird's (2007) framework, the main co-production mode within which the Friendship Centre operated between 1966 and 1971 involved professionals as the primary planners and deliverers of services. The SMIFC referred most clients to mainstream services; however, through funds the centre raised itself, it was able to provide some services in the co-production category, where community members were the sole planners and deliverers of services. In response to assumptions about the irrelevance of Aboriginal cultures to urban life, individuals involved with the Friendship Centre used their limited means to move away from assimilationist goals towards creating a centre in which Aboriginal cultures could be celebrated. Promoting Aboriginal cultures in the city was in direct opposition to assumptions that Aboriginal people would give up their cultures in favour of mainstream cultural beliefs and practices.

New Challenges for the Friendship Centre, 1972-77
The Friendship Centre faced new challenges and opportunities between 1972 and 1977. These included the challenge of working with the heterogeneity

posed by First Nations and Métis objectives and goals, opportunities created by the gradual introduction of service delivery roles into the centre, and increasing amounts of money raised by the centre itself.

While the early boards in the Friendship Centre had a majority of First Nations members, 1972 elections produced a board with a majority of Métis members, including a Métis president. The *Newbreed*, a Métis publication, noted: "Up until awhile ago there was no Métis or Non-Status Indian voice on the Board but with a lot of hard work they got a voice and are now in the majority" ("Saskatoon Friendship Centre," *Newbreed*, 9 October 1972). In addition, the Friendship Centre now had new organizations using its premises, including the Native Alcohol Centre, which was a Métis initiative, and Métis Local 11, which was a political organization of the Saskatoon Métis (Trotchie 1972; "Saskatoon Friendship Centre," *Newbreed*, 9 October 1972).

By 1973, probably resulting from the fact that the existing board held its annual meeting and board election on 28 December 1972, there were no First Nations representatives on the board of directors. The *Star Phoenix* reported that the result was a March occupation of the Friendship Centre by the Native Youth Movement, the Urban Indians Association, and the Saskatchewan Native Women's movement (Goertzen 1973). During the one-week sit-in, the purpose of which was to break up the all-Métis board, there were heated meetings and discussions. Six of the nine board members resigned in December 1973 and left the Friendship Centre. As a result, Métis Local 11, a group that had previously held meetings at the Friendship Centre, split off into a new organization and pursued separate programming. A new, temporary board of directors was elected at the Friendship Centre on 17 January 1974, and a permanent board was elected in March of that year ("Centre Elects New Directors," *Saskatchewan Indian*, 19 January 1974). Both of these new Friendship Centre boards had representation from the Métis and First Nations communities.

The struggle over board control demonstrated the tensions built into government assumptions about the homogeneity of urban Aboriginal populations. While the mainstream population did not understand the cultural and political differences between First Nations and Métis, many First Nations and Métis people felt that they were politically stronger if they functioned separately. By forming separate organizations, some First Nations and Métis people felt that they could pursue programming for members of their own communities and address issues that were unique to their cultures and histories. A participant (participants were guaranteed anonymity) interviewed for this project (12 July 2007) recalled that the friction in the

Friendship Centre was created because everyone wanted control, and, as a result, groups spilt away from the centre to create their own organizations. However, the respondent reflected that this was not a negative thing for Aboriginal people in Saskatoon in the long run because it meant that organizations could focus on providing different services. Discussions became heated because there was so much passion involved.

> *Well they had their hearts in it you know? They fought for what*
> *they believed in and there was a group of them that believed in the*
> *same thing so they just went after it and that's, like, housing and*
> *how it got started. Those guys [Métis Local 11] moved away from*
> *the Friendship Centre but that [housing] started, and then you guys*
> *[Friendship Centre] were able to continue on and build this up. And*
> *they built the other end and so now in Saskatoon we've got a really*
> *nice place for people to come and their kids to do things and you've*
> *got housing on the other side. So, and then we had alcohol [the*
> *Native Alcohol Treatment Centre], we were starting to look after*
> *that too, so we sort of really started branching out.* (SIMFC Focus
> Group, 10 February 2009)

However, the formation of new organizations also created competition for funding. As one respondent recalled:

> *Competition for funding ... from those levels of government,*
> *federal and provincial ... created a dog-eat-dog world.* (interview,
> 10 July 2007)

As a result, the Friendship Centre was no longer the only place for Aboriginal people to go to be with other Aboriginal people. Within its own organization, the Friendship Centre faced the challenge of heterogeneity as it had a bylaw that stipulated equal representation of First Nations and Métis board members. In 1976, a bylaw was passed stipulating that the board would be represented by five Métis individuals and five First Nations individuals, with one additional representative, who could be Métis, First Nations, or non-Aboriginal ("Saskatoon Centre Board Is Dominated by Métis Members," *Saskatchewan Indian*, 7 July 1976).

During this period, the Friendship Centre began to deliver provincial services to urban Aboriginal people. At the end of March 1972, the Friendship Centre reported a total income of $35,650 – more than double that of the previous year (City of Saskatoon Clerk's Office 1973). The main source of the increase appears to have been the federal government's new Migrating Native Peoples Program (City of Saskatoon Clerk's Office 1973). In a February 1972 letter to the *Newbreed* (Trotchie 1972, 2), the president of the Friendship Centre noted that there had not been much activity at the centre because of the hold-up in funding but that, now that it had received its funding, it could hire new people and develop new programs. According to the *Newbreed*, the executive director reported in October of the same year that "the people of Saskatoon seem to think that the Friendship Centre is a hang-out for Native people and that nothing of real importance goes on there. He says he is going to change that" ("Saskatoon Friendship Centre," *Newbreed*, 9 October 1972). As a result of the additional funding, the Friendship Centre planned to hire more staff, including three court workers, a secretary, a director, an assistant director, four lunch counter workers, and a janitor (Ibid.; Trotchie 1972).

Possibly because of debates about board membership, program and employment records for the 1973 and 1974 fiscal years are sparse. However, a 1975 report to the Saskatoon City Clerk's Office (1975) demonstrates that, while the Friendship Centre continued to act in a referral role, it had also been successful in negotiating the delivery of a number of provincial programs to urban Aboriginal residents. The Friendship Centre was assigned the role of referring Aboriginal families to twenty-four low-rental housing units set aside by the Saskatchewan Housing Corporation for Aboriginal people. With a provincially funded family worker, the centre provided assistance to the provincial departments of Indian affairs, social services, and human rights as well as the Saskatoon Legal Assistance Clinic. The Friendship Centre also referred individuals to the Native Alcohol Centre, which was administered by Métis Local 11. The Friendship Centre acted as trustee for the incomes of individuals receiving support from the Department of Services and Welfare who had difficulty budgeting their money, and these people also received counselling from the family worker at the centre. Provincially funded programs delivered by the Friendship Centre included hospital visits, interpretation, and transportation to allow individuals to look for housing, attend appointments, or get to the bus or the train. The Friendship Centre also delivered the provincial Courtworkers Program for Aboriginal people, providing advice to accused individuals about their rights and assisting them in the courts.

Behind this seemingly straightforward reporting of new programming lays an important change in Friendship Centre-government relationships. Initially, friendship centres had been established strictly as referral organizations and not as program delivery agents. During the 1972 review of friendship centre organizations that preceded the development of the Migrating Native Peoples Program, researchers heard that Aboriginal people were frequently referred to friendship centres because existing mainstream organizations did not feel that they had the expertise to work with Aboriginal clients. While friendship centres argued that they should be able to deliver services, the terms of reference for the Migrating Native Peoples Program defined them solely as referral organizations (Peters 2002). The administration of these new programs meant that the Friendship Centre had moved towards a more active role in co-production: the community delivery of professionally designed services.

Between 1972 and 1977, the Friendship Centre also expanded its efforts to generate its own revenues to support activities the board and membership considered important. In 1972, the Friendship Centre board applied for and was granted a licence to hold a weekly bingo at the centre to create revenue and to serve as a social occasion (City of Saskatoon Clerk's Office 1972). By 1974, the centre began holding bingos twice a week (City of Saskatoon Clerk's Office 1974). The Friendship Centre was able to use funds from bingos to celebrate various holidays, support sports and cultural activities, and help people in the community on a case-by-case basis.

In 1972, the *Newbreed* reported that the Friendship Centre hosted dry dances every Saturday night and talent shows on Sunday afternoons ("Saskatoon Friendship Centre," *Newbreed*, 9 October 1972). Among the sports listed in the report to City Council were basketball, bowling, boxing, and hockey. The centre's 1975 report to the Saskatoon City Council indicates the importance of sports activities and the efforts of the Friendship Centre to build community in the city:

> Two evenings a week are taken up in boxing, pool, table tennis, weight lifting and just general exercise. Youth bowling takes place every Saturday sponsored by the centre. Curling is on Sundays on a cost sharing basis with the participants. Hockey is on a planned basis at present due to a shortage of ice and should be operating toward the end of November. (City of Saskatoon Clerk's Office 1974)

The same report also describes extensive cultural activities:

> An Indian social family night takes place the first Friday of each month and
> a regular dance is being held each third Friday of the month sponsored by
> the Indian group of the centre. Other dances are also held on a basis of
> about once a month ... Crafts and culture are now on a planned program for
> later November or early December ... A talent show and children's Christmas
> party are also planned for December. (Ibid.)

In 1976, the Friendship Centre added a youth group, guitar lessons, all-
Indian drama, summer camp for children and youth, and a cribbage night
for elders ("Saskatoon Centre Board Is Dominated by Métis Members,"
Saskatchewan Indian, 7 July 1976). It also used these funds to provide meals
and clothing to individuals requiring these in emergency situations.

The ways in which the Friendship Centre used the financial support it
raised itself undermined initial assimilationist goals. In part, this was
because activities in the Friendship Centre passed on First Nations and
Métis traditions through a variety of cultural practices. The extensive sports
and recreation program also helped to create community in urban areas.
Aboriginal people were able to engage in activities with other urban
Aboriginal residents and to compete as Aboriginal teams or as Friendship
Centre-sponsored competitors. Rather than assimilating into sports and
recreation opportunities available in the mainstream community, urban
Aboriginal people were able to create their own activities. The importance
of these activities was reflected in the fact that, in 1976 and 1977, the
Friendship Centre began seeking support to relocate to a larger building.

Solidifying a Role for the Friendship Centre, 1977-82
In 1978, the Friendship Centre employed an executive director as well as an
accountant, a program director, a secretary, two family workers, three
court workers, three home and school liaison workers, and five employees
funded by the Canada Works Program (Thomas 1978). One participant
noted that this was a good-sized staff and that the Friendship Centre received provincial Worker Initiative funding. Wages were about four hundred dollars a month,

> *but that was good wages for a lot of our people ... [who] were coming
> off welfare.* (interview, 23 July 2007)

In other words, the Friendship Centre provided benefits to community members not only by delivering services but also by offering employment.

Several other developments demonstrated the evolution of co-production between governments and the Friendship Centre. In 1978, the Friendship Centre announced its Home School Liaison Program. The program emerged from a number of meetings in which parents spoke of their concern about the high dropout rates of Indian and Métis students. The main objectives of the program were to implement home visits and to work with Aboriginal families in Saskatoon; to improve communications between Aboriginal students, parents, and teachers; and to compile and chart statistics concerning Aboriginal students (Thomas 1978). The program was funded by the federal Canada Works Project. By 1979, this program had led to the Friendship Centre's participation in an attempt to create an alternative school for Aboriginal students (Saskatoon Indian and Metis Friendship Centre 1979, 22).

In 1980, the Friendship Centre applied to the City of Saskatoon for a licence to establish a day care centre (City of Saskatoon Clerk's Office 1980). Citing the needs of Aboriginal families attending the Indian Social Work Education Program and the Indian Teacher Education Program, the Friendship Centre indicated that it had thirty-four children registered and a waiting list of twelve. Despite some protests from local businesses, City Council approved a licence. There is little further documentation of this initiative, and the day care centre does not appear to have survived for very long, but the attempt to establish a day care provides an indication of the centre's changing role in the urban Aboriginal community.

Another initiative also responded to local needs. In cooperation with the Friendship Inn, a non-profit organization providing daily meals and other services to individuals in poverty, and the Saskatchewan Human Rights Association, the Friendship Centre introduced the Streetworkers Program. The intent of the program was to work with youth who gathered in public places in the inner city and to offer them an alternative to street life. This was the first evidence of cooperation between the Friendship Centre and other non-profit organizations in order to meet local community needs, and, like the Home and School Liaison Program, it marked the Friendship Centre's growing movement away from being a centre whose purpose was solely to refer people to government programs and towards being a centre whose purpose was to design and deliver its own programs.

These initiatives demonstrate a marked departure from the Friendship Centre's earlier participation in service delivery. Friendship Centre staff, recognizing issues of particular concern to local Aboriginal residents, designed programs to meet their needs. Here, the centre moved from delivering programs designed by non-Aboriginal professionals to designing, finding government funding for, and delivering programs tailored to specific community needs. Material accompanying the Friendship Centre's 1978 application for funding to the Saskatoon City Council underscores its role change. So far from limiting the Friendship Centre's objectives to referring people to existing mainstream services, the executive director emphasizes that it is

> to act as a catalyst for identifying Native concerns and needs; to assist and encourage Native people to organize themselves to receive the required assistance to deal with these concerns and to meet their needs. (City of Saskatoon Clerk's Office 1978a)

In moving to a role in which it defined local community needs, designed a program, and worked with various government and non-governmental organizations to find funding and support, the Friendship Centre moved closer to a self-government role in the urban Aboriginal community.

This new programming meant that additional space was even more important, and, in 1979, the Friendship Centre was finally able to move to its 168 Wall Street location, where it is currently located. The Friendship Centre was able to secure significant funding from municipal, provincial, and federal governments for the purchase of this building, demonstrating that it had solidified its role in the city (City of Saskatoon Clerk's Office 1980; "Friendship Centre Opens," *Star Phoenix*, 28 September 1979).

Conclusion

As the first Aboriginal service organization in Saskatoon, the Friendship Centre had a colourful history. It began as a result of the community's advocating for a centre and was eventually supported by federal, provincial, and municipal governments; however, because this was uncharted territory, the relationship was not always an easy one.

While government assumptions about the inevitability and desirability of assimilation were apparent in the early days of the Friendship Centre, it worked against these assumptions from its very inception. Initially, this resistance involved supporting First Nations and Métis cultural activities, languages, and communities, largely through fundraising and volunteer activities. Fundraising allowed the Friendship Centre to control its own funds, which was very important as, without this, it would have been unable to offer many programs, particularly culturally based programs. The involvement of volunteers was also important. The Friendship Centre was able to offer the services that it wanted to because community expertise, in the form of volunteers, allowed it to run programs for which it lacked formal funding agreements. This type of co-production allowed the Friendship Centre to offer community members services that government funders might not understand or value. Increasingly, over the years, self-generated funding helped the Friendship Centre to expand these activities. Towards the end of the period examined here, the Friendship Centre began to use government funding to deliver services it designed to meet local community needs, moving towards greater self-determination.

Assumptions about the homogeneity of urban Aboriginal populations meant that the Friendship Centre was mandated to provide services to all Aboriginal people, with no distinction made between First Nations and Métis people. The Friendship Centre initially worked well because First Nations and Métis worked together towards a common goal: to help newcomers and to create an Aboriginal meeting place in Saskatoon. However, once this goal was achieved, unique histories and legal status made further development difficult. First Nations groups were concerned with the protection of treaty rights in the city, while Métis leaders were concerned with the socio-economic development of their own community members (Dosman 1972; Schilling 1983). As a result, organizations split off from the Friendship Centre to pursue their own initiatives, and the centre itself had to put into place strategies to ensure equal representation on its board.

During this time frame, the Friendship Centre's role in co-production shifted dramatically. Initially, co-production involved only Friendship Centre referrals to professionally designed and delivered mainstream services, and the culturally focused services centre staff and volunteers were able to design and deliver. These arrangements reflected the assumption that Aboriginal cultures could not successfully adapt to urban life and, therefore, that services designed and administered by Aboriginal people would be neither effective nor desirable. As the centre gained more experience, it built the capacity to engage in much higher levels of co-production, but the groundwork occurred during its early days. Relationships were formed and, consequently, opportunities for further control emerged as time wore on. Greater Friendship Centre involvement in co-production occurred when the centre began to deliver a variety of professionally designed services rather than serving primarily as a referral organization. By 1982, the Friendship Centre had moved to designing and delivering services, being funded by various levels of government, and responding to expressed community needs. Thus, the centre moved towards greater self-determination. The shift in the relevance of Aboriginal culture with regard to successfully adapting to urban life was signalled in a presentation the Friendship Centre's executive director made to a 1978 conference (City of Saskatoon Clerks Office 1978b): "It is a fact that it is preferable that one knows the Indian culture and the Indian urban experience to work as a staff member or as a Board member of the centre." In other words, rather than being a disadvantage, knowledge and experience of Aboriginal cultures is a prerequisite for the successful design and delivery of appropriate services.

In its evolution during this period, the Friendship Centre challenged mainstream assumptions about the nature of urban Aboriginal identities. It resisted ideas about the inevitability and desirability of assimilation by strongly supporting cultural activities and traditions. With its sports and recreation programs, crafts and language classes, and programs for all ages, it created an Aboriginal community that did not disappear into the rest of the urban population. Recognizing and accommodating the challenge of the heterogeneity of the urban Aboriginal population and the different objectives created as a result of varying histories and legal status, the Friendship Centre created a board structure that mandated the equal representation of First Nations and Métis peoples. Finally, the Friendship Centre board and staff demonstrated the capacity for, and the beginning of, self-government by negotiating increased responsibility for program delivery and, eventually, for the design and administration of government-funded programs. As the first formal Aboriginal organization in Saskatoon, the Friendship Centre created a foundation for the subsequent development of a host of Aboriginal organizations whose purpose is to attempt to meet the needs of urban Aboriginal communities.

Note

This research was funded by a SSHRC Strategic Research Grant entitled Urban First Nations and Métis Identities.

References

Abele, F., and K. Graham. 2012. Federal urban Aboriginal policy: The challenge of viewing the stars in the urban night sky. In *Urban Aboriginal policy making in*

Canadian municipalities, ed. E.J. Peters, 33-52. Montreal and Kingston: McGill-Queen's University Press.

Brudney, J.L., and R.E. England. 1983. Toward a definition of the co-production concept. *Public Administration Review* 43(1): 59-65.

Bovaird, T. 2007. Beyond engagement and participation: User and community co-production of public services. *Public Administration Review* 67(5): 846-60.

City of Saskatoon Clerk's Office. 1970. Reports: Grants to Organizations, Indian and Métis Friendship Centre, file C.4-29, City Council meeting minutes, 16 February.

–. 1971. Submission of support of request by the Saskatoon Indian and Métis Friendship Centre, n.d., accompanying "Grant-in-Aid," City Council meeting minutes, 22 March.

–. 1972. Grants-in-Aid, City Council meeting minutes, 27 March.

–. 1973. Carole Feargue, Assistant Director of the Saskatoon Indian and Metis Friendship Centre, to Mr. Fraser, City Clerk's Office, 30 July.

–. 1974. Application for a licence to hold a bingo, Indian and Métis Friendship Centre, file C.12-8-2, City Council meeting minutes, 28 January.

–. 1975. D.V. Vandale, Program Director, Indian and Métis Friendship Centre, to Mr. J. Kolynchuk, Secretary, Legislation and Finance Committee, 27 January.

–. 1978a. Attachment regarding application for a Saskatchewan Recreational and Cultural Facilities Grant. Peter Gardippi, Executive Director, SIMFC, to Susan Coley, Secretary, Planning and Development Committee, City Clerk's Office, City Hall, 1 August.

–. 1978b. Resume of the Intercultural Dialogue and Action Planning Workshop. 28 April.

–. 1980. Saskatoon Indian and Métis Friendship Centre – Program Fund, Revenue and Expenditure. Attachment. Solinus Jolliffee, Assistant Director/Program Director, SIMFC, to Susan Coley, Secretary, Legislation and Finance Committee, 12 February.

Cooper, T., and P. Kathi. 2005. Neighbourhood councils and city agencies: A model of collaborative co-production. *National Civic Review* 94(1): 43-53.

Dey, I. 2004. Grounded theory. In *Qualitative research practice,* ed. C. Seale, G. Gobo, J.F. Gubrium, and D. Silverman, 80-93. London: Sage.

Dosman, E.J. 1972. *Indians: The urban dilemma.* Toronto: McClelland and Stewart.

Goertzen, H. 1973. Indians continue to occupy centre. *Star Phoenix,* 13 March.

Hall, L. 2009. The early history of the Winnipeg Indian and Métis Friendship Centre, 1951-1968. In *Prairie metropolis: New essays on Winnipeg social history,* ed. E.W. Jones and G. Friesen, 223-41. Winnipeg: University of Manitoba Press.

Hylton, J.H. 1999. The case for self-government: A social policy perspective. In *Aboriginal self-government in Canada,* ed. J.H. Hylton. Saskatoon: Purich.

Johnson, J.T. 2008. Indigeneity's challenges to the white settler-state: Creating a third space for dynamic citizenship. *Alternatives* 33: 29-52.

LaGrand, J.B. 2002. *Indian metropolis: Native Americans in Chicago, 1945-75.* Chicago: University of Illinois Press.

Nagler, M. 1970. *Indians in the city.* Ottawa: Canadian Research Centre for Anthropology, St. Paul University.

Newhouse, D. 2000. From the tribal to the modern: The development of modern Aboriginal societies. In *Expressions in Canadian Native studies*, ed. R.F. Laliberte, P. Settee, J.B. Waldram, R. Innes, B. Macdougall, L. McBain, and F.L. Barron, 395-409. Saskatoon: University of Saskatchewan Extension Press.

Parks, R.B., P.C. Baker, L. Kiser, R. Oakerson, E. Ostrom, V. Ostrum, S.L. Perry, M.B. Vandivort, G.P. Whitaker, and R. Wilson. 1981. Consumers as co-producers of public services: Some economic and institutional considerations. *Policy Studies Journal* 9: 1001-11.

Peters, E.J. 2002. "Our city Indians": Negotiating the meaning of First Nations urbanization in Canada, 1945-1975. *Historical Geography* 30: 75-92.

Price, J.A. 1975. US and Canadian Indian urban ethnic institutions. *Urban Anthropology* 4(1): 35-52.

Proulx, C. 2003. *Reclaiming Aboriginal justice, identity and community.* Saskatoon: Purich.

Royal Commission on Aboriginal Peoples. 1996. *Perspectives and realities. Report of the Royal Commission on Aboriginal Peoples.* Vol. 4. Ottawa: Minister of Supply and Services.

Sanderson, F., and H.A. Howard-Bobiwash, eds. 1997. *The meeting place: Aboriginal life in Toronto – In celebration of the Native Canadian Centre of Toronto's 35th anniversary.* Toronto: Native Canadian Centre.

Saskatchewan Archives Board. 1979. Collection R-1453, Indian and Native Affairs Secretariat, file 3.10, "Appendix: Funding History and Background."

Saskatoon Indian and Metis Friendship Centre. 1979. Saskatoon Friendship Centre offers various programs and services. *Saskatchewan Indian* 9(8): 22-23.

Satzewich, V., and T. Wotherspoon. 1993. *First nations: Race, class, and gender relations.* Scarborough, ON: Nelson.

Schiellerup, P. 2008. Stop making sense: The trials and tribulations of qualitative data analysis. *Area* 40(2): 163-71.

Schilling, R. 1983. *Gabriel's children.* Saskatoon: Saskatoon Métis Society.

Silver, J., P. Ghorashi, J. Hay, and D. Klyne. 2006. *In a voice of their own: Urban Aboriginal community development.* Ottawa: Canadian Centre for Policy Alternatives.

Thomas, V. 1978. Saskatoon Friendship Centre commences new program. *Saskatchewan Indian* 8(1): 43-45.

Trotchie, C.J. (President, Local 11). 1972. Letter to the editor. *New Breed,* 2 February.

Urban Aboriginal Task Force. 2007. *Urban Aboriginal Task Force final report.* Toronto: Ontario Federation of Indian Friendship Centres.

Walker, R. 2008. Aboriginal self-determination and social housing in urban Canada: A story of convergence and divergence. *Urban Studies* 54: 185-205.

Walker, R., J. Moore, and M. Linklater. 2009. More than stakeholders, voices and tables: Creating good urban Aboriginal affairs policy in Manitoba. Paper presented at the Aboriginal Policy Research Conference, Ottawa, Ontario, 9-12 March.

Weibel-Orlando, J. 1999. *Indian country, LA: Maintaining ethnic community in complex society.* Rev. ed. Chicago: University of Illinois Press.

7

Increasing the Depth of Our Civic Identity
Future Seeking and Place Making
with Aboriginal Communities

RYAN WALKER

Aboriginal identities should be articulated and shared, and they should meaningfully affect the lives of Aboriginal and non-Aboriginal citizens as well as the unique sense of place that each city evokes for residents and visitors. Ideally, Aboriginal and non-Aboriginal identities would create, reproduce, and mutually reinforce a shared civic identity palpable and meaningful to each city's residents. How can Aboriginal peoples and the non-Aboriginal mainstream engage one another as partners in the dynamic process of future seeking and place making in the twenty-first-century city?

This chapter explores how Aboriginal identities can be fully embraced in a city's future-seeking processes (e.g., planning and policy making) and in its implementation of place-making endeavours (e.g., urban design). I argue that, by embracing the cultural project of Aboriginality in both future seeking and place making,[1] urban Aboriginal communities and the cosmopolitan mainstream will flourish by adding depth to their local civic identities.[2]

The next section examines how the concept of the co-production of urban plans and policies – at the municipal, provincial, and federal levels – can advance the articulation of Aboriginality in the local civic identity. This is followed by a discussion of how implementing expressions of Aboriginality in the built environment can contribute to the advancement of the post-colonial Canadian city.

While the Constitution Act, 1982, may have marked Canada's transition to a postcolonial state, "internal colonialism" persists in a no less powerful colonial mythology and non-overt forms of Canadian democratic racism (Adams 1999; Moore, Walker, and Skelton 2011; Sandercock 2003; Walker 2006). As Leonie Sandercock (2003) points out, our twenty-first-century cities are the sites in which we need to rewrite the Canadian story in a way that embraces Aboriginal cultures and viewpoints, much in the way that, more broadly, Denis's (1997) cultural project of Aboriginality requires. I conclude with some comments about how to advance the place of Aboriginality in the local imaginary and civic identity.

Future Seeking through the Co-Production of Urban Plans and Policies

Co-production of policies and plans occurs when state actors who have jurisdiction over a specific policy or planning field (e.g., municipal, provincial, or federal departments) join up with community forces outside of the government apparatus (Brudney and England 1982; Casey and Dalton 2006; Nyland 1995; Ouart, this volume). The partnership between state actors and community-based actors is fundamental to co-production. In the ideal scenario, this partnership begins as early as the identification of a problem or issue; extends through the process of setting priorities and implementing programs and services; and culminates in shared monitoring and evaluation of the production. Typically, co-production is employed when the government apparatus with jurisdiction over a policy or planning field perceives value in sharing the responsibility for defining issues and priorities.

In this chapter, the concept of co-production refers to a normative principle for engaging in future seeking (i.e., planning and policy making) with urban Aboriginal communities (see Belanger and Walker 2009). The argument that co-production serves as a normative principle for creating and implementing urban Aboriginal policies or plans is based upon the right of self-determination. Aboriginal community self-determination reflects group rights and associated jurisdiction emanating from prior occupancy, treaties, and constitutional arrangements made between settlers and Aboriginal peoples to create and reproduce the modern settler state of Canada. The United Nations (2007) makes it clear that Aboriginal peoples, as self-determining political communities, have the right to "full and effective participation in all matters that concern them." Indigenous scholars in Canada and internationally consistently argue that, at the most fundamental level, facilitating self-determination and forging relationships based on mutual recognition and respect are necessary for strengthening relations between Aboriginal society and the settler state (Durie 2003; Green 2005; Hunter 2006; Maaka and Fleras 2005; Royal Commission on Aboriginal Peoples 1996).

Aboriginal self-determination in urban communities has a legitimate basis within political communities that have been shaped and reproduced through common histories, contemporary social and cultural interaction, and shared future aspirations (Andersen and Denis 2003; Walker 2006). Indian and Métis friendship centres in Canadian urban areas, starting in the 1950s but more widely in the 1960s and 1970s, were instrumental in building urban political communities. Friendship centres provided a place for service referrals, advocacy, and social, cultural, and recreational programs for Aboriginal people in cities and towns.

Over the past couple of decades, scholars have considerably advanced our understanding of how cultures of Indigenous peoples in settler states manifest themselves in urban life through the development of culturally appropriate institutions that address everything from housing, health, economy, law, and education to arts and culture. This process is supported by community networks that transcend urban-reserve boundaries (e.g., Maaka 1994; Morgan 2006; Newhouse and Peters 2003; Peters 2010; Walker 2008; Wilson and Peters 2005). Aboriginal urban identities specific to the city as a home-place are now also being reinforced by the courts (e.g., *Canada v. Misquadis*; Belanger, this volume). I use three examples to demonstrate the extent to which co-production, and its normative foundation, is distinguishable in urban plans and policies developed by the municipal, provincial, and federal governments in Winnipeg, Manitoba.

The Failure to Co-Produce Winnipeg's Municipal Aboriginal Pathways

In 2003, the City of Winnipeg launched what was at the time the most ambitious Canadian municipal policy aimed at strengthening the working relationship between City Hall and Aboriginal urban communities. The initiative was led by councillors Dan Vandal (Métis) and Jenny Gerbasi, and former mayor Glenn Murray. Murray was known for being an activist mayor during his term in office, having instituted an ambitious municipal housing policy and program and having led the development of First Steps: Municipal Aboriginal Pathways (MAP). MAP "defines a policy framework – based on a number of key principles – to open the door to a new era of co-operation between the City and Winnipeg's Aboriginal community" (City of Winnipeg 2003, 1). The city's principal long-range policy and decision-making document, Plan Winnipeg 2020 Vision, includes a policy statement to "Promote Self-Reliant Aboriginal Communities." MAP was launched as a secondary plan to guide council activities in achieving the objective articulated in Plan Winnipeg 2020 Vision. MAP had five policy platforms (i.e., pathways): employment, economic development, safety, quality of life, and outreach and education. Each pathway had three "strategic initiatives" aligned with it, alongside which specific action plans were supposed to be developed by responsible departments shortly after the release of MAP. Action planning would also have involved developing implementation mechanisms, resourcing strategies and timelines to targets.

When council instructed staff to begin work on MAP, an early issue for municipal officials was the extent to which consultation with Aboriginal communities should occur and at what point in the policy production process. One scenario considered was whether to consult with Aboriginal stakeholders to learn what their priorities might be. However, it was determined that this could lead to a number of requests for intervention – requests with which the municipal government was ill-equipped to deal. Instead, the five pathways and the strategic initiatives were drafted in-house and brought to the Aboriginal community for feedback. Mayor Murray and councillors Gerbasi and Vandal met with roughly 350 Aboriginal and non-Aboriginal community members at an inner-city high school to present the draft and to receive input.

The pathways received mixed reviews. The concept of creating a working partnership between City Council and the Aboriginal communities in Winnipeg was well received; however, the pathways and strategic initiatives outlined fell short of community expectations. To this criticism, councillors and the mayor responded that MAP represented the first steps towards a longer-term constructive partnership. Its implementation would involve using municipal programming and resources to address some areas, but it would rely on partnerships with other levels of government to realize others. That partnership with other governments would come in the form of the Winnipeg Partnership Agreement (see below), which was brought into effect shortly after MAP was released.

It is unfortunate that the process of formulating MAP was not more carefully contrived. The logic of deciding in-house what strategic initiatives would be possible and then taking those out to present to the community was a major flaw, and it was even less justifiable given that no funding was ultimately attached for implementation. Given the lack of resources to implement MAP, what might have had greater staying power would have been an exemplary process of relationship building directed towards establishing a long-term collaborative partnership between City Hall and the Aboriginal communities. Creating a full secondary plan with specific principles and implementation objectives cannot be a legitimate basis for "opening the door to a new era of co-operation between the City and Winnipeg's Aboriginal community" if the Aboriginal community is not a full co-producer.

In consultations with Aboriginal community leaders in Winnipeg in 2007, four years after MAP's launch, many either did not remember MAP at all or noted that it sounded familiar but that they could not remember specifics. They may well have vaguely recalled it as a public meeting at a high school that did not translate into much on the ground. Had the MAP process focused first on creating a strong collaborative partnership with Aboriginal leaders that was based on mutual respect and driven by a desire to articulate shared objectives, it might have become a foundation for Aboriginality in future-seeking processes and been appreciated as taking the "first steps" towards a deeper civic identity.

A Missed Opportunity to Co-Produce a Provincial Urban Aboriginal Program Framework

Winnipeg has a long history of tripartite agreements to combat decline in its inner city. In the 1980s and early 1990s, there were two tripartite Winnipeg Core Area Initiatives. In the period from the mid-1990s to the new millennium, the Winnipeg Development Agreement continued to bring resources and leadership from all levels of government to bear on inner-city economic and social development in a relatively seamless intergovernmental fashion. In 2004, the governments of Canada, Manitoba, and Winnipeg entered into another five-year tripartite agreement, called the Winnipeg Partnership Agreement (WPA), to continue this tradition. While the creation of all past inner-city development agreements involved some form of interaction with Aboriginal communities, the WPA was the most ambitious in its Aboriginal advisory mechanism and its focus on Aboriginal programming as one of four of its components. The four components of the WPA were: Aboriginal participation in the Winnipeg economy and community; building sustainable neighbourhoods; downtown renewal; and supporting technology and innovation.

The genesis of the WPA is linked to a combination of factors, including the lineage of past tripartite programs and their success in intergovernmental cooperation and achieving results in a shared political space. There is a shared appreciation among governments that downtown Winnipeg is an area that requires sustained public investment in economic and community development. Senior staff in all governments had experience working together in Winnipeg with tripartite models, and, as the prior Winnipeg Development Agreement wound down in 2001, there was considerable pressure from community groups to continue investing in the core. For my purposes, the genesis of the Aboriginal participation component of the WPA is of greatest interest because it offers us lessons on how to improve future urban Aboriginal program frameworks of this kind.

Manitoba's minister for Aboriginal and northern affairs, Eric Robinson, had been lobbied for an urban Aboriginal strategy for Winnipeg for some time prior to the inception of the WPA. According to a senior government official involved in the process, Robinson was supportive but interactions between Aboriginal political organizations in Winnipeg were divisive, and he felt that he could not work constructively with them. At the same time, in 2003, negotiations were under way between governments to create the WPA. This was seen by Manitoba Aboriginal and Northern Affairs as an opportunity to include an Aboriginal component in the WPA, and, fortuitously, the federal government was beginning to pilot its Urban Aboriginal Strategy in Winnipeg at that time.

Robinson opted to work with his senior officials instead of with the leadership of Aboriginal political organizations – the Manitoba Métis Federation, the Assembly of Manitoba Chiefs, the Aboriginal Council of Winnipeg, and the Mother of Red Nations Women's Council of Manitoba – to create the Aboriginal Participation component of the WPA. It was not co-produced with Aboriginal leaders. However, an Aboriginal Partnership Committee – composed of representatives from the Assembly of Manitoba Chiefs; the Manitoba Métis Federation; the Aboriginal Council of Winnipeg; the Mother of Red Nations; five Aboriginal community members at large (mostly from Aboriginal community-based organizations); two Aboriginal youth; two representatives from the Aboriginal business community; representatives from the three governments; the United Way; the Winnipeg Foundation; and Aboriginal Elders (non-voting) – made recommendations on implementing the resources dedicated under the Aboriginal Partnership component of the WPA. Decisions under the Aboriginal Participation component started with the Aboriginal Partnership Committee (APC), which advised the WPA Management Committee (made up of senior government officials). This committee, in turn, took direction from the Policy Committee, which was made up of politicians from all three governments. Proposals for program and project funding under the Aboriginal participation component were reviewed by the APC, and the APC's recommendations were taken under advisement by the Management Committee.

At the outset, Aboriginal political organizations were opposed to the APC model because they felt that they should be able to administer a portion of the Aboriginal participation component's resources on behalf of their peoples. Further, the APC included community members at large (and often from community-based Aboriginal service organizations), government officials, and representatives from non-Aboriginal philanthropic organizations on an equal footing with Aboriginal political leaders. Despite some criticisms of the model, once it was concluded that the APC would serve as the mechanism for Aboriginal input into decision making, some on the committee then argued that it should have authority to make binding recommendations to the Management Committee with regard to funding decisions. One of the rationales for the argument in favour of granting the APC more decision-making powers was similar to an earlier argument made by Aboriginal political organizations in favour of Aboriginal autonomy over resource management. It was argued that the Aboriginal representatives should have the authority to act on behalf of Aboriginal communities and to make determinations, that they should not be restricted to an advisory function. The APC was a compromise between a desire to initiate concerted activity in urban Aboriginal affairs and a governance mechanism perceived by state decision makers to be able to circumvent what was previously taken as a prohibitive conflict between Aboriginal political organizations.

The Aboriginal participation component of the WPA misses the mark as far as being a tool for engaging Aboriginal communities in a process of policy co-production. The process for administering the Aboriginal participation component was derived without the involvement of Aboriginal communities. The designated places on the APC for political organizations, community members, and other business and non-Aboriginal philanthropic organizations did not emanate from consultation with the Aboriginal community.

If consultation had occurred (beyond initial discussions between provincial government officials and Aboriginal political organizations – which were perceived by provincial officials to be overly laden with the inefficiency of multi-party conflict), the decision-making and advisory mechanisms would, perhaps, have been different. The presence of Aboriginal political organizations may have been reduced, non-Aboriginal organizations may have been left off, and the presence of policy and program experts from among the many Aboriginal community-based organizations in Winnipeg might have been increased. Or perhaps, though it would seem unlikely, the decision-making/advisory mechanisms would have remained the same. A normative basis in co-production offers a pathway to future seeking that involves a partnership between Aboriginal and non-Aboriginal communities. The route taken and the destination become inextricably linked.

Approaching Co-Production of Federal Aboriginal Youth Programming at Canadian Heritage

The Urban Multipurpose Aboriginal Youth Centre (UMAYC) Program, which recently ended, was directed at supporting the development of cultural strength and leadership among the growing population of Aboriginal urban youth. It was administered through a third-party agreement with the National Association of Friendship Centres across much of Canada. But in the largest urban centres across Manitoba, Saskatchewan, and Alberta, including Winnipeg, it was administered directly by the Department of Canadian Heritage. This was a political decision attributed to Ralph Goodale, former Liberal cabinet minister from the Prairie regions, who determined that friendship centres were not appropriate representative bodies within Aboriginal urban communities in the large Prairie cities, where First Nations, Métis, and urban Aboriginal political and service constituencies were most varied. Whether delivered by friendship centres or by the Department of Canadian Heritage, decision making on local program priorities and project proposals was conducted through the Aboriginal Youth Advisory Committee (AYAC).

There were ten members on AYAC in Winnipeg, with each member sitting for a two-year term. Members were selected by a general call for nominations through Aboriginal organizations, schools, and universities. In selecting the committee members from nominees, the Department of Canadian Heritage tried to strike a balance between genders and between Métis and First Nations peoples. While they were on the committee, AYAC members represented Aboriginal youth, not political organizations. One of the major differences that participants saw between AYAC and the APC (of the WPA) was that AYAC was made up of informed Aboriginal youth, whereas the APC tended to be weighted more heavily towards representatives of Aboriginal political organizations (more so than might have been the case had community nominations been used).

Canadian Heritage officers deferred to AYAC with regard to the appraisal of community relevance and for the ranking of project proposals, and they implemented its recommendations for projects (provided that the financial risk and budgets stood up to scrutiny from standard department financial-review processes).

In Winnipeg, three examples of successful programs (from among many) to receive a significant proportion of their funding from UMAYC are: the Winnipeg Aboriginal Sport Achievement Centre, run by the Winnipeg Aboriginal Sport and Recreation Association; the Big HART (Heritage, Arts, and Recording Technology) Program, run by the Winnipeg Métis Association; and Growing Together: Youth Helping Youth Mentorship Program, run by the Ma Mawi Wi Chi Itata Centre, an organization providing culturally relevant supportive programs and services to Aboriginal families.

It is unclear who originally set the agenda for the UMAYC initiative nationally and whether it involved Aboriginal leaders in Ottawa or in communities across the country. It is difficult to say, therefore, whether policy co-production occurred nationally, beginning with issue identification and goal setting. It is clear, though, that at the local level in urban communities across Canada, Aboriginal youth advisory committees working with local friendship centres (or with the Department of Canadian Heritage directly in some Prairie cities) found project selection and implementation permissive enough in the context of local priorities that the principle of self-determination and some measure of co-production were approximated. A commonly perceived strength of UMAYC was that Aboriginal political organizations were not involved in adjudicating proposals and that the process relied on youth in the community who had been nominated by their peers for their skills and leadership abilities.

Place Making by Implementing Aboriginality in Built Form

When marginalized groups begin to see their contributions to the city represented in the city's form, they may be more willing to participate in planning processes. (Rahder and Milgrom 2004, 40)

The concept of "place" is understood as a meeting point for social and cultural relations and physical form. Place is connected intimately to identity and belonging (Lynch and Ley 2010; Relph 1976). People's love of place flourishes from the meaning they attach to relationships between culture, environment, and time in space (Lynch and Ley 2010; Tuan 1974). A sense of place is created by a combination of many facets of the built and socio-cultural environment and is physically and socially constructed "with continuously circulating meanings among different groups reflecting history and supporting identities" (Lynch and Ley 2010, 327).

Underpinning urban Aboriginal policy making and planning with a normative basis that includes recognition of the pursuit of self-determination and the process of co-production can set the groundwork for the meaningful implementation of Aboriginality in built form. In turn, the palpable experience of moving through an urban environment that reflects the cultural presence of Aboriginal peoples can contribute to Aboriginal peoples' greater engagement in civic processes. The policy, planning, and program processes examined in the previous section all contribute to place making to the extent that they build relationships and, through project implementation, change the social, cultural, and built environment of the city. In this section, I use two examples from Saskatoon, Saskatchewan, to demonstrate the potential transformative effect of Aboriginality in urban design on what citizens perceive to be the depth of their shared civic identity: (1) urban design at River Landing, the hallmark public district in that city's downtown, which is currently under development; and (2) the development of urban reserves, an innovation for which the City of Saskatoon and the Muskeg Lake Cree Nation are given pioneering credit across Canada.

Aboriginal peoples in urban areas are often characterized in terms of social problems, making it difficult to turn the corner in Aboriginal-settler relations to a place of mutual respect. The social disparities research that has a near monopoly on urban Aboriginal studies and representation in the mainstream media eclipses the strong communities Aboriginal peoples comprise: communities with aspirations, traditions, and contributions to make towards enhancing our collective, shared, urban-place identity.

Aboriginal culture is a tremendous yet under-appreciated civic asset that can provide a rich entry point to strengthening interactions between Aboriginal and non-Aboriginal urban communities. Culture itself has become a preoccupation of postindustrial economic development approaches in cities across Canada (e.g., Baeker 2010). Expanding the collective civic imagination and depth of identity to bring to the fore Aboriginal culture in planning and urban design, public art and monuments, street and park naming, civic history and consciousness-raising could have a transformative effect on the ways in which Aboriginal peoples in cities relate to local civics in general. Moreover, it could have a dramatic effect on how the non-Aboriginal mainstream sees itself in relation to a larger and more deeply situated sense of place and the strength of the Aboriginal peoples that contribute much to its positive reproduction.

In 2006, the Urban Design Section in the City of Saskatoon's Land Branch established a community group made up of five elders from Cree and Dakota First Nations in the Saskatoon area to work with designers and to create a set of eight tree grate designs for implementation in phase one of the River Landing site. The broad goals for urban design elements at River Landing were to reflect local site features, "to tell the stories of the River Landing location, to draw attention to its unique character, to interpret its rich history, and most importantly, to express the genius loci or spirit of the place" (City of Saskatoon 2006, 2).

The elders provided secular stories about what kinds of activities would have taken place at the River Landing site prior to intensive European urban settlement, which began in the 1880s. The narratives conveyed by the elders inspired the visual elements within each of the eight different tree grate designs. The implementation of the project brought new depth to the perceptible and shared understanding of the site and of the spirit of the place, which is a hallmark public development for the city as a whole. The tree grate design project won the Premier's Award for Design Excellence in 2007.

There are over thirty urban reserves in Saskatchewan, with roughly fifty more planned, in communities ranging from villages to large urban centres (Barron and Garcea 1999; Belanger 2013). Urban reserves referred to here are not principal reserves that have, perhaps, had a city grow up around or beside them, such as the Tsuu T'ina First Nation on the fast-growing City of Calgary's southwestern boundary. Instead, "urban reserve" refers to the urban lands acquired by First Nations through land claim settlements or purchase for economic development (or other social, cultural, or political goals) that serve the interests of the principal reserve community, which is often located some distance away.

The federal government's Additions to Reserves Policy and Saskatchewan's Treaty Land Entitlement Framework Agreement, signed in 1992 by federal, provincial, and more than two dozen First Nations band governments, set out provisions and processes for the creation of urban reserves. Among the key issues that a municipality and a First Nation must negotiate when an application is made to the federal government for a parcel of urban land to be transferred from freehold property to urban reserve status are: compensation paid for the loss of local taxes; financing of municipal services on the reserve parcel; bylaw compatibility between the municipality and reserve parcel; and a joint consultative process for maintaining good neighbour relations between the First Nation and municipal governments (Sully et al. 2008).

The first urban reserve in a Canadian city was developed in 1988 in Saskatoon by the Muskeg Lake Cree Nation on fifteen hectares of land in the Sutherland industrial area. The City of Saskatoon and the Muskeg Lake Cree Nation were able to work through the four issue areas noted above in good faith, and this pioneering relationship between a First Nation and an urban municipality has remained a strong one. There are several other properties in Saskatoon that are urban reserves or that are in the process of becoming reserves. They include undeveloped land in an area of potential future growth at the city's border, gas stations, and office towers in the central business district. The potential exists for future residential development on urban reserves, though this concept has not yet been implemented in a large Saskatchewan city.

In cities across Canada, urban reserves can create a positive and tangible presence in the built environment that can foster cultural, economic, and social development for Aboriginal and non-Aboriginal citizens. The commercial complex on the Muskeg Lake Cree Nation's urban reserve in the Sutherland neighbourhood of Saskatoon, for example, has had a positive impact on surrounding property values off the reserve parcel, and it provides a range of services and jobs for area residents (Sully et al. 2008). Augmenting our sense of place by giving physical manifestation to the situated histories and contemporary presence of Aboriginal cultures in the city through developments like urban reserves and design treatments such as the tree grates at River Landing is a promising area of interest for urbanists.

Conclusion

Are we operating at diminished capacity in our Canadian cities, particularly in Prairie cities such as Winnipeg and Saskatoon, by denying ourselves access to one of the most deeply situated future-seeking and place-making assets we have at our disposal – the full articulation of urban Aboriginality in policy, planning, programming, and built environment? Particularly as "urban Aboriginal" identities of second- and third-generation urbanites become more prominent in urban populations generally (see Andersen, this volume), how will this manifest itself in our governance and design?

This chapter explored the role that the co-production of policy and design can play at all levels of government jurisdiction as well as how tangible place-making projects that articulate Aboriginal identities in the shared built environment can deepen our civic identity. As Kelly Greenop and Paul

Memmott (this volume) point out, considerable potential exists for intercultural forms to emerge in the urban landscape and in relationships between peoples. Ron Laliberte (this volume) ponders a similar potential in
the context of an emerging urban Métis identity, which he sees as a distinctive feature of Canadian culture and identity. Our future in the postcolonial
twenty-first-century Canadian city depends on how well we can collectively
understand and articulate the strength of Aboriginal peoples' historic and
contemporary culture in our common civic identity.

Notes

The research assistance of James Moore and Maeengan Linklater is gratefully acknowledged. Some of the material in this chapter is taken from empirical work funded by a SSHRC major collaborative research initiative on multilevel governance and
public policy making in municipalities, led by Robert Young, University of Western
Ontario. The results of that work are to be found in *Urban Aboriginal Policymaking
in Canadian Municipalities*, edited by Evelyn Peters and published in 2011 by
McGill-Queen's University Press. The chapter of specific interest is entitled "More
Than Stakeholders, Voices, and Tables: Towards Co-Production of Urban Aboriginal
Policy in Manitoba," by Ryan Walker, James Moore, and Maeengan Linklater.

1 In this chapter, the meaning of the term "Aboriginality" is drawn from the work of
Claude Denis (1997), who uses it to signify a comprehensive cultural project that
brings the inherency of Aboriginal ways of life and the basic right to continued
self-determination to bear on how we understand the relationship between Euro-
Canadians and Aboriginal peoples. His ideas around Aboriginality contrast it with a
mono-cultural modern myth of universal Canadian citizenship, which eclipses the
vitality of Aboriginal social, cultural, and governance structures. The cultural project
of Aboriginality is a basis for decolonization in partnership with settler society.

2 The phrase "increasing the depth of our civic identity," which is used in the title of
this chapter, is one that I have adapted from a 2007 conversation with Jeanna South
while she was manager of urban design for the City of Saskatoon. She used the
phrase while describing the potential that Aboriginal cultures had for expanding our
shared (Aboriginal and non-Aboriginal) sense of place, history, and culture in
Saskatoon.

References

Adams, H. 1999. *Tortured people: The politics of colonization*. Rev. ed. Penticton, BC:
     Theytus.
Andersen, C., and C. Denis. 2003. Urban Natives and the nation: Before and after the
     Royal Commission on Aboriginal Peoples. *Canadian Review of Sociology and
     Anthropology* 40: 373-90.

Baeker, G. 2010. *Rediscovering the wealth of places: A municipal cultural planning handbook for Canadian communities.* St. Thomas, ON: Municipal World.

Barron, F.L., and J. Garcea, eds. 1999. *Urban Indian reserves: Forging new relationships in Saskatchewan.* Saskatoon: Purich.

Belanger, Y. 2013. *Ways of knowing: An introduction to Native studies in Canada.* 2nd ed. Toronto: Nelson Education.

Belanger, Y., and R. Walker. 2009. Interest convergence and co-production of plans: An examination of Winnipeg's "Aboriginal pathways." *Canadian Journal of Urban Research* 18(1) Supplement: 118-39.

Brudney, J., and R. England. 1982. Urban policy making and subjective service evaluations: Are they compatible? *Public Administration Review* 42: 127-35.

Canada (Attorney General) v. Misquadis, 2003 FCA 370.

Casey, J., and B. Dalton. 2006. The best of times, the worst of times: Community-sector advocacy in the age of "compacts." *Australian Journal of Political Science* 41: 23-38.

City of Saskatoon. 2006. *River Landing interpretive elements: Tree grate design.* Saskatoon: City of Saskatoon.

City of Winnipeg. 2003. *First Steps: Municipal Aboriginal Pathways.* Winnipeg: City of Winnipeg.

Denis, C. 1997. *We are not you: First Nations and Canadian modernity.* Peterborough, ON: Broadview.

Durie, M. 2003. *Ngā Kāhui Pou: Launching Māori futures.* Wellington: Huia.

Green, J. 2005. Self-determination, citizenship, and federalism as palimpsest. In *Reconfiguring Aboriginal-state relations. Canada: The state of the federation, 2003,* ed. M. Murphy, 329-52. Montreal and Kingston: McGill-Queen's University Press.

Hunter, A. 2006. The politics of Aboriginal self-government. In *Canadian politics: Democracy and dissent,* ed. J. Grace and B. Sheldrick, 24-39. Toronto: Prentice Hall.

Lynch, N., and D. Ley. 2010. The changing meanings of urban places. In *Canadian cities in transition: New directions in the twenty-first century.* 4th ed., ed. T. Bunting, P. Filion, and R. Walker, 325-41. Toronto, Oxford University Press.

Maaka, R. 1994. The new tribe: Conflicts and continuities in the social organisation of urban Māori. *Contemporary Pacific* 6: 311-36.

Maaka, R., and A. Fleras. 2005. *The politics of Indigeneity: Challenging the state in Canada and Aotearoa New Zealand.* Dunedin, NZ: University of Otago Press.

Moore, J., R. Walker, and I. Skelton. 2011. Challenging the new Canadian myth: Colonialism, post-colonialism, and urban Aboriginal policy in Thompson and Brandon, Manitoba. *Canadian Journal of Native Studies* 31(1): 17-42.

Morgan, G. 2006. *Unsettled places: Aboriginal people and urbanisation in New South Wales.* Kent Town, AU: Wakefield.

Newhouse, D., and E.J. Peters, eds. 2003. *Not strangers in these parts: Urban Aboriginal peoples.* Ottawa: Policy Research Initiative.

Nyland, J. 1995. Issue networks and non-profit organisations. *Policy Studies Review* 14: 195-204.

Peters, E.J. 2010. Aboriginal people in Canadian cities. In *Canadian cities in transition: New directions in the twenty-first century*, 4th ed., ed T. Bunting, P. Filion, and R. Walker, 375-90. Toronto: Oxford University Press.

Rahder, B., and R. Milgrom. 2004. The uncertain city: Making space(s) for difference. *Canadian Journal of Urban Research* 13(1) Supplement: 27-45.

Relph, E. 1976. *Place and placelessness*. London: Pion.

Royal Commission on Aboriginal Peoples. 1996. *Report of the Royal Commission on Aboriginal Peoples*. Ottawa: Minister of Supply and Services.

Sandercock, L. 2003. *Cosmopolis II: Mongrel cities in the 21st century*. New York: Continuum.

Sully, L., L. Kellett, J. Garcea, and R. Walker. 2008. First Nations urban reserves in Saskatoon: Partnerships for positive development. *Plan Canada* 48: 39-42.

Tuan, Y. 1974. Space and place: Humanistic perspective. *Progress in Geography* 6: 211-52.

United Nations. 2007. United Nations Declaration of the Rights of Indigenous Peoples. Report of the Human Rights Council. UN Doc. A/61/L.67/2007.

Walker, R. 2006. Interweaving Aboriginal/Indigenous rights with urban citizenship: A view from the Winnipeg low-cost housing sector, Canada. *Citizenship Studies* 10(4): 391-411.

–. 2008. Aboriginal self-determination and social housing in urban Canada: A story of convergence and divergence. *Urban Studies* 45(1): 185-205.

Wilson, K., and E.J. Peters. 2005. "You can make a place for it": Remapping urban First Nations spaces of identity. *Society and Space* 23: 395-413.

PART 2

American Indian Urbanization in the United States

AS IN MANY NATION-STATES, in the United States Indigenous nations signed treaties with the US government that were, more often than not, honoured in their breech. One significant impact of these treaties in the United States, however, included the widespread creation of "reservations" within which tribal collectivities resided. Often these reservations incorporated small parts of larger traditional territories, but in many cases they did not. They did, however, allow for a continued communal lifestyle. While we may take Snipp's argument (this volume) that "urbanization" is hardly a recent phenomenon for American Indians (Snipp, in fact, argues that, in many cases, *de*urbanization long preceded the urbanization that characterizes the twentieth and twenty-first centuries), the nineteenth and (especially) twentieth centuries have borne witness to a massive migration of American Indian people from reservations to urban centres (both large and small). In his excellent *Indian Metropolis,* James LaGrand (2002) argues that, while long-standing social scientific and historical research has tended to position such population movements as mere epiphenomenal reflections of federally produced American Indian policy (in both the nineteenth and twentieth centuries) and their effects in terms of dispossession, poverty, and general anomie (e.g., Waddell and Watson 1971), the reality is a good deal more complicated. LaGrand argues that four major factors precipitated movement from reservation/tribal communities into urban ones. And, while these factors are powerfully rooted in US "Indian" policy, they also bear the stamp of agentic decisions and networks of power specific to tribal, gendered, and geographical proximities.

The first major factor stems from tribal reactions to the Dawes Act, 1887. This act, which "de-communalized" tribal land and opened it up both for individual allotment (leasing to non-tribal members) and eventual sale, effectively destroyed the collective land base so important to tribal sovereignty. In turn, this produced dispossession, economic marginalization, poverty, and disease – all of which, LaGrand (2002, 19) argues, contributed to migration from reservations. The effects of the Dawes Act forced many tribal members to migrate from the reservation in search of work, much of which tended to be wage-based (particularly agrarian and timber). While this produced a "life of mobility" (2002, 24), LaGrand argues that it could easily have been understood as a simple adaptation of pre-existing seasonable practices. Having said that, such wage labouring tended to take place near reservations so that those involved could travel with relative ease back and forth between reservation and work, maintaining both family and larger kin links to the tribal community. The scale of such urbanization tended to be small, and those who moved away for work tended to reside in smaller communities on the edge of towns (which meant little contact with non-tribal people) – "cities," in this sense, were understood as temporary homes for work while the "real" home was still the reservation.

LaGrand (2002, 28) argues that, while tribal people were being integrated into the US national economy through their wage labouring, this consisted of "tentative steps and temporary engagement." Likewise, it produced increased interaction with non-tribal people, which solidified a pre-existing prejudice and ensconced racist social relations within these temporary communities. LaGrand argues that many moved to larger cities to escape the problems af-flicting these smaller ones. Similarly, Fixico (2006, 19) highlights the creation of the Civilian Conservation Corps, which encouraged Indian men to leave the res-ervations for work, and this, he suggests, produced a growth in off-reserve em-ployment. In sum, until the Second World War, the loss of land, the development of novel wage labour patterns, and changing demographics all played their role in increasing the urbanization of tribal people (LaGrand 2002, 32).

Yet, these factors all paled in comparison to the impact of the Second World War on the lives and mobility patterns (both social and geographical) of tribal peoples (a point made by Snipp, this volume). Socially, the experience of the Second World War both at home and on the varied battlefronts changed the expectations of American Indian people. Those who enlisted met new people and experienced new kinds of relationships with non-tribal people that were largely free of the racism and discrimination they experienced back home. For those on the home front, the Second World War produced both a massive labour shortage and a coincidental pressing need for massive amounts of ma-chinery, munitions, and foodstuff. Indians were paid better than they had been, and Indian women, in particular, filled labour roles (in defence industries in par-ticular) that had previously shut them out. The impact of the war cannot be overstated: Indian people's enhanced socio-economic position allowed them to purchase consumer items formerly out of their reach, and they engendered relations with non-Indians, many of whom they befriended (and even married). LaGrand (2002, 38) argues that wartime experiences, both at home and abroad, raised expectations for the postwar period in terms of political, social, and eco-nomic improvements.

Immediately following the end of the Second World War in 1945, labour shortages were curtailed and Indian people found themselves once again shut out of industries in which they had proven to be successful only months before. Following the war, Indian policy changed in important ways as well, particularly with respect to the termination and relocation ethos that buttressed them. Specifically, a "voluntary" relocation program (begun in 1952) played a massive role in encouraging the migration of literally thousands of tribal members into major US cities, part of a larger assimilation ethos that had begun to take hold in government policy silos. This program, which offered to assist new migrants in finding employment, temporary housing, and relief payments, proved attractive to more than 100,000 people between 1952 and 1972 (Fixico 2006, 22). As one of Weibel-Orlando's (1991, 24) participants notes, however, the program offered only one-way tickets to the city.

LaGrand (2002) notes that, as a harbinger of contemporary relations, tribal members were deeply conflicted about leaving their reservation homes. On the one hand, it constituted a place of kin and friends; on the other, while it cannot be reduced to such pathologies, successive generations of US policy had rendered it a locale of deeply rooted social and economic malaise. The economic diversity and perceived opportunities of large cities engendered a powerful "pull" for those living in impoverished communities. And, while many have argued that urbanization meant that American Indian people entered cities on the lowest rung and stayed there, this was evidently preferable to the hopelessness of attempting to improve one's material comfort on reservations. However, it was American Indian peoples' reaction to the relocation program, rather than the program itself, that often dictated migration choices. LaGrand (2002, 90) argues that decisions to move and to stay or return were complex and were made in discussion with family and friends, whether they had relocation experiences or not: people often moved in groups and moved to locations in which they already knew family or friends.

However, dreams of a better life did not always square with reality. For example, Thornton, Sendefur, and Grasmick (1982, 27) note that "urbanization [did] not necessarily improve economic conditions." Early research seems to indicate that those coming to the city with skills and training were far more likely to benefit economically from urban life than were those without such skills (which were even more important than formal education). In either case, American Indians lagged behind (often significantly) the socio-economic status of their non-Indian neighbours, while enjoying a significantly higher status than that of their reservation-based kin. Equally, though research is clear that the urban Aboriginal communities that developed in some of the major US cities are distinctive in relation to those geographical and socio-demographic locales, they share a number of characteristics. These include: (1) they are the centre of a proliferation of Aboriginal organizations (usually formalized, usually non-profit); (2) they are multigenerational; (3) they are multi- (and in certain circumstances inter-) tribal; (4) they have links to pre-existing homelands; (5) they experience increased economic and class diversity; (6) they have a recognized urban history (see Lobo 2001, 78–80); and, often, (7) they experience a "scatteredness" within the larger sea of other ethnic minorities. The urbanization of Aboriginal peoples, far from producing the assimilation it was expected to engender, "brought Indians from different tribes together in one place, giving them a chance to create new communities and to bridge tribal differences that had interfered with community organizing in the past" (Ramirez 2007, 2).

References

Fixico, D. 2006. *Daily life of Native Americans in the twentieth century.* Westport, CT: Greenwood Press.

LaGrand, J.B. 2002. *Indian metropolis: Native Americans in Chicago, 1945-75.* Urbana: University of Indiana Press.

Lobo, S. 2001. "Is urban a person or a place? Characteristics of urban Indian country." In *American Indians and the urban experience,* ed. S. Lobo and K. Peters, 73-84. Walnut Creek, CA: AltaMira Press.

Ramirez, R. 2007. *Native hubs: Culture, community, and belonging in Silicon Valley and beyond.* Durham, NC: Duke University Press.

Thornton, R., G.D. Sandefur, and H.G. Grasmick. 1982. *The urbanization of American Indians: A critical bibliography.* Urbana: Indiana University Press.

Waddell, J., and O.M. Watson. 1971. *The American Indian in urban society.* Perdue: Little, Brown and Company.

Weibel-Orlando, J. 1991. *Indian country, LA: Maintaining ethnic community in complex society.* Chicago: University of Illinois Press.

8

American Indians and Alaska Natives in Urban Environments

C. MATTHEW SNIPP

The urbanization of Indigenous people, particularly American Indians and Alaska Natives, is significant for a number of reasons. One of these is that urbanization is a direct reflection of the extent to which American Indians and Alaska Natives participate in the everyday life of American society. Most Americans live in cities, and urban living now represents the quintessential American experience. The presence of American Indians and Alaska Natives in modern American cities signifies the degree to which they have lives that differ little from those of other Americans. Another reason that urbanization is especially significant for American Indians and Alaska Natives is that it reflects a certain disconnection from the lived experience of tribal life on reservations, in villages, and in other areas regarded as "Indian Country," conventionally thought to express the "ground zero" of American Indianness. For some urban Indians, this disconnection is complete in every possible respect; for others, it is less complete, and possibly temporary. Yet, no matter how temporary, urban living is still a disconnection from tribal life. Finally, urbanization also represents a challenge to tribal communities insofar as tribal members return to their home communities and bring knowledge and lifestyles that may or may not be welcome in the tribe. An unwelcome change, for example, might be the introduction of urban gang culture to reservation youth. Alternatively, urban Indians also can bring much needed human and social capital such as job skills, education, work experience, and a familiarity with modern American society.

The subject of this chapter is the urbanization of American Indians and Alaska Natives in the United States. I begin with a brief historical overview of the urbanization of American Indians. I then offer statistical data for American Indians and Alaska Natives and compare them with data for whites and African Americans in order to give the reader a sense of the social and economic position of the former in urban environments. I conclude with some observations about the larger implications of American Indian and Alaska Native urbanization.

Historical Background

Taking a long view of history, American Indians, in particular, have lived in urban areas since before the time of Columbus. The archaeological record attesting to the urbanization of American Indians clearly indicates that North America was the site of a number of large pre-Columbian settlements – the largest of course were those sited in what is now Mexico. There is also evidence, however, that the Natives north of the Rio Grande lived in settled, urban communities.

Throughout the southwest, the Anasazi, ancestors of the modern Pueblo communities, resided in relatively large settlements. The ruins at Mesa Verde National Park is the largest and most well developed example, though such settlements can be found at a number of locations in the states known now as Utah, Colorado, and New Mexico. Perhaps the largest settlement in what is now the United States was located just east of modern-day St. Louis, across the Mississippi River, and known as Cahokia.

The Cahokia site was occupied approximately between 700 CE and 1400 CE, and it probably attained its peak development around 1250 CE (Pauketat 2009). Contemporary scholars have since identified the pre-1400 residents of the settlement as representatives of the Mississippian culture, and the remnants of their civilization include a variety of large and elaborate earthen mounds for burial and ceremonial purposes. At its peak, the City of Cahokia included perhaps as many as 120 mounds built across an area of about fifteen square kilometres. The population of Cahokia probably numbered, conservatively, around ten to fifteen thousand people at its apex. For the sake of comparison, this number is slightly smaller than estimates for London, England, in roughly the same time period, making Cahokia a city comparable in size and population to medieval London.

However, London obviously endured, but for a variety of complex reasons, the City of Cahokia failed, and, by 1400, it was all but abandoned. The reasons for Cahokia's failure are outside the scope of this discussion, but suffice it to say that by the time white settlers arrived in the Mississippi River Valley, Cahokia had ceased to exist. However, while Cahokia failed, the Mississippian mound-building culture had extensive subsequent influence. Indeed, in this way, nascent urban places can be seen throughout the southeastern United States and its eastern seaboard. The Spanish explorer Hernando DeSoto, for example, encountered settled villages during his southeastern expedition (Driver 1969). Similarly, to the north, the six nations of the Iroquois Confederacy – as well as other tribes – were organized in permanent towns. Small by modern standards, these settlements prefigured the first urban communities in North America.

After the arrival of Europeans, the struggle for the possession and control of land, along with frequent epidemics, decimated these communities. In particular, the southeastern removals of the early nineteenth century destroyed these towns as tribes such as the Cherokee and the Chickasaw were forcibly uprooted and marched west to the Indian Territory (Foreman 1972). For example, the Cherokee Nation was forced to abandon its capital of New Echota in Georgia and to re-establish a new one in what is now Tahlequah, Oklahoma.

The history of Tahlequah offers a template for the experience of American Indians in the Indian Territory and elsewhere. In its early years, Tahlequah was a relatively large settlement, and it boasted the first public school system west of the Mississippi River (McLoughlin 1993). However, with the passage of time, growing numbers of white settlers gradually surrounded and overwhelmed the Cherokee in their own territory. The Indian Territory was dissolved in 1907, and, while the rest of the United States grew larger and more urbanized, Tahlequah grew comparatively smaller, more isolated, and less Cherokee. At the turn of the twenty-first century, the total population of the City of Tahlequah was slightly over fourteen thousand – a small town by modern standards – with American Indians forming barely over a quarter of the total population.

The experience of the Cherokee in Tahlequah was replayed in a variety of scenarios across the United States as whites and American Indians fought for possession of the land. For most of the nineteenth century, forced removals, relocations, and resettlements forced the American Indian population into often remote settlements, almost always far from the growing and increasingly urban mainstream of the United States. By the twentieth century, the American Indian population was fully contained in the rural backwaters of American society, left behind by the growth of the nation's urban industrial economy (Snipp 1989). The de-urbanization of American Indians was complete.[1]

The 1930 census was notable because it was the first census to show that the majority of Americans lived in cities. Yet, while over one-half of all Americans lived in urban areas, barely 10 percent of the American Indian and Alaska Native population could be found in cities (Snipp 1989). In the early decades of the twentieth century, relatively few American Indians resided in cities, and this did not begin to change until after the end of the Second World War.

The postwar urbanization of American Indians and Alaska Natives proceeded quickly and was fuelled by three developments. The first was the war itself. Approximately twenty-five thousand American Indians, mostly men, served in the armed forces. Another forty thousand went to work in war-related industrial production (Bernstein 1991). For many of these American Indians, involvement in the war was an opportunity to leave their reservations and to experience urban life first-hand. Exact numbers are unavailable, but many of these young men and women opted to remain in the city rather than to return to the reservation. Others returned to their reservation only to later return to an urban area in search of employment. A second development was the passage of the GI bill near the end of the war. This bill provided returning war veterans with financial support to complete their education, to attend college or vocational school, and with low-cost loans to buy a home or start a business. A substantial number of American Indians and Alaska Natives took advantage of these programs (Bernstein 1991). However, reservation life offered few jobs or opportunities. For those American Indians who attained a college degree or wished to start a business, moving to an urban area represented their only viable option.

A third push towards the cities emerged in the years following the Second World War. In the late 1940s and early 1950s, Congress and policy makers in the federal government enacted a series of initiatives known today as the policies of Termination and Relocation. The basic idea behind these policies was to end the special legal and political status of American Indians and Alaska Natives with three measures. First was the establishment of a special commission to settle pending claims filed by tribes against the federal government. Second, Congress unilaterally mandated the abolition of reservations with all due speed. And finally, in the early 1950s, the Bureau of Indian Affairs introduced a series of programs designed to induce relocation from reservations to pre-selected urban areas.[2] In exchange for leaving the reservation, American Indians and Alaska Natives were offered a short-term stipend, job training, and assistance with finding housing and employment. These programs operated at their peak levels in the 1950s and 1960s. During the period between 1952 and 1972, well over 100,000 American Indians and Alaska Natives were resettled in urban areas (Sorkin 1978).

The relocation programs were sharply criticized for being ineffective insofar as they took poorly educated and unemployed reservation Indians and turned them into poorly educated and unemployed urban Indians. An unknown number of these relocated Indians did not remain in cities, while others found themselves in urban slums plagued by substance abuse and other social ills (Fixico 1988; LaGrand 2002). Additionally, many have faulted these relocation programs for undermining labour forces and impeding economic development projects on reservations as American Indian workers who had the skills and education necessary to fill reservation jobs were relocated to cities.

In the 1970s, the relocation programs were scaled back and finally ended in the Reagan administration. However, the cessation of the relocation programs did not abate the movement of American Indians to cities in subsequent decades. Indeed, in every census taken since the Second World War, there has been a steady increase of American Indians in US cities; and, in recent decades, these migratory flows have mirrored the southern and westerly movements characteristic of the rest of the American population (not to mention internationally – see Taylor, this volume; Kukutai, this volume; Norris, Clatworthy, and Peters, this volume). There can be no doubt that American Indians and Alaska Natives are no less immune to the economic and other demographic forces shaping migration across the United States than is any other population. In the remaining discussion, I present empirical data to show how the urbanization of American Indians has most recently unfolded and where urban Indian populations are situated and most heavily concentrated. I also offer some summary characteristics of these populations.

A Statistical Overview of Urban American Indians and Alaska Natives

In connection with the preceding historical narrative, an examination of the data showing temporal changes in urban residence for American Indians and Alaska Natives is a logical place to begin this discussion. The data to follow are derived from sources produced by the US Census Bureau, which represents the single best and most comprehensive source of information about American Indians and Alaska Natives. Although conceptually easy to envision, temporal comparisons of urban change for any group or population are fraught with a host of methodological problems. In particular, readers should be mindful of two concerns.

An especially important inter-censal change involved the modification of the categories used to designate racial heritage. Among other changes, the 2000 census allowed persons to identify with more than one race. That is, some persons may identify as only American Indian while others may identify with two or more races, for instance American Indian and white or American Indian and black. There were approximately 2.5 million persons who reported "American Indian or Alaska Native alone" as their race, and another 1.7 million who claimed one or more races in addition to American Indian and Alaska Native.[3] Readers should also be mindful that, in the data presented below, in a very crude way, this measure captures very different kinds of identities for American Indians and Alaska Natives.

In particular, the personal circumstances and the networks of social relations for persons who identify as American Indian or Alaska Native along with another race almost certainly may vary dramatically from the social environments and circumstances of persons identified only as American Indian or Alaska Native. For example, one might contrast the conditions and life experiences of a person identified as American Indian and African American living in Atlanta, Georgia, with those of an American Indian living in Phoenix, Arizona. It would be easy to dwell too long on this point, but one can imagine the many complex ways that a person of part-Indian and part-black heritage in Atlanta, a southern city deeply influenced by African-American culture, might differ from a person for whom only American Indian is reported and who lives in a city and region with large numbers of American Indians, tribal lands, and a considerable Native presence in the local culture (for a similar discussion in a Canadian context, see Andersen, this volume).

Another concern that readers should note is the meaning of the term "urban." The federal government periodically revises the definition and criteria used to designate an area as urban. As these definitions and criteria change, new urban areas are created while others may disappear (Yaukey, Anderton, Lundequvist 2007, 349-55). After the Second World War, for example, the San Francisco Bay area emerged as a major metropolitan area due to the rapid growth of three adjacent cities linked by surrounding suburban areas: San Francisco, Oakland, and San Jose. In addition, urban areas often change their boundaries, usually to annex adjacent areas experiencing population growth. In some cases, an area such as a reservation may exist just outside a city – a common situation in southern California, for example – then later become part of an urban area as the adjacent city expands its boundaries. The reservation proper will remain distinct and separate from the city, but, for statistical purposes, its residents are now considered part of an urban area, making the reservation residents "urban" without their ever having changed residence. Admittedly, this is not a common occurrence, but it does illustrate the perils of comparing urban areas over time.

Table 8.1 shows the numbers and percentages of American Indians and Alaska Natives residing in urban areas and in Metropolitan Statistical Areas (MSAs). The most striking feature in this table is that, in the aggregate, about two-thirds of the American Indian and Alaska Native population now resides in cities.

However, there are several other noteworthy details embedded within this table. First, the numbers for MSAs do not differ greatly from those of urban areas. This is noteworthy because, in anticipation of the 2000 census, the Census Bureau revamped its definition of urban areas to make it more consistent with an intuitive understanding of the circumstances connected with city living (for instance, a large densely settled area). In previous censuses, "urban" places could be as small as twenty-five hundred persons and included a sizable number of small towns. For this reason, many analysts eschewed statistics for urban areas in favour of data for MSAs. The latter are more closely aligned to large cities, including places of 250,000 or more among a number of other criteria required for the designation of MSA. However, as this table indicates, the differences between urban areas and MSAs are relatively small. Accordingly, for the balance of this chapter, data for MSAs and for urban areas are presented. However, data for urban areas appear most often because of their ready availability in published census material.

Another detail in Table 8.1 concerns a notable difference between American Indians and Alaska Natives who are identified with no other racial group, on the one hand, and American Indians and Alaska Natives who are identified in combination with one or more other races, on the other. Specifically, multiracial American Indians and Alaska Natives are more likely to reside in urban areas or in MSAs than are American Indians and Alaska Natives who are identified with only one race. This is an important distinction that becomes more apparent in subsequent tables, which show that persons identified as multiracial American Indians and Alaska Natives have a sizable material advantage over American Indians and Alaska Natives for whom only one race is reported.[4]

C. Matthew Snipp

TABLE 8.1
Distribution of American Indians and Alaska Natives, alone or in combination with another race, in metropolitan statistical areas and urban areas

	Metropolitan statistical areas	Urban areas
American Indians or Alaska Natives alone	1,432,750 (57.9%)	1,497,402 (60.5%)
American Indians or Alaska Natives in combination with another race	1,289,458 (78.5%)	1,277,314 (77.7%)
Total	2,722,208 (66.1%)	2,774,716 (67.4%)

Source: US Census Bureau, 2000 Decennial Census, Summary File 2.

Finally, it is worth noting that the rural-urban gap between multiracial American Indians and Alaska Natives and those who are identified as only American Indian and Alaska Native is somewhat smaller for the MSA-/Non-MSA difference. This is because 58 percent of the single-race American Indian and Alaska Native population lives in MSAs, and slightly more, 61 percent, can be found living in urban areas. However, virtually identical percentages of multiracial American Indians and Alaska Natives live in MSAs and in urban areas – 79 and 78 percent, respectively.

The next table (Table 8.2) shows temporal change in the urbanization of American Indians and Alaska Natives in MSAs compared with that of blacks and whites from 1980 to 2000. In the course of a generation, the white and African-American populations have continued to become more concentrated in large urban areas. For example, in 1980, 73 percent of the white population lived in MSAs, and, by 2000, this number had grown to 79 percent. Similarly for African Americans, 81 percent lived in MSAs in 1980, and, twenty years later, this figure had grown to 88 percent. By any measure, these are substantial increases in the concentration of these populations, even allowing for the fact that some of this change may reflect nothing more than changes in the definition of an MSA. However, the urbanization of American Indians and Alaska Natives continues to lag behind these groups, though this gap has decreased significantly in the past twenty years.

Although the urbanization of African Americans and whites increased in past decades, the increase in the percentage of American Indians and Alaska Natives living in MSAs was staggering – growing by more than one-third – especially because most of this change came between 1990 and 2000. In

1980, just slightly less than one-half of the American Indian and Alaska Native population resided in MSAs, and by 1990 this number had increased to 51 percent. However, by 2000, about two-thirds of the American Indian and Alaska Native population could be found in MSAs. There may be a number of factors that account for this dramatic increase. The most likely explanation may be the effect of "ethnic drift" within the American Indian and Alaska Native population (Guimond 2003). A detailed discussion of the phenomenon of ethnic drift, also known as ethnic mobility, is beyond the scope of this chapter. However, it is well known that much of the growth in the American Indian and Alaska Native population since 1960 has been due to individuals switching their racial heritage from white or black to American Indian (Eschbach, Supple, and Snipp 1998). Evidence of this drift is manifest in the difference percentages for persons identified as only American Indian or Alaska Native and for persons identified with another race in addition to American Indian or Alaska Native. The drift appears most evident in urban areas, and the causes of this are undoubtedly complex. However, mixed-race marriages and relationships are more common in urban areas (Snipp 1989), and these unions are responsible for there being a larger number of persons in urban areas who have the option of identifying with more than one race. The introduction of a race question allowing more than one race for a response on the census may have induced a number of persons who would not have identified as American Indian or Alaska Native in the past to now include this heritage as one to be reported.

Comparing the percent of American Indians and Alaska Natives living in MSAs in 1980 with persons identified as only American Indian and Alaska Native in 2000 yields a pattern of urbanization similar to increases among African Americans and whites, from 49 percent in 1980 to 58 percent in 2000. This is a plausible comparison because ostensibly, in 1980, only one race could be reported for each person in a household. Comparing the multiracial American Indian and Alaska Native population with the 1980 American Indian and Alaska Native population is more problematic, but clearly, the former is a highly urbanized population with 79 percent living in MSAs. From this, it seems quite likely that much of the urbanization that took place between 1980 and 2000, especially the aggregate numbers, is due to at least two components, the first of which is a general tendency experienced across American society – the movement to large cities, especially in the south and west. Even in 1980, migration patterns of American Indians and Alaska Natives resembled those of other Americans, so it is entirely plausible that there are now more American Indians living in cities

TABLE 8.2

Percent of American Indians and Alaska Natives, African Americans, and whites residing in metropolitan statistical areas, 1980-2000

	1980	1990	2000
American Indians and Alaska Natives	49.0	51.3	66.1
Alone	n/a	n/a	57.9
In combination	n/a	n/a	78.5
African Americans*	81.1	83.7	87.5
Whites*	73.3	74.8	79.2

* Includes persons who identified as white or African American alone or in combination with another race for year 2000.
Sources: Snipp (1989, 1996); US Census Bureau, 2000 Decennial Census, Summary File 2.

than was the case in past decades (Snipp 1989). Some of this increase may also be owing to changing definitions of MSAs. However, the dramatic magnitude of this increase is also almost certainly due to ethnic drift, the second component of urbanization between 1980 and 2000. This is especially plausible owing to the fact that, in 2000, for the first time, persons with some degree of American Indian or Alaska Native heritage, no matter how tenuous or far removed the connection, could be identified as American Indian or Alaska Native. This gave persons who might have been identified only as black or white in a previous census the opportunity to add American Indian and Alaska Native to their racial heritage (for similar situations in a Canadian context, see Clatworthy, Norris, and Peters 2011).

Table 8.3 shows the twenty-five MSAs with the largest American Indian and Alaska Native populations. The first two columns of Table 8.3 show the cities with the largest populations of persons who were identified in the 2000 census as American Indian or Alaska Native only. The second two columns show the cities with the largest populations of persons identified as American Indian or Alaska Native in combination with another race. For both of these groups, the largest numbers are found in the Los Angeles-Riverside-Orange County metropolitan area located in southern California. This area was a relocation centre in the 1950s and 1960s, and it has been the site of the largest urban American Indian and Alaska Native population since at least the 1970 census (Snipp 1989). It is also noteworthy that all of the cities selected to be relocation centres in the original Bureau of Indian Affairs programs are represented in this table. Cleveland is a notable exception insofar as it was a relocation centre yet is ranked only twenty-second with respect to the size of its multiracial American Indian and Alaska Native population. It does not have a sufficiently large number of persons identified as only American Indian or Alaska Native to be included in the twenty-five largest populations for this particular group.

Another notable feature of Table 8.3 is the heterogeneity in the list of cities boasting large populations of multiracial and monoracial American Indians and Alaska Natives. Very roughly, the five or ten cities with the largest American Indian and Alaska Native populations have large numbers of multiracial American Indians and Alaska Natives as well as of those identifying only as American Indian. However, among those metropolitan areas with smaller populations, a number have large populations of multiracial American Indians and Alaska Natives and significantly smaller numbers of persons identified only as American Indian or Alaska Native. For example, the Philadelphia area has nearly twenty-three thousand persons identified as American Indian or Alaska Native in combination with another race and is ranked eleventh in size. However, in this same area, slightly more than thirteen thousand persons were identified as only American Indian or Alaska Native. In contrast, Albuquerque, New Mexico, has nearly forty thousand persons who were identified only as American Indian or Alaska Native, and it ranked eighth in size. But the multiracial American Indian and Alaska Native population of Albuquerque was not sufficiently large to be included in the twenty-five largest cities for this group. Finally, it is notable that Honolulu, Hawai'i, has the twenty-first largest population of multiracial American Indians and Alaska Natives (about fourteen thousand), just behind Minneapolis-St. Paul, Minnesota, at twentieth. However, the latter has a much larger number of persons identified only as American Indian or Alaska Native, about twenty-two thousand persons, seventeenth largest in this list. Not surprisingly, the number of monoracial American Indians and Alaska Natives in Hawai'i is not sufficiently large to appear in this ranking.

The next table and figure show the relative differences among American Indians and Alaska Natives residing in metropolitan and non-metropolitan areas. Table 8.4 shows differences in the educational attainment of these populations. There are two general conclusions that can be drawn from these data. One is that urban American Indians are, on average, better educated than are their counterparts residing in non-metropolitan areas. In the latter group, the modal category of educational attainment is a high school diploma or its equivalent. About 32 percent of American Indians and Alaska Natives in rural areas have completed high school, regardless of how they identified. In metropolitan areas, the percentage of American Indians and

TABLE 8.3
Metropolitan areas with the twenty-five largest American Indian and Alaska Native populations, alone and in combination with another race (rank)

Rank	Metropolitan area	American Indians and Alaska Natives alone	Metropolitan area	American Indians and Alaska Natives in combination with another race
1	Los Angeles–Riverside–Orange County, CA	142,083	Los Angeles–Riverside–Orange County, CA	116,906
2	Phoenix–Mesa, AZ	70,740	New York–Northern New Jersey–Long Island, NY–NJ–CT–PA	91,209
3	New York–Northern New Jersey–Long Island, NY–NJ–CT-PA	70,515	San Francisco–Oakland–San Jose, CA	60,423
4	Tulsa, OK	55,772	Seattle–Tacoma–Bremerton, WA	40,227
5	San Francisco–Oakland–San Jose, CA	45,990	Washington–Baltimore, DC–MD–VA–WV	35,764
6	Oklahoma City, OK	45,382	Detroit–Ann Arbor–Flint, MI	32,815
7	Seattle–Tacoma–Bremerton, WA	41,731	Chicago–Gary–Kenosha, IL–IN –WI	31,341
8	Albuquerque, NM	39,992	Tulsa, OK	30,346
9	Flagstaff, AZ–UT	33,255	Dallas–Ft. Worth, TX	27,391
10	Dallas–Ft. Worth, TX	29,629	Oklahoma City, OK	26,544
11	Tucson, AZ	27,178	Sacramento–Yolo, CA	23,443
12	Chicago–Gary–Kenosha, IL–IN–WI	24,364	Portland–Salem, OR–WA	23,127
13	San Diego, CA	24,337	Philadelphia–Wilmington–Atlantic City, PA–NJ–DE–MD	22,922

▶

◄ **TABLE 8.3**

Rank	Metropolitan area	American Indians and Alaska Natives alone	Metropolitan area	American Indians and Alaska Natives in combination with another race
14	Denver–Boulder–Greeley, CO	22,900	San Diego, CA	21,840
15	Washington–Baltimore, DC–MD–VA–WV	22,621	Phoenix–Mesa, AZ	20,780
16	Portland–Salem, OR–WA	22,119	Boston–Worcester–Lawrence, MA–NH–ME–CT	19,867
17	Minneapolis–St. Paul, MN–WI	21,590	Denver–Boulder–Greeley, CO	19,523
18	Houston–Galveston–Brazoria, TX	20,671	Houston–Galveston–Brazoria, TX	18,960
19	Detroit–Ann Arbor–Flint, MI	19,611	Atlanta, GA	16,486
20	Sacramento–Yolo, CA	19,077	Minneapolis–St. Paul, MN–WI	16,396
21	Anchorage, AK	18,941	Honolulu, HI	13,743
22	Fresno, CA	16,002	Cleveland–Akron, OH	12,662
23	Las Vegas, NV–AZ	15,264	Kansas City, MO–KS	12,206
24	Philadelphia–Wilmington–Atlantic City, PA–NJ–DE–MD	13,384	Las Vegas, NV–AZ	11,645
25	Boston–Worcester–Lawrence, MA–NH–ME–CT	12,862	Tampa–St. Petersburg–Clearwater, FL	11,067

Source: US Census Bureau, 2000 Decennial Census, Summary File 2.

TABLE 8.4
Educational attainments of American Indians and Alaska Natives, alone
or in combination with another race, by place of residence

	Metropolitan area		Non-metropolitan area	
	Alone	In combination with another race	Alone	In combination with another race
8th grade or less	10.5	6.7	12.0	8.4
9th grade to 12th grade; no diploma	17.0	13.0	19.5	15.9
High school graduate (includes equivalency)	27.3	24.9	32.1	32.0
Some college; no degree	24.8	28.3	21.9	25.4
Associate degree	6.9	7.7	6.1	6.7
Bachelor's degree	8.9	12.1	5.7	7.3
Post-graduate degree	4.7	7.3	2.6	4.3
Total	100.0	100.0	100.0	100.0

Source: US Census Bureau, 2000 Decennial Census, Summary File 2.

Alaska Natives with a high school education is smaller than it is in non-metropolitan areas, but this is because these areas have a significantly larger share of the population with a college education. For example, for persons in metropolitan areas identified as American Indian alone, about 45 percent have attended college or completed a degree, compared to only 36 percent of such persons outside of metropolitan areas. The reason for this difference is almost certainly due to two facts. One is that colleges and universities are more often than not located in large urban areas and the graduates of these institutions often settle in nearby places. More important is that the employment prospects for college-educated persons are better in cities than in rural areas: there are more jobs in cities and the demand for highly skilled and educated workers is higher in urban areas than in rural places.

Although the educational differences between American Indians and Alaska Natives in metropolitan and non-metropolitan areas can be attributed to the qualities of these areas, there is another set of differences in Table 8.4 that deserve comment: these are the disparities manifest between the

FIGURE 8.1 Median household incomes of American Indians and Alaska Natives (AIAN), whites, and blacks in metropolitan and non-metropolitan places, 2009 dollars

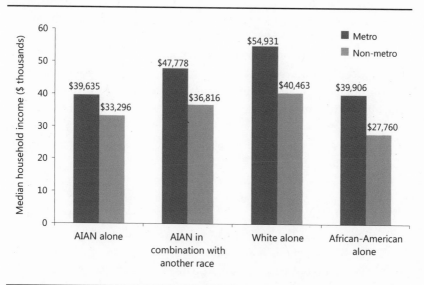

Source: US Census Bureau, 2000 Decennial Census, Summary File 4. Medians interpolated from grouped data.

populations identified as American Indian or Alaska Native alone and those identified as American Indian or Alaska Native in combination with another race. Regardless of location, the latter population is significantly better educated than the former. These gaps are smaller than those for place of residence, but they are still noteworthy. Again, focusing on those persons with college experience throws these differences into sharp relief. As noted above, 45 percent of persons identified as American Indian alone in metropolitan areas have attended college, but 55 percent of American Indians or Alaska Natives who also identify with another race have attended college. A similar, though smaller gap exists in non-metropolitan areas as well.

The last data in this series (Figure 8.1) further articulate the gaps in economic well-being in urban and rural areas. Figure 8.1 shows the median household incomes for several types of households in metropolitan and non-metropolitan areas – namely, American Indian and Alaska Native alone; American Indian and Alaska Native identified with another race; whites; and blacks. There are two broad conclusions that can be drawn from this figure. One is that, regardless of race, persons living in metropolitan areas enjoy significantly higher household incomes than do persons living outside of urban areas. The economies of metropolitan areas offer a diverse mix of job opportunities and, especially, jobs for highly educated and well-paid workers in professional, technical, and managerial positions.

The race-specific median incomes reflect the economic advantages enjoyed by white households, who have the highest median household incomes regardless of place. In metropolitan areas, white households have a median income of nearly $55,000. The next highest median household income is found among American Indians and Alaska Natives who also identify with another race – $47,778. This group is followed by African-American households, with a median income of $39,906. Households consisting of persons identifying only as American Indian or Alaska Natives show a median income of $39,635.

While the data for metropolitan areas are unsurprising, the data for non-metropolitan areas yield several unexpected findings. One is that there is a pronounced race-specific income gap between metropolitan and non-metropolitan areas. The largest gap exists within the African-American population: metropolitan households enjoy median incomes 44 percent higher than those of their non-metropolitan counterparts. For whites and for mixed-race American Indians and Alaska Natives, the median household incomes are 36 and 30 percent, respectively, higher in metropolitan areas than in non-metropolitan areas. The gap is smallest for households identified only as American Indian or Alaska Native insofar as their median household income in metropolitan areas is only 18 percent higher than in non-metropolitan areas. However, this is consistent with past research showing that American Indian workers in urban areas enjoy only small economic benefits compared to those working outside of urban areas, owing to the human capital deficits of American Indian workers relative to other workers in urban labour markets (Snipp and Sandefur 1988).

While households identified only as American Indian or Alaska Native in urban areas may not benefit in urban labour markets as much as other households, especially whites, the relatively small gap also reflects a relative advantage enjoyed by American Indians and Alaska Native (alone) households in non-metropolitan areas. For example, median household income for American Indians and Alaska Natives (alone) in metropolitan places is about 28 percent lower than it is for white households in similar areas. In non-metropolitan areas, this gap shrinks to 17 percent. More surprising is that American Indian and Alaska Native (alone) households in non-metropolitan areas have median household incomes that are decidedly higher than those of their African American counterparts, about 20 percent higher. This is surprising for two reasons. One is that American Indian and Alaska Native (alone) households and African-American households in metropolitan areas have nearly identical median household incomes. Even more surprising is that, nearly twenty years earlier, they were similar in non-metropolitan areas as well (Snipp 1989). No doubt, this reflects the success that some reservations have enjoyed with respect to developing their local economies, especially through gaming and tourism, over the past decades.

Concluding Remarks

Although the urbanization of American Indians and Alaska Natives has often been treated as a post-Second World War phenomenon, the history of Native settlement in permanent towns and villages predates the arrival of Europeans in the Western Hemisphere. This erroneous view partially reflects a lack of knowledge about the history and complexity of Native America, particularly among scholars and social scientists who should know better. It also reflects a common urge among many scholars to present an image of Native Americans as a group of innocent primitives swallowed up by the juggernaut of the urban United States.

While this view is not entirely accurate, neither is it entirely wrong with respect to the twentieth century: most problematic is that it fails to take a longer view of history and neglects to take into consideration the diversity of Native people, which has existed since time immemorial. For instance, in some parts of the continent, the Natives of the Western Hemisphere foraged for their subsistence in small nomadic band societies, while, in other areas, Native peoples lived in well-organized permanent settlements. Of course, the largest and most complex pre-Columbian cities developed in places south of what is now known as the Rio Grande River. North of the Rio Grande, the urban settlements were not as vast as were those to the south; however, they were still substantial and commonplace in what is now the southwestern United States as well as in the Mississippi River Valley.

The arrival of Europeans, of course, brought profound changes to Native America and to the places where Native Americans lived. Disease and warfare led to the outright destruction of many of these places. The Puritan settlers who arrived to establish Plymouth colony, for example, believed that divine providence left behind the remnants of a town, including food that helped them survive the first year in their new home. In reality, this was a former Massachusetts community abandoned in the wake of a smallpox epidemic (Thornton 1987).

The de-urbanization of Native people was also helped along in less dramatic ways. Forced removal in the early nineteenth century caused many tribal towns to be abandoned and reoccupied or dismantled by ever-growing numbers of white settlers. In the aftermath of removal, many tribes re-established their communities in the Indian Territory. Over time, white settlers came to outnumber Natives, and, by the end of the nineteenth century, Indian communities were small in relative numbers and marginalized in the places where they were established.

As the nation industrialized in the late nineteenth and early twentieth centuries, great cities grew rapidly across the Midwest and the East. With a few exceptions, the West, where most American Indians were now concentrated, remained a rural backwater mainly valuable as a source of raw material for industrial production in the East. This did not begin to change until the conclusion of the Second World War brought rapid growth to many places in the West. American Indians and Alaska Natives, like other Americans, were swept up in this tide of urbanization. The war and postwar federal policies precipitated a massive shift in the American Indian and Alaska Native population away from their reservation communities and into large cities such as Los Angeles, Phoenix, and Minneapolis, to name just a few. Today, more American Indians and Alaska Natives live in cities than in the places that were reserved for them in the nineteenth century.

The selective migration associated with urbanization, the opportunities presented by urban labour markets, and contact with diverse populations of non-Indians has produced an urban American Indian and Alaska Native population that differs substantially from its counterparts living outside of cities. In material terms, urban American Indians and Alaska Natives are better educated and enjoy a higher standard of living than do those who live outside of cities. However, contact with non-Indians has also produced a substantial number of persons who identify with multiple racial heritages. These individuals are particularly well-off compared to other American Indians and Alaska Natives, regardless of where they live, underscoring the fact that the population of persons who call themselves American Indians or Alaska Natives is breathtaking in its diversity and complexity.

In the years ahead, it remains to be seen whether the contemporary urbanization of American Indians and Alaska Natives will continue at the same pace as it has in the recent past. The impact on tribal culture and Native customs – a topic outside the scope of this chapter – also remains to be seen. Nonetheless, the impact is likely to be palpable and deserving of careful consideration in the future, both by scholars and by Native people in rural and urban communities alike.

Notes

1 Of course this is not intended to suggest that all American Indians lived in permanent settlements. Many tribes were hunter-gatherers and never lived in anything remotely approaching an urban settlement. The point of this statement is that settlements established by and for American Indians largely languished and were eclipsed by Anglo-Americans during the American industrialization in the late nineteenth and early twentieth centuries.
2 These cities included Chicago, Cleveland, Dallas, Denver, Los Angeles, Oakland, San Francisco, San Jose, Seattle, Tulsa, and Oklahoma City (Sorkin 1978).
3 The exact number of persons identified as American Indian or Alaska Native alone is 2,475,956. Another 1,643,345 persons identified as American Indian or Alaska Native in combination with another race. The total number of persons identified as American Indian or Alaska Native alone or in combination with another race is 4,119,301.
4 It is important to note that, in this context, multiracial American Indians are persons for whom more than one race is reported. There may be, in fact, within the single-race American Indian and Alaska Native population a sizable number of persons whose true ancestry includes more than one race. Still, for statistical reporting purposes, these individuals identified only with a single racial designation, indicating only American Indian or Alaska Native with no other race reported.

References

Bernstein, A.R. 1991. *American Indians and World War II.* Norman: University of Oklahoma Press.

Driver, H.E. 1969. *Indians of North America.* 2nd rev. ed. Chicago: University of Chicago Press.

Eschbach, K., K. Supple, and C.M. Snipp. 1998. Changes in racial identification and changes in the educational attainment of American Indians, 1970-1990. *Demography* 35: 35-43.

Fixico, D.L. 1988. *Termination and relocation: Federal Indian policy, 1945-1960.* Albuquerque: University of New Mexico Press.

Foreman, G. 1972 [1932]. *Indian removal.* Norman: University of Oklahoma Press.

Guimond, E. 2003. The demographic explosion of Aboriginal populations: Looking at the contribution of ethnic drifters. In *Aboriginal conditions: Research as a foundation for public policy,* ed. J. White, P. Maxim, and D. Beavon, 91-107. Vancouver: UBC Press.

LaGrand, J.B. 2002. *Indian metropolis: Native Americans in Chicago, 1945-75.* Urbana: University of Illinois Press.

McLoughlin, W.G. 1993. *After the trail of tears: The Cherokee's struggle for sovereignty, 1839-1880.* Chapel Hill: University of North Carolina Press.

Pauketat, T.R. 2009. *Cahokia: Ancient America's great city on the Mississippi.* New York: Penguin.

Snipp, C.M. 1989. *American Indians: The first of this land.* New York: Russell Sage Foundation.

–. 1996. The size and distribution of the American Indian: Fertility, mortality, residence, and migration. In *Changing numbers, changing needs: American Indian demography and public health,* ed. G.D. Sandefur, R.R. Rindfuss, and B. Cohen, 17-52. Washington, DC: National Academy Press.

Snipp, C.M., and G.D. Sandefur. 1988. Earnings of American Indians and Alaska Natives: The effects of residence and migration. *Social Forces* 66: 994-1008.

Sorkin, A.L. 1978. *The urban American Indian.* Lexington, MA: Lexington.

Thornton, R. 1987. American Indian holocaust and survival: A population history since 1492. Norman: University of Oklahoma Press.

Yaukey, D.A., D.L. Anderton, and J.H. Lundequist. 2007. *Demography: The study of human population.* Long Grove, IL: Waveland.

9

"Being Indian in the City"

Generational Differences in the Negotiation of Native Identity among Urban-Based American Indians

NANCY LUCERO

This chapter examines a number of interrelated elements that, together, result in urban Native identities being both complex and, at times, contradictory. The work in this chapter is based on a qualitative study that examined how cultural identity may be evolving over generations in an urban area with a long-established American Indian community as well as how urban living may be affecting this identity (Lucero 2009).

Contrary to the common belief that the lingering remnants of American Indian tribes remain on reservations well removed from the mainstream of American life, a large percentage of American Indians have, in fact, become part of the contemporary urban United States. The majority of American Indian people now live in cities and not on tribal lands; the 2000 US Census estimated that 64 percent of all American Indians reside in urban areas (United States Census Bureau 2004), and this figure is not expected to diminish. This study was conducted in Denver, Colorado, where 42,423 American Indians reside within the Denver-Boulder-Greeley metropolitan area. This figure includes both individuals who identified on the 2000 US Census form as "American Indian or Alaska Native alone" and those who identified as "American Indian or Alaska Native in combination with another race" (see Snipp, this volume). In addition, in a 2007 community needs assessment conducted by the Denver Indian Family Resource Center, it was found that the city is home to individuals who indicate affiliation with more than 250 different federally recognized tribes and Alaska Native villages as well as individuals from Canadian First Nations groups and Indigenous peoples from Mexico and Central America (Denver Indian Family Resource Center 2007). However, Lakotas/Dakotas and Navajos are the tribal groups whose members form the largest percentage of the Native population living in Denver.

Andersen (this volume) identifies twelve contextual elements that shape aspects of contemporary urban Aboriginal communities. The majority of these elements can be seen as in some way shaping the identities of study participants and their relationship to the Denver Indian community. For example, the Denver Indian community is experiencing a growth in its professional and middle-class segments, and members may include an "Indian professional" identity as a component of their Native identity; several participants identified themselves as a part of this group.

Meanwhile, a large majority of the community continues to suffer from severe poverty and economic marginalization, including some study participants. Participants often referred to the social exclusion, as well as the type of economic marginalization of Native people pointed out by Andersen (this volume) as "invisibility." In addition to the diversity in tribal affiliation discussed previously, community members can be found occupying places on a wide continuum of level of assimilation or acculturation and strength of Native identity. Furthermore, the legal diversity Andersen identifies is exemplified by a growing number of the Denver Indian community who consider themselves to be Indian but, for a variety of reasons, are not tribal members in a legal sense. Some of these individuals no longer meet eligibility requirements for tribal enrolment (e.g., younger members of tribal families whose blood quantum has fallen below the minimum established by the tribe for membership). There are also individuals and entire families who consider themselves to be culturally Indian but may not be able to identify the specific tribe from which their heritage descends, often because of the past adoption of older family members by white families. Differences in legal status may position community members in opposition to one another around the question "who is really Indian" and may create cases in which those who lack tribal membership, but feel strong cultural identity and affiliation, struggle to understand how individuals who have legal status yet little, if any, Native identity should still be recognized as Indian.

American Indians have a relatively long history of residing and working in Denver. The city's centralized location in relation to a number of reservations to the north, south, east, and west has allowed relatively easy travel between tribal communities and the city, and the presence of railroad, agricultural, construction, and other types of employment has been a strong draw. However, two primary waves of American Indian movement into Denver appear to have formed the foundation of the city's Native community. Snipp (this volume) notes factors that contributed to the movement of American Indian veterans of the Second World War into urban areas, and, consistent with his discussion, the first major wave of Indian urbanization in Denver consisted of Indian veterans who began settling in the city shortly after the war.

The second wave consisted of relocatees from the Bureau of Indian Affairs (BIA) Voluntary Relocation Program (known as "Relocation"), who began arriving in the early 1950s. The Relocation Program began officially in 1952 and resulted in thousands of American Indians leaving their reservations for employment and training in targeted US cities, which, besides Denver, included Chicago, Los Angeles, St. Louis, San Francisco, Oakland, San Jose, Dallas, Cincinnati, Cleveland, Tulsa, and Oklahoma City. Whereas numerous sources agree that the contemporary movement of American Indians from their reservations and tribal communities into small towns as well as major metropolitan areas began well before the official start of the Relocation Program (LaGrand 2002; Officer 1971; Tyler 1973; Weibel-Orlando 1999), the program is commonly agreed to have been the major force behind the existence of many of the urban Indian communities seen today across the United States.

American Indian cultural identity is commonly considered to have been negatively affected by urban living: "Urbanization has seemingly brought about some decreased emphasis on Native American tribal identity" (Thornton 1997, 39). Frequently, a pan-Indian identity is pejoratively ascribed to American Indians living in tribally diverse urban settings. "Pan-Indianism" is variously thought of as identification with a wider intertribal collective of Native people or as a generalized and "detribalized" Indian identity that melds beliefs, values, and practices from various tribal groups, while lacking identification with any specific tribe (Nakao 2002). A common belief running through Indian Country and the mainstream United States is that American Indians who reside in urban areas are "less Indian" than are those individuals residing on reservations and that living in an urban area implies that an individual has lost a great deal of his or her cultural identification. Urban Indians are often conceptualized by others as being conflicted about their ethnic identity or as having little remaining "authentic identity"

– and that identity is frequently questioned, even to the point of asking whether an American Indian living in an urban area can still be considered "Indian" (Peroff and Wildcat 2002).

The dominant discourses on Relocation and urbanization tend to implicate these processes as attempts by the dominant culture to break down tribal cultures and to assimilate American Indians into the mainstream. The contention between forces of assimilation and resistance to them (through a strong adherence to cultural values and practices that were contested in the Relocation era) continues in the lives of urban Indians; however, the power of the assimilation process may be lessening. Snipp (1992, 359) saw attention shifting away from "the anticipated dissolution of Indian culture toward explanations for the apparent persistence and vitality of cultural traditions in urban environments." Several contemporary authors have also begun to conceptualize urbanization as a dynamic process in the evolution and development of distinctively urban Indian communities and identities that blend tribal practices and values with their own evolving traditions, cultural practices, and histories (Fixico 2000; Lobo 1998; Thrush 2007; Weibel-Orlando 1999). In addition, multi-generational views of American Indian identity contribute important perspectives to the American Indian cultural identity literature, beginning with Schulz's (1998) study of generational differences in cultural identity among tribally based Navajo women. Jackson's (2002) work is especially notable in this area as it was one of the first studies to emphasize the important role of generationally based experiences in the formation of urban Indian identity.

The lived experiences related by participants in the current study embody many of the points made by the scholars reviewed above. The use of a phenomenological rather than an ethnographic design for the current study is intended to reveal the types of cognitive and emotional schemas constructed by urban-based American Indians as individuals who are attempting to make meaning of Native identity in relationship to their social location. The analysis of participant narratives sheds light on how deeply complex, nuanced, dynamic, and evolving urban American Indian identities are when examined at the cognitive and psychological levels and in relation to the psychosocial functioning of the individual. This perspective both supports existing Native identity work conducted in other social science disciplines, such as anthropology and sociology, and presents additional observations and insights that have their basis in psychology and social work.

Methodology and Findings

The qualitative study upon which this chapter is based (Lucero 2009) was designed to examine changes over generations in the cultural identity of American Indians whose families had lived continuously in an urban area for three to four generations. It did this by exploring the following two questions: "How do urban American Indians construct and maintain their cultural identities?" and "What differences related to cultural identity can be found between generations of American Indians whose families have maintained long-term residence in an urban area?" Eighteen individuals, who were members of families from five different tribes and who resided permanently in Denver, Colorado, participated in the study.

The study sought to draw its sample from a group of American Indians with long-term and stable urban residence. Data from previous studies of the Relocation Program, presented in Neils (1971), appeared to indicate that the population of American Indians in Denver prior to 1952 was negligible and that the program was responsible for the presence of American Indians in the city and the establishment of the Denver Indian community. Consequently, I, as the author of the study, originally planned for participants to come from families with a member who had participated in the Relocation Program and in which subsequent generations had remained in the Denver area. However, in the course of recruiting relocation families, I learned from several Lakota Sioux informants that American Indians from a number of tribes had been living in the city in sizeable numbers since the 1930s. These informants had lived in the city since the early to mid-1940s and also had family members who had moved to Denver during the Depression in order to find work. The informants recalled that there had been several waves of American Indian migration to the city prior to the arrival of the first relocatees. One such group was made up of Indian veterans of the Second World War, who began settling in the city around 1945. A second group was composed of Lakota and Dakota families who came to the city from their reservations in North and South Dakota and Nebraska due to the devastation wrought by severe blizzards in 1948 and 1949, and who had chosen to remain. The informants also remembered a sizeable community of Navajo living in Denver prior to the 1950s. However, the informants did not know why these families were in Denver because they recalled that, in those years, Indian people in Denver did not regularly interact with individuals from tribes different from their own.

These additional perspectives on American Indian urbanization in Denver resulted in my widening the parameters of the study sample to include families who had a member come to live permanently in Denver during the twenty-year period from the late 1940s through the late 1960s, regardless of their impetus for moving to the city. I then refocused the current study onto the experiences of cultural identity development and maintenance in the wider group of American Indian families who have experienced living in an urban area over the course of three to four generations rather than on just those who relocated to the city through participation in the Relocation Program. The final sample was comprised of five families, representing five different tribes.

It is worth noting that, among families in this sample, urban situatedness was expressed as quite intentional. Unlike Madison, a young man whose narrative is presented in Morgan's chapter (this volume) and whose life had been "punctuated by frequent movements between Redfern and 'up home,'" study participants, beginning with those in the second generation, saw themselves as having been firmly positioned, often, in their words, "by choice," in the urban environment for most, if not all, of their lives. There was little desire expressed by any participant, regardless of generational group, to return to live permanently on the family's reservation or to live a lifestyle punctuated by the frequent back-and-forth movement between the city and tribal community that other authors in this volume have identified as a component of the urban Indigenous experience.

Data were collected through in-depth interviews with at least one member of each generation in each family, using narrative inquiry strategies suggested by Singer (2004) and conversational interview guidelines from Kvale (1996). Philosophically, the stance of the phenomenological researcher is that the structures of experience of a phenomenon emerge from the biographical, contextual, and personal data contained in a narrative interview (Giorgi 1975). Thus, the interviewing approach that was utilized was intended to support and encourage participants to develop detailed descriptions of their experiences and to reflect upon and interpret these experiences in relation to their cultural identity.

Narratives were analyzed using Giorgi's steps for achieving the phenomenological reduction of psychological and experiential sociological data (von Eckartsberg 1986). Giorgi (2003, 213) urges a move towards conceptualizing the outcome of the phenomenological reduction as revealing of presences or key constituents (Giorgi and Giorgi 2003, 255) of the structure of a psychological phenomenon (i.e., cultural identity) rather than as producing a set of invariant structures or essential constituents. In doing this, Giorgi seeks to address the charge that phenomenological inquiry is reductionist or essentialist and to demonstrate that, instead, phenomenology leads to a fuller and more encompassing examination of a phenomenon. He emphasizes that, when using phenomenological methodology, one should be "seeking the psychological essence or structure of the phenomenon and not the universal essence or the essence as such" (Giorgi 2003, 250). He emphasizes that, in regard to psychological phenomena, uncovering the nature of the experience and the functions it serves in the life of the individual, rather than simply identifying a set of essential components, is of primary importance in phenomenological studies. He contends that, from this perspective, "respect for the complexity of the experience and the refinement of psychological understanding are two consequences of the phenomenological analysis" (Giorgi and Giorgi 2003, 255).

Analyses of participant narratives yielded highly detailed and multifaceted data about the experience of being an urban-based American Indian. Reducing the data through Giorgi's descriptive phenomenological methodology resulted in multiple layers of findings, each growing more complex and detailed the deeper I delved into them. What emerged from the process of phenomenological reduction was an in-depth understanding of the complexity inherent in each participant's identity and her/his experiences as an urban-based American Indian. Also, there emerged a description of the range and variety of ways that urban Indians think about and engage with their Indianness, both spatially and relationally, while living in a context that is often considered foreign, alienating, and marginalizing for Native peoples.

Study participants who originally left their reservations or tribal communities and moved to Denver to settle permanently at a point between 1948 and 1968 are referred to as "Generation 1 participants." Generation 1 participants represent (a) the parents of Generation 2 participants, (b) the grandparents of Generation 3 participants, and (c) the great-grandparents of Generation 4 participants. References to participants as being from Generations 2, 3, or 4 thus relate to their position within their own families rather than to their position within a larger societal cohort. As a collective group, all study participants who represent a discrete generation in a particular family are referred to as a generational group. Together, the members of a specific generational group are also referred to as "Generation 1s, 2s, 3s, or 4s."

Intergenerational Comparisons of Cultural Identity

Although many similarities were found between Generations 1 and 2 with regard to cultural identity, growing differences between Generations 2, 3, and 4 were identified. These same differences were even more pronounced when comparing Generation 1 to Generations 3 and 4, indicating a growing divergence of experience and changes in the conceptualization of Indian identity across the span of two to three generations of urban residence. The ways that these differences manifest themselves in several areas are illustrated in the following subsections.

Thinking, Feeling, and Identifying as "Indian"

When asked about his identity, one Generation 2 participant simply stated, "Being Native is who I am." This expression would appropriately characterize the cultural identity stance of members of his generational group as well as those of Generation 1. In contrast, Generations 3 and 4 participants were more likely to say that they "felt good" or "felt proud" of being Indian and that having an Indian identity was something that made them unique or set them apart from non-Indians. Members of all four generational groups expressed the belief that one's Indian experiences and connections with family and other Indian people were the core elements of an Indian identity.

Generation 1 participants were likely to consider that Indian identity was automatically conferred through one's relationships to ancestors and family members and through connections to the historical experiences of one's tribe. In this sense, identity did not have to be developed or maintained in any particular way. This generational group generally believed that a person did, however, come to understand the meaning of his or her identity as he or she matured – a sentiment that was echoed by most participants in Generation 2.

Generation 2 participants tended to see their Indianness as "just who we are and have always been." Family provided a foundation for Indian identity, which then became an internalized core state of being and, as such, did not really need to be maintained. Most did not feel that they had to work hard at being Indian, but they had considered deeply what it meant to be Indian in relation to their living in an urban area.

Although Generation 3s and 4s understood Indian identity to be an internal state, they felt they also had to put a conscious effort into developing and maintaining their American Indian identity, unlike the generations before them. Many Generation 3s and 4s were also engaged in a conscious process of embracing culture and making it a part of their lives. They often relied on "doing Indian things" to affirm their identity, whereas members of prior generations simply "were Indian" without the emphasis on cultural activities.

Participants from Generations 3 and 4 relied to a greater extent on external affirmations of their Indianness and reported spending less time reflecting on being Indian or what it meant than participants in Generation 2, who were engaged in internal processes that continually sought understanding of their identity and thereby reaffirmed it. Like participants in Generation 2, Generation 3s and 4s believed that family provided a foundation for Indian identity, that learning about one's culture helped identity develop, and that identity developed and matured over the course of an individual's lifetime.

All participants in Generation 1 identified themselves as American Indian, or simply as "Indian," and, specifically, as being from their respective tribes. They expressed feelings of general relatedness to other Indians, regardless of tribe, and this did not diminish their tribal-specific identity or lead them towards a pan-Indian type of identity. Among participants in Generation 1, maintaining a tribal-specific identity while living in an urban area was not dependent upon being around other members of their tribes. Instead, identity represented a firmly ingrained sense of who the individual was – a sense that had remained strong despite, as was the case for two Generation 1 participants, their being the only members of their tribe (other than their own children) to have lived in Denver since they arrived more than forty years ago.

Beginning with participants in Generation 2 and continuing with those of Generations 3 and 4, the way an individual identified his or her Indian identity began to stem from a feeling that one had either (a) a collective or shared Indian identity through which one considered him- or herself to belong to the greater group of American Indian peoples, or (b) a tribal-specific identity as a member of a distinct tribe with a unique history and tribal culture. Various participants then went on to describe having only a tribal-specific identity, only a collective Indian identity, or to hold a combination of the two but with one aspect's being predominant. Adjoining the collective or tribal-specific identity, an individual might also have an "urban-Indian identity" or one of a number of Indian subcultural identities such as "powwow" or "Indian professional." (The role of powwow in urban Native identity formation, expression, and strengthening is discussed in depth in Johnson, this volume.)

Although individuals in Generations 3 and 4 appeared to be more likely to state that they believed an urban-specific Indian identity was emerging and embraced it as one of the various Indian identity choices they felt were available to them, members of Generations 1 and 2 used the term "urban Indian" more as a way of situating themselves than as an expression of their cultural identity.

Participants in Generations 3 and 4 were unique among the generational groups in that, when it came to their ethnic identity, they saw themselves as having choices that prior generations did not consider themselves to have. Generations 3 and 4 participants were all of mixed ancestry and, when initially asked how they described themselves as an Indian person, were likely to mention being biracial. They often believed that their mixed bloodedness gave them a range of cultural identity choices that they could negotiate simultaneously alongside their Native identity. Unlike participants in Generation 2, who appeared to see identifying as American Indian to be their only option, those in Generations 3 and 4 appeared to (a) view biracialness as natural, (b) see identifying as a biracial Indian as an option, (c) have *chosen* to identify as American Indian instead of with their other racial/ ethnic group, and (d) be relatively comfortable managing multiple ethnic identities.

Biculturality and Assimilation

Prior to relocating to Denver, experiences in boarding schools, on jobs in reservation border towns, in the military, and through interactions with non-Indians living on or near their reservations or tribal communities socialized Generation 1 participants to the expectations of the urban setting. Most Generation 1 participants arrived in Denver already having achieved a high degree of biculturality, and they did not consider themselves unprepared for living outside their reservation or tribal community. Participants in this generational group considered being able to adapt to city ways and being flexible in their interactions with the dominant culture to be necessary in order to live successfully in an urban area. Members of this older generational group internalized the message that being able to function in both Indian culture and the dominant culture was something they must strive for.

Generation 1s passed on to their children – Generation 2 participants – the importance of biculturality. Generation 2s, like their parents, grew up having to negotiate both mainstream culture and Indian culture, although Generation 2s began this in the urban context rather than in the tribal setting of their parents. Living as an Indian person in an urban area required

Generation 2s to master the social norms of both cultures and to understand the different behavioural expectations of each, something Generation 1s may have achieved outside the urban context. Generation 2s considered being bicultural a necessary skill that had to be developed, and they often discussed its achievement in terms of having found a "balance" between Indian and mainstream worlds.

In contrast, biculturality came across as ingrained or integrated, rather than as having been developed, in most Generations 3 and 4 participants. These participants appeared, for the most part, to have automatically internalized much of the balance between Indian and mainstream culture that the prior generational group had striven for, and being bicultural often seemed to be taken for granted by these Generation 3s and 4s. Other Generation 3s and 4s, though, could be characterized as struggling much more than prior generations but in an opposite way as they were attempting to achieve a balance by bringing in more elements of Indian culture to offset a predominance of dominant culture socialization. Although many individuals in Generations 3 and 4 still indicated that living in an urban area required that one successfully negotiate both cultures and that knowing how to act in both cultures continued to be a necessary skill for urban Indians, they appeared most concerned with learning how to act in Indian culture.

Resisting assimilation was important to all generational groups, despite their biculturality, and was expressed by Generation 1s and 2s through highly developed psychological processes. For Generation 1s, these processes arose prior to the individual's arrival in the city and were not aimed directly at maintaining one's cultural identity while living in an urban area. Generation 1 participants had all attended boarding schools and lived through a historical era during which assimilation into the dominant culture was an active government policy. The manifestations of this policy had personally touched each one, and, as a group, they tended to see that all Indians had been affected by assimilation, regardless of where they lived, just by being part of modern society. Despite this, and in seeming contradiction to the importance they associated with resisting assimilation, Generation 1s did not seem to worry much about being assimilated themselves, and they tended to see their children as having resisted assimilation to the greatest degree possible, given that they grew up in an urban area.

Generation 2s felt what one participant termed "the pull of assimilation" as a constant in their lives. Members of this generational group, similar to Generation 1s, also felt that most Indians were assimilated to some degree. Whereas most Generation 2s considered themselves less assimilated than many other Indians in the city, some even considered themselves less assimilated than those they knew who lived on reservations. Many Generation 2s expressed the attitude "I'm not assimilated, but a lot of other Indians are." These individuals believed that it was possible to combat the assimilative pull by engaging in psychological and political resistance and by retaining traditional ways.

Generation 2s also articulated the idea that it is not possible to be like those in the dominant culture and still be Indian; to them, an urban Indian person had to do some of the things whites do but, psychologically, had to fight becoming like them. In contrast, many participants in Generations 3 and 4 felt that embracing aspects of the dominant culture and engaging with that culture did not automatically lead to assimilation if one maintained an attitude of resistance, remembered he or she was Indian, and practised cultural ways. An attitude expressed within these latter two generational groups could be characterized as: "I can be outwardly like members of the dominant culture in many of the things I do, but that doesn't mean I'm assimilated or think like them." The psychological resistance that those in Generation 2 had to develop appeared to have been passed down to Generations 3 and 4, where it had been internalized and reconciled with the need to interact within the dominant culture.

Effects of Urban Environments on Indian Identity

Generation 1s came to the city with a firmly established Indian identity that was neither threatened nor diminished by living in an urban area. Many stated plainly, "Moving to Denver did not affect my identity." They felt that *their* Indian identity was not tied to a physical location but that the Indian identity of their children and grandchildren was. Many Generation 1s believed that their children and grandchildren, because of their urban status, *might* have to do things Generation 1s did not have to do in order to develop and maintain an Indian identity. Generation 2s did not share the concern of their parents that their own Indian identity might somehow be compromised by growing up in an urban area. However, like their parents, they, too, were concerned that their children and grandchildren might not develop a strong Indian identity. Consequently, they often took steps to assist their children and grandchildren to do so.

As a result, participants from Generations 1 and 2 felt they had a stable core Indian identity that allowed them to transition smoothly between Indian and non-Indian settings. These participants saw themselves as engaged in balancing the demands of the dominant culture with the more traditional value systems they felt they lived by, and they believed they could do so successfully in the urban environment with relatively little effort. Overall, members of these two generational groups felt that the urban setting had little, if any, negative effect on their identities.

Two primary identity tasks for many of the Generations 3 and 4 participants were seeking cultural knowledge and learning tribal traditions. Members of these generational groups were often attempting to re-embrace traditional values and practices or felt they must eventually do this as part of claiming an Indian identity. For these individuals, the urban environment was considered to be a barrier to accomplishing these two tasks and to have a much greater effect on identity than Generation 1s and 2s thought that it had. Members of these younger generational groups believed city living presented challenges to developing an American Indian identity that they felt neither their reservation-based peers nor their parents and grandparents had faced. This led most to believe strongly that it was easier and more natural to have an Indian identity if one lived on the reservation.

Differences between Urban and Reservation Indians

Generation 2s saw themselves, from a cultural identity perspective, as not much different from their reservation-based peers, whereas participants in Generation 1 might be likely to say they were like them due to having similar early experiences and a common background. Generations 3s and 4s were more likely to think there was a difference between themselves and their reservation-based peers and to lack perspective on what it felt like to be an Indian person living on a reservation or in a tribal community.

Participants from both Generations 1 and 2 were nearly identical in the differences and similarities they saw between reservation and urban settings, including with regard to the people who resided in each. In these two groups, opinions about the differences between the urban and reservation/ tribal community contexts were based on actual lived experiences, although the opinions of Generation 2 participants may have been formed from less extensive observation and obtained primarily while visiting during childhood and adolescence. Although both of these earlier two generational groups regarded their urban-based Indian peers as not that different from their counterparts on the reservation, in an obvious contradiction, some participants in both groups looked at Indians who did not relocate to the city as being less motivated and more content with government dependency than those, such as their family members, who had left the reservation for a new life in the city. Both groups also considered urban-based Indians to have a better work ethic, to be harder working, and to be more adaptable than Indians living on their reservations.

In contrast, Generations 3 and 4 participants tended to see bigger differences between themselves and their reservation-based peers, as mentioned earlier, although their opinions in this area were likely to have been based on few actual encounters with their reservation counterparts. Generation 3s and 4s were likely to opine that urban-based Indians thought and acted differently than their reservation-based peers, whereas participants in Generation 2 believed urban Indians had to make a conscious decision to think and act differently than their reservation-based peers in order to live successfully in the urban setting.

Participants in Generation 2 seemed very aware of differences between urban and reservation contexts, and they were able to provide detailed explanations of these differences as well as the differences between Indian and non-Indian ways. Generation 3s and 4s appeared less aware of differences between the urban and reservation contexts, but, like their parents, grandparents, and great-grandparents, they were quite adept at distinguishing and verbalizing very nuanced differences between Indian and non-Indian ways of thinking and acting.

Finally, although participants in Generation 1 made distinct references to experiences of racism and discrimination while living on their reservations or in their tribal communities, they made little mention of these kinds of experiences happening to them in Denver. When asked specifically about this, one Generation 1 participant responded:

> White people in Denver didn't have the same racist attitudes and beliefs about Indians as they did in South Dakota. During the time of Relocation, the White people in Denver were just beginning to learn about and deal with Indians. They weren't already used to treating Indians bad the way a lot of people in South Dakota were.

Generation 2s expressed being very aware of discrimination based on non-Indians' beliefs and stereotypes about reservation-based Indians, and some expressed concern that these stereotypes would be improperly applied to them. Interestingly, however, participants in both Generations 1 and 2 expressed beliefs about reservation-based Indians (e.g., that they lacked ambition, took advantage of government handouts, or were lazy and had a poor work ethic) that were similar to stereotypes many Indians might typically consider some non-Indians to hold about them.

Generation 3s and 4s reported having experienced discrimination due more to their misidentification as a member of another ethnic minority group than because they were American Indian. They, too, expressed some of the same negative beliefs about reservation-based Indians as did the two prior generational groups.

Vignettes

The following short vignettes, which illustrate several study participants' understanding of their Native identity, begin to demonstrate the complexity and range of the identities of contemporary urban-based American Indians whose families have lived in a large metropolitan area for multiple generations. They provide insight into the emotional and psychological efforts these individuals have undertaken to develop and maintain their Native identity while living in a context that frequently marginalizes and may even negate it. Additionally, these efforts encompass attempts to resist not only assimilation into the dominant culture but also the pressures that may seek to absorb Native people into a multicultural urban mixture in which distinctive ethnic and cultural boundaries become blurred.

Angela, a member of the third generation of her family to live in the city, believes that the urban environment offers American Indian people choices regarding which cultural identities to embrace. She considers Indian identity in the city to be different than Indian identity on the reservation because, to her, being Indian in a collective, rather than tribal-specific, sense is what defines Indianness in an urban setting. Recently, however, Angela has chosen to develop her tribal-specific identity in addition to continuing to identify with Indians generally, but she sees her cultural identity as more complex than simply having a tribal-specific and a generalized Indian identity. In addition to these, she describes herself as an "urban convenience Indian" and sees her enjoyment of the resources of the city as part of an urban-specific Indian identity.

As a second-generation urban Native, Marie's Indian identity is based in large part on seeing herself as similar to members of her large extended family who continue to live on the reservation. Her Native identity is not connected to being physically located on her reservation, nor is it affected by living in an urban area. "I can be Lakota anywhere – even on the moon," she says. The foundation of her cultural identity, she believes, was established as a young child through interactions with her Indian extended family members both on and off the reservation. Her identity then became firmly internalized over time through exposure to elements of her culture, such as language and the environment. On a day-to-day basis, Marie resists involvement in mainstream culture because it is inconsistent with the Lakota values she lives by and, therefore, also inconsistent with her identity as a Lakota woman. This being the case, Marie also realizes that, as an urban Indian, she must be flexible and adaptable in order to survive in the urban environment. She has constructed an Indian identity that allows her to adapt to the urban environment by knowing how to act in the mainstream culture without losing her Indian values, her sensitivity to cultural norms and modes of behaviour, and the ways she expresses her Indianness. In order to do this, she has had to analyze and become acutely aware of the differences between Indian culture and its values and the dominant culture and its values. She sees this process as having been instrumental in strengthening her cultural identity.

Since childhood, William, another second-generation individual, has identified as a member of his tribe, even though he is of mixed American Indian and European heritage. When asked by others about his ethnicity, he will identify both sides of his heritage and then give his specific tribal affiliation. William's desire to identify as a member of his small tribe has been growing since he was a child, but he identifies political factors, such as the tribe's loss of federal recognition and absorption into another tribe, as making it difficult for him to maintain a strong tribal-specific Indian identity. As a result, William also maintains a collective Indian identity, which he feels is stronger at this point in his life than his tribal-specific identity. Identifying with and seeking out connections with other Indian people is an important part of his cultural identity, and social involvement with other Indians, working in Indian-focused jobs, volunteering in the Indian community, and researching his tribe are all elements that contribute to strengthening William's Indian identity.

Cheryl experiences her American Indian identity as problematic because she considers cultural identity to be tied, in large part, to physical appearance. A member of the third generation of her family to live in the city, Cheryl has experienced others having difficulty in identifying her as Indian because of her light skin and phenotypically white appearance. These characteristics also cause her to feel that she does not fit in around other Indians. Not looking Indian has held Cheryl back from developing an Indian identity that includes elements of social connectedness to other Indian people;

instead, she sees her cultural identity simply as an internal state of being that is grounded in her spirituality and family history.

The decision to embrace his Indian identity, rather than some other identity that may have been available to him in the urban environment, was a conscious choice Jason made in his twenties after realizing that he was proud to be Native. Jason, from the second generation in his family, believes that he is "growing up" into his Indian identity as he passes through the years of his adult life, and he considers this to be the way that identity develops for Indian people. He also feels that Indian identity is based, in part, upon each individual's experiences of being American Indian, and he recognizes that Indian people may express their Indian identities in many different ways. Deep questioning and self-reflection have led him to believe that having an Indian identity while living in an urban area is not solely about maintaining one's traditions and connections to one's heritage but, rather, is about maintaining a balance between engaging with Indian culture and engaging with modern society.

Discussion

Findings from this study point to urban American Indian identity as an internalized state or core component of the self that, in generational groups 2, 3, and 4, has been affected in a number of ways by the urban context. One impact of living in an urban area, revealed in participant narratives, was a growing divergence in experiences related to being Indian between those individuals comprising Generation 1, who had grown up in a tribal community or on a reservation, and their children, grandchildren, and great-grandchildren, most of whom had lived exclusively in the city. These changing experiences seemed to play a part in the shift in how participants conceptualized, situated, and then negotiated their cultural identity. One example of this is the change in identity stance whereby Generation 1 participants considered that American Indian was the only identity possible for them, but Generation 3 and 4 participants had come to believe that they had choices of ethnic or cultural identities and that they could successfully negotiate multiple identities.

It was striking to note the amount of time, and mental and emotional energy, that participants from all generational groups had devoted to reflecting on their cultural identity and what it meant to be American Indian. These endeavours had occupied a prominent place in the lives of most participants for many years. The majority had begun the quest to understand their identity during their teenage years, and this had continued into their young and middle adult years as an important developmental task. It was evident that individuals comprising Generation 2, as well as those from Generations 3 and 4, had worked diligently to construct a cultural identity that made sense to them, had determined the values and behaviours that would support that identity, and were engaged in continual efforts to maintain or refine that identity.

Similar to those of several of the young men that Morgan interviewed (this volume), a number of study participants' Native identities began to take shape appreciably in the late teen years and throughout young and middle adulthood. However, participants did not indicate that they had gone through a period in their lives when they had been indifferent about being Native. This contrasts with the sense of diffidence in regard to Aboriginal identity that several of the young men in Morgan's study had experienced for a good part of their younger lives. Yet, participants in both the current study and Morgan's were similar in that a significant life event occurring in their late teens or early twenties had often led to a firming up or strengthening of Native or Aboriginal identity.

Generation 2 participants may be best thought of as members of a transitional generation in relation to urban-based American Indian cultural identity. Most Generation 2 participants were born in the city. Consequently, unlike their parents, who came to the city with established cultural identities, Generation 2s were firmly situated within the urban setting. Their continuing ties to their families' tribal communities and extended family living there necessitated not only that they develop an Indian identity appropriate to the urban context but also that they develop one that would allow them to smoothly transition between the reservation and the city. They were challenged, however, to determine how this could be done because they had few, if any, prior examples.

The outcome of the identity development process of Generation 2 participants, as seen in the their narratives, was that this generational group appeared to have achieved the most highly developed, complex, and adaptable American Indian identities of any of the four generational groups that were examined in this study. Further research on urban American Indian cultural identity may determine that the cultural identities of members of this generational group, and the ways in which they constructed their cultural identities, are distinct from those of the generational groups both before and after them.

Urban American Indian Cultural Identity Discourses

There is no argument that powerful identity discourses and societal messages about who American Indians are (or should be) have had an impact upon members of this group for hundreds of years. The lived experiences of study participants revealed the influence of many of these identity discourses, both those coming from the wider American society and those generated from within the American Indian world.

Most notable of the discourses that appeared to affect the cultural identity of study participants, beginning with those from Generation 2, is one that stresses that living in an urban area inherently affects cultural identity in a negative way. This discourse includes messages such as (a) an American Indian is somehow less Indian if he or she lives in an urban area than if he or she lives on a reservation or in a tribal community; (b) one is at risk of quickly losing one's Indian identity by being in the city; and (c) it is difficult to acquire an Indian identity if one is an urban Indian. Consequently, if an urban Indian does develop a cultural identity, this identity may not be genuine or may simply have been "made up" out of unconsciously internalized elements of what non-Indians think Indians should be.

In the study, the author recognized another identity discourse that was having an impact upon participants from Generations 2, 3, and 4. This discourse rose to prominence during the late 1960s and spoke to the need to re-traditionalize, retribalize, and revive Indian cultures. It contains a powerful message that participants heard as saying that, in order to truly be American Indian, one must embrace traditional cultural values, practices, and spirituality; profess pride in one's Indian heritage; and demonstrate one's Indianness through vigorous involvement in culture-focused activities.

The message to retraditionalize, retribalize, and revive Indian cultures may have been one impetus for the development of urban Native institutions in Denver similar to those discussed by Andersen (this volume) and which he identifies as playing a critical role in the production of urban Native identity. Although not discussed specifically in this chapter, study participants from all generational groups identified their connections to these types of institutions, beginning with the formation of the original Denver Indian Center in the early 1970s, as providing the social connections with other Indian people that are a critical component of Native identity.

Study participants from Generation 2 were teenagers and young adults at the time that this discourse arose and while it grew more powerful. Their narratives spoke to the impact that the messages contained within the discourse had upon their cultural identity development. These narratives also spoke to the confusion each participant had to resolve when the messages of this discourse about what one must do to be Indian conflicted with those messages of the discourse that spoke to the difficulty of having an Indian identity as an urban-based Native person. Thus, cultural identity development for many Generation 2 participants was a much more daunting task than it had been for their parents. Despite the enormity of this task, most Generation 2 participants felt that they had met and resolved its challenges successfully, and they considered themselves to have achieved a strong and positive American Indian cultural identity.

Participants from Generations 3 and 4 currently find themselves tasked with developing their cultural identity under conditions within the urban environment that are much different than were those encountered by prior generational groups. The twenty-five to thirty years that have passed since Generation 2s were young adults have been witness to exponential changes in American society. Predominant among these is a lifestyle that is much faster paced, more complex, and more diverse than that of the 1960s and 1970s. A number of current social and economic factors make it challenging for Generation 3 and 4 individuals to find and sustain relationships with other Indian people. Job and financial responsibilities now require many to work long hours, and often at more than one job, further limiting community and social involvement. Moreover, American Indians have come to be dispersed across the wide geographical space of the metropolitan Denver area as well as to be absorbed within its large population through intermarriage with non-Indians and increasing mixed bloodedness.

Social changes and their challenges have also filtered down to urban Indian communities in such a way that young adult participants in Generations 3 and 4 now find themselves part of an Indian community that is more socially, economically, and educationally diverse than it was thirty years ago. Many times, also, the relational ties through family, kin, clan, or tribe that once created closeness and affiliation in this urban Indian community have been disrupted through social, emotional, and geographical distance. These changes are reflected in the lived experiences of Generation 3 and 4 participants and speak to the accuracy of one of the intracultural messages that this generational group has heard – that it is harder to find and connect with other Indians in the city and that an urban Indian must work hard to find a place where he or she fits in as an Indian person. This challenge remains an important factor in whether or not Generation 3 and 4 participants, and others like them, are able to develop an American Indian identity that serves to support and empower them.

Growing up during the civil rights era, experiencing the Red Power movement first-hand, and having access to individuals who had recently lived on the reservation may have made it somewhat easier for Generation 2 participants than for those from the two next generations to engage with the cultural revitalization movement. However, Generation 3 and 4 participants have still firmly internalized the message that they are responsible for being engaged with cultural values and traditional practices and spirituality and that they, too, must not only play their part in keeping Indian culture alive and vital but also pass it on to future generations. Although many of the Generation 3 and 4 participants told the interviewer that it is difficult for them to find the activities and events through which they might do this, they appeared to be compensating for this difficulty by expecting themselves to develop cultural knowledge by other means, such as through reading, higher education, and developing political consciousness.

Conclusion

The contemporary movement of American Indians from reservations and tribal communities to urban areas began in the early decades of the twentieth century and gained increasing momentum from the 1950s onward. At present, the majority of American Indians live in urban areas, and the existence in many cities of sizeable and well-established communities of American Indians is readily acknowledged. Accordingly, the presence of large numbers of American Indians in urban areas calls for increased examination of how this Native diaspora is affecting the cultural identity of urban-based American Indians.

Significant gaps continue to exist in our understanding of how urban living shapes American Indians' cultural identities and how culture is transmitted intergenerationally outside the tribal community. This chapter (and the earlier qualitative study upon which it is based) represents a first step towards increasing this understanding by exploring the lived experiences of individuals whose families have resided in a large US city for forty to fifty years and who were negotiating an American Indian identity from an urban standpoint. Their narratives identified generational differences in the conceptualization of Native identity as well as how this identity has been affected by long-term urban residence. These narratives also provided a brief look at how members of a group of urban-based American Indians living in a large US metropolitan area have, over generations of urban living, come to develop, maintain, and understand their cultural identities. Although its qualitative methodology prevents broad generalization to similar groups, findings reveal a number of areas that are worthy of future inquiry not only with other urban-based American Indians groups but also with Indigenous peoples in other countries who are experiencing an urbanization process.

References

Denver Indian Family Resource Center. 2007. Denver Indian Family Resource Centre circles of care: Keeping the circle whole – adult community survey data results. Appendix B. Lakewood, CO: Denver Indian Family Resource Centre.

Fixico, D.L. 2000. *The urban Indian experience in America.* Albuquerque: University of New Mexico Press.

Giorgi, A. 1975. Convergence and divergence of qualitative and quantitative methods in psychology. In *Duquesne studies in phenomenological psychology,* vol. 2, ed. A. Giorgi, C.T. Fischer, and E.L. Murray, 72-79. Pittsburgh: Duquesne University Press.

–. 2003. A phenomenological psychological approach to research on hallucinations. In *Imagination and its pathologies,* ed. J. Phillips and J. Morley, 209-24. Cambridge: MIT Press.

Giorgi, A.P., and B.M. Giorgi. 2003. The descriptive phenomenological psychological method. In *Qualitative research in psychology: Expanding perspectives in methodology and design,* ed. P.M. Carmic, J.E. Rhodes, and L. Yardley, 243-73. Washington, DC: American Psychological Association.

Jackson, D.D. 2002. *Our elders lived it: American Indian identity in the city.* DeKalb, IL: Northern Illinois University Press.

Kvale, S. 1996. *InterViews: An introduction to qualitative research interviewing.* Thousand Oaks, CA: Sage.

LaGrand, J.B. 2002. *Indian metropolis: Native Americans in Chicago, 1945-1975.* Urbana: University of Illinois Press.

Lobo, S. 1998. Is urban a person or a place? Characteristics of urban Indian Country. *American Indian Culture and Research Journal* 22(4): 89-102.

Lucero, N.M. 2009. "Creating an Indian space in the city": Development, maintenance, and evolution of cultural identity and cultural connectedness among multiple generations of urban American Indians. PhD diss., University of Denver.

Nakao, A. 2002. *Census 2000: Who we are. SFGate.com,* 13 February. http://articles.sfgate.com/.

Neils, E.M. 1971. *Reservation to city: Indian migration and federal relocation.* Chicago: University of Chicago, Department of Geography.

Officer, J.E. 1971. The American Indian and federal policy. In *The American Indian in urban society*, ed. J.O. Wadell and O.M. Watson, 9-65. Boston: Little, Brown.

Peroff, N.C., and D.R. Wildcat. 2002. Who is American Indian? *Social Science Journal* 39: 349-61.

Schulz, A.J. 1998. Navajo women and the politics of identity. *Social Problems* 45(3): 336-55.

Singer, J.A. 2004. Narrative identity and meaning making across the adult lifespan: An introduction. *Journal of Personality* 72 (3): 437-60.

Snipp, C.M. 1992. Sociological perspectives on American Indians. *Annual Review of Sociology* 18: 351-71.

Thornton, R. 1997. Tribal membership requirements and the demography of "old" and "new" Native Americans. *Population Research and Policy Review* 16: 33-42.

Thrush, T. 2007. *Native Seattle: Histories from the crossing-over place.* Seattle, WA: University of Washington Press.

Tyler, S.L. 1973. *A history of Indian policy.* Washington, DC: United States Department of the Interior, Bureau of Indian Affairs, US Census.

United States Census Bureau. 2004. *Census 2000 special tabulation: American Indian and Alaska Native population by place of residence: 2000.* http://www.census.gov/.

von Eckartsberg, R. 1986. *Life-world experience: Existential-phenomenological research approaches in psychology.* Washington, DC: Centre for Advanced Research in Phenomenology and University Press of America.

Weibel-Orlando, J. 1999. *Indian country LA: Maintaining ethnic community in complex society.* Urbana: University of Illinois Press.

10

Dancing into Place

The Role of the Powwow within
Urban Indigenous Communities

JAY T. JOHNSON

> *Every weekend of the year Indian people gather in one place
> or another to share their dances and songs, renew friendships,
> and reaffirm their shared experiences as members of a tribe,
> organization, family, or community. Whether in large metro-
> politan arenas, university gymnasiums, small community
> buildings, or isolated rural dance grounds, the powwow has
> become a way for Indian people to remember their past,
> celebrate the present, and prepare for the future.* (Ellis,
> Lassiter, and Dunham 2005, vii)

The powwow movement has become a central expression of Indigenous
identities in North America, particularly over the past several decades. The
dances that began on the Great Plains over a century ago have now co-
alesced into a movement of people across the continent to participate and
compete, to celebrate and remember. Despite its birth on the Plains, powwows are now celebrated in every corner of the continent and beyond.
Dozens of powwows are held from Nova Scotia to southern California every
weekend of the year. Many of these celebrations are rural and continue to
centre around reservation/reserve communities, but as Native American
and First Nations peoples have moved into urban centres, the powwow has
moved with them.

This chapter sets out a discussion of the role of the powwow in urban Native American and First Nations communities in North America, particularly with regard to how the powwow is creating Indigenous places within a setting that has been described as alienating to Native peoples. This chapter has grown out of a personal interest and participation in the powwow movement. As an urban Native American who has lived in various parts of North America and beyond, I have found that the powwow is one way for me to express my identity and to create meaning in places far from my tribal homelands.

As Native Americans and First Nations have moved from rural reservation/reserve settings to urban centres, tribally specific expressions of identity have, to some extent, been transformed into pan-tribal identities (Wilson and Peters 2005, 407). Some of this pan-tribalism is necessitated by the diversity of Native urban communities, while its genesis is likely founded upon authentic cultural commonalities. As Lucero (this volume) notes, pan-tribalism can play an important role in promoting unity among urban Indigenous communities and the persistence of urban Indigenous identities. My central question here is: As a pan-tribal movement, what role does the powwow play in creating Native places within urban environments and to what extent does it assist urban Natives to maintain their Nativeness?

As a graduate student living in Honolulu, Hawai'i, I became familiar with and participated in the various powwows held throughout the islands every year. The Honolulu Intertribal, which started in 1974, and other Hawai'i powwows serve as an excellent example of utilizing this pan-tribal phenomenon – the powwow – to create Native North American places within urban settings far from tribal lands. They created for me, and for many of the other participants, temporary Native American places that served to revive our connections not only with each other but also with homelands far removed.

Urbanization

The rural/urban dichotomy is a false expression of Indian reality, yet it has been one of the molds that has continued to shape research and writing. (Lobo and Peters 1998, 3)

Before examining the powwow movement, I want to spend a moment discussing the urbanization of Indigenous peoples, particularly in North America. This dichotomy between urban and reserve is, as Wilson and Peters (2005) describe, a creation of the settler-state and is employed to delineate between the spaces of European civilization and the spaces reserved and set apart for the "primitive, backward, and often savage" First Nations (398). With the creation of reserve spaces, the state confined the Native within clearly established boundaries – boundaries that not only delineated "civilized" and "primitive" but that also served to empty all the lands in between for "settlement, materially and conceptually" (399; see also Harris 2002). Another side effect of this delineation of space between the settler-state and First Nations is the creation of urban spaces as exclusively settler spaces. This dichotomy between the civilized urban centres of the settler-state and the primitive reserve spaces of First Nations identifies urban areas as places where Indigenous identity is out of place (see Wilson and Peters 2005).

Despite this discourse establishing the urban centres of North America as the fledgling home for European civilization in the "New World," Native peoples have been establishing themselves in these same urban centres since the beginning of the colonial era. While the laws of the settler-states have attempted to curtail such settlement, and did for some decades slow or control the movement of Native peoples into the cities, the cities of North America today all have Native populations of some size. Some cities, particularly those close to sizable reserve/reservation populations as well as those identified by the United States as Urban Relocation Centres in the 1950s, have sizable Native populations. What is perhaps unique about Native urban populations is that individual and familial connections with reserves/reservations are rarely lost completely (see Lobo 1998). Renya Ramirez (2007) refers to this maintenance of connection with tribal communities as transnationalism, meaning the ability to simultaneously live within the urban environment of the settler-state while preserving a tribal identity. One method for maintaining connections with reserve/reservation communities is through periodic migration between urban centres and the generally rural reserve areas. Movement between reserve and urban centre can occur on seasonal, annual, or less frequent cycles (Wilson and Peters 2005). These migrations aid in maintaining tribally specific identities and community affiliation. One may suspect that, over generations, this transnational identity might fade or disappear entirely, but current research among urban Natives demonstrates a strong ongoing connection with tribal/Native identity. Lucero's research (this volume) demonstrates that third- and fourth-generation urban Natives feel that they have greater choices in how they express their Nativeness than did their parents and grandparents.

It is important to note, as does Matthew Snipp (this volume), that some of the First Nations of the Americas developed large urban centres prior to

European contact. These ancient urban centres rivalled European cities of the same era in size. The Indigenous peoples of the Americas were dispossessed of these urban centres through the process of colonization, which brought with it virgin soil epidemics and forced relocations. The urbanization of First Nations people over the last several decades is, in some ways, merely a reclaiming of our rightful place within urban centres. Unfortunately, though, these are not urban centres of our own creation; rather, they are places produced through the colonial projects of the settler-state inheritors of our lands.

The modern movement of Native peoples from the rural locations reserved by colonial administrations for their containment to urban centres has been, until recently, a slow and highly controlled process. Despite the variation in the timing of the movement of Native peoples from reservation/ reserve to urban centres found between the United States and Canada, currently, both countries have relatively high urbanization rates among their Indigenous populations. In Canada's 2006 census, the urbanization rate for First Nations, Métis, and Inuit was roughly 50 percent, a 10 percent increase over the 1991 census figures (Peters 1998, 665; Statistics Canada 2008). In the United States, the rate is even higher, with 61 percent of Native-identified individuals living outside of reservations, most in highly urbanized areas, according to the 2000 Census (Ogunwole 2002). Urbanization has been occurring among Native Americans over a greater period of time than it has among First Nations, mainly because US law did not prohibit the movement of Natives from reservations to urban areas, as did Canadian law (through a pass system designed to control movement off reserves in western Canada) (Barron 1988). Despite this rapid urbanization, though, it is important to note that Native peoples in Canada and the United States still have the lowest urbanization rates of any ethnic group in their respective countries. In addition, their rates are significantly lower than are the figures for New Zealand, where 84 percent of Māori live in urban centres (Statistics New Zealand/Tatauranga Aotearoa 2006), and in Australia, where 76 percent of Aborigines live in non-remote areas (Australian Bureau of Statistics 2009).

The issue of identity has become a major concern and focus for research in the face of the rapid urbanization of First Nations peoples over the past few decades. With recent arguments concerning Indigenous identity flowing quite prolifically from anthropology journals over the past decade, the academic audience has been instructed by Kuper (2003) that an Indigenous identity is one that only truly exists *outside of* the modern, urban context (Wilson and Peters 2005, 398).[1] It is one that *must* remain temporally fixed in an ahistorical past and geographically fixed within non-urban locations, those created through treaty negotiation or dispossession by the settler-state. Indigenous identities are portrayed as weak identities that must be "preserved" against the corrupting influences of modernization. They are identities defined by their remoteness from all things civilized and modern.

While I recognize that Indigenous activists, in some parts of the world and at some moments in time, have employed essentialist tactics to protect the survival of their communities against colonial and neocolonial projects, I agree with Dean and Levi (2003, 3) when they assert "that those who would force a choice between authenticity and political participation traffic in stereotypes and perpetuate a false dichotomy." As Greenop and Memmott (this volume) observe, the process of colonial encounter has rendered the nature of the relationship between colonizer and colonized ineluctably intercultural. What I think is more interesting than the debates concerning whether or not the "Indigenous" continues to exist in our modern world (because I think it obvious that it does), is why people choose to hold on to these identities. Perhaps it is as Peters, Maaka, and Laliberte (2009, 3) state, that we need to shift "the focus from a debate about the sources of Aboriginal identities to a discussion of how Aboriginal people draw on their cultural heritage and their experience of colonialism to make sense of their place in contemporary society." What motivates them and, for the purposes of this chapter, how do they go about creating Indigenous places within urban environments in order to perpetuate Indigenous identities?

Powwow: A Brief History

> The dance circle draws us in. The powwow has now spread coast to coast, and while some see it as a pan-Indian fabrication, I now see that it serves as a vital catalyst for cultural renewal ... No matter how we dance, how we dress, or how we live, for a few moments of the song we stand together as a people, united by tradition and connected in the certain belief that dance is essential to the expression of ourselves. (Hill 1996, 8)

The history of the powwow is intimately intertwined with the history of Native North America over the past century. The English word "powwow" has come to mean everything from a medicine man/woman or spiritual leader to a gathering or meeting of almost any type. The word "powwow" is derived from the Massachusetts (*powwow*) and Narragansett (*powwaw*) languages and originally referred to a Native priest or leader of medicine ceremonies (Gibbs 1841, 30). Early European colonists, interested in the medicinal knowledge of tribes in the northeastern United States, used the term to describe any ceremony or dance believed to impart healing. Today, though, the modern powwow, while still ceremonial at its core, has evolved into a significant social, cultural, and economic movement in Native North American communities, whether rural or urban. As Clyde Ellis observes, "Whether as social, cultural, psychological, economic, or political statements, powwows have become one of the most powerful expressions of identity in the contemporary Indian world" (Ellis, Lassiter, and Dunham 2005, 11). This quest for a powerful expression of identity has grown in recent years beyond the Native North American community to include considerable powwow gatherings by non-Native peoples in North America (see Aldred 2005) and in various parts of Europe as well (Watchman 2005). While the interest shown by non-Native peoples in participating in the powwow is a fascinating subject, in this chapter I focus on the powwow as a Native North American expression of identity, primarily within urban centres.

The modern powwow can be defined as a dance or series of dances, in different styles, organized around a designated and consecrated dance arena. Some of these dance styles are derived from Warrior Society or related women's dances, which are perhaps several hundred years old (or more). Some of the dance styles that are now a part of the powwow movement, though, have developed over the past one hundred years. Besides open, or intertribal, dances, there are also dance competitions within particular dance styles and age ranges. Some adult dancers travel around the powwow circuit, particularly during the summer months, competing at times for significant cash prizes.

There are various accounts of the birth of the intertribal powwow movement. As Tara Browner (2002) notes in *Heartbeat of the People: Music and Dance of the Northern Pow-Wow*, some groups are asserting claims that go back as far as two hundred years, as in the case of the Omaha tribe, with regard to hosting the oldest continuous intertribal powwow. Certainly, some of the dances that are now intertribal in nature originated with the Omaha tribe; but, as Browner asserts, it is not accurate to say that these early nineteenth-century gatherings were intertribal in nature. In the mid- to later parts of the nineteenth century, as the Canadian and US settler governments began increasingly to interfere in the ceremonial life of Native tribes, the Warrior Dance societies of the Great Plains, along with many other tribal dances, were banned (Ellis 2005, 12). These dances were described as the vestiges of an uncivilized life. The banning of these societies largely grew out of the settler society's fear, perhaps not entirely unfounded, that some of these dances were held as precursors to new attacks on European settlements (Herle 1994). Particularly, some of the millennial dances that developed during this period, such as the Ghost Dance,[2] were based on ceremonies that were geared towards the elimination of settler society (see Carroll 2007). In order to circumvent the bans on these dances and ceremonies, tribes began to take the gatherings beyond the gaze of government Indian agents.

With the birth of the Wild West shows in the 1880s, a clear and easy avenue for the revitalization and sharing of these Warrior Society dances presented itself (Ellis 2005, 13). These shows visited all of the major cities of North America and eventually also toured much of Europe. The sharing of dances was not only through the performances for European and settler audiences but also with other Native performers in the shows who came from a wide variety of tribes. The sharing, or gifting, of dances between Native performers began the transfiguration of tribally specific dances into their intertribal forms. Slowly over the latter half of the nineteenth century and into the beginning of the twentieth, Warrior Society dances began to evolve into the dance styles we know today. The Grass Dance developed from the Omaha tribe's Warrior Dance. The men's southern straight dance evolved from the Osage tribes' Ilonshka. Some women's dance styles connect back to dances performed by women on the northern and southern Plains during men's Warrior Society dances. Some are entirely new dances either meant to provide more energetic dance styles for women or, like the Jingle Dress, are the product of newer spiritual ceremonies.

As the powwow movement began to evolve away from the Wild West shows and into tribal and intertribal events, its events were organized primarily on reservations and reserves away from settler audiences. This is particularly true in Canada, where the ban on powwows and potlatches lasted longer than it did in the United States. Some historians credit the relocation of tribes from throughout the Northeast, Southeast, and Plains regions of the United States to Indian Territory (now known as Oklahoma) as another important catalyst in the development of the intertribal powwow (see Howard 1955).

Despite the need by some tribes to continue to hold their dances in secret, some tribal powwows were intentionally performed in full sight of non-Native audiences in order to demonstrate their willingness to participate in settler-state society by performing dances that were geared, in some respect, towards entertainment (see Warren 2009). These dances also portrayed the Native dancers and communities as strongly patriotic by incorporating American flags into the beaded designs on dancers' regalia and by holding powwows on national holidays, such as the fourth of July. As Browner and another western historian, Benjamin Rader (2004), assert, the first large intertribal and off-reservation powwow organized by Native peoples was the homecoming powwow held in 1926 at Haskell Institute, which, at the same time, was evolving from a government-run boarding school for primary and secondary education into a government-run school focused on postsecondary and vocational education. Today Haskell Indian Nations University is an accredited four-year institution that still hosts intertribal powwows for the urban Native community of Lawrence, Kansas, which makes up approximately 4 percent of the city's total population.

The powwow movement continues to include both rural and reservation settings as well as an ever-growing number of urban events. With over 60 percent of Native Americans and over 50 percent of Canadian First Nations living in urban areas, and with these numbers continuing to grow, the powwow movement will become increasingly focused in urban centres. As Wilson and Peters (2005) observe, though, urban areas are still perceived as places where Indigenous peoples are conceived as "out of place." The central question I am hoping to answer is: What role does the powwow play in aiding Native urban populations in creating "Native place"?

Place Making, Native Identity, and Powwow

> Indian people from all walks of life, from all kinds of communities, with all kinds of interests, see the powwow as a source of renewal, joy, strength, and pride. For them the powwow has become a singularly important cultural icon in their lives. (Ellis and Lassiter 2005, vii)

For the Native peoples of North America, a sense of place is crucial to the development and interpretation of their individual and social characters as well as their identity (see Basso 1996; Thornton 2008). Within Native homelands, this sense of place is created through the experience and, particularly, the knowledge of storied place names. These storied landscapes contain the critical information required for perpetuating and educating individuals into the social network of the community (Johnson 2012). As individuals and families leave the reservation/reserve for urban centres, the role of the storied landscape in perpetuating tribal identity is diminished, if not lost entirely. Some, though, maintain strong contacts with their homelands even while making their home in a city. For them, the lessons of distant named places continue to "stalk" them, reminding them that living in balance requires "constant care and attention" (Basso 1996, 60). However, many who have moved to the cities have little knowledge of the storied landscapes of their homeland and turn to other avenues to understand what it might mean to embrace a Native identity.

It is evident that the social, linguistic, economic, and ritual structures of Indigenous peoples throughout the Americas, Eurasia, Africa, and Oceania are vital conduits for place making (Thornton 2008). Even for immigrant and diasporic peoples far from their homelands, these same structures, particularly ritual structures, continue to aid in making individual and communal sense of the new places in their landscape. The same is true for First Nations who have moved to cities. The cultural structures they take with them aid in the perpetuation of their cultural identity. The performance of tribally specific rituals serves as one method of maintaining tribally specific cultural identity.

As a few authors have noted in their work on Native urban identity production, the preservation or adaptation of tribally specific ceremonies serves as one element that enables urban Natives to maintain distinct identities in places that can be strongly anti-Native (see Lobo 1998). Susan Krause (2001), in writing about the urban Native community in Rochester, New York, notes that this community's collective identity remains strongly connected with and protective of its foundation in the Haudenosaunee, or Iroquois Confederacy. Community dances and ceremonies there do not include the pan-tribal powwow but instead maintain the dances of the local tribal traditions. Wilson and Peters (2005) note, though, that many urban Native people decide to embrace pan-tribal ceremonies as one method of maintaining Native identity within urban environments. The powwow plays a crucial role for some urban Native communities in providing a widely accepted pan-tribal ceremony around which to gather. As Howard (1983, 72) notes, "the principal vehicle for the diffusion of Pan-Indian music, dance, and costumes styles is the intertribal pow-wow."

I think that it is important to note, as do Ellis, Lassiter, and Dunham (2005, ix), that "powwows can reflect 'a powerful synthesis of related traditions' ... [T]hey also simultaneously encourage tribally specific and community-specific senses of identity as well." Specific tribal distinctions exist within the movement. Some powwows incorporate tribal dances, such as the Haudenosaunee Smoke Dance, within the powwow itself. Other powwows incorporate culturally specific dance traditions, such as Stomp Dancing, a dance style from the southeastern United States, through the overnight hours following the end of powwow style dancing (see Jackson 2005). Even within intertribal dance styles, tribally specific regalia, facial painting, and dance technique can identify an individual's tribal background as well as some aspects of her or his personal history. Thus, tribally specific forms of expression are maintained within the pan-tribal powwow movement.

As someone interested in how Indigenous peoples create meaning in places and how they then use these Native places for social and political purposes, and as a powwow dancer myself, I have become interested in how places are created and transformed through the embodied ceremony of the dance. As Browner (2002, 95) describes it:

> The grounds for each powwow, including the arena and its surrounding areas, are laid out according to a preconceived blueprint and create a consecrated performance space for participants. Powwow grounds are blessed by members – usually the elders – of each community, who perform that function by burning tobacco or sage, an act accompanied by prayers and songs. By doing so the grounds are cleared of negative spirits and influences, a business of utmost importance because consecrated spaces are considered neutral grounds where all personal hostilities are to be put aside.

As illustrated in Figure 10.1, though, the spaces created through the powwow, while they may be transparent to most Native participants, are only partially apparent to non-Native participants. The differences between how Native and non-Native participants perceive the spatial arrangement of the powwow grounds is not only a difference in cultural competence but also perhaps demonstrates a significant ontological disconnect, particularly in that Native participants include "spirits" as the outermost ring of the powwow while non-Native participants do not perceive their presence (or even, perhaps, their existence).

The creation of a Native place through participation in the powwow, through the consecration, through embodied dance and drum, and through the gossip and conversation of the audience creates a place for all to come together, both the living and the non-living. Despite the powwow's modern and evolving form, many perceive it as providing an avenue that enables one to connect to an ancestral past. In this way, it not only creates a temporary

FIGURE 10.1   Typical non-Indian perception and meaning of powwow space
(left) and George Martin's (Ojibwe) concept of powwow space (right)

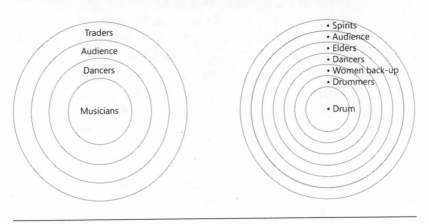

Source: Based on the work of Tara Browner (2002).

Native place but also succeeds in transcending the linear time of the modern, settler-state city. As Ramirez (2007, 65) notes from her research with urban Natives: "Powwows function as more than places to renew one's Native culture, community, and identity. In my interviews with Native Americans, they also explained how powwows could take on spiritual meanings."

By embracing the pan-tribal nature of the powwow, urban Natives are able to become integrated into a movement that not only serves to aid in identity production and/or preservation but also serves to create temporary bounded Native places. By demarking the powwow dance area with ceremonies that create "blessed ground," one makes a distinct purpose and place from what might otherwise be a basketball court within a large urban arena (see Weibel-Orlando 1999). These temporary places of Native identity serve multiple purposes, and, as Young (1981, 68) notes, perhaps one of the most significant purposes the powwow serves is in raising the "quality of life of its participants through improved mental health and social contacts." For urban Natives, the social contacts made and continued through the powwow can play a crucial role in the cultural survival of individuals and communities. Ramirez (2007, 58) envisions urban Native networks, such as those created through urban powwows, as "hubs" through which urban Natives gather together to preserve "culture, community, identity, and belonging within interconnected relationships across space." These contacts also cut across cultural boundaries, communicating what it means to be Aboriginal to a non-Native audience (Buddle 2004, 32).

The powwow is an embodied, intentional form of place making: not the place ballet or taskscapes described by various phenomenologists but, rather, a conscious and empowered act of somatic engagement (cf. Ingold 1993; Seamon 1980). The powwow is a conscious attempt at being in place together, creating togetherness from often disparate segments of Native society. As Axtmann (2001) notes, the creation of these bounded Native places within urban environments, albeit temporary in nature, serves as a powerful form of resistance to oppression. It is not merely the competitive performance of pan-tribal dances in order to gain individual notoriety or wealth, it is also the expression of a troubled present and the remembering of painful histories in acts of embodied survival. The "point" to dance lies, in the words of the geographer Nigel Thrift (1997, 147), in being able to "articulate complexes of thought – with – feeling that words cannot name." These emotional geographies of dance provide a profound means for expressing what it is to be Native.

The urban powwow is by definition a temporary place – a transitory manifestation of Native identity within what can frequently be a Native-unfriendly environment. The powwow's sacred core, surrounded by a semi-sacred space for audience members, exists within this non-Native urban environment, providing a transitory place for connection and belonging (Weibel-Orlando 1999, 145). In conjunction with the other events that bring urban Natives together, the powwow becomes one of many "collecting centers, or hubs, of urban Indian culture, community, identity, and belonging" (Ramirez 2007, 64). These Native hubs within the urban setting alter the landscape in subtle but significant ways that provide places for Native identity to persist and, perhaps, even thrive.

Conclusion

I think that it is obvious from recent publications, both inside and outside of the academy, that the powwow plays a significant role in the construction and maintenance of Native identity throughout North America. It is also apparent that this pan-tribal form plays an even more crucial role within urban Native communities. The creation of Native places within the fabric of the urban landscape provides venues for an embodied performance of Nativeness, whether or not one chooses to participate in the dance itself. It is also apparent that these Native places play an important role in increasing the emotional and social life of urban Natives. What remains unclear is exactly how significant the powwow is for urban Natives in preserving cultural identity.

While anthropologists have begun to explore the role of the powwow in identity production and preservation among urban and rural Native communities, there remains a wide range of topics that could best be addressed through geographical approaches. One of these topics is the way in which the powwow arena is divided off from the surrounding area, particularly in urban settings, and how this production of a "blessed ground" affects the audience and participants. Another important topic from a geographical perspective is the migratory movement of those who follow the powwow trail around the continent and the impacts this movement has on participants' identity, livelihood, and community life. Related to this are the financial and social impacts this movement and large urban powwows have on local communities. While this chapter may not answer as many questions as it poses, I hope that it has succeeded in spurring more interest in understanding the role of the powwow in urban Native communities, particularly on the part of the geographical community.

Notes

1 Kuper's 2003 article, "The Return of the Native," in *Current Anthropology* has initiated a dialogue concerning the relevance and continuing applicability of the definition "Indigenous" for any contemporary group of people globally. Proulx (2006) demonstrates the problems with Kuper's arguments, as do several other cultural and social anthropologists (e.g., Merlan 2009).
2 "In dream-cult dancing people enacted their visions through dancing. The most noted dance of this type was the Ghost dance, the vision of a Paiute prophet named Wovoka, who believed it would revive the old Indian ways, return the buffalo and eliminate the European intruders. The Sioux developed sacred ghost dance costumes which, they believed, would protect them from bullets, a belief tragically destroyed by the massacre at Wounded Knee in 1890" (Herle 1994, 59).

References

Aldred, L. 2005. Dancing with Indians and wolves: New agers tripping through powwows. In *Powwow*, ed. C. Ellis, L.E. Lassiter, and G.H. Dunham, 275-302. Lincoln: University of Nebraska Press.

Australian Bureau of Statistics. 2009. National Aboriginal and Torres Strait Islander social survey. Canberra: Australian Bureau of Statistics.

Axtmann, A. 2001. Performative power in Native America: Powwow dancing. *Dance Research Journal* 33(1): 7-22.

Barron, F.L. 1988. The Indian pass system in the Canadian west, 1882-1935. *Prairie Forum* 13(1): 25-42.

Basso, K.H. 1996. *Wisdom sits in places: Landscape and language among the Western Apache*. Albuquerque: University of New Mexico Press.

Browner, T. 2002. *Heartbeat of the people: Music and dance of the northern powwow*. Urbana: University of Illinois Press.

Buddle, K. 2004. Media, markets and powwows: Matrices of Aboriginal cultural mediation in Canada. *Cultural Dynamics* 16(1): 29-69.

Carroll, K. 2007. Place, performance, and social memory in the 1890s Ghost Dance. PhD diss., University of Arizona.

Dean, B., and J.M. Levi. 2003. *At the risk of being heard: Identity, Indigenous rights, and postcolonial states*. Ann Arbor: University of Michigan Press.

Ellis, C. 2005. "The sound of the drum will revive them and make them happy." In *Powwow*, ed. C. Ellis, L.E. Lassiter, and G.H. Dunham, 3-25. Lincoln: University of Nebraska Press.

Ellis, C., and L.E. Lassiter. 2005. Introduction. In *Powwow*, ed. C. Ellis, L.E. Lassiter, and G.H. Dunham, viii-xv. Lincoln: University of Nebraska Press.

Ellis, C., L.E. Lassiter, and G.H. Dunham, eds. 2005. *Powwow*. Lincoln: University of Nebraska Press.

Gibbs, J.W. 1841. Contributions to English lexicography. *American Journal of Science and Arts* 16(3): 28-31.

Harris, R.C. 2002. *Making native space: Colonialism, resistance, and reserves in British Columbia*. Vancouver: UBC Press.

Herle, A. 1994. Dancing community: Powwow and pan-Indianism in North America. *Cambridge Anthropology* 17(2): 57-83.

Hill, R. 1996. Light in the forest. In *Powwow: Images along the red road*, ed. B. Marra, 8. New York: Abrams.

Howard, J.H. 1955. Pan-Indian culture of Oklahoma. *Scientific Monthly* 81(5): 215-20.

–. 1983. Pan-Indianism in Native American music and dance. *Ethnomusicology* 27(1): 71-82.

Ingold, T. 1993. The temporality of landscape. *World Archaeology* 25: 152-74.

Jackson, J. B. 2005. East meets west. In *Powwow*, ed. C. Ellis, L.E. Lassiter, and G.H. Dunham, 172-97. Lincoln: University of Nebraska Press.

Johnson, J. 2012. Place-based learning and knowing: A critical pedagogy grounded in Indigeneity. *GeoJournal* 77(6): 829-36.

Krause, S.A. 2001. Traditional Iroquois socials: Maintaining identity in the city. *American Indian Quarterly* 25(3): 400-08.

Kuper, A. 2003. The Return of the Native. *Current Anthropology* 44(3): 389-402.

Lobo, S. 1998. Is urban a person or a place? Characteristics of urban Indian country. *American Indian Culture and Research Journal* 22(4): 89-102.

Lobo, S., and K. Peters. 1998. Introduction. American Indians and the urban experience. Special issue. *American Indian Culture and Research Journal* 22(4): 1-15.

Merlan, F. 2009. Indigeneity: Global and local. *Current Anthropology* 50(3): 303-33.

Ogunwole, S.U. 2010. *The American Indian and Alaska Native population: 2000*. United States Census Bureau 2002, http://www.census.gov/.

Peters, E.J. 1998. Subversive spaces: First Nations women and the city. *Environment and Planning D: Society and Space* 16(6): 665-85.

Peters, E.J., R. Maaka, and R. Laliberte. 2008. "I'm sweating with Cree culture not Saulteaux culture and there goes the beginning of Pan Indianism": Urban Aboriginal cultural identities. Paper presented at Aboriginal Demography Project, University of Alberta.

Proulx, C. 2006. Aboriginal identification in North American cities. *Canadian Journal of Native Studies* 26(2): 405-38.

Rader, B.G. 2004. "The greatest drama in Indian Life": Experiments in Native American identity and resistance at the Haskell Institute homecoming of 1926. *Western Historical Quarterly* 35(4): 429-50.

Ramirez, R.K. 2007. *Native hubs: Culture, community, and belonging in Silicon Valley and beyond*. Durham: Duke University Press.

Seamon, D. 1980. Body-subject, time-space routines, and place-ballets. In *The human experience of space and place*, ed. A. Buttimer and D. Seamon, 148-65. New York: St. Martin's.

Statistics Canada. 2008. *Aboriginal Peoples highlight tables, 2006 Census*. http://www12.statcan.ca.

Statistics New Zealand/Tatauranga Aotearoa. 2006. QuickStats about Māori. Wellington: Statistics New Zealand/Tatauranga Aotearoa.

Thornton, T.F. 2008. *Being and place among the Tlingit*. Seattle and Juneau, AK: University of Washington Press/Sealaska Heritage Institute.

Thrift, N. 1997. The still point: Resistance, expressive embodiment and dance. In *Geographies of resistance*, ed. S. Pile and M. Keith, 124-51. London and New York: Routledge.

Warren, S. 2009. "To show the public that we were good Indians": Origins and meanings of the Meskwaki Powwow. *American Indian Culture and Research Journal* 33(4): 1-28.

Watchman, R. 2005. Powwow overseas: The German experience. In *Powwow*, ed. C. Ellis, L.E. Lassiter and G.H. Dunham, 241-57. Lincoln: University of Nebraska Press.

Weibel-Orlando, J. 1999. *Indian country, LA: Maintaining ethnic community in complex society*. Urbana: University of Illinois Press.

Wilson, K., and E.J. Peters. 2005. "You can make a place for it": Remapping urban First Nations spaces of identity. *Environment and Planning D: Society and Space* 23(3): 395-413.

Young, G.A. 1981. Powwow power: Perspectives on historic and contemporary inter-tribalism. PhD diss., Indiana University.

PART 3

Aboriginal Urbanization
in Australia

AS IS OFTEN THE CASE, the use of "Indigenous" to refer to Australia's original owners and residents masks a startling diversity of societies and languages. Beginning near the end of the eighteenth century (1788), these nations were incrementally displaced and dispossessed of their lands and resources. Unlike the Indigenous peoples in Canada, the United States, or New Zealand, however, the Indigenous peoples of what was eventually to become Australia did not benefit from treaties or any other formal negotiated processes that might produce what Jeremy Webber (1995) elsewhere refers to as "inter-societal norms" that presuppose and produce equitable relations between Indigenous and settler societies. Instead, their societies were incrementally displaced in light of an advancing (if nascent) agricultural/industrial society (Taylor and Bell 2004, 14). Altman and Sanders (1995, 206) suggest that direct contact and, with it, disease decreased the precontact population by as much as 75 percent so that, by the beginning of the twentieth century, the Indigenous population was outnumbered by Australia's growing settler population by a ratio of about twenty to one.

Australian colonial administrative attempts to "govern" the lives of Indigenous people in the name of "protection" bear a striking resemblance to philosophies used in early colonial Canada. Altman and Sanders (1995) suggest that, while each of the different Australian states was free to produce its own internal methods of governing, they all engaged in a large-scale attempt to exclude Indigenous people from settler society. As in both Canada and the United States, in Australia "reserves" were set aside for Indigenous occupation and, with other pieces of legislation, Indigenous people became heavily surveilled and regulated in light of the governing rationalities contained in these pieces of legislation (though the gap between paper and practice could be vast). Likewise, Australian Indigenous children suffered a fate similar to that of the children affected by Canada's oft-termed "sixties Scoop" and the residential school era that long preceded it, which enforced the involuntary removal of Aboriginal children from their homes and families and their placement in foster homes and institutions (such as boarding schools and children's homes). In Australia, the victims of this process, which lasted from the beginning of the twentieth century up until the 1970s, came to be known as the "stolen generation."

Taylor and Bell (2004) note that, while settler administrators fully expected Indigenous collectives to disappear, by the 1930s the "protection" era had been displaced by *cultural* assimilation. The latter had become the preferred option through which to precipitate the movement of Indigenous people into settler society and its norms. And, indeed, following the Second World War, Australian Indigenous people began to migrate to the cities. Though the patterns for doing so differed greatly by city – both between large and small cities and by region – such movement was largely positioned by authorities to indicate a wish to assimilate (or at least the inevitability of assimilating) into the body politic and social norms of Australia's booming urban population. As McGregor (2004, 291) puts it, following the Second World War, "Aborigines were expected, or compelled, to adhere to and internalize the social norms and cultural competencies of the national community."

Paralleling the gradual movement of official policy away from assimilation (particularly in its postwar incarnation) towards the beginnings of self-government – or at least self-management – talk from the 1970s onward was of the rise in the number and proportion of urban Indigenous people. Taylor and Bell (2004, 15) note that, while this urbanization process mirrors in some ways the demographic shift undergone by "settler" Australians, it nonetheless retained a distinctiveness, particularly with respect to the circular movement patterns, the disproportionate number of Indigenous people living in smaller cities, and the enormous demographic complications caused by "ethnic mobility." In any event, scholars argue that the growth in urban Aboriginal communities in Australia was borne on the back of a set of complex "push/pull factors": the promise of employment, housing, and social services in urban centres and the depressed socio-economic conditions on "reserves" conspired to produce a large-scale migration from rural to small- and large-city locales.

More specifically, Morgan (2008) traces the racially tinged motivations behind government efforts to increase Indigenous urbanization. In particular, officials attempted to persuade so positioned "enlightened" Indigenous individuals (and their families) to serve as models for other Indigenous families – a practice engaged in by US relocation officials during a roughly similar period: officials "represented Aboriginal people as eager to move from humpy to house, from backwardness to modernity, and doing so without ambivalence" (76). And, while he notes the far more painful realities and the continuation of everyday racisms suffered by these families both from neighbours and from surveilling officials (see Morgan 1999), the movement was often precipitated by a set of complex push-pull factors that varied by region and era.

In one of the first serious treatments of urban Aboriginal communities as a distinctive object of analysis, Gale (1972, 4-5) suggests six major reasons that Indigenous people and their families migrated specifically to the City of Adelaide. She suggests that, most important, kinship and family patterns (referred to as "chain migration") shaped decisions about when and where to live, followed by dependence on church and welfare, medical/health services, large-scale increases on proximately located reserves (and, with it, declining labour opportunities), a larger criminal justice infrastructure, and formal educational opportunities. In addition to this, Morgan (2008) argues that, in the particular context of Sydney, many Indigenous people made the decision to relocate to Redfern in the interest of escaping the raw frontier-style racism they encountered and grew up with in smaller towns (see also Rowse 2000). Gale (1972, 4-5) notes: "Under such circumstances the capital city becomes the inevitable Mecca for prospective migrants. It seems to offer work, housing, schools, medical care, opportunities for a younger generation, and fun and stimulus" (see Smith and Biddle 1975 for a similar discussion of Indigenous people in Brisbane; and see Anderson and Jacobs 1997).

The socio-demographic characteristics from the 1970s onward paint a bleak picture of these growing communities. Smith and Biddle (1975, xi) note that, while urban Indigenous people living in Brisbane were better off than were their rural and small town counterparts, their quality of life was nonetheless far below that of their non-Indigenous neighbours. And, in many cases, those moving to cities were forced to the lower-rung neighbourhoods, often marked by "decaying pre-Federation housing, large terraces which had been neglected by their slum landlords" (Morgan 2006a, 376). However, while historically scholars have painted urban Aboriginal communities in Australia in predictable ways (i.e., offering deficit-based discussions that highlight the cultural difference of Indigenous transplants and the pathologies wrought by dislocation [see Gale 1972; Smith and Biddle 1975]), some (Langton 1981) argue that these (mal)adaptions are as much a reaction to the racism and discrimination experienced as to any pre-existing cultural deficits.

Be that as it may, in the past three decades most Indigenous people in Australia have lived in cities, though they continue to comprise a majority of the populations in many of the smaller and more remote communities. And, as Cowlishaw (2009) notes, while urban Indigenous communities tend, socio-economically, to have more in common with remote communities than with their non-Indigenous urban neighbours, she also notes the vibrancy, resilience, and distinctiveness of these communities, both from other urban Indigenous communities and from those of smaller locales and rural areas. Again, while this is city-specific (both in relation to its size and to its historical relationships with the urban Indigenous community), the distinctiveness of these communities remains as apparent to outsiders as it does to insiders.

That is to say, the values, lifestyles, and practices of these communities' members – particularly with respect to expectations about appropriate (read: sedentary) residential patterns and nuclear family dwellings – differ markedly from those of many of their non-Aboriginal neighbours and, in certain ways, those of their non-urban kin. Indeed, many Indigenous people who moved to the city did not stay, and those who did stay often returned to "home" communities, whether for seasonal work, family commitments, or ceremonial business. Taylor and Bell (2004, 17) refer to this demographically as "circular mobility" – movement patterns that require a complex set of decisions on the part of individuals, families, and communities about how to weigh or balance their various commitments to different (and necessarily competing) locales. Birdsall (1988) addresses similar issues in a more anthropological context. Nonetheless, much of contemporary Aboriginal political activism can be traced to the urban communities and the particular incarnation of anger, resentment, and political consciousness they produced (not least including the Commonwealth Games protest in Brisbane in 1992 and the TJ Hickey protests in Redfern in 2004), and this production is especially interesting in light of the significant residential segregation taking place in Australian cities that mark "white" from "Indigenous" spaces.

The notion that kinship continues to play a prominent role in the shaping of urban communities is well documented in the literature. Likewise, others have discussed the role played by formal organizations in creating (and maintaining) the sinews of attachment through which "community" is experienced (see Pierson 1977; Plater 1995). Yamanouchi (2010) notes, however, a tension between urban Indigenous issues scholars who focus primarily on this "push/pull" factor (e.g., kin ties) and others (Morgan 2006b; Schwab 1988) who suggest a more pan-Aboriginal understanding of these communities. Morgan (2006b, 66) argues, for example, that a new "urban Aboriginal vernacular" sprang up in the post-Second World War era in addition to antecedent, kinship based identities. Indeed, he traces the political difficulties experienced by urban activists who fail to take sufficient account of the differences that continue to exist locally. Morgan (2006a, 382) argues that many urban Aboriginal residents possess "multiple belongingness," a point echoed by Yamanouchi (2010), who suggests that traditional forms of identification are unmoored in urban contexts, producing an ambiguity among its residents about what "counts" as Aboriginal (the two primary modes of affiliation being kinship and organizations).

References

Altman, J.C., and W. Sanders. 1995. From exclusion to dependence: Aborigines and the welfare state in Australia. In *Social welfare for Indigenous populations*, ed. J. Dixon and R.P. Scheurell, 206-29. London: Routledge.

Anderson, K., and J.M. Jacobs. 1997. From urban Aborigines to Aboriginality and the city: One path through the history of Australian cultural geography. *Australian Geographical Studies* [now *Geographical Research*] 35(1): 12-22.

Biddle, N. 2009. *Location and segregation: The distribution of the Indigenous population across Australia's urban centres.* Canberra, AU: Centre for Aboriginal Economic Policy Research, Australian National University.

Birdsall, N. 1988. All one family. In *Being black: Aboriginal cultures in "settled" Australia,* ed. I. Keen, 137-58. Canberra: Aboriginal Studies Press.

Cowlishaw, G. 2009. *The city's outback.* Sydney: UNSW Press.

Gale, F. 1972. *Urban Aborigines.* Canberra: Australian National University Press.

Langton, M. 1981. Urbanizing Aborigines: The social scientists' great deception. *Social Alternatives* 2(2): 16-22.

McGregor, R. 2004. Governance, not genocide: Aboriginal assimilation in the postwar era. In *Genocide and settler society: Frontier violence and stolen Indigenous children in Australian history,* ed. D. Moses, 290-310. Oxford, UK: Berghahm.

Morgan, G. 1999. The moral surveillance of Aboriginal applicants for public housing in New South Wales." *Australian Aboriginal Studies* 17(1): 3-14.

–. 2006a. Aboriginal politics, self-determination and the rhetoric of community. In *Returning (to) communities: Theory, culture and political practice of the communal,* ed. S. Herbrechter and M. Higgins, 367-86. Amsterdam: Rodopi.

–. 2006b. *Unsettled places: Aboriginal people and urbanisation in New South Wales.* Kent Town, SA: Wakefield.

–. 2008. Aboriginal migration to Sydney since World War II. *Sydney Journal* 1(3): 75-82.

Pierson, J.C. 1977. Voluntary organisations and Australian Aboriginal urban adaptations in Adelaide. *Oceania* 48: 46-58.

Plater, D. 1995. Aboriginal people and "community" in the Leichhardt municipality. In *Minorities: Cultural diversity in Sydney,* ed. S. Fitzgerald and G. Wotherspoon, 35-49. Sydney: State Library of New South Wales Press.

Rowse, T. 2000. Transforming the notion of the urban Aborigine. *Urban Policy and Research* 18(2): 171-90.

Schwab, J. 1988. Ambiguity, style and kinship in Adelaide Aboriginal identity. In *Being black: Aboriginal cultures in "settled" Australia,* ed. I. Keen, 77-96. Canberra: Aboriginal Studies.

Smith, H., and E. Biddle. 1975. *Look forward, not back: Aborigines in metropolitan Brisbane, 1965-1966.* Canberra: Australian National University Press.

Taylor J., and M. Bell. 2004. *Population mobility and Indigenous peoples in Australasia and North America.* London and New York: Routledge.

Webber, J. 1995. Relations of force and relations of justice: The emergence of normative community between colonists and Aboriginal peoples. *Osgoode Law Journal* 33: 623-60.

Yamanouchi, Y. 2010. Exploring ambiguity: Aboriginal identity negotiation in South Western Sydney. *Environment and Planning A* 42(2): 285-99.

11

Indigenous Urbanization in Australia

Patterns and Processes of Ethnogenesis

JOHN TAYLOR

A central assumption behind the policy of assimilation was that those who chose to live in the cities and towns thereby signaled a preparedness to cede their Indigenous identities and become absorbed into the social mainstream. (Morgan 2006, 55)

In demographic terms, the process of urbanization is marked by an increasing concentration of population in towns and cities and a concomitant proportional decline in rural residence. From this perspective, the Indigenous population of Australia has experienced rapid urbanization since the middle of the last century due to the combined effects of migration from rural areas, natural increase, and increased census identification. This chapter charts the rise in this urbanization and establishes the contribution made by different components of growth. In the larger cities it finds that social processes associated with enumeration and male exogamy now contribute more to urbanization than do spatial processes involving migration, while at the lower end of the settlement hierarchy, especially in remote areas, government policies of centralization have the potential to bring about a new wave of rural-urban migration (Taylor 2009b). Whatever the context, it is clear that, rather than resulting in diminished Indigenous identity, as authorities clearly expected and intended, the process of urbanization has served more to reinforce identity. A demographic measure of this is provided by the observation of a steady rise in Indigenous urban numbers based on self-identification in successive census counts. This increase has been substantially beyond that accounted for by natural increase and in-migration and is a marker of what Rowse (2000, 184) has referred to as "Aboriginal ethnogenesis."

Mobility Transition

One of the more obvious transformations of the Australian Indigenous population in the second half of the twentieth century involved a shift in the balance of continental geographic distribution away from remote and rural areas towards urban and metropolitan centres and, consequently, from the north and west to the south and east of the country. Over the longer term, this redistribution may be viewed as an outcome of the incorporation of Indigenous people into modernizing institutions of the Australian state. Over the shorter term, since the 1970s, uncertainty exists as to whether it is spatial mobility, ethnic mobility, or simply better enumeration of already urban-based populations that has been the main contributor to increased urban numbers. Such issues are inherent in attempts to circumscribe an Indigenous demography (Taylor 2009a).

In Australia, an urban centre is defined as a population cluster of more than one thousand persons. Against this measure, the rate of Indigenous urbanization has been very high for several decades and is among the highest in the world. According to census counts, in 1971 the urban population was just 51,400; by 2006 it was 335,400. This represents an annual growth rate of 5.5 percent. Today, only three countries exceed this rate of urban growth (Burundi, Laos, and Liberia). Among Indigenous populations around the world, this parallels the very high rate of urbanization that occurred among Māori from the mid-1920s through to the present and that saw the proportion of Māori population in urban areas rise from 7 percent in 1936 to 84 percent today (Bedford and Pool 2004, 56; Kukutai, this volume). By contrast, on the same measure of residence in settlements over one thousand population, Indigenous peoples in Canada are today only roughly 50 percent urban.

In Australia, a reliable picture of urbanization emerges only since the 1971 census onwards, when consistent census recording of self-identified Indigenous status became the norm. The 1971 census indicated that 44 percent of the Indigenous population was urban; at the most recent census (2006) it was 76 percent (Figure 11.1). Numerically, most urban dwellers live

FIGURE 11.1   Indigenous urban/rural population distribution, 1971 and 2006

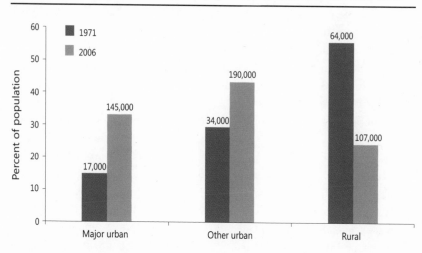

Source: Australian Census of Population and Housing, 1971 and 2006.

in smaller urban centres (fewer than 100,000), but the greatest proportional increase over the past thirty-five years has occurred in major cities (over 100,000). In the meantime, while the rural proportion has fallen dramatically, it is clear from Figure 11.1 that the actual population in rural areas has almost doubled.

If anything, these figures understate both the extent and rapid rise in urban numbers, especially in terms of proximity to metropolitan centres and larger cities. This is because the criteria used by the Australian Bureau of Statistics (2008) to classify statistical units as urban or rural are based on measures of population density, land use, and spatial contiguity. Consequently, many people who may reasonably be regarded as forming part of a city or town region are not classified as urban dwellers. If those in such peri-urban areas are included, then the Indigenous urban share is closer to 80 percent – not far short of the level of 89 percent urban recorded for the non-Indigenous Australian population, which is among the most urbanized in the world. Having said that, international comparison of urbanization is fraught due to the application of widely differing definitions of what constitutes an urban place. Nonetheless, it is undeniable that, as a group, Indigenous Australians are a predominantly urban population, far more so, for example, than many populations in many developing countries and many other Indigenous populations who remain predominantly rural. This shift from a mostly rural residential base to an overwhelmingly urban one reflects a rapid process of demographic transition that has occurred among Indigenous Australians, as it has among many other Indigenous populations, and it parallels an equally compressed mobility transition involving rural-urban migration but with sustained high mobility (Bedford and Pool 2004; Taylor 2003; Taylor and Bell 1996).

In the 1960s, a series of survey- and census-based analyses highlighted what had been perceived as occurring for some time: the Indigenous population resident in major cities had been growing rapidly due to net migration gains from small towns and rural areas. In the definitive study, based on Adelaide, this process was seen to commence in the 1950s, and it was argued that movement from mission and government reserves was stimulated by a search for employment opportunities and the attraction of better social services, especially housing (Gale 1967, 1972; Gale and Wundersitz 1982). Once metropolitan links were established, movement out of rural areas was sustained by a process of chain-migration involving kin networks. Similar sets of push-and-pull factors, with particular emphasis on the search for employment, were reported from migrant surveys in other cities (Beasley 1970; Brown, Hirschfeld, and Smith, 1974, 19; Burnley and Routh 1985; Smith and Biddle 1975, 42-53).

The clearest spatial example of such rural-urban migration occurred among Torres Strait Islanders (Taylor and Arthur 1993). Until the end of the Second World War, Torres Strait Islanders were restricted by law and administrative arrangements to residing in scattered communities across the Torres Strait archipelago. This is despite notable exceptions, such as those Islanders who seasonally ventured further afield across northern Australia as crews on pearling luggers. Due to legislative change and subsequent out-migration for employment, however, as well as increase of the Islander population on the mainland, this pattern of distribution is now almost completely reversed. In 2006, almost 85 percent of all Torres Strait Islanders were resident on the mainland. Furthermore, the pattern of settlement that has emerged from this redistribution is quite distinctive, being focused primarily on the larger urban centres of North Queensland as well as metropolitan Brisbane and Sydney.

Notwithstanding this obvious and rapid urbanization, perhaps the more remarkable observation is the degree of continuity that has been sustained in rural and, particularly, in remote residence. Basically, in reaction to centralizing forces of government policy under policies of assimilation, there emerged in the 1970s a "return-to-country" movement involving the spontaneous re-settlement of traditional Indigenous clan estates across much of central and northern Australia. This very tangible expression of preferred livelihoods was enabled by the emergence of land rights and self-determination policies and involved small clan-based groupings moving away from polyglot "mod-ernizing" townships. Initially, and until quite recently, this manifestation of Indigenous agency was encouraged and fiscally supported by federal and some state governments; but, as state ideology and policy goals in relation to Indigenous affairs have shifted in recent years away from self-determination towards attempts at mainstreaming Indigenous outcomes, the prospects and practicalities of dispersed remote living have been increasingly called into question. This has brought into sharp relief a range of policy tensions around the nature and meaning of Indigenous peoples' development in con-temporary Australia and has "placed" urban locations on one side of a policy discourse as desirable destinations. By so doing, it has highlighted the vul-nerability of government-supported non-urban settlement in the face of ideological limits to diversity (Taylor 2009b).

It is interesting to consider the origins of this discourse in the 1960s and to reflect on what the prominent social science of the day thought of the plight of rural Indigenous populations towards the end of the policy period of assimilation. Conscious of a growing mood for change, the (then) Social Science Research Council of Australia sponsored a series of studies on "Ab-origines in Australian Society" that focused, among other things, on docu-menting the dire social and economic conditions that prevailed in remote reserve locations in which Indigenous people had been required to live. One of the more influential of these studies describes the various mission and government settlements established for Indigenous people at that time as instrumental in "frustrating" their urbanization. Such places were viewed negatively as "holding institutions," serving to prevent the inevitable migra-tion of Indigenous people to towns and cities (Rowley 1971, 84).

With the benefit of more than thirty years' hindsight, during which time Indigenous people have been free from the institutional and legislative shackles that governed their place of residence, this proposition is only par-tially upheld. While migration from the bush to towns and cities has un-doubtedly occurred, the overall net flow of migration to urban areas has been only marginally positive since the 1970s. Consequently, much of the substantial growth in urban Indigenous population that has been observed in recent decades mostly reflects an increase in the enumeration of already

FIGURE 11.2 Indigenous and non-Indigenous population distribution
by remoteness category, 2006

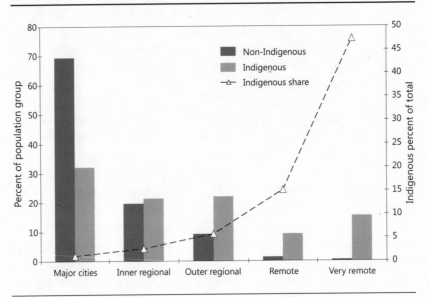

Source: Australian Bureau of Statistics, 2008.

urban-based Indigenous people (Taylor 2003). That being so, the increased
dispersion of Indigenous population to clan-based settlements on traditionally owned lands is striking because it runs counter to expectation and to
the standard theory of mobility transition (Taylor and Bell 2004). This unique
social outcome provides an example of strategic engagement by Indigenous
peoples with processes enacted by the state, whereby principles of self-
determination have enabled a persistence of customary practice despite inevitable pressures for change. Sahlins (1999) depicts such engagement as an
"Indigenization of modernity," and, in Australia, it has (so far) culminated in
a very different distribution of Indigenous population compared to that
overall, as shown in Figure 11.2.

To interpret this chart it is necessary to understand that Australian census geography defines remoteness for each location using a relative index of
accessibility to goods, services, and population. This produces five broad
categories, with major cities classified as the least remote. On this basis, as
shown in Figure 11.2, almost one-third of Indigenous Australians are resident in remote areas compared to a very small proportion of the rest of the
population. In very remote areas (which cover almost 80 percent of the

FIGURE 11.3 Indigenous and non-Indigenous urbanization rates
by Australian states and territories, 2006

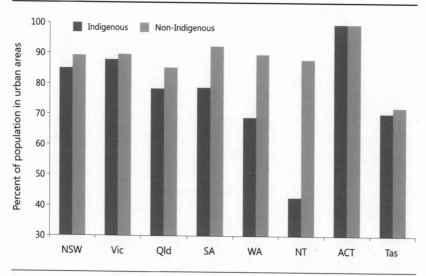

Source: Australian Census of Population and Housing, 2006.

continent), Indigenous peoples constitute almost half of the resident population; although, away from the thinly scattered mining and service towns,
they are very much the majority. Such areas have been referred to as an
"Indigenous domain" to reflect a space where social closure acts as a form of
resistance to state dominance and where Indigenous peoples and their institutions predominate (Trigger 1986).

The effect of this rural resistance to change is shown in the varying degrees of Indigenous urbanization between Australian jurisdictions (Figure
11.3). Thus, in New South Wales and Victoria, where the impact of colonization has been longest and most comprehensively felt, Indigenous urbanization rates are well above 80 percent and close to non-Indigenous
rates. Elsewhere, non-Indigenous urbanization remains high but Indigenous rates fall away, first in Queensland and South Australia, and then more
noticeably in Western Australia and, especially, the Northern Territory,
where most Indigenous people remain in rural areas. The two exceptions
are the Australian Capital Territory, where, for obvious reasons in a city-
jurisdiction, Indigenous and non-Indigenous rates are both high; and
Tasmania, which has the lowest overall rates of urbanization.

A Revisionist View of Urbanization

While there is no doubting the steady rise in urban numbers or the clear empirical evidence of rural out-migration due to push factors such as agricultural reform (Castle and Hagan 1984) and pull factors such as access to social services and kin (Gale 1967, 1972; Morgan, this volume), a revisionist view of this spatial redistribution has emerged. This regards postwar migration to major cities as only a temporary wave during the 1950s and 1960s and one that contributed less to Indigenous urban population growth than previously claimed (Gray 1989, 130-33). Suspicion that much of the apparent shift in population distribution since the 1960s could have been due to an increased tendency for city-based Indigenous people to self-identify in census enumerations, as much as to net migration, was first raised by Smith (1980a, 202; 1980b, 252) and Gray (1989, 130), based on the fact that early studies of Indigenous urbanization focused solely on flows towards cities with no corresponding analysis of counter-streams of people who may have been leaving metropolitan areas.

This point was addressed in detail by Gray (1989), who demonstrated emphatically that, if migration were ever a major factor leading to an increased Indigenous presence in major cities, then, from 1976 onwards, it was far less so. The same point was acknowledged by Gale and Wundersitz (1982, 96), who noted that mobility patterns focused on Adelaide were not unidirectional but, rather, included a good deal of movement back out to country areas. They also concluded that migration flows to the city peaked during the 1960s, with subsequent growth in urban areas due more to the effects of natural increase (39). For the contemporary period, Gray (1989), Taylor and Bell (1996), Taylor (forthcoming), and Biddle (2009) have recorded consistently low overall effectiveness ratios of migration flows between metropolitan and non-metropolitan areas, with census results variously indicating either slight overall net gain to capital cities or slight net loss.

Also observed are very different patterns of net migration flows in the various major cities. Sydney, for example, has regularly experienced sizeable net losses of Indigenous people to the rest of New South Wales since the 1970s. Likewise, Melbourne has regularly lost to the rest of Victoria. By comparison, the other major cities of Brisbane, Adelaide, Perth, and Canberra have consistently experienced substantial net migration gains, again mostly due to interaction with their jurisdictional hinterlands, except in the case of Canberra, given its unique catchment as the national capital. Interestingly, this variation between major cities mirrors the pattern observed for the Australian population as a whole, though for quite different reasons.

Population Turnover

In contrast with the pattern observed in the general population, high inter-regional turnover rates for the Indigenous population, involving half or more of a region's population at times, tend to be associated with metropolitan areas, notably Brisbane, Perth, Melbourne, and Adelaide. The Indigenous populations of the smaller Territory capitals (Canberra and Darwin) also display relatively high rates of turnover, even in these typically migrant cities. For example, the rate of turnover of the Indigenous population of Canberra in 2006 was 1.5 times that of the rest of the population. This high turnover is attributed largely to movement generated between cities and their respective state hinterlands, as opposed to involving long-distance inter-metropolitan movement, as it does more frequently for the non-Indigenous population. One view of this is that it undermines the notion of an "urban Indigenous population" as distinct from any other (Gray 1989, 133). The suggestion is that Indigenous people in the city are not just similar to those in country areas – to a large extent, they are the same people spatially displaced at different stages of their lives. This turnover also reflects the diasporic impact of colonialism, especially in more closely settled parts of the country, and the socio-spatial networks that this has generated, many of which are focused on the location of urban-based kin (Gray 2004; Andersen, this volume).

The demographic basis for this observation of turnover is available from the age distribution of net flows in and out of cities, with two broad patterns in evidence (Gray 1989; Taylor 2006). The first of these is found in the large metropolitan centres of Sydney and Melbourne and involves a cycle of young single people moving to the city then returning to country areas maybe ten years later, taking their new families with them (Gray 1989). The second pattern is focused on Brisbane and the smaller cities of Adelaide and Perth and involves more permanent migration across all age groups. Reasons for consistently higher net gains in these cities have not been established, although Gray (1989) points to the existence of active Indigenous social housing programs in Adelaide and Perth as possible reasons.

If we examine large urban areas as a group (Figure 11.4), there are net gains at almost all ages and a clear concentration in the 15-24 age group, suggesting an economic imperative associated with education, training, and

FIGURE 11.4 Indigenous net migration gains by age and sex in large
urban centres (>10,000 population), 2006

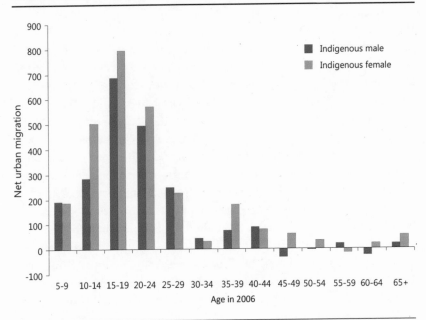

Source: Biddle (2009).

job search. However, the notable feature of this net shift is the prominence
of females at almost all ages and, especially, at younger ages of 10-24 years.
This is observed in many urban areas and is likely to reflect higher female
rates of schooling and tertiary education participation as well as an increasing tendency (and capacity) for females to establish independent means of
living through employment and social security arrangements and access to
social housing.

The experience of Indigenous people tends to undermine classical models
of urban migration that portray migrants as income maximizers in undiffer-
entiated labour markets. That is not to say that job search and depressed
economic conditions in rural communities have not been significant stimu-
lants to Indigenous urbanization, but even here emphasis can be placed as
much on the strength of government agency in directing or enabling migration flows as it can on individuals as free agents (Gray 2004; Morgan 2006).
Alternate economic approaches that relate mobility to risk minimization
within highly segmented labour markets present a more realistic framework

for Indigenous populations as they highlight the distinctiveness of Indigenous economic participation, mostly in secondary labour markets, and give prominence to the role of social networks in facilitating movement. Given the persistently low socio-economic status of Indigenous peoples in Australia, this relationship between marginalization and mobility is becoming a key public policy question around the conundrum of whether mobility reflects socio-economic status or whether socio-economic status reflects mobility.

Urbanization: Demographic and Social Components of Change

As might be expected, a strong positive relationship exists in the Australian population between regional net migration gain and regional population growth. Put simply, regions that experience growth in population do so largely because of net gains from migration. Conversely, those regions experiencing decline do so mostly because of net migration losses. In line with this, an R^2 of 0.89 has been established between regional net migration rates and population growth rates for the non-Indigenous population (Taylor 2003). While the form of this relationship also holds for the Indigenous population, the association is much weaker with many regions, especially those focused on metropolitan areas or with mostly urban populations, experiencing population growth above expectation given their net migration rate. This discrepancy can be substantial at times. For example, between 1991 and 1996, the metropolitan area of Sydney experienced a 31 percent increase in its Indigenous population despite experiencing a net migration loss. Given that rural-urban migration provided the early impetus for urbanization, the question arises as to how much this is still the case: If migration is now less of a factor than it used to be, what now are the key drivers of urbanization?

Figure 11.5 begins to provide a perspective on this question by outlining the size and direction of Indigenous population flows between four major settlement categories: two at the base of the settlement hierarchy and two at the top. Clearly, the overall flow of population is up the hierarchy towards city areas, although large regional towns experience the highest rate and absolute level of net migration gain.

This movement into regional, as opposed to metropolitan, Australia is very much focused on a number of important service towns where there has been a history of deliberate government attempts to redirect populations

FIGURE 11.5 Size and direction of Indigenous population flows, 2001-6

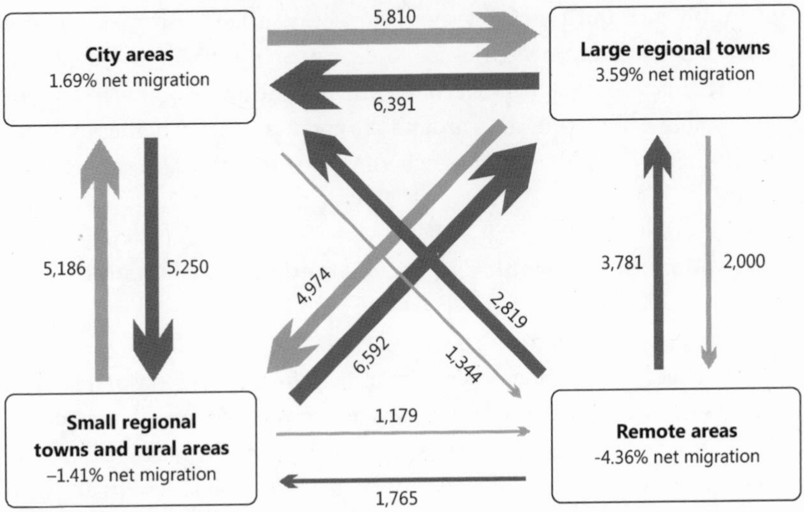

Source: Biddle (2009).

from remote areas via welfare and public housing policies (Mitchell and Cawte 1977; Gray 2004; Morgan 2006). This has built up social networks with defined catchments that are now leading to enhanced step-wise migration into regional centres such as Dubbo, Port Augusta, and Kalgoorlie. In these sorts of places (half-way between remote areas and metropolitan areas) Indigenous population growth is far outstripping non-Indigenous growth, and, as a consequence, the Indigenous share of population in these centres is rising (Taylor 2006). The long-run prospect for such places is towards an increasingly prominent Indigenous profile and identity given the differential population dynamics under way between Indigenous and non-Indigenous residents due to a combination of relative ageing and migration. This trend has major implications for the nature of services delivered in many of Australia's regional centres as well as for the role that Indigenous residents will play in terms of their social life, governance, and economy.

In contrast, small towns and rural and remote areas experience net migration loss. While this structural pattern of net flow has long been observed, the key point to note alongside this is that the scale of redistribution due to migration is much lower than might be expected compared to the relative growth in population counts in cities and large regional towns (see also Norris, Clatworthy, and Peters, this volume). Also noteworthy is the substantial gross migration that occurs, especially between cities and regional areas.

A further indication of migration impact is provided in Figure 11.6, which shows the numeric contribution of natural increase and then natural increase plus net migration to overall Indigenous population change in major cities, large regional towns, and small regional towns. In all three urban settings, there is a substantial residual population increase after accounting for demographic inputs. This is most noticeable in small regional towns, given that a net migration loss is observed. Clearly, in urban areas generally, something other than demography is contributing to Indigenous population growth. In order to establish a more precise measure of this latent effect on rates of urban population increase, a regression model of the contribution of natural increase and net migration to population change has been developed by Taylor and Biddle (2010), using a small-area statistical geography (Indigenous Areas), and this is used to allocate residuals to an urban classification.

The Taylor-Biddle model reveals a strong spatial pattern. It shows that negative residuals (census "undercount," in the sense that the change in census count was lower than predicted based on intercensal natural increase and net migration) are heavily concentrated in remote and rural areas, whereas in urban areas positive residuals (census "overcount," in the

FIGURE 11.6 Contribution of demographic processes to Indigenous population change by remoteness area, 2001-6

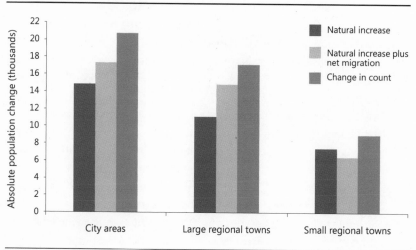

Source: Taylor and Biddle (2010).

sense that the change in census count was higher than predicted based on intercensal natural increase and net migration) tend to predominate. By grouping Indigenous Areas into an aggregated "urban" category, an overall measure of urban overcount (growth in census count in excess of net migration and natural increase) can be established. In this way, the overall contribution to Indigenous urban population growth between 2001 and 2006 is estimated at 76 percent due to natural increase, 10 percent due to net migration, and 14 percent due to non-demographic factors (Taylor and Biddle 2010), with net migration and non-demographic factors dominant in cities and large urban centres (Figure 11.6).

The tendency in official statistical reporting in Australia has been to attribute this latter component to a shift in the propensity of Indigenous people to self-identify in census counts (Ross 1999; Snipp, this volume), although it is also suggested that it reflects variable census coverage (Gray 1997, 2002). The first of these is suggestive of behavioural change while the latter alludes more to administrative factors. Either way, explanation has been confounded by a lack of appropriate data, although one set of observations does seem to undermine the proposition that behavioural factors associated with identity are prominent. This stems from a comparison of single-year age-specific growth in Indigenous population counts for successive censuses from 1991 to 2001, showing highly systematic movements in the distribution of growth across the entire age distribution that are simply not compatible with socio-demographic processes (Kinfu and Taylor 2005). In line with Gray (1997, 2002), what they do suggest is variable-capture by census enumeration but a capture of whole households rather than of random individuals – hence the systematic shifts across the age distribution. As to processes that might explain this, no information exists except to say that the Australian Bureau of Statistics has developed strategies over time to improve its Indigenous enumeration in both rural and urban settings (Taylor 2002).

Notwithstanding such efforts, volatility over time in census counts is almost a defining feature of the self-identified Indigenous population. Since 1971, intercensal change in recorded numbers has been negative on one occasion and is often excessively positive. Given the tendency for high error of census closure among self-identified populations (Passel 1996), successive census data effectively report the characteristics, including those pertaining to migration, of different populations. While some scope exists for estimating the compositional impact of newcomers on the population using fixed population characteristics such as "age left school" (Eschbach, Supple, and Snipp 1998), for characteristics that are variable over time, such as movement status, this is simply not possible. A fundamental and unresolved difficulty for tracking Indigenous urbanization processes is therefore the lack of consistent calibration of migration effects.

Natural Increase

Further complexity is generated by the maternal composition of Indigenous births. As indicated, fertility accounts for a large share of the intercensal increase in urban population. However, there are two components to Indigenous births that derive from different fertility dynamics, one of which considerably favours urban (especially metropolitan) over rural natural increase. In the Australian vital registration system, a birth is declared as Indigenous when one or both parents self-identify as Indigenous, and this leads to a distinction between Indigenous fertility and Indigenous births. The latter includes births of Indigenous children to non-Indigenous mothers that arise from Indigenous male exogamy. Since male exogamy rates are highest in major cities (Sydney 82 percent, Melbourne 82 percent, Brisbane 79 percent, Adelaide 71 percent, Perth 57 percent, Hobart 82 percent compared to 52 percent overall), this provides an additional boost to urban births and therefore an added impetus to Indigenous urban growth that is linked directly to formal expression of identity (see Snipp, this volume). As noted, over the 2001-06 intercensal period, the contribution of births to overall Indigenous urban growth was estimated at 76 percent. Two-thirds of these births were to Indigenous mothers and one-third were to non-Indigenous mothers. This latter contribution is almost certain to continue increasing, given the dynamics of male exogamy and continued self-identification, and this is one of the reasons that recent Indigenous population projections point to a steady rise in urbanization (Biddle and Taylor 2009).

Conclusion

In terms of residential location, Indigenous Australians are a predominantly urban population. This reflects a postwar transformation stimulated initially by rural-urban migration but now sustained mostly by natural increase and the growing impact of Indigenous male exogamy, especially in major cities. Although the phase of high rural-urban migration is now over, many regional towns still remain the focus of Indigenous in-migration from surrounding hinterlands, and this is given prominence by the fact that non-Indigenous populations in these same places tend to be moving out, leading to an "Indigenization" of urban areas in inland Australia (Taylor 2006). Potential also exists for government-induced migration to select growth centres in remote Australia (Taylor 2009b).

With migration now less prominent as a contributor to urbanization, in order to establish the demographic components of urban growth with more precision there is a particular need to determine fertility rates according to the differing partnering relationships of Indigenous and non-Indigenous women resident in urban areas. This can be done using own-children data from the census (Kinfu and Taylor 2005). Less certain are estimates of non-demographic contributions to population change. Here it is significant that current projections of Indigenous population that point to sustained growth in urban shares tend to produce this outcome without such estimates suggesting that future urbanization may be even higher than currently predicted.

While the focus here is on urbanization as a demographic and spatial process, it may also be viewed as a behavioural process, with towns and cities identified as centres and agents of social change. Interestingly, in this regard, until the 1960s, Australian government policy paid little attention to the growing urban Indigenous population. As we have seen, the view was that those who chose to live in towns and cities were considered to have signalled a preparedness to cede Indigenous identity. The "real" Indigenous population, and therefore the focus of government policy at this time (some might say still), were those who lived on rural reserves in government and mission settlements. Cities were sites of transition from tradition to modernity (Morgan 2006). However, rather than shedding their culture, many people were involved in a process of cultural production combining old and new, and, rather than breaking with communities of origin, they were building broader communities of association based on commonalities in Aboriginal life (Langton 1981, 21-22; Anderson and Jacobs 2002; Morgan 2006; Greenop and Memmott, this volume).

The congregation of Indigenous peoples from different regions in high-density population clusters such as the suburb of Redfern in Sydney produced new solidarities and adaptive cultures of resistance (Langton 1981). This common purpose to assert Indigenous identity saw the expression of a new Aboriginality closely associated with a renegotiation of the place of Indigenous people in urban spaces, and it was reflected in the rise of Indigenous political and cultural organizations such as Aboriginal legal services, housing associations, medical services, arts groups, and land councils (Anderson and Jacobs 2002; Andersen this volume). Reflecting the historic importance of this cultural resistance and reinvigoration, Indigenous politician Linda Burney recently described the Redfern-Waterloo neighbourhoods of Sydney as "truly the birthplace of self-determination" (Parliament of New South Wales 2004, 130-36). What may be seen, then, as a transformation from a demographic perspective has actually served to reinforce Indigenous identity both directly in terms of population numbers and indirectly via the formation of new cultural institutions. Thus, the proposition, and the colonial aspiration, that urbanization would necessarily negate Indigeneity is revealed to be not only misplaced but manifestly inverted.

References

Anderson, K., and J. Jacobs. 2002. From urban aborigines to Aboriginality and the city: One path through the history of Australian cultural geography. *Australian Geographical Studies* 35(1): 12-22.

Australian Bureau of Statistics. 2008. *Experimental estimates of Aboriginal and Torres Strait Islander Australians, June 2006.* Catalogue no. 3238.0.55.001. Canberra: Australian Bureau of Statistics.

Beasley, P. 1970. The Aboriginal household in Sydney. In *Attitudes and social conditions*, ed. R. Taft, J. Dawson, and P. Beasley, 133-86. Canberra: Australian National University Press.

Bedford, R., and I. Pool. 2004. Flirting with Zelinsky in Aotearoa/New Zealand: A Māori mobility transition. In *Population mobility and Indigenous peoples in Australasia and North America*, ed. J. Taylor and M. Bell, 44-67. London and New York: Routledge.

Biddle, N. 2009. The geography and demography of Indigenous migration: Insights for policy and planning. *CAEPR Working Paper No. 58.* Canberra: Centre for Aboriginal Economic Policy Research, Australian National University.

Biddle, N., and J. Taylor. 2009. Indigenous population projections, 2006-2031: Planning for growth. *CAEPR Working Paper No. 56.* Canberra: Centre for Aboriginal Economic Policy Research, Australian National University.

Brown, J.W., R. Hirschfeld, and D. Smith. 1974. *Aboriginals and Islanders in Brisbane.* Canberra: Australian Government Publishing Service.

Burnley, I.H., and N. Routh. 1985. Aboriginal migration to inner Sydney. In *Living in cities: Urbanism and society in metropolitan Australia*, ed. I.H. Burnley and J. Forrest, 199-211. Sydney: Allen and Unwin.

Castle, R.G., and J.S. Hagan. 1984. Aboriginal unemployment in rural New South Wales, 1883-1982. In *Unemployment in the eighties*, ed. R.G. Castle and J. Mangan, 82-95. Melbourne: Longman Cheshire.

Eschbach, K., K. Supple, and M.C. Snipp. 1998. Changes in racial identification and the educational attainment of American Indians, 1970-1990. *Demography* 35(1): 1-9.

Gale, F. 1967. Patterns of post-European Aboriginal migration. *Proceedings of the Royal Geographical Society of Australasia, South Australian Branch* 67: 21-38.

–. 1972. *Urban Aborigines.* Canberra: Australian National University Press.

Gale, F., and J. Wundersitz. 1982. *Adelaide Aborigines: A case study of urban life, 1966-1981.* Canberra: Development Studies Centre, Australian National University.

Gray, A. 1989. Aboriginal migration to the cities. *Journal of the Australian Population Association* 6(2): 122-44.

–. 1997. The explosion of Aboriginality: Components of Indigenous population growth, 1991-1996. *CAEPR Discussion Paper No. 142.* Canberra: Centre for Aboriginal Economic Policy Research, Australian National University.

–. 2002. The future history of Aboriginal families. In *The Aboriginal population revisited: 70,000 years to the present,* ed. G. Briscoe and L. Smith, 109-32. Aboriginal History Monograph No. 10. Canberra: Aboriginal History.

–. 2004. The formation of contemporary Aboriginal settlement patterns in Australia: Government policies and programmes. In *Population mobility and Indigenous peoples in Australasia and North America,* ed. J. Taylor and M. Bell, 201-19. London and New York: Routledge.

Kinfu, Y., and J. Taylor. 2005. On the components of Indigenous population change. *Australian Geographer* 36(2): 233-55.

Langton, M. 1981. Urbanizing Aborigines: The social scientists' great deception. *Social Alternatives* 2(2): 16-22.

Mitchell, I.S., and J.E. Cawte. 1977. The Aboriginal family voluntary resettlement scheme: An approach to Aboriginal adaptation. *Australian and New Zealand Journal of Psychiatry* 11: 29-35.

Morgan, G. 2006. *Unsettled places: Aboriginal people and urbanisation in New South Wales.* Adelaide: Wakefield.

Parliament of New South Wales. 2004. Parliamentary debates (Hansard) 17 November. Sydney: Parliament of New South Wales.

Passel, J.S. 1996. The growing American Indian population, 1969-1990: Beyond demography. In *Changing numbers, changing needs: American Indian demography and public health,* ed. G.D. Sandefur, R.R. Rindfuss, and B. Cohen, 79-103. Washington. DC: National Academy Press.

Ross, K. 1999. *Population issues, Indigenous Australians.* Catalogue no. 4708.0. Canberra: Australian Bureau of Statistics.

Rowley, C.D. 1971. *The remote Aborigines.* Canberra: Australian National University Press.

Rowse, T. 2000. Transforming the notion of the urban Aborigine. *Urban Policy and Research* 18(2): 171-90.

Sahlins, M. 1999. What is anthropological enlightenment? Some lessons of the twentieth century. *Annual Review of Anthropology* 28: i-xxiii.

Smith, L.R. 1980a. New black town or black new town: The urbanization of Aborigines. In *Mobility and community change in Australia,* ed. I.H. Burnley, R.J. Pryor, and D.T. Rowland, 193-209. St. Lucia: University of Queensland Press.

–. 1980b. *The Aboriginal population of Australia*. Canberra: Australian National University Press.

Smith, H.M., and Biddle, E.H. 1975. *Look forward not back: Aborigines in metropolitan Brisbane, 1965-1966*. Canberra: Australian National University Press.

Taylor, J. 2002. The context for observation. In *Making sense of census data: Observation of the 2001 enumeration in remote Indigenous Australia*, ed. D. Martin, F. Morphy, W. Sanders, and J. Taylor, 1-12. Canberra: Australian National University E Press.

–. 2003. Indigenous Australians: The first transformation. In *The transformation of Australia's population: 1970-2030*, ed. S.E. Khoo and P. McDonald, 17-39. Sydney: UNSW Press.

–. 2006. Population and diversity: Policy implications of emerging Indigenous demographic trends. *CAEPR Discussion Paper No. 283*. Canberra: Centre for Aboriginal Economic Policy Research, Australian National University.

–. 2009a. Indigenous demography and public policy in Australia: Population or peoples? *Journal of Population Research* 26: 115-30.

–. 2009b. Limits to diversity: The State, Indigenous settlement and mobility in remote Australia. Paper presented at the European Science Foundation Conference, Moved by the state: Perspectives on relocation and resettlement in the circumpolar North, University of Lapland, Rovaniemi, August.

–. Forthcoming. The political economy of Indigenous mobility. In *Australians on the move*, ed. M. Bell, G. Hugo, and P. McDonald. Aldershot: Ashgate.

Taylor, J., and W.S. Arthur. 1993. Spatial redistribution of the Torres Strait Islander population: A preliminary analysis. *Australian Geographer* 23(2): 26-39.

Taylor, J., and M. Bell. 1996. Indigenous peoples and population mobility: The view from Australia. *International Journal of Population Geography* 2(2): 153-69.

–. 2004. Continuity and change in Indigenous Australian population mobility. In *Population mobility and Indigenous peoples in Australasia and North America*, ed. J. Taylor and M. Bell, 13-43. London and New York: Routledge.

Taylor, J., and N. Biddle. 2010. Estimating the accuracy of geographic variation in Indigenous population counts. *Australian Geographer* 41(3): 469-84.

Trigger, D. 1986. Blackfellas and whitefellas: The concepts of domain and social closure in the analysis of race relations. *Mankind* 16(2): 99-117.

12

Aboriginal Identity and Place in the Intercultural Settings of Metropolitan Australia

KELLY GREENOP AND PAUL MEMMOTT

This chapter provides a brief overview of colonial and postcolonial intercultural manifestations of place in metropolitan Australia, which have been forged by the dynamic cultural interactions between Indigenous and non-Indigenous cultural systems over two centuries. Such interactions have been prompted by the urban growth and morphological transformations of these cities as well as by the succession of government policies imposed on Indigenous people, including removalism, assimilation, and, most recently, Native title. Using the case studies of the suburbs of South Brisbane and Inala in the Queensland state capital of Brisbane, we examine the evolution of contemporary Indigenous identities, kinship, socio-spatial behaviours, song and dance, and other classical symbols of place making within highly intercultural settings despite such policies.

In particular, we take up the concluding remarks of John Taylor in the chapter immediately preceding our own. He says that many of those Australian Indigenous people who moved to the cities became "involved in a process of cultural production combining old and new, and, rather than breaking with communities of origin, they ... [built] broader communities of association" (252) instead of undergoing assimilation, as was prescribed by mid-twentieth-century government policy.

Beginning with Barwick's work (1962, 1963), and gathering strength from the late 1980s, anthropologists have been arguing for the recognition of Indigenous culture within "settled Australia," notably through Keen's collection (1988), the work of Macdonald (1986), Birdsall-Jones (1991), and, more recently, Yamanouchi (2007, 2010) and Cowlishaw (2009, 2010). These studies assert the need to acknowledge, record, and analyze urban Indigenous cultures, despite persisting narratives of Indigenous culture loss within popular media and Native title legislation in Australia. They argue that, rather than focusing on the loss of culture from the point of British sovereignty, an acknowledgment of the ever-changing nature of all cultures reveals that Indigenous people in urban areas have dynamic cultures rooted in a classical heritage.

We therefore use the term "intercultural" in this chapter to address the dynamic and mutually constitutive cultural processes that have occurred in Indigenous and non-Indigenous communities since colonization. Recently, anthropologists such as Merlan (1998, 2005) and Hinkson and Smith (2005) have discussed the need to conceptualize both Indigenous and non-Indigenous cultures as part of a realm perpetually in flux rather than as cultures comprised of a dichotomy between fixed cultural blocs. Others, such as Sullivan (2005), even question the ability to distinguish what is intercultural in the entangled lives of contemporary people. What is, perhaps, most important is to view these entanglements as part of the normal cultural dynamics that occur within every culture.

An intercultural focus also alerts those examining Indigenous cultures and lifeways that non-Indigenous cultures and their interaction with, influence on, and responses to Indigenous peoples also require attention. This perspective is often narrowly focused on an analysis of the interactions between the state and Indigenous people (e.g., Lea 2008), with only a few attempts to truly engage in the everyday interactions between Indigenous and non-Indigenous people on a public and everyday scale (e.g., Kowal 2008). Analysis of the ways in which both Indigenous and non-Indigenous cultures have been influenced by and through one another allows us to assess a more diverse range of cultural expressions in contemporary urban environments, which have been previously underrepresented in the analysis of Indigenous Australia.

We begin this chapter with an analysis of the historical, social, political, and policy factors affecting urban Indigenous people in Brisbane, based on historical literature and Aboriginal accounts from these eras. Next, we undertake a qualitative analysis of two case study suburban areas, South Brisbane and Inala,[1] examining the creation of places significant to Indigenous people in these two suburbs of Brisbane through looking at the common factors of social and kin networks, the assertion of traditional rights, and intercultural activities that create place. Through these examinations, we argue that the "traditional imagination" pervades the diverse cultural forms evident in our Brisbane case studies.[2]

Types of Urbanized Settlement in Indigenous Australia

In classifying types of Indigenous settlements in Australia, we can consider two broad types: discrete bounded settlements (especially including remote settlements) and dispersed urban housing across towns and cities (Memmott and Moran 2001). While discrete bounded settlements are distributed mainly through the remote north and centre of Australia, dispersed settlements occur mainly in capital cities and on the fertile east coast, where the majority of Australian cities and towns lie.[3] Dispersed settlement patterns within metropolitan settings usually see Aboriginal people congregating in rental and private housing. In 2006, 43 percent of Australia's Indigenous population lived in housing dispersed through the coastal capital cities and major regional centres, especially on the east coast. While bounded settlements do occur in cities (see, for example, such exemplar enclaves as "the Block" at Redfern in Sydney, also discussed by Morgan, this volume), this chapter focuses upon Indigenous people in dispersed housing in capital cities. The housing occupied by Indigenous people within these centres is a mixture of community, public, and private rental as well as home-owner housing. Public rental housing was used by governments in Australia as a vehicle for the assimilation policies of the 1950s and 1960s, and Indigenous households were scattered across urban areas in the larger centres to encourage social integration (Memmott 1991a, 135, 136; Morgan 2000). Nevertheless, a strong correlation eventually emerged between the location of Indigenous housing precincts and low socio-economic status suburbs (Taylor 1993a, 1993b; Hunter 1996; Memmott and Moran 2001).

Historical Background on Brisbane

Brisbane, the capital of the State of Queensland in Australia, is contiguous with the cities of Logan and Gold Coast in the south, Caboolture and Sunshine Coast to the north, and Ipswich to the west, forming a two-hundred-kilometre-long megalopolis with a combined total of 2.9 million people (Australian Bureau of Statistics 2009). Brisbane has a majority white (Anglo) population, with only 1.4 percent of its population being Indigenous Australians.

At the time of early colonization in the nineteenth century, Aboriginal fringe camps were a feature of most, if not all, of the newly established Australian towns, while larger towns had several satellite camps of up to several hundred people (Reynolds 1978, 167). Brisbane, established as a British penal colony in 1824, was no exception. The socio-spatial structures of such fringe camps evolved from, and were often a continuation of, large traditional camps (Memmott 1996, 7; Memmott 2007).

During the early twentieth century, Aboriginal people became largely excluded from the City of Brisbane after the Queensland government implemented a succession of legislative acts controlling their behaviour (often simplified to "the Act" by Aboriginal people) and confining them to rural missions or reserves unless specially exempted.[4] This situation gradually changed after the Second World War as more people gained exemption from the Act, allowing them to work in urban areas. However, as Aird (2001, 17) points out, gaining work and changing to conform with Western expectations was a survival technique for Aboriginal people, "for they lived with the fear of having their children taken from them and placed under the control of government officials." During this time, Aboriginal people from South East Queensland gradually congregated in public rental homes in several lower-class Brisbane suburbs and established a set of places within those suburbs where the place-making activities of events, people, and identity were bound together to add to their traditional meanings and importance.

Government policies imposed from the 1950s to the early 1970s were aimed at culturally assimilating Aboriginal people. With the advent of the Queensland Aboriginals Act, 1971, statutory mechanisms formerly preventing Indigenous people from leaving reserve communities were relaxed. Rural people began to drift gradually to regional centres throughout the 1960s and 1970s based on a progression from a traditional place of residence to missions, to fringe camps on the outskirts of the city, and, finally, to suburbs such as South Brisbane and Inala. A study of Aboriginal people originally from the Myora Mission, a discrete settlement of the Nunukul, Ngugi, and Koenpul on North Stradbroke Island off the coast of Brisbane, describes this kind of gradual movement into Brisbane. Whereas other Australians in the area had come from almost all suburbs of Brisbane, the Aboriginal populations had arrived at their present homes via settlements, fringe-dwellings in country towns, urban fringe-dwellings (e.g., Cribb Island and Acacia Ridge), South Brisbane, and finally Inala, where the housing commission homes are located (Keats et al. 1966, 39).

FIGURE 12.1   Location of places in South East Queensland

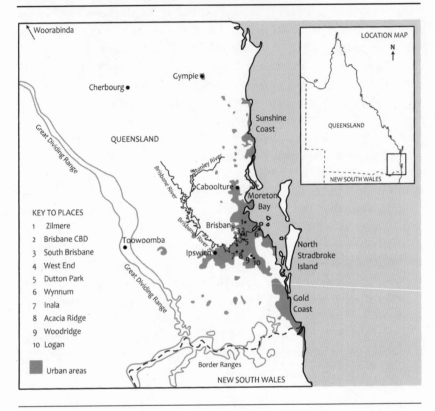

A pattern of dispersed Indigenous residence was established in Brisbane that has since grown more populous and complex. Morgan (this volume) notes that Sydney's Aboriginal population adopted a chain migration pattern from the 1940s, choosing to settle in areas of Sydney where established family and social contacts were based, creating a "heart" of Indigenous occupancy and cultural life in Sydney's Redfern (cf. Anderson 1994; Shaw 2007). A similar development occurred in Brisbane, where the gravitation of Indigenous people to specific urban locales was not the result of simply choosing low-rental suburbs and designated state housing developments but also involved making conscious social choices, such as to return to familiar family residential areas and to kin networks, "reserve" community groups (e.g., from Cherbourg [see Figure 12.1] and Woorabinda, further to the north), or to others of similar lifestyle. Negative forces, such as racist

landlords and neighbours, reinforced Indigenous perceptions that residing close to other Indigenous people was safer and more fulfilling than was
residing in other places.

The Formation of Urban Social and Kin Networks across Brisbane

Various studies have indicated a propensity for urban Indigenous households to locate their housing close to kin and family, whether it be in country towns or metropolitan centres (Gale 1972; Gale and Wundersitz 1982;
Memmott 1991a), and individuals may take several years of patiently relocating from one rental housing unit to another to gain that proximity.
The tendency to cluster together in this way can be termed "informal segregation," by which we mean the concentration of Aboriginal people into
particular suburbs of regional and capital cities due to a combination of
economic forces and housing rental policy as well as a motivation to live
in proximity to other Aboriginal people, particularly kin. McCrae (2009)
argues that homophily, the desire to live near others who are similar, as it
typically occurs in South East Queensland, is driven by structural factors
such as housing type, facilities, and schools rather than by social factors
such as kin and ethnicity of neighbours. This is in contrast to our findings for
the Indigenous residents of South East Queensland, whose housing choices
are clearly influenced by social and cultural drivers. This process simultaneously generates strong internal social capital and group identity among
Aboriginal residents within an Aboriginal suburb, but, potentially, it also
produces a degree of social isolation (e.g., a lack of social bridging or net-
working in the social capital parlance) and even the stigmatization of the
suburb and its Indigenous residents by non-Aboriginal people.

This phenomenon of segregation has recently been analyzed at a quantitative level across Australia from the Centre for Aboriginal Economic Policy
Research, Australian National University, particularly in Biddle's (2009) recent work, which examines the segregation of Aboriginal populations in
Australia's urban centres. However, the current study, made from within
our own research centre (the Aboriginal Environments Research Centre,
University of Queensland), takes a qualitative approach and demonstrates
that, while these outcomes of segregation do occur, intercultural processes
also take place over a period of generations, which facilitates both changes
in Indigenous city cultures and mutual interaction between Indigenous
people and other groups within such suburbs.

In addition to kinship links between households within urban areas, people also maintain ties with specific, discrete Indigenous settlements outside of the city. There is considerable ongoing mobility between locales, even for those born in the city, with high levels of in-migration into urban areas counterbalanced by high levels of out-migration (see Taylor, this volume).

In Brisbane, social organization became characterized by multiple, overlapping kin-based communities located across numerous suburbs and by high internal transformation as members moved across the city or returned to home settlements in many parts of the state. New arrivals to such communities built on kinship and home-town links at first but then formed other community networks around a range of other social bonds, such as affiliation to sporting clubs and government and Indigenous community organizations. Acceptance into the group partly relied on familiarity with its social norms. Group membership was also dictated by lifestyle circumstances, as in the case of alcoholic, low-income street groups. More permanent features of Brisbane Indigenous social organization are stable matrifocal families with long-term residential links (Memmott 1991b, 261).

The Indigenous people of Brisbane include a number of core families of long-term residence, some having lived there for ninety years or more and some tracing their residency back to the early twentieth-century missions (discrete settlements) of Deebing Creek and Purga near the City of Ipswich and Myora on North Stradbroke Island (Memmott 1991b, 253, 254). These historical families have come to take on a special status in social structures, as is seen later in the chapter. A significant proportion of the Brisbane population is from Cherbourg, the nearest large extant discrete settlement in Queensland, some 330 kilometres away, and which had a population of over one thousand people in 2006 (Australian Bureau of Statistics 2007b). Only a minority of Brisbane Aboriginal people can now claim to be descended from the original Brisbane traditional-owner tribal groups, such as the Yuggera, Turrbul, and Jagera (see map in Figure 12.2).

Social and Kin Networks in South Brisbane and Musgrave Park

The South Brisbane area, which contains the area of Musgrave Park, is one section of the city that became home to many Indigenous families, and it has been central to the development of the street- and park-dweller lifestyle mentioned earlier. Musgrave Park was established very early in Brisbane's town planning and is located near one of the city's two Boundary streets,

FIGURE 12.2   Location of traditional owner group Native title claim areas

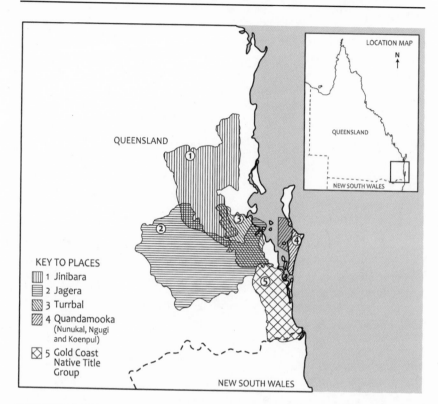

Source: Based on the map by National Native Title Tribunal, entitled "Queensland South Native Title Applications and Determinations Areas as per the Federal Court (31 March 2005)," published by the National Native Title Tribunal, Canberra.

which were laid out in the mid-1800s as part of a square containing the original town of Brisbane and marking the area inside which Aboriginal people were forbidden to trespass after dark (Greenop and Memmott 2007). It seems that from this original Public Recreation Reserve, at what is now Musgrave Park, Indigenous people could gain a foothold in the new colonial settlement as they were tolerated in this location even during the era of the Act (see Figure 12.3). It became a place where people could gather and exchange information and socialize. Aboriginal people have, from its earliest days, turned the colonial planning of this area to their own uses.

That area of South Brisbane, just inside the former Boundary Street exclusion zone, had become, over the course of fifty years, the suburb of West

FIGURE 12.3 An 1878 map showing the location of what is now Musgrave Park as a Recreation Reserve in the southwestern corner, bordering Boundary Street

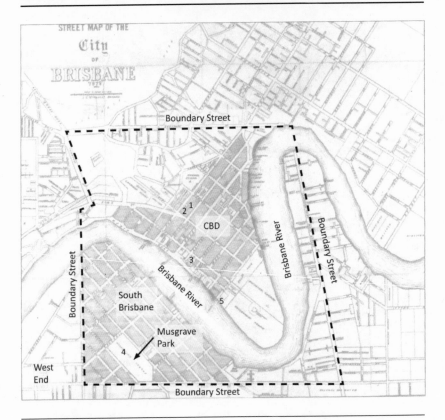

Key: 1 = King George Square, 2 = Brisbane City Hall, 3 = Queens Park, 4 = Musgrave Park, 5 = O'Connor
Boathouse (pre-1970)
Source: Adapted from "Street Map of the City of Brisbane, Queensland, 1878," John Oxley Library of
Queensland, negative no. 185673.

End, a working-class inner suburb popular with migrants and other non-Anglo residents, including many Aboriginal families. The multicultural mix of the suburb made it attractive to some Aboriginal people because they were subject to less racism than in the newer, Anglo-dominated outer suburbs (Aird 2001, 106).

The South Brisbane Aboriginal community had a "beat" (after Beckett 1988) of several locations, at which one was sure to find friends or relatives. As one resident described it in the 1930s:

We used to get mud crabs up around the [Dutton Park] cemetery. Set the dillis up there.[5] We would go around to South's [Leagues Club] and we would fish there and get whiting and stuff. Then we would go to Musgrave Park ... [T]hey would all be there of a Sunday morning sitting in Musgrave. (quoted in Aird 2001, 28)

During the 1940s and 1950s, Aboriginal elders from all over South East Queensland used Musgrave Park as a meeting place for the discussion of "law business" (sacred beliefs and ritual practices).[6] Outstanding individuals were Uncle Willie McKenzie, or Gaiarbau (b. 1873),[7] an elder of the Jinibara (Dungidau subgroup) from near the junction of the Brisbane and Stanley rivers; Charlie Moreton, or Mookin, of the Koenpul of North Stradbroke Island (b. 1861); and his sister Janie Sunflower, or Winyeeba. As elders and leaders, all three were instrumental in cultural transmission within a continuing, albeit transforming, regional Aboriginal law system. While there may be a lack of data regarding how early Aboriginal leaders influenced the colonial settlement of Brisbane (Greenop and Memmott 2007), their retention of traditional knowledge has contributed to the contemporary pool of Aboriginal customary knowledge, enabling various Native title claims to be launched in Brisbane today.

During the 1960s, Musgrave Park and the South Brisbane hotels were still popular with local Aboriginal people, and a "beat" of well-known places, including hotels, eating places, community organizations, and rental residences, was used to establish regular movement and predictable meeting places for some Aboriginal social groups (Aird 2001, 28). These beats helped to maintain social cohesion as people always knew where to look for companions. While many Aboriginal people remained under the rule of the Act, and their movements were restricted even into the 1970s, the commitments of city-dwelling Indigenous people did not necessarily diminish, despite their having been dispossessed of traditional lands owing to settler invasion and later removal under the Act. Many travelled every year, or even more frequently, to return to their spiritual homes in different parts of Queensland (Aird 2001, 9, 42). Place significance resided not only in locations within Brisbane but also in the home country, the territory of traditional tribal affiliation and ancestors. Residents returning to home countries were often prompted to discuss cultural practices that were not normally discussed in metropolitan settings and to pass on such knowledge to members of the younger generations when they visited their traditional places (31). Movement was partly prompted by the associations and activities in traditional places, which retained their importance.

Connections with missions and other places to which Aboriginal people were removed under the Act were still valued, despite the occupants' having been originally forcibly moved to these places. Cherbourg, despite its early history as a place of virtual imprisonment, remains highly valued by those people who raised their children there and stayed for many years. A shared history of hardship and joy means that it is regularly visited by people associated with its history. After the abolition of the Act, those people within the sector of the Brisbane Aboriginal community who were from Cherbourg continued to share a common identity. Circular mobility between Brisbane-based Aboriginal families and Cherbourg kin was a recurrent demographic pattern (Memmott, 1991b; Aird 2001 33, 35; Huggins and Huggins 1994 76-78, 137-38).

Intercultural Activities Creating Place

Later in the twentieth century, returning and immigrant Aboriginal populations began to make new connections with Brisbane as an urban place in a modern cultural context and not just as a place with traditional importance. "The Boathouse," a popular dance hall by the river in inner Brisbane, for example, attracted large numbers of Aboriginal people who worked as domestics during the late 1950s and 1960s. The place retained its significance and meaning for some Aboriginal people long after it was demolished (Huggins and Huggins 1994, 51).

As the century progressed, cultural change came full circle to return to resistance, protest, and demands for a range of human rights for Aboriginal people. In 1969, employing an intriguing mix of both Indigenous and settler land systems, a young Aboriginal activist named Marcia Langton staked a miner's claim on a section of Queen's Park in the central business district of Brisbane. Within a four-peg, roped enclosure she held up a banner with the words "Land Rights for Aborigines" and canvassed the public, handing out pamphlets ("Park Protest over Aboriginal Rights," *Telegraph*, 15 April 1969; Aird 2001, 105). By combining both Aboriginal and Western land systems in her protest, Langton demonstrated that, even by white standards, she had rights that she could use. But these were denied her as the police carried her away. Her approach, which could be described as intercultural in its method of appropriating Western land systems for the benefit of her own struggle, in no way implies that she gave up her customary Aboriginal rights or place values in the process.

Many public protests for Aboriginal rights followed. These were deemed illegal by the state government, resulting in recurring arrests and police violence. The 1971 South African Springbok Rugby Tour led to protests in Brisbane calling for rights for Indigenous people within Australia as well as for black South Africans under the apartheid regime.[8] In 1981, an Aboriginal tent embassy calling for land rights was established in King George Square, opposite the Brisbane City Hall, the city's symbol of civic authority (*Courier Mail* 1981 [various editions]).[9] The 1982 Commonwealth Games in Brisbane precipitated demonstrations and rallies, with street marches from King George Square across the river to Musgrave Park, which was also the site of a camp protest with public speakers and performances for the duration of the Games (Aird 2001, 116). The Bjelke-Petersen Queensland Government countered by legislating the Commonwealth Games Act, giving police the power to remove placards and T-shirts that featured the Aboriginal flag (Aird 2001, 117).[10]

Nevertheless, protests continued during 1988 when Brisbane hosted World Expo in South Brisbane,[11] and Aboriginal deaths-in-custody protests commenced in the early 1990s (Aird 2001, 126; *Koori Mail*, 1 December 1993). When the National Aboriginal and Islander Day of Commemoration Week celebrations were instated, they were first held at Musgrave Park. Continuing there for a number of years,[12] these actions reinforced the nature of the park not only as a place of protest but also as a place to celebrate community values.

The advent of World Expo marked the beginning of the gentrification phase in South Brisbane and the West End. Property prices began to escalate and would continue escalating for some decades, while poorer socioeconomic groups (Vietnamese, Greeks, Aboriginal people) were forced to relocate to outer suburbs. However, Musgrave Park continued to be a place of Aboriginal protest as well as a place of social gathering, which involved uniquely Aboriginal uses of place. People from out of town sometimes camped at Musgrave Park (Aird 2001, 127), and resistance to, and rejection of, settler values was demonstrated through the flouting of laws and through public drinking, swearing, and fighting. Not only is resistance demonstrated here but also persistence of values (Keefe 1988; Macdonald 1988; Langton 1988)[13] – and a unique set of place values, which is modern and still living and changing.

Such is the significance of Musgrave Park that proposals for an Aboriginal cultural centre to be built there have been advanced for several decades, although as yet there has been no building constructed in this significant and richly laden cultural place. Musgrave Park is intercultural in nature, created and shaped not only by Indigenous values displayed by gathering together, sustaining laws and customs, and celebrating and protesting but also by non-Indigenous forces such as the Boundary streets, racist colonial laws, the enforcement of the Act, and events prompting both protest and celebration. The diverse nature of such shaping forces does not diminish the authenticity of cultural expressions but, rather, highlights the mutually constitutive nature of Indigenous and non-Indigenous domains.

Assertion of Traditional Rights in Metropolitan Brisbane

Despite the relatively small number of Indigenous people resident in South East Queensland, a number of traditional-owner groups, such as the Turrbul, Yuggera, and Jagera people of Brisbane; the Kombumerri people of the adjacent Gold Coast area; and the Quandamooka people of Moreton Bay, Stradbroke, and Moreton Islands (see Figure 12.2) have, in recent decades, undertaken various activities in order to assert their traditional rights over these now urban territories. These have included mapping sacred sites in their countries, forming their own tribal corporations, and maintaining a strong sense of Aboriginality despite the fact that their tribal territories fall within areas that have experienced maximum historical contact since the early 1820s. Since the mid-1990s, their activities have also involved making Native title claims.

In Australia, local planning authorities (i.e., city and municipal councils) have been legally obliged to recognize and cooperate in certain ways with local traditional-owner groups who have a registered Native title claim under the Native Title Act, 1993, both until the matter is resolved in the Federal Court (which can take ten years or more) and after Native title is granted. Such local owner groups are empowered to enter into Indigenous Land Use Agreements with developers who are implementing urban development projects within the claimant area, which, in various ways, can provide streams of income for those Aboriginal groups. In metropolitan settings, the impact of this Act has, in many cases, resulted in a revitalization of cultural identity among traditional-owner groups as well as in a contestation of rights both with non-traditional owner groups and between competing traditional-owner groups.

The re-emerging role of Indigenous people in environmental and land management processes for the first time since the early colonial contact period is occurring as a result of the recognition of Native title rights. The impact of existing and spreading human settlements on the natural environment, including river catchments, forests, and coastal areas, as well as on Indigenous sacred sites and heritage places in towns, are all matters related to Native title rights. Indigenous groups, through the Native title process, are negotiating degrees of involvement with all levels of government in environmental decision making. The cooperative approach to environmental planning and management has been openly embraced by many city and shire councils, including in Brisbane, where many Indigenous Land Use Agreements have been struck. Such initiatives are examples of the increasingly intercultural nature of environmental planning processes, which were previously exclusionary government practices.

Social and Kin Networks in Inala

Inala is a suburb in the outer southwest of Brisbane, which has a 7.3 percent Indigenous population (Australian Bureau of Statistics 2006), a much greater proportion than for Brisbane overall, which has 1.4 percent. Inala is a hub of Indigenous residence within a belt of suburbs (favoured by Indigenous people) that runs from the city of Ipswich (thirty kilometres to the west of Brisbane) southeast to Logan, a city twenty-five kilometres south of Brisbane's central business district but contiguous with its southern suburbs. As Morgan notes in the case of Sydney, and as Biddle (2009) recently discusses in a nationwide context, these Brisbane suburbs have a set of similar features, including large Indigenous populations, high levels of recent migrant population, and higher than average levels of financial disadvantage.[14] The wider population of Brisbane characterizes these places in a negative manner. However, internally, Inala is characterized by a strong sense of positive identification with place, community pride, and "battler" spirit.[15]

In Inala, the preference to live near family and social networks, rather than near places of employment or services provided within the suburb, holds true for many Aboriginal individuals (Greenop 2009a, 2010). Although facilities and infrastructure, including public rental housing, drive the choice of suburb in which to live among the general population in South East Queensland (McCrae 2009), additional social factors are at work in Inala. Indigenous people sometimes choose to stay in Inala in order to maintain family and social ties, despite being able to afford the higher costs

of private rental housing in alternate suburbs. Indigenous people still experience significant discriminatory barriers when trying to gain access to
the private rental sector, although there is a shortage of in-depth research
into this problem (Focus Pty Ltd 2000).

Identification with kin is also central to the identity of many Indigenous
people within the city. Naming family members and enquiring about family
well-being is an important part of Inala greetings and protocols, particularly
among older generations (Greenop 2009a). Traditional kinship networks
are still very strong, and some describe them as constituting "an urban tribe."
Others feel that their identities have altered from traditional versions, and
yet others feel they have no connections to a "tribal" identity. Yet, even for
families who do not consider themselves as having an "urban tribe" identity,
family and kinship ties remain very strong.

The family is usually defined in terms of extended kin, including one's
siblings, cousins, aunts and uncles, grandparents, and other relations (such
as second- or third-generation cousins and adopted family members).
Traditional family kinship terms are maintained in urban environments; for
example, it is common in Inala for traditional classificatory terms and relationships of responsibility to be maintained unselfconsciously. All of one's
mother's sisters are called "mothers," and all of one's father's brothers are
called "fathers," a practice that extends to parallel cousins, who are called
"brothers" or "sisters," and to great aunts and uncles of one's grandparents'
generation, who are called "grandparents." As one Inala woman puts it, "we
are Nanas to *all* them kids," who must call all members of the generation by
the correct title, thus emphasizing the closeness, authority, and obligations
associated with that relationship.

A sense of Indigenous community unity is also generated through the
expression of classificatory relationships. At times of stress or joy, non-
family members (i.e., those with neither cognatic nor affinal relations) may
be referred to as "sis" or "bro," emphasizing the connectedness of the Indigenous community and the obligations and respect that accompany it.
This can move beyond the boundaries of Indigeneity when, for example,
an Indigenous person calls a non-Indigenous person "sister girl" or "my
white sister" as a demonstration of closeness – a reward for helping or a plea
for assistance. Younger people can also be called "bub" by elders, or "cuz" by
those not related, demonstrating inclusion and a particular place within an
Indigenous social system. Obligations and reciprocity can extend beyond
the Indigenous-only world into the intercultural connections and relationships that are inevitable in the urban setting (Greenop 2009a).

Assertion of Traditional Rights in Inala

Prior to European settlement, Inala was part of the territory of the Yuggera-speaking peoples, whose lands extended through much of the Brisbane Valley (see Figure 12.2). The Jagera subgroup of the Yuggera make a particular claim to the Inala area. Today a number of families within Inala are still recognized as the traditional owners of the country.

While the majority of Inala's Indigenous residents are not traditionally from Inala, there are a number of acknowledged traditional-owner Jagera families who live in Inala and have the right to "speak for" the community with traditional owner status. These Jagera families are called upon with regard to the relatively new custom known as the "Welcome-to-Country" ceremony, performed nationwide at the start of official state, Indigenous, and non-Indigenous community events since the late 1980s.[16] While some may view Welcome to Country ceremonies as token gestures or as an opportunity to deliver tactical bureaucratic speeches, Everett (2009) notes that the meaning of the ceremonies cannot be fully contained by the state and that the implications of prior ownership and sovereignty constitute their underlying meaning.

The Welcome to Country ceremony is usually quite short and takes the form of a traditional owner's identifying him- or herself as a properly entitled person, asserting his/her ownership and right to host and then welcoming other people into his/her country and inviting visitors to feel at home (Greenop 2009a). However, the Welcome to Country ceremony in Inala has developed its own specific tradition, which is not always in line with a pan-Aboriginal version. At some events in Inala, the Welcome to Country has been conducted not by a traditional owner but, rather, by a "historical owner" of Inala (Greenop 2009a). These are usually people of elder status who have lived in the suburb for many decades, often dating back to the original influx of people in the 1950s and early 1960s. Historical ownership may seem like a break with tradition, yet it reflects a classical practice of Aboriginal ownership, whereby rights to country can be activated by long-term residence and caring for country. Such rights may not develop into the primary traditional-owner rights of being able to "speak *for* country," but they do allow a certain amount of being able to "speak *about* country" (Sutton 1998).

During 2008, there were competing versions of tradition in Inala as local historically important people came into conflict with non-local people who wanted to ensure that traditional-owner protocols were observed at the opening ceremony for an Indigenous civic event. Local historical people had opened this event for a number of years, but new non-local group members asserted that, in fact, the event should be opened by a traditional owner of country. Nevertheless, local historical people persisted with their practice of "follow[ing] our Inala tradition" rather than catering to a restrictive pan-Aboriginal set of rules – rules that had been supplanted in Inala by modified values associated with connection to place. A subtle aspect of this practice is that the local historical owner acknowledgment welcomes people to the community of Inala, as opposed to the traditional country in which Inala is placed. But, like the owner's Welcome-to-Country ceremony, this ceremony also acknowledges the traditional owner group, usually names the members of that group as the rightful owners of the land, and recognizes the status of elders who have died as well as of those who are still alive. These ceremonies illustrate the intercultural practices that are forming in places like Inala. Both versions reinforce continuing ownership and care for country by traditional owners and both reveal the underlying Indigenous geography over which the colonized landscape of the urban environment has been imposed, but which it can never erase. Traditional and historical ownership rights may coexist, although they do so with differing responsibilities and levels of contingency (cf. Sutton 2003, 19).

Affiliation with other pan-Aboriginal values has also emerged since colonization, such as: a broad affiliation to an Australia-wide Indigenous community; an acknowledgment of the importance of kin, sharing, and reciprocity; and a shared history of struggle against oppression. These values are expressed in various symbols, such as the popular Aboriginal flag, designed in 1971 by Harold Thomas, and the subsequent Torres Strait Islander flag, designed by Bernard Namok in 1992. The colours of the respective flags have become symbolic of Indigeneity, and the flags themselves have become well known, are officially recognized by Australian governments, and are used in both celebration and protest. In Inala, this is evident in the prevalence of the use of flag colours for clothing and jewellery (and other design items) as well as for identifying organizations, clubs, and individuals as Aboriginals or Torres Strait Islanders (Greenop 2009b).

Intercultural Activities Creating Place

In Inala, many customary traditions of Indigenous culture persist and remain strong, including the everyday practices of linking to a wider Indigenous social network, claiming traditional country, and maintaining strong connections with a specific kin-based social group. Also prominent is self-displaying, often referred to as "representing" oneself as Indigenous through housing location, decoration and décor, speech, and dress styles (Greenop 2009a, 2009b). Some of these practices have their origin in classical Indigenous traditions, while others have developed in the contemporary urban context; however, we maintain that both have an Indigenous basis, which maintains their authenticity, and we emphasize the intercultural circumstances in which the latter have developed.

In the mid-1950s, Indigenous people were among the first people in Inala to settle into state government public housing, which also included postwar refugee families from countries such as Italy, Greece, Poland, and Russia. According to Indigenous residents who were children at that time, there was a great mixing of people of many nationalities and a sense of acceptance between people of diverse cultures, similar to the robust working-class culture described by Morgan (this volume). One Inala resident said that she felt privileged to be Indigenous as both her parents had jobs and could speak English, whereas some neighbouring families struggled to find employment and had to adjust to a new language and environment. During the 1970s, there were further intakes of migrants, including a significant and now thriving Vietnamese community. More recently, there have been Pacific Islander and Sudanese migrants, who have added layers of multiculturalism and change to the Inala community. However, the Indigenous community has remained distinct and has established community services and infrastructure that support its cultural and social traditions, including a kindergarten, churches, sporting clubs, and Aboriginal and Torres Strait Islander community organizations (Greenop 2009a).

One emerging aspect of identity found among some Inala residents is the shift in primacy of "claiming" land: it has moved away from claiming what are often distant home countries (claimed by ancestors up to three or four generations ago) to that of claiming Inala as the first location of one's identity. As one resident put it, "I claim Inala first, then I claim [my family's traditional] country." This, however, is part of a fluid, politically sensitive and contingent identity construction. Some of those who have an Inala-based identity feel concerned that family elsewhere would sanction them for openly relegating primary connections to home country areas.

What is significant is that Inala has become a place symbolic of Indigenous cultural strength, similar to Redfern in Sydney, which Morgan (this volume) describes as a "heart" of Indigenous community spirit. Inala has become a significant symbolic space in Indigenous Brisbane, from which it is possible to claim an Indigenous identity, however contingent (Greenop 2009a).

Other outer suburbs of Brisbane that hold this status as places of urban Indigenous identity are Acacia Ridge, Woodridge, and Zillmere as well as Ipswich, Stradbroke Island, and Cherbourg in the wider South East Queensland region.

In Inala, specific socio-spatial identities developed in the 1970s and 1980s around particular geographic locations within the suburb. Teenage gangs affiliated with their local suburban territories centred on sets of shops within neighbourhoods, and these groups became the self-appointed urban "traditional owners," defending, demarcating, and speaking for these areas. Although these are play-versions of true traditional ownership, the dedication people have to these areas and their social identities has become more serious and long-term as the teenagers have become established members of the Inala community and have become recognized as important "Inala families" by traditional owners. These specific areas of Inala have become meaningful places of significance to some local families, with second-generation offspring also seeking housing there in order to retain their affiliations. In this way, they remain not only in Inala but also in a specific neighbourhood that they associate with social identity and security (Greenop 2009a, 2009b).

Inala as a place of belonging for the Indigenous community is, clearly, very strongly established. This may also be due to the suburb's refuge quality. It has been a place of acceptance for many people who have moved there, and one of the most commonly repeated stories told by interviewees is that Inala is the place to which they fled after financial difficulty, racist abuse, and/or illness. People, of all racial groups, from Inala often feel branded by the fact that this is where they reside, that they are marked as "not the same," as "poor" and "rough" (Peel 2003). Inala residents take this to heart and take pride in their toughness as well as in their collective identity – a type of oppositional identity that aligns with that reported in the literature for other Indigenous groups (e.g., Keefe 1988). Many more recently arrived residents state that they were initially reluctant to come to Inala because of its reputation, but some are now happily there "for life" and have found it to be a place of security and close community – something that they had not anticipated. In this process of urban integration and identification, the importance of public housing in providing dependable residency access and a place of physical security cannot be underestimated.

Emerging contemporary identity practice includes graffiti tags of Inala's postcode "4077," "OIB" (for Original Inala Boy, referring to families that have been in Inala for more than two generations), "Inala Girlz," and other tags that are used to mark out geographic areas and to provide a unified expression of group identity. In previous generations, self-executed body tattoos identified social groups specific to Inala, whereas, today, designs are commissioned from professional tattoo artists to express popular geographic, social, and kin identities (Greenop 2009a). These emerging practices are new in content, but their aim is to assert a "traditional place" in Inala.

Aboriginal and white residents, along with other non-Indigenous groups (e.g., Vietnamese), share both the shame and the pride of being from Inala. The identity created in being an "Inala Boy" (or an "Inala Girl") is a substantial claim in Inala, one that few people who have married into Inala families are prepared to make. Significant political and social clout is gained with Inala Boy/Girl status, but it is cautiously avoided by those who do not wish to "big-note" themselves or to overstate their importance (Greenop 2009a). Claiming Inala in this way can be seen as an assertion of historical ownership. Yet the term is intercultural, albeit contested. Some non-Indigenous men, like those who have grown up, been schooled, and remained in Inala, along with their Indigenous friends, claim status as Inala Boys. Though denied by some, others recognize that "he grew up with us, he went to school with me," so his status becomes generally accepted and acknowledged. The extraordinary pull of attachment to Inala continues to capture a multiracial group of people, and this attachment, while seen by Indigenous residents as primarily an Indigenous one, cannot be neatly bounded by that Indigeneity. It is too entangled in its geographic area. The Indigenous community is too porous, too embedded within the fabric of the multiracial suburb, to exclude all others.

Conclusion

While urban life has attractions for many Indigenous people, it can also be compelling for those who need to undertake a variety of predominantly city-based activities, such as tertiary education, professional vocations, hospitalization, or other urban services. Australian Aboriginal academic Marcia Langton (1981, 16) once claimed that a feeling for the people and country "back home" – that is, away from the city – is always maintained. We argue, drawing on our research, that this may have changed in recent decades and that contemporary Indigenous identities may, in some cases, now be city-based and, thus, not rely upon a connection to traditional country. However, this change is uneven throughout the Indigenous population and is dependent upon personal and family histories.

In some areas, such as Musgrave Park in South Brisbane, urban locations have become centres from Indigenous cultural, social, and political life. Both Inala and South Brisbane have become, for some people, "Aboriginal places," in part through developing Indigenous traditions and in part through state-supported services such as housing, social and welfare agencies, festivals and community events, communal civic amenities, and the sanctioning of Indigenous organizations. There is uneven acceptance of new identities and practices within Inala and variations of place significance. Some Indigenous Inala residents regard such newer emerging traditions as spurious. "They just need to find out who they are and where they come from, that's it," one person said, implying that the links to a traditional country should come before any links to Inala and that dances and other traditions should come from those proper sources and not be self-consciously constructed by people in the contemporary intercultural setting. However, the range of response differences seems to reflect the many paths into Inala, the varying lengths of residence, and the diversity of experiences. This diversity does not imply an invalidation of Inala as a place of importance for many people, only that there are numerous identity forms, place significances, and traditions, and that they are not universally embraced.

Some contemporary Inala identities are, in fact, drawn from classical Indigenous traditions such as kinship, and many urban immigrants have retained their cultural identity based on home country places and hope to return to their home communities in their later lives, if local housing shortages or other preventative factors can be overcome. However, there are alternate patterns of socialization, such as for those persons with similar economic and diasporic histories. There is a danger of being tempted to classify people and places along racial lines, yet there has been significant intercultural development between Indigenous people and their non-Indigenous partners, neighbours, service providers, and governments in both Inala and South Brisbane. Inala Indigenous culture embraces a mix of cultural traditions but varies according to family history, personal associations, and life patterns (Greenop 2009a), while in South Brisbane the historical forces that have shaped places like Musgrave Park have involved complex interactions between Indigenous cultural imperatives and the laws, planning, and funding regimes of the state.

While we have not examined South Brisbane as a site associated with an emerging Indigenous identity, its location as a historically significant site and symbol of Indigenous persistence within the heart of the city does position it as a site for the production of Indigenous identity. Festivals, protests, and services there maintain an Indigenous presence, while, over multiple generations, knowledge of the history of the site has created significance.

Symbolic links to the classical past are being sought in both South Brisbane and Inala, and, although they differ in precise content, those seeking them do so to construct a reinterpretation of past practices, which, in turn, gives meaning to contemporary lives. Where past identities have been deliberately severed or strained through processes of colonization, new identities and expressions are being both spontaneously and self-consciously created by urban people in an attempt to provide frameworks that mirror practices whose roots are in the past.

Notes

Kelly Greenop's research was proudly supported by the Queensland Government's Growing the Smart State PhD Funding Program and may be used to assist public policy development. However, the opinions and information contained in the research do not necessarily represent the opinions of the Queensland Government or carry any endorsement by the Queensland Government. The Queensland Government accepts no responsibility for decisions or actions resulting from any opinions or information supplied. The Australian Institute of Aboriginal and Torres Strait Islander Studies, the University of Queensland's School of Architecture, and the Ceridwen Greenfield and University of Queensland Return to Research scholarships provided other financial assistance. The research would not have been possible without the generous assistance of the Inala Indigenous communities, organizations, and individuals who participated in the research, whom we thank wholeheartedly. Particular thanks go to Patricia Conlon, Chelsea Bond, John Brady, Daniel Wagg, Gerry Lomas, Davida Lomas, Joeline Neil, Lynette Douglas, Daniel Paton, Tamara Egert, Ross Bell (RIP), Russell Simpson (RIP), Sandra Bond, Ray Thomsen, Leah Andersen, Elwyne Reid, Barbara Toby, Uncle Albert Holt, Uncle Kevin Bond and the Inala elders, Inala Wangarra, Inala State School, St. Mark's School Inala, Wandarah Preschool, and those who participated but wish to remain anonymous.
1 Greenop's analysis of the place attachments of Inala's Indigenous people is based on ethnographic interviews, participant observation, and the mapping of significant places for Indigenous people in suburban Brisbane, all of which were conducted as part of her PhD research from 2005 until the time of writing. Memmott's case study of West End is based on his experience of the specific area, formal ethnographic interviews regarding Native title claims, participant observation, and interactions with Aboriginal people in Brisbane from the 1970s until the present.
2 The term "traditional imagination" follows Holcombe (2004, 163), who analyzes the processes through which the Amanturrngu (Mt. Leibig) community in central Australia has "re-territorialized" particular places, using what she terms "the traditional imagination." She describes how the community, relocated from its traditional territories, uses symbols, activities, and conceptions of community in local, creative ways to construct new affiliations and identities.

3 Or, more specifically, cities having both an Indigenous and non-Indigenous population count greater than two thousand, respectively (see Biddle 2009).
4 The Queensland "Aboriginal Acts" included the Aboriginal Protection and Restric-
   tion of the Sale of Opium Act, 1897; the Aboriginal and Torres Strait Islanders Preservation and Protection Act, 1939; the Aborigine's and Torres Strait Islander's Affairs
   Act, 1965; the Aborigines Act, 1971; and the Community Services (Aborigines) Act,
   1984.
5 A "dilli" is a traditional Aboriginal woven bag or net.
6 Personal communication to Paul Memmott from Quandamooka interviewees who
   were acquaintances and relatives of Willie McKenzie, Willie's associate Janie Sunflower, and Janie's brother Mookun. All three frequented Musgrave Park at times.
7 Uncle Willie Mackenzie, Gaiarbau, was interviewed by Winterbotham (1957).
8 One of the authors (Paul Memmott) was present during this incident. It was documented in 2006 as a Museum of Brisbane exhibition: Taking to the Streets: Two
   Decades That Changed Brisbane, 1965-1985.
9 The protesters emulated the Aboriginal Tent Embassy in Canberra, established
   in 1972.
10 Joh Bjelke-Peterson was the premier of Queensland at the time. He was vehemently
   opposed to Indigenous land rights as well as to other basic forms of civil rights, such
   as the right to gather in public places for political speech.
11 Land rights in Queensland, however, were not legislated until the Aboriginal Land
   Act (Qld) and Torres Strait Islander Land Act, both in 1991. However, the government then applied them in a limited way in the more remote Far North Queensland
   and never allowed them to be exercised in metropolitan settings.
12 See the *Koori Mail* (26 July 2000, 8 August 2001, 16 July 2003, 28 July 2004).
13 See Keefe (1988) for an analysis of Aboriginal identity maintenance using the techniques of "persistence" and "resistance."
14 Inala's statistics relating to income are significantly lower than are those of the
   Brisbane-wide population (2006 Census QuickStats: Inala [Brisbane City] [State
   Suburb]). This trait is also shared by suburbs such as Woodridge, in Logan to
   the south (2006 Census QuickStats: Brisbane [Local Government Area]; 2006 Census
   QuickStats: Woodridge [Logan], http://www.abs.gov.au). Both these areas also share
   a higher than average percentage of overseas-born populations for Brisbane.
15 In Australia, a "battler" is a person, usually from a working-class background, who is
   lauded for his or her hard work, honesty, and unselfish, modest achievements. He or
   she stoically "battles" through life.
16 Culminating with the 2009 "Welcome to Country," performed at the opening of the
   Australian Parliament prior to the national apology to the Stolen Generations
   (Everett 2009).

References

Aird, M. 2001. *Brisbane blacks.* Southport: Keeaira Press.
Anderson, K. 1994. Constructing geographies: "Race," place and the making of
   Sydney's Aboriginal Redfern. In *Constructions of race, place and nation,* ed. P.
   Jackson, and J. Penrose, 81-99. Minneapolis: University of Minnesota Press.

Australian Bureau of Statistics. 2006. *2006 Census.* Canberra. http://www.abs. gov.au.

–. 2007a. Population distribution, Aboriginal and Torres Strait Islander Australians. Report No. 4715.0. Canberra.

–. 2007b. 2006 Census QuickStats: Cherbourg (S) (Indigenous Area), 25 October 2007. Canberra.

–. 2009. Population by age and sex, regions of Australia, Report No. 3235.0. Canberra.

Barwick, D. 1962. Economic absorption without assimilation: The case of some Melbourne part-Aboriginal families. *Oceania* 33(1): 46-58.

–. 1963. A little more than kin: Regional affiliation and group identity among Aboriginal migrants in Melbourne. PhD diss., Australian National University.

Beckett, J. 1988. Kinship, mobility and community in rural New South Wales. In *Being black: Aboriginal cultures in "settled" Australia,* ed. Ian Keen, 117-36. Canberra: Aboriginal Studies.

Birdsall-Jones, C. 1991. All one family: Family and social identity among urban Aborigines in Western Australia. PhD diss., University of Western Australia.

Biddle, N. 2009. Location and segregation: The distribution of the Indigenous population across Australia's urban centres. *Centre for Aboriginal Economic Policy Research, Working Paper No. 53.* Canberra, Australian Capital Territory, Australia.

Cowlishaw, G. 2009. *The city's outback.* Sydney: UNSW Press.

–. 2010. Mythologising culture. Part 1: Desiring Aboriginality in the suburbs. *Australian Journal of Anthropology* 21(2): 208-27.

Everett, K. 2009. Welcome to country ... not. *Oceania* 79(1): 53-64.

Focus Pty Ltd. 2000. Rental market failure: Investigating the failure of the private rental housing market in meeting the needs of Indigenous households. Proposed methodology and preliminary observations. Report prepared for State and Territory Housing Authorities, Mt. Crosby, Queensland, April.

Gale, F. 1972. *Urban Aborigines.* Canberra: Australian National University Press.

Gale, F., and J. Wundersitz. 1982. *Adelaide Aborigines: A case study of urban life, 1966-1981.* Canberra: Development Studies Centre, Australian National University

Greenop, K. 2009a. Inala traditions: People, places and history in urban Indigenous communities. *International Association for the Study of Traditional Environ-ments Working Paper Series* 216: 26-48.

–. 2009b. Housing and identity in an urban Indigenous community: Initial findings in Inala. Paper presented at SAHANZ 26: Cultural Crossroads Conference Proceedings, Auckland, New Zealand.

–. 2010. "I'm Biota Mob": Place meaning, attachment and identity in contemporary Indigenous Inala, Queensland. Unpublished manuscript. St. Lucia, Queensland: Aboriginal Environments Research Centre, University of Queensland.

Greenop, K., and P. Memmott. 2007. Urban Aboriginal place values in Australian metropolitan cities: The case study of Brisbane. In *Past matters: Heritage and planning history – Case studies from the Pacific Rim,* ed. C. Miller and M. Roche, 213-22. Cambridge, UK: Cambridge Scholars.

Hinkson, M., and B. Smith. 2005. Introduction: Conceptual moves towards an inter-cultural analysis. *Oceania* 75(3): 157-66.

Holcombe, S. 2004. The sentimental community: A site of belonging. *Australian Journal of Anthropology* 15(2): 163-84.

Huggins, R., and J. Huggins. 1994. *Auntie Rita*. Canberra: Aboriginal Studies Press.

Hunter, B. 1996. Indigenous Australians and the socio-economic status of urban neighbourhoods. Discussion Paper No. 106/1996. Canberra: Centre for Aboriginal Economic Policy Research, Australian National University.

Keats, J., H.M. Smith, C.C. Rogers, and G.P. Rowe. 1966. *Dunwich: A study of Aboriginal and European integration*. St. Lucia: University of Queensland Press.

Keefe, K. 1988. Aboriginality: Resistance and persistence. *Australian Aboriginal Studies* 1: 67-81.

Kowal, E. 2008. The politics of the gap: Indigenous Australians, liberal multiculturalism, and the end of the self-determination era. *American Anthropologist* 110(3): 338-48.

Langton, M. 1981. Urbanising Aborigines: The social scientists great deception. *Social Alternatives* 2(2): 16.

–. 1988. Medicine square. In *Being black: Aboriginal cultures in settled Australia*, ed. Ian Keen, 201-26. Canberra: Aboriginal Studies Press.

Lea, T. 2008. *Bureaucrats and bleeding hearts. Indigenous health in northern Australia*. Sydney: UNSW Press.

Macdonald, G. 1986. The Koori way: The dynamics of cultural distinctiveness in settled Australia. PhD diss., University of Sydney.

–. 1988. A Wiradjuri Fight Story. In *Being black: Aboriginal cultures in settled Australia*, ed. Ian Keen, 179-210. Canberra: Aboriginal Studies Press.

McCrae, R. 2009. Explaining socio-spatial patterns in South East Queensland, Australia: Social homophily versus structural homophily. *Environment and Planning A* 41(9): 2201-14.

Memmott, P. 1991a. *Humpy, house and tin shed: Aboriginal settlement history on the Darling River*. Sydney: Ian Buchan Fell Research Centre, Department of Architecture, University of Sydney.

–. 1991b. Queensland Aboriginal cultures and the deaths in custody victims. In *Regional report of inquiry in Queensland, Royal Commission into deaths in custody*, ed. L. Wyvell, 171-289, app. 2. Canberra: Australian Government Printer.

–. 1996. From the 'curry to the 'weal: Aboriginal town camps and compounds of the western back-blocks. *Fabrications* 7: 1-50.

–. 2007. *Gunyah, goondie and wurley: Australian Aboriginal architecture*. St. Lucia: University of Queensland Press.

Memmott, P., and M. Moran. 2001. *Indigenous settlements of Australia*. Environment Australia (Technical Papers), Canberra, http://www.ea.gov.au.

Merlan, F. 1998. *Caging the rainbow: Places, politics, and Aborigines in a North Australian town*. Honolulu: University of Hawaii.

–. 2005. Explorations towards intercultural accounts of socio-cultural reproductions and change. *Oceania* 75(3): 167-82.

Morgan, G. 2000. Assimilation and resistance: Housing Indigenous Australians in the 1970s. *Journal of Sociology* 2: 187-204.

Peel, M. 2003. *The Lowest rung: Voices of Australian poverty.* Melbourne: Cambridge University Press.

Reynolds, H. 1978. Townspeople and fringe dwellers. In *Race relations in North Queensland,* ed. H. Reynolds, 167-79. Townsville: Department of History, James Cook University of North Queensland.

Shaw, W.S. 2007. *Cities of whiteness.* Carlton, Victoria: Blackwell.

Sullivan, P. 2005. Searching for the intercultural, searching for the cultural. *Oceania* 75(3): 183-94.

Sutton, P. 1998. *Native title and the descent of rights.* Perth: National Native Title Tribunal.

–. 2003. *Native title in Australia: An ethnographic perspective.* Cambridge: Cambridge University Press.

Taylor, J. 1993a. The relative economic status of Indigenous Australians, 1986-91. *Research Monograph No. 5.* Canberra: Centre for Economic Policy Research, Australian National University.

–. 1993b. Regional change in the economic status of Indigenous Australians. *Research Monograph No. 6.* Canberra: Centre for Economic Policy Research, Australian National University.

Yamanouchi, Y. 2007. Searching for Aboriginal community in south-western Sydney. PhD diss., University of Sydney.

–. 2010. Kinship, organizations and "wannabes": Aboriginal identity negotiation in south-western Sydney. *Oceania* 80(2): 216-28.

13

Aboriginal Youth, Work, and Aspiration in Sydney's Redfern-Waterloo Region

GEORGE MORGAN

This chapter investigates the lives of young Aboriginal men living in the Redfern-Waterloo (RW) district of inner Sydney, where urban renewal programs are taking place around them, and pays particular attention to their relationship to paid employment. RW has long been the symbolic centre of the Aboriginal community in New South Wales and a central base of the pan-Aboriginal political movement that emerged in the second half of the twentieth century. However, it has long been a place of intense social disadvantage (particularly for young men), with very high rates of unemployment, crime, addiction, and family breakdown. While similar conditions exist for most Aboriginal people in rural and remote areas (where there are also usually fewer opportunities), the experience of living in a deprived neighbourhood in a prosperous global city sharpens a sense of relative disadvantage. In addition, RW's history as a centre of Indigenous protest culture has encouraged the formation of resistant identities among the area's young Aboriginal people. Public authorities guiding RW's renewal have stated their intention to preserve its Indigenous character and to provide economic and cultural opportunities for existing residents. However, the experience of traditional communities and disadvantaged groups in places that have undergone similar processes of regeneration does not provide grounds for optimism.

This chapter draws on biographical narrative interview data to explore the attitudes of young urban Aboriginal men to employment. Although special public funding and affirmative action policies have provided employment opportunities, much more than opportunity is needed for some to escape the cycle of disadvantage. It also requires, among other things, the ability to conceive of the possibility of surviving the rigours of youth (particularly in cities, where kinship networks are perhaps less influential than they are in regional areas) and then to build vocational aspirations. The case studies presented here demonstrate the varying levels of difficulty experienced by four Aboriginal men in responding to these challenges. They face a landscape very different to that of fifty years ago, with the decline in blue-collar working-class jobs and the rise in precarious labour and the "new economy," in which much employment is in the service, "creative," and technology fields.

The regeneration discourses of RW feature the vocabulary of creativity very prominently. These discourses interpolate Aboriginal people as cultural subjects able to contribute to the development of the creative industries seen as pivotal to the area's renewal. However, it is not clear what kind of cultural recognition they will be granted in this new landscape, nor how the benefits of urban renewal will trickle down to them. To what extent will young Aboriginal men become the entrepreneurial/opportunistic workers of the new economy and be inclined to seek employment based on Indigenous identification?

Redfern-Waterloo: Setting and Context

Redfern-Waterloo has long been an area of poor housing, accommodating largely the Irish Catholic working class and, at various times, ethnic minority groups (notably Lebanese). Significantly, it is the hub and centre of the New South Wales (NSW) urban *koori* (Indigenous people of southeast Australia) community and a base for pan-Aboriginal politics in the post-Second World War period (Morgan 2006; Anderson 1993; Shaw 2008). The precise patterns and extent of early and mid-twentieth-century Indigenous migration to Sydney are difficult to determine as much took place beneath the official radar. Until the 1960s, the Aborigines Welfare Board of New South Wales administered Indigenous affairs on the basis that those who moved into towns and cities had implicitly accepted an obligation to assimilate – a viewpoint that appeared to animate much of the colonial understandings of Aboriginal migration the world over (see Andersen, this volume; Peters, this volume). For much of the twentieth century, Aboriginal people were not separately enumerated in the Commonwealth Census and,

although some were prepared to "pass" and burn their bridges with Indigenous communities,[1] most were not. Those who remained openly
Aboriginal sought out family and friends already living in the city (see
Lucero, this volume, for a similar migration ethos in the US context).
Settlement trends reflected points of origin, and most of those who moved
to RW came from the state's west (see Taylor, this volume, for a discussion
of urban Aboriginal demographic trends in Australia). Additionally, many
of those who had been removed from their parents as children (the "Stolen
Generation") travelled to RW in search of family members. The RW area has
long been (and still is) a meeting place, the symbolic heart of Aboriginal
Sydney, going back to the days when Aboriginal people worked in the nearby Eveleigh Railway workshops (Taksa 2003). Anecdotal accounts indicate
that, between the wars, the growth of the inner-city Indigenous population
was gradual and largely prompted by the closure or reduction in size of various government reserves (similar to "reserves" in Canada and "reservations"
in the United States) in rural NSW and the displacement of those who lived
there. Urban migration increased in the 1940s and 1950s, when labour
shortages in Sydney meant that Aboriginal people could earn higher wages
there than were available in the bush (Morgan 2006, chap 3; see also Greenop
and Memmott, this volume, for a discussion of migration patterns for the
Brisbane region).

Chain migration created overcrowding in the run-down, inner-city
housing that provided the only genuine rental option for Aboriginal people.
Racist letting practices by landlords and agents precluded those who identified and/or were identified as Indigenous from obtaining tenancies in better dwellings. The neighbourhoods in which Aboriginal people made their
homes were often shared with members of the poor white working class –
many from Irish Catholic backgrounds – and these districts were characterized by lively street culture and robust local social life.

In 1974, in response to plans to redevelop the area around Eveleigh
Street for private housing, Indigenous leaders, in coalition with local
priests, approached the Whitlam federal Labour government to set up an
area of dedicated Aboriginal housing. This led to a government grant, the
formation of the Aboriginal Housing Company, and the purchase of the
area that became known as the Block (Anderson 1993). Original designs
for the Block embodied utopian aspirations – fences between gardens were
to be demolished to produce communal space. Community affairs were to
be directed through participatory democracy, embodying counter-cultural

ideas that were popular among young people in this era. Aboriginal activists made links between alternative/collective lifestyle aspirations of the counter-culture and the social arrangements that prevailed in a traditional Aboriginal setting, and the Block became the heart of the Indigenous community in Sydney, giving a symbolic space in the city to Aboriginal people from various areas, whose identities were tied to their homelands. RW became a centre of political activity, especially from the late 1960s, when the Black Power movement in Australia began to challenge the paternalism that had characterized the administration of Aboriginal affairs. A range of important community organizations were set up in RW, and the area provided the activist energy for many key protests that led to significant political and legal gains (see Hokowhitu, this volume, for a similar discussion of the political elements of Māori urbanization).

But, as with many utopian visions, plans for the Block went awry. The politics of the Housing Company was later afflicted by a bitter factionalism, along with allegations of corruption and nepotism, as has been the case with many Aboriginal organizations in recent history (Australian Broadcasting Commission, AM Radio Current Affairs, 1999). More destructive, however, was the influence of drugs and crime among young people. The Block became a centre of drug dealing and addiction in the 1980s and 1990s, which was graphically and sensationally documented in media reports through this period. These resurrected long-held middle-class popular fears about slums and their potential to generate inner-urban social decay and disorder. The drug culture of the area was associated with street crime and sporadic violence, and the policing of these problems was often heavy-handed and culturally insensitive. A low point was reached in the early 1990s, when the Aboriginal community was locked into a pattern of brooding and intractable conflict with the police. The Aboriginal areas of RW resembled the classic, depressed city fringe areas described in Park's classic concentric ring theory of urban development, amidst the comprehensive gentrification of surrounding suburbs (Park et al., 1925). In recent years, much of the original housing in the Block has been demolished.

On the stifling night of 15 February 2005, young people threw bricks and Molotov cocktails at police in Redfern following the death of Aboriginal teenager TJ Hickey, which the young people believed was the result of a police chase. The graphic media images from the event resembled the Brixton and Harmondsworth riots in Britain in the 1980s and in Los Angeles in 1991. When, in the wake of the troubles, John Brogden, the NSW Opposition leader, called for the "slums" of Redfern to be bulldozed and for the rioters to be dealt with severely, he joined a long line of moral entrepreneurs who have fulminated against the Aboriginal community in the area. No urban minority in Australia has been so feared or stigmatized for so long as have the residents of the Block.

Work, Identification, and Aspiration: Four Case Studies

Unemployment and Urban Renewal

Sydney, like many Western cities, has undergone change as it moved away from a manufacturing-based economy towards a service/technology/knowledge creative economy. The problem for young people, and for young men from working-class and minority groups in particular, is that the pathways into productive work are not all that clear. Part of the brief of the Redfern-Waterloo Authority – the body formed by the NSW government to oversee the area's renewal – is to enhance education, training, and employment opportunities for the Aboriginal population. Youth unemployment is particularly high among the Indigenous community (16 percent in Redfern and 33 percent in Waterloo) and the low levels of workforce participation hide a much more substantial problem of long-term unemployment and welfare reliance (Redfern Waterloo Authority 2006).

This problem is particularly acute for young Aboriginal men, for several reasons:

1 Low levels of participation in formal education mean that young Aboriginal men lack the credentials to be competitive in the job market.
2 Many have grown up in family/community contexts in which long-term unemployment is the norm. Young men have few role models, particularly male role models, to encourage them to develop ambitions, work habits, and life skills commensurate with steady employment in the current economy.
3 There has been a steady erosion of traditional male jobs (manufacturing trade, agricultural/pastoral work, etc.). The parallel growth in service industries is of little benefit to young Aboriginal men because employment in these sectors is largely feminized (Watson et al. 2003).
4 Unemployment also results from an inability to form individual narratives of aspiration and to see pathways into the adult world. This is a significant problem for young Aboriginal men who have left school early, been branded as failures, and for whom peer-group activities, some of

which are illegal and/or dangerous, are much more attractive than are formal education or work.

Numerous questions can be asked about the role Indigenous Australians might play in the regeneration/gentrified landscape of RW. How can those who, by all sociological yardsticks, are severely disadvantaged share the fruits of urban renewal? Will they enjoy the "trickle down" suggested in much of the literature and policy documents on the new economy? How will they interact with the new, more socially privileged people who come to live and work in the area? How will they be employed, if at all? Urban renewal strategies – in contrast with rural areas, where employment remains centred on primary production – seek to encourage the development of creative industries in the RW area and suggest that those who can take advantage of their "cultural skills" are best placed to prosper in the transformed environment. But what sorts of opportunities will be available to Aboriginal people? Will their culture be conscripted only in clichéd touristic performance/marketing of Aboriginality? To become new economy workers or cultural entrepreneurs, young Indigenous people in RW will need to identify as Aboriginal, develop cultural/aesthetic skills based on that identity, recognize them as skills, conceive of how they might be transferable to other settings, and incorporate them into a narrative of aspiration. This is particularly difficult for those who feel excluded from the opportunities afforded to most Anglo-Australians. In other words, can those who are steeped in the vocabularies of resistance be conscripted to form dispositions and identities commensurate with the post-Fordist city? Even if they can surmount these obstacles, will Aboriginal youth ever be able to move beyond the precarious employment associated with the creative economy? For all of the talk about creativity forming the basis of economic regeneration, only a very few creative workers will cross the large divide between the secondary and primary labour markets.

Method and Sample
In what follows, I present four vignettes drawn from research funded by the Australian Institute of Aboriginal and Torres Strait Islander Studies and conducted in the RW area. Life history interviews were conducted with sixteen young men, who ranged between their late teens and early thirties, each of whom has been involved in creative activities/skills training in RW. Many studies in the social sciences have turned to narrative and discursive methods to explore the ways in which people talk about, and make sense of,

their lived experiences (Andrews et al. 2000; Chamberlayne, Rustin, and Wengraf 2002; Riessman 2008; Wengraf 2001). This approach understands subjectivity to be, in part, constituted through narrative forms located in specific historical, political, and social moments. These influence the way experience is lived and made meaningful. Life history narratives are social accomplishments shaped by socially available narratives and discourses (Allen and Doherty 2004). Attention to these can inform an understanding of the subject and the social and historical circumstances through which work/worker subjectivities are constituted, understood, and performed. The central problem to be explored through these case studies is whether, and under what conditions, Aboriginal men are able to produce narratives of aspiration; what obstacles they confront to finding vocational momentum; and, if these are overcome, what is the shape of their ambitions and do these fit with the challenges of the "new economy"? These challenges are much more keenly felt by Aboriginal people in cities – and particularly in a deindustrialized inner-city area like RW – than by those in regional and remote communities, where pastoral, agricultural, and mining occupations continue to predominate, as they have since colonization.

Warren: Rural Childhood to Urban Adulthood

We conducted interviews at the Yaama Dhiyyan Catering College in Redfern. One of the directors of Yaama Dhiyyan, Murray, is enthusiastic about the prospects of Indigenous cultural enterprise. With very few restaurants in Sydney offering traditional native ingredients and "Bush tucker," he is keen to encourage his students to take up the opportunities in the hospitality industry associated with their Aboriginality. However, this requires them both to have entrepreneurial skills/inclinations and to be prepared to shape their vocational aspirations around their Indigenous identities.

We interviewed Warren, a Ngunnawal man in his early/mid-twenties, dark-skinned, and thickly set. He grew up in West Wyalong, was one of five children from a working-class background, and had employed siblings working in low-skilled jobs. With only a small number of families identifying as Aboriginal in the town, Warren told us that he experienced little racism in his childhood and youth, and it was apparent that his identification was not particularly strong. He told us:

> Growing up, I knew nothing about my culture, nothing really, until I moved in with my uncle.

This happened when he travelled to Sydney to take up an electrician apprenticeship. He still lives there with his uncle, a long-time Indigenous rights activist who works in Aboriginal education. He excelled in his studies and was the only Aboriginal person in his apprenticeship cohort. He was chosen to travel to Canberra, the seat of government, to be part of an event showcasing apprenticeships:

> *"Today's Skills, Tomorrow's Leaders," it was for Group Training*
> *Australia and they picked apprentices from each state and we got*
> *shipped down to Canberra just for a lunch with the Governor*
> *General, and I got picked to do that because they said we will pick*
> *you because you are Aboriginal, we will pick this one because she is*
> *a woman, and we will pick this bloke because he was a Muslim,*
> *and so we will put you three out there, and then yeah they picked*
> *me in the end and sent me down there.*

This narrative illustrates the discursive construction of Aboriginality. Warren recounted it with a tone of slight incredulity – as if his participation was somewhat tokenistic – and we got the impression of the reductive effects of affirmative action policies. Someone for whom Aboriginality was not a particularly strong identity – far stronger were the categories of apprentice, worker, and country town resident – was conscripted to play a role in exemplifying the way that minorities should be included in the high-skill vision for Australia's future. However, despite being a high-achieving student, Warren much preferred informal mimetic learning to formal classroom learning:

> *I prefer this because ... if they sit down with you and it is kind of*
> *like more hands-on with your learning and all that ... I actually*
> *probably was one of the top students there but it didn't really stay*
> *in my head all the information, but yeah they just stand at the*
> *board just write it down copy it and did all that crap.*

He worked for a short time on the construction of Sydney's cross-city tunnel and then for two years at a race track. He enjoyed the camaraderie of both workplaces, where he was the only Aboriginal employee. He talked fondly about the community of practice:

It was a lot of fun. We'd always do stuff together ... they always looked out for you ... at Rosehill ... they taught me a lot, they kind of took me under their wing out there.

However, he was made redundant because of the economic downturn and had trouble finding another job in his trade. We met him when he was studying at Yaama Dhiyan, taking a short course to make young Aboriginal people job-ready for the hospitality industry (providing "Responsible Service of Alcohol" [a mandatory requirement for bar work] and Barista Certificate training, basic food preparation, and kitchen-hand qualifications). The college also educates the students in traditional ingredients and bush-tucker cuisine and encourages them to think about how this creative niche, much underdeveloped in the contemporary restaurant/catering scene, might form the basis for vocational ambitions:

Question: *I am just wondering ... whether you think that the cultural knowledge that you are learning here, whether that is something you feel like you will have a chance to use in the future?*

W: *Yeah I'm not sure eh, it is to learn more about who I am and my people and all that and the Aboriginal culture ... Yeah it could be, you could bring some ideas for a new place.*

This was a half-hearted response. It is clear that the significance of the course, for Warren, was not the training in aspects of Aboriginal culture but the generic training in hospitality skills. When asked about how he intended to use these skills, Warren made a connection with his previous employment:

Working in a club or something like that, because working at Rosehill I've seen all the big functions so I would like to work in something like that ... It would be fun, just like an RSL or a big club like that ... Either as a kitchen hand or in the bar or something like that yeah.

Trying to elicit a sense of whether he might see creative employment opportunities around his Aboriginality, how his cultural skills might form the basis for ambitions, we pushed Warren to imagine what might happen in future:

I am still not too sure, I don't know ... I haven't really thought about that long term.

When pushed about possible entrepreneurial ambitions, Warren was reticent:

> *Oh I would like to but when I am like older, you know, when I am*
> *almost forty I would like to start my own business but yeah, no, now*
> *I would rather work for someone for a while.*

He described conventional plans for a family and a house in the suburbs, wanting stability of employment in order to raise children. He loves Sydney and wishes to remain living there.

This interview reveals, first, that Warren's Aboriginality was not a particularly strong badge of identity. Like many young Aboriginal men, Warren is exposed to official/institutional processes through which his Aboriginality is interpolated. Opportunities present themselves to him because of his Aboriginality, but he is still diffident about forming a sense of his future based on that identity position. Our impression is that class/occupational identity was at least as important. The interview process was about eliciting his experiences and aspirations as an Aboriginal worker, but his story was fairly typical of young men of a certain background who undertake apprenticeships. Second, Warren did not demonstrate a particularly entrepreneurial disposition. His narrative of aspiration was not particularly well formed, and there is little of the confidence and chutzpah required of the ideal worker in the new economy. So while we are told that there are all sorts of creative opportunities available for Aboriginal people in the redevelopment of RW, it does not appear that Warren is particularly well suited to take advantage of them. He was certainly not the ideal post-Fordist new worker, seeking out a niche market for his skills.

Madison: Living between City and Bush

Madison met us at the Redfern Community Centre close to his home on The Block. He is in his late teens, left school early, and in many ways his life is typical of that of other young Koori men of his age. His life has been punctuated by frequent movements between Redfern and "up home," a small town on the NSW north coast. In an article published in the early 1980s, Marcia Langton (1981) questions the category "urban Aborigine," contending that it does not acknowledge the itinerate character of Indigenous life worlds and that it works with a concept of residence and settlement that does not do justice to Aboriginal experience of place. Madison exemplifies this. Born in Redfern, he was taken back to his home town, where he

spent his early primary school years. He grew up without a father around –
just his mother and older brother. When he was ten, his mother, a strong
woman who struggled as a single mother, brought her sons back to live in
RW. Here they remained, but in his mid-teens Madison had trouble at the
inner-city school and moved back to his home town, intending to finish his
education there. But this did not happen because he got into trouble with
the police:

> I was doing good up there until all the blackfellas got together and
> decided to do a few shops over. 'Cos there's nothing to do up there ...
> The only thing there is to do in small towns like that is break-in and
> drink.

So he returned to RW, where he was engaged in casual building work. This
was low-paid labouring for a small builder, involving some bricklaying and
cement mixing and pouring on local home renovation projects. When
pressed about whether he would consider taking a building skills course
that is run in the area, he showed little enthusiasm, saying that he already
had the skills and did not need to take a course. It appears that, like many
young Aboriginal men, the conflict and alienation he experienced at school
made him diffident about further formal education. In a Canadian context,
Andersen (this volume) notes this conflict and alienation as a larger feature
of urban life for Aboriginals. Madison told us:

> I did a bit of acting. They went around and got a lot of young blokes
> from Redfern Waterloo and they filmed us ... They paid us on the
> spot. It was just for a showing at the community centre.

We asked Madison whether he might like to pursue this further, or any of
his other interests, such as information technology, music, and so on. But,
like many young Aboriginal men, he seemed reluctant to express any creative ambition that might lead him to be "shamed" – that is, to experience
embarrassment due to efforts to stand out from the crowd. The interview
discloses no trace of the agential individualist subject of the new economy.
The closest he came to expressing vocational aspiration was when he discussed the work he did for his uncle, who runs a small racing car team in
Bowraville. Madison has mechanical and driving skills and told us he cov-
eted a professional role in motor sport, although he had very little sense of
how this might be achieved. This is a very common ambition for young

Australian men from working-class backgrounds, and it flows from their participation in "petrol-head" (i.e., car enthusiast) subcultures in towns and suburbs.

Madison's Aboriginal identification is strong, but he has what many would perceive as an embattled, belligerent character. He spoke of the conflict in the local school he attended between the Koori kids and those from "Asian" and "Indian" backgrounds. Broadly speaking, Aboriginality and ethnicity come to define youth gang membership, and he expressed concern that the teachers were favouring the children from immigrant, rather than from Indigenous, backgrounds, thus alienating the latter. He appeared not to identify strongly with the postcolonial political definitions of Aboriginality and had very little interest in "traditional" Indigenous culture; rather, for Madison, Aboriginality was based largely on street solidarities that often morphed into involvement in criminal activities.

With a girlfriend now pregnant, Madison expressed a desire to break with the patterns of recent years, but this transition to responsibility is not easy to effect. In the following passage, he appears to express a yearning for structured implacable authority that was missing in his mid-teens. Not capable of self-discipline, he seeks an external authority structure to give him direction:

M: I was gonna join the army but my Mum said that she'd ring them up and say that I've got a mental problem. My brother wanted to join the army too but she said she'd do the same thing ... So we can't join the army.

G: So what was that all about? Why join the army?

M: There's a lot of young fellas feel a lot of anger these days because of racism and prejudice.

G: You reckon that's a way of getting rid of anger you might have.

M: Yes.

G: What do you reckon about going up to fight in Iraq or Afghanistan or somewhere like that?

M: I'd jump at the chance.

G: Hard life in the army, you know. You can't sleep in 'til 10 or 11 o'clock. Don't you reckon you'd experience racism in the army?

M: If there was racism I'd probably do something to them. But they teach you discipline in the army.

G: You reckon that's what you need?

M: Yes. -

There is a good deal of pathos in this quote. Madison appears to lack confidence in his ability to break with the pulls of gang subculture and crime. Unable to deal with the responsibilities of adulthood, including the need to hold down a job, he looks to military discipline to effect a transformation.

Ray: Commuting and Culture

Ray grew up in the lower Blue Mountains area on the western edge of Sydney, the son of an Aboriginal father (Gamiloroi, from the small town of Gunnedah) and a non-Aboriginal mother in an area with a small Aboriginal population. He recalled that, during his childhood and teenage years, Aboriginality was only a low-level identification:

> *No you know growing up in the Western Suburbs for me it was hard to really get a good grasp of my culture, it wasn't really until going to, you know, to Eora in Redfern where I really got to learn a lot more about my culture, so it was really, you know, up to, you know, the age of eighteen where I got to really learn a whole lot more and really immerse myself.*

There was no memory of a particularly acute experience of racism, and while he was always ready to identify when the question arose, Aboriginality was not particularly central to his sense of self as a teenager. However, he contrasted himself with another local boy whom he knew to be from an Aboriginal background but who appeared inclined to conceal his Aboriginality. Ray's father was a teacher and Ray remained at school and matriculated, but his academic achievements were not particularly high, and he was not at first inclined towards further education. He worked while still at school, something that is common among Australian teenagers:

R: Well yeah, you know I have always, I have been working since I was sixteen, I have worked at a petrol station and held that job all the way through high school, so I was still working there and I thought, you know, had wanted to sort of get some more shifts. I knew some friends that worked in a warehouse that I played rugby with. He said, you know, come across have a go and so I worked at the warehouse there, and the warehouse supplied camping goods to a store. And then I ended up working at one of the stores, you know, I just put my résumé into another store. So, you know, basically it was just, you know, it was a job for me to do so I had money to go out ... and have a good time.

I: Yeah, so at that stage you weren't really sure where you were going to end up.

R: No, I had no plans, and you know at that stage I probably was just considering staying in retail and learning the retail industry, but you know, obviously I am glad it didn't turn out that way but ...

He remained in this job throughout his subsequent period of postschool study and was recognized as a good worker. The income from this wage labour supported him throughout his period of education. Like many students, particularly postschool, he combined work and study.

At his father's suggestion, in his early twenties, Ray enrolled in a film and television course at Eora College. The college, which is located in Redfern and is for Aboriginal students, is part of the mainstream technical education system and specializes in fine and performing arts. He enrolled in a hands-on training course in skills associated with the production of film/video (camera techniques, editing, production, etc):

> *I just thought it could be something fun, you know it wasn't any-thing as serious as that, I just thought I would give it a go, see what it was like, you know, and get a certificate out of it. So it was just something I thought I would give a try just while I was working.*

This gave Ray a good practical grounding, and he gradually developed ambitions associated with film and television, making the sort of transition that is sometimes more difficult for young people from poorer backgrounds who are afraid to be "shamed" by declaring creative vocational intentions. Here he met his future partner, an Aboriginal woman, and they developed a shared passion for film. He talked about the solidarities and friendships that he built up through the college:

> *It just felt like a big house, everyone was friends there and got on ... And you know you slowly learn, you know, just in general conver-sation you learn more and more about your culture without you knowing it.*

The Eora Centre, therefore, provided an informal pan-Aboriginal education as well as formal cultural-vocational training. It also served to encourage identification, in a way that does not occur in places like the lower Blue Mountains, which has a smaller Aboriginal population and few organizations with the capacity to involve young people in building Aboriginal solidarities. In a sense, the RW area is a place where such institutions of education/culture/service provision are concentrated, and it is a key site for the constitution of contemporary pan-Aboriginal solidarities (see Ouart, this volume, for a similar discussion of the role of institutions in a Canadian context). This is not to overstate the role of space/place: while RW is an area of relatively high Indigenous population, it is important to note that Ray lived outside the area while taking the course. For him, Indigenous solidarity was institutionally mediated. This contrasts with Madison, who grounded his Aboriginality in delinquent street subcultures.

Ray completed his two-year certificate course but soon realized that he could not find work in the film/television industry. He was encouraged to enrol in a bachelor of communications program at the nearby University of Technology and to develop his skills at the tertiary level. He found the theoretical content of much of the early part of the course particularly challenging and recalled that he was on the verge of withdrawing during the first semester. However, the presence of key Aboriginal mentors at the university provided the sort of personal support and tutoring in the intricacies of academic requirements (such as referencing) that he needed to pass the courses. Again, the informal sphere – in this case, an Indigenous section of a mainstream institution – served to sustain Ray and prevent him from resisting and dropping out. As a result of his earlier training, he excelled in the practical courses associated with the degree and indeed recalled being consulted by lecturers and asked for assistance on technical matters because his skills were more up-to-date than their own. He completed the degree and is now working in the film and television industry and has plenty of work with National Indigenous Television, most of which has involved covering sporting events. He has made documentary films and was selected by Film Australia for a short trainee course where he was able to make a range of industry contacts.

When asked whether his ambitions were restricted to working in the sphere of Aboriginal media, he responded emphatically that they were not. He talked about his plans to travel to the United States with his partner and to settle in Los Angeles for a time and to work in the mainstream film industry. He discussed the way in which Aboriginal actors tend to be cast in roles in dramas based on race rather than crossing over into roles in which their Aboriginality is only incidental or even not acknowledged at all. He is happy to work in Indigenous media for now but has a larger mainstream ambition.

Jarrod: Local Solidarities

Jarrod is in his early thirties, fair skinned, and grew up in Redfern. His father was a Scottish merchant seaman and his mother is a Wiradjuri woman from Wellington, in Central West NSW, who had six other children. As Jarrod said:

> *Two sisters are working, my four brothers they don't work.*

His parents never lived together and split up when Jarrod was six months old. And, like many young men in RW, Jarrod grew up in a matriarchal household:

> *Mum worked on and off ... [but was mainly] taking care of the kids.*

He went to local schools and recalled enjoying study, particularly English and history. When asked about his exposure to Aboriginal studies, he recalled experiencing a sense of diffidence:

> *On small occasions we worked on Aboriginal culture ... but it doesn't stick in my mind so yeah I can't say that there was a lot because it doesn't stick, you know.*

But he had clashes with teachers, some of which became physical. He did not conform to the expectations of respect and discipline ("probably my mouth getting me into trouble") and was suspended before he could complete his junior high school qualification. He enjoyed sport, excelled at rugby league, and harboured ambitions to play professionally. These dreams were never realized due to the troubles he experienced later.

When he left school, he had a number of short-term labouring jobs ("unloading containers and things like that") but nothing that lasted more than a few weeks. His mother, concerned that he lacked a role model to get him used to the rigours and expectations of wage labour, sent him off to stay with "relatives who worked so as to get [him] familiar with work." He told us of his early ambivalence about his Aboriginality. Even though he grew up hanging out on the streets with many other young, predominantly Aboriginal people, Aboriginality was not a central badge of identity:

> *That, yeah, that is the only way I have learned about my culture, I mean living in Redfern, you know, it is an Aboriginal community*

*and being a black fella I have struggled with, like my identity at
times, you know, so only growing up in the Aboriginal community
more or less has, you know, it took a while to notice that I actually
lived as a black fella, you know what I mean ... It is something
that only over time I have grown to realize. So even though I have
struggled to identify it but in the end you know it is within me, so
yeah, I grew up on the street learning about the culture, you know.*

This statement indicates the extraordinary existential complexities that
Jarrod faced as a young man. He did not understand the solidarity of the
street or the problems he experienced with the police as being based around
race/colonial oppression. Later in the interview, he revealed that his Aboriginality was firmed up when he spent time in jail and forged bonds with other
Indigenous inmates. He now calls himself

*Gadigal ... even though that tribe has been wiped out I am Sydney
born and bred so that is what I class myself as. My mum is Wiradjuri
but I still class myself as Gadigal.*

During his time in jail he took a university bridging course and qualified
as a fork-lift driver. When released from prison, he resolved to develop some
momentum and aspiration, which he described in the following terms:

*Well, I have never been a goal-orientated person and the goal is to
keep setting goals ... I have got a small family that, you know, I have
got to take care of so, you know, I have got to start being a man and
living life as a young man now. Yeah, my goal is to grow up and
take responsibility, you know, so yeah it might sound ... One friend
that has turned his life around and, you know, he is learning out
of jail, but he did it pretty young so, you know, yeah, he is a good
friend, so he has turned his life around, I know it can be done. My
two sisters are an example, they didn't go and study but they have
turned their life around, keeping out of jail and drugs, and now
they have been working for a few years and turned their life right
around so I know it can be done.*

It is often said that work is central to the development of self-esteem and
public purpose, especially for men. This quote illustrates how it is tied up
with ideas of maturation, responsibility to family, the ability to imagine a

future organized around accomplishment ("setting goals"), and the possibility of surviving beyond youth into adulthood. Work ambitions are associated with a move away from an impulsive way of life.

Jarrod associated the period of his life in which he embraced his Aboriginality, and retreated into the Aboriginal community in the RW area, with a withdrawal from the prospect of paid employment:

> *In the Aboriginal community there wasn't many people working,*
> *they were all criminals, you know, but outside in the general*
> *population a lot of my friends worked. Like I said, I lost contact*
> *with them at a certain, you know, at an important stage, and I*
> *think that was at a time when I was going through my identity*
> *phase, you know, so I kind of stayed in the Aboriginal community*
> *kind of thing. Yeah, so when I look back say, you know, I had a few*
> *struggles with my identity back then, so I think that stopped me*
> *progressing, you know, with work and employment and things.*

This suggests that Indigenous male bonding is incompatible with conventional aspiration. In a setting in which the great majority of people are unemployed and in which criminal activities are common, young men can make a virtue out of their marginality. To undertake paid employment – or even to seek it – can signify an aspiration to social mobility that threatens to distance you from your brothers, to mark you out as a "coconut" or an "uptown black," one who has abandoned community for the mainstream. In Jarrod's narrative, community appears as a limiting force. Indeed, he sees his goal of taking responsibility, of being a man, as associated with building non-Indigenous contacts, networks rather than community, and social capital rather than subcultural solidarity:

> *You know you can't be pigeonholed, you know, in one community.*
> *At stages of my life I ... just got stuck in the Aboriginal community,*
> *you know, and I lost a lot of my friends outside of that so ... [to]*
> *grow and to be successful, I mean, not everyone wants to be*
> *successful but, you know, to be, I don't know, yeah, to grow I think*
> *you have got to, yeah, you have got to mix.*

In many ways, Jarrod expresses the dispositions and vocabulary of the new economy. The rhetoric of goal-setting and of resisting the fatal pulls of community is central to the individualism that is encouraged by those who give vocational advice. Social theorists like Beck (1992) and Giddens (1991) argue that those who are best equipped to overcome the precariousness of the late modern world are those who struggle against the cultural gravity of community, avoid reproducing the habits associated with class and ethnicity, and manage their lives in a way that requires reflexivity and a preparedness to be flexible, entrepreneurial, and open to the possibility of lifelong education. "The first step is to get the qualification and then, you know, look at things after that," Jarrod tells us. He has many ambitions and interests but is concerned about dissipation, about lacking clear direction or resolution associated with training and working life:

> *Well, through my experience welfare would be a good choice, you know, and I have also dreamt about doing business, you know, so, that is the funny thing with me, I have got so many dreams that I tend to confuse myself, you know, and that is what stops me kind of thing. So if I can just pinpoint something and stick to it I think that is my best way to go. But I am still struggling with that, you know.*

However, we interviewed Jarrod at a point at which he had nearly completed a nine-week course in basic maritime skills. This was done under the auspices of the Tribal Warrior Association, which runs Aboriginal cultural tours (in the ship of the same name) as well as being a publicly funded training organization. Many of the trainees – who are both Aboriginal and non-Aboriginal – have been exposed to the criminal justice system and, in working with the Tribal Warrior Association, are exposed to a demanding environment in which hard work and cooperation are crucial to the success of the enterprise. In the words of the coordinator, Shane Phillips, the perfunctory chain-of-command "toughens-up" the youngsters and "makes them thick skinned." There is little room for sentiment or for bruised egos. Nobody is treated as special, and the individual is subsumed within the collective enterprise. This is a "community of practice" (Lave and Wenger 1991), similar to that operating on the factory floor or among groups of stockmen or shearers. It is based on on-the-job training. The Tribal Warrior is a resolutely masculine space, with the only woman involved employed in decorative work on the ship.

Analysis

The narratives of Warren and Madison demonstrate that, despite Aboriginal people's being exhorted by cultural brokers and those in charge of urban renewal to take advantage of the opportunities that might arise in the gen-trified Redfern area, many young Indigenous people are only inclined to develop prosaic ambitions. Jarrod is struggling to overcome the problems of earlier life and, while reconstructing his sense of self around a responsible orientation to the future, is struggling to take the first steps towards voca-tional stability. In some ways, Jarrod sees cultural identity based on a certain kind of masculine solidarity as a hindrance to social mobility. Madison has difficulty imagining any stable adult role for himself at all and has only the vaguest sense of how to navigate the path towards stable paid employment. Mired in his youthful awkwardness and habitual behaviour, he seeks firmer direction for himself so that he can face up to his familial responsibilities. Despite encouragement to become entrepreneurial and to plan a future based on cultural identity, Warren simply wants to undertake steady work in mainstream industries. His mindset is that of the Fordist worker, and he is not inclined towards seeking employment based on his Aboriginality. Ray is unusual in his ability to assimilate to the new world of work and educa-tion. Of the four, he is best placed to take advantage of the creative industry opportunities that are emerging in inner Sydney. Like Warren, having grown up in a family with both parents living at home and working, and in a less disadvantaged area than RW, there was less opportunity for participation in resistant street cultures and less intensive policing of young people. His ability to stay in the education system to the point of university gradua-tion has to do with the stability associated with his earlier life and the role models provided by his parents, particularly his father. While Madison and Jarrod got into trouble as young men in RW, for Ray and Warren, paradox-ically, the process of urbanization was associated with strengthening identi-fication. Taking courses through Aboriginal organizations in RW entailed being exposed to a pan-Aboriginal politics and culture that was not particu-larly significant in the rural and regional areas in which they grew up. For both Madison and Jarrod, identification was associated with delinquent pan-Aboriginal street solidarities, in contrast with the more kinship-based solidarities in rural areas, but these were complicated and have not pro-duced the sort of Aboriginality that is easily incorporated into the changing landscape of RW.

Conclusion

From the 1970s onwards, Australian governments encouraged Aboriginal people to move into cities. This corresponded with the rapid decline of urban manufacturing and job opportunities, particularly in traditional male blue-collar occupations. While Aboriginal women have remained pivotal in family and communal life, men have struggled to find fulfilling social roles, either through or outside paid work. Addiction, incarceration, and family breakdown were common consequences. Many young Indigenous people in cities have grown up in single-mother, welfare-dependent households without guidance in the habits needed for paid labour. Young men, in particular, suffer high levels of unemployment not only from lack of opportunities but also from an inability to form individual narratives of aspiration – to see pathways into the adult world. This chapter reports on research on young Aboriginal men in the RW area of Sydney. It considers the forces that encourage and discourage the formation of vocational momentum. The discourses of the new economy that are shaping the redevelopment of RW suggest that there might be niche employment or small enterprise opportunities available to people from culturally diverse backgrounds, particularly Aboriginal backgrounds. However, the four case studies illustrate the complexities associated with identification among young men, and they show how such identities are not necessarily compatible with demands for flexibility, individualism, and an entrepreneurial inclination. Many of the men in RW might not be able to share in the fruits of the area's renewal, not from lack of formal "opportunities" but because their upbringing, dispositions, and cultural inclinations do not allow them to see such employment niches as opportunities at all.

Note

1 A process perhaps best described in Morgan's (1987) autobiographical account of growing up in a "passing" family in Perth.

References

Allen, J., and M. Doherty. 2004. Learning through work, discourse, and participation: Storied lives, self, and social-changing cultures. *Australian Journal of Adult Learning* 44(2): 158-78.

Anderson, K. 1993. Constructing geographies: Race, place and the making of Sydney's Aboriginal Redfern. In *Constructions of race, place and nation*, ed. P. Jackson and J. Penrose, 81-99. London: UCL Press.

Andrews, M., S.D. Sclater, C. Squire, and A. Treacher. 2000. *Lines of narrative*. London: Routledge.

Australian Broadcasting Commission. 1999. AM Current Affairs Program, 1 July. http://www.abc.net.au/.

Beck, U. 1992. *Risk society: Towards a new modernity.* London: Sage.

Chamberlayne, P., M. Rustin, and T. Wengraf. 2002. *Biography and social exclusion in Europe.* Bristol: Policy Press.

Giddens, A. 1991. *Modernity and self-identity: Self and society in the late modern age.* Cambridge: Polity.

Langton, M. 1981. Urbanising Aborigines: The *social* scientists' great deception. *Social Alternatives* 2(2): 16-22.

Lave, J., and Wenger, E. 1991. *Situated learning.* Cambridge: Cambridge University Press.

Morgan, G. 2006. *Unsettled places: Aboriginal people and urbanization in New South Wales.* Adelaide: Wakefield Press.

Morgan, S. 1987. *My place.* Fremantle, WA: Fremantle Arts Centre Press.

Park, R.E., E.W. Burgess, R.D. McKenzie, and L. Wirth. 1925. *The city: Suggestions for investigation of human behavior in the urban environment.* Chicago: University of Chicago Press.

Redfern Waterloo Authority. 2006. *Redfern and Waterloo Employment and Enterprise Plan.* http://www.redfernwaterloo.nsw.gov.au/.

Riessman, C.K. 2008. *Narrative methods of the human sciences.* London: Sage.

Shaw, W. 2008. *Cities of whiteness.* New York: Blackwell.

Taksa, L. 2003. "Pumping the life-blood into politics and place": Labour culture and the Eveleigh railway workshops. *Labour History* 79: 11-34.

Watson, I., J. Buchanan, I. Campbell, and C. Briggs. 2003. *Fragmented futures: New challenges in working life.* Sydney: Federation Press.

Wengraf, T. 2001. *Qualitative research interviewing: Biographical narrative and semi-structured methods.* London: Sage.

PART 4

Māori Urbanization
in New Zealand

THE MĀORI OF NEW ZEALAND probably constitute the most homogeneous of Indigenous groups in the countries featured in this volume. They share many similar cultural attributes and a single language, although there are variations in dialect. Nevertheless, the use of the term "Māori" to refer to all of the Indigenous peoples of New Zealand only occurred in about 1850 in order to differentiate Māori from Pākehā (i.e., European) settlers (Williams 1971). Before the arrival of Pākehā, Māori identity revolved around a combination of tribal groupings with shared common characteristics: "they were based on kinship, claiming descent from a common ancestor, and they lived within a designated territory" (Maaka 1994, 313). The emergence of a collective Māori identity was supported by re-sistant political and religious movements constructed around collective Māori sovereignty, the homogenization of tribal specificity, and the construction of a pan-tribal Māori culture by Pākehā ethnographers (Meredith 2000). As indicat-ed by Coombes, Kukutai, and Hokiwhitu (all in this volume), the role of the tribe in urban Māori identities is a contested one.

When Europeans began to settle in New Zealand in the 1790s, they were dependent on Māori good will and their economic and social support. The Treaty of Waitangi (often referred to simply as "the Treaty"), signed between the British and most Māori tribes "had the potential to deliver benefits to all parties" (Durie 2005, 15). However, in the 1850s, the newly established settler govern-ment attempted to revamp Māori land tenure and impose British concepts of title and ownership. Māori who resisted had their lands forcibly confiscated. Durie states that:

> By 1900, land alienation had eroded tribal estates from 29,880,000 hectares to a mere 3,200,000 hectares; fishing rights had been presumed to amount to no more than non-commercial fishing rights; and subsurface rights, as well as rights to harbours and the foreshore, had been claimed by the Crown. (14)

Standards of living among Māori declined to the extent that Māori popula-tions began to decrease in the 1870s. Durie (2005, 16) notes that, despite ex-pectations that the Māori were destined for extinction, new institutions emerged that contributed to a resurgence of Māori populations, cultures, and political influence. The 1900 Māori Councils Act, which set up local Māori authorities, was introduced in order to diffuse the challenge of Māori attempts to promote self-government. With increased attention to Māori health issues as a result of the act, Māori populations began to increase. The rural economy could not sup-port a growing labour force, and while the Great Depression created hardships for all New Zealanders, it took a particularly heavy toll on Māori communities.

In 1933, the estimated Māori unemployment rate was at 33 percent, compared to 12 percent for the Pākehā population (Tremblay and Forest 1993, 39).

Unlike treaties signed in Canada and the United States, the Treaty of Waitangi did not make provision for the establishment of reserves or reservations. Despite this, Māori were a rural people during the nineteenth century and for the first half of the twentieth century. In the 1920s, convinced of the negative consequences of Māori urbanization, the New Zealand government began to introduce policies to ensure that Māori remained in rural areas. According to Barcham (2004, 164) "the ultimate outcome of policies aimed at keeping Māori out of urban environments was the creation of state-funded Māori farming." Prior to the Second World War, approximately 90 percent of the Māori population lived in rural areas, mostly in tribal territories (Walker 1990).

Several interrelated factors contributed to rapid Māori urbanization following the Second World War: demand for manufacturing and service labour grew more quickly than the non-Māori labour force could supply; Māori population growth outstripped the resource capacity of Māori communities; the subdivision of Māori land meant that many farms were unable to provide adequate economic support; and the areas most heavily populated by Māori experienced a generally slow rate of economic development (Butterworth 1991). In 1951, almost a quarter of the Māori population lived in urban areas (Metge 1964). The Hunn Report (Hunn 1960), released in 1961, signalled a dramatic change in the New Zealand government's approach to Māori urbanization. Like Canada's Hawthorn Report (Hawthorn 1966-67), the Hunn Report viewed urbanization as a means of bridging gaps in health, employment, and education between Māori people and other New Zealanders. In contrast to earlier policies of segregation, the New Zealand government's policy now emphasized integration through urbanization. The key idea behind "integration" was that Māori should adopt Western cultural norms and behaviours in order to succeed in urban society. Relocation policies, like those in Canada and the United States, actively encouraged Māori movement into urban areas and provided financial and other support to migrants. By 1966, two-thirds of Māori were living in urban areas, the results of what Pool (1991) describes as the most accelerated movement experienced by any population.

Early Māori urbanization resulted in some cultural dislocation as migrants were separated from supportive rural community relationships and faced with the demands of a wage labour economy. In response, voluntary associations emerged in the form of Māori culture clubs, sports clubs, religious and tribal associations, Māori executive committees and councils, Māori wardens, and the Māori Women's Welfare League (Walker 1979). Working against state

expectations of integration through assimilation, the objective of these voluntary associations was cultural continuity and the survival of the growing Māori
community (Walker 1990). The 1960s saw the widespread establishment of
urban *marae*, consecrated grounds and meeting places and the location for
important celebrations and ceremonies based on voluntary association and co-
location rather than on the kinship and descent organization of rural *marae*.
Language and educational opportunities created cultural support in urban
areas (Kukutai, this volume). According to Durie (2004, 22), "Māori were now
less closely defined by tribal affiliation than by locality and occupation."
Beginning in 1984, Māori in a number of cities established multitribal urban
Māori authorities to foster the economic, social, and commercial development
of urban Māori communities. Urbanization provided a catalyst for the development of new forms of social institutions.

As occurred in other countries, in New Zealand Māori rights activism that
focused on rural issues had an important urban history. According to Barcham
(2004, 168-69), urbanization was accompanied by an increase in the number of
Māori tertiary graduates who, "raised in the urban environment and unsure of
their position in New Zealand society, were dissatisfied with the status of Māori
and began in the late 1960s to actively agitate for change." This new protest
movement influenced the passage of the Treaty of Waitangi Act, 1975, which
established the Waitangi Tribunal to allow Māori to pursue grievances concerning the Treaty (see Hokowhitu, this volume). Increasingly, activists also argued
for Māori control of the resources allocated to them by the government, in-
sisting that they understood their own needs best and could deal with them
more effectively than government agencies. In the environment of devolution
and then contracting out of government services to service providers in New
Zealand in the 1980s, urban Māori authorities were able to assume the management of programs in the areas of employment, welfare, and economic development. In 1998, the Waitangi Tribunal recommended that urban Māori authorities
should have the same rights to receive grants and to deliver services as did
traditional tribes. In the same year, however, a series of court cases determined
that only *iwi* (traditional tribes), and not urban Māori authorities, could benefit
financially from treaty settlement. As a result, there are continuing tensions concerning rights and representation between iwi and urban pan-tribal organizations (Maaka 1994). Coombes (this volume) argues that the contemporary
emphasis on iwi as representing Māori interests positions urban Māori as less
authentic and not rights-bearing communities, and undermines their abilities to
influence the environmental conditions of their communities in urban areas.

In contrast to assumptions that Māori identities would dissolve with urbanization, Durie (2005) characterizes Māori urbanization as one of a number of transitions made by Māori peoples over their histories. Recognizing continuity as well as re-creation, he notes:

> Fifty years of urbanization have demonstrated that it has been possible to live side by side with other New Zealanders without being assimilated into a homogenous way of life. It has been possible to retain links with whānau (extended family) and hapū (clan). It has been possible to recreate a sense of community that is not dissimilar to whānau. (24)

References

Barcham, M. 2004. The politics of Māori mobility. In *Population mobility and Indigenous peoples in Australasia and North America*, ed. J. Taylor and M. Bell, 163-83. New York: Routledge.

Butterworth, G.V. 1991. *Ngā Take I Neke Ai Te Māori: A journeying people.* Wellington, NZ: Manatu Māori.

Durie, M. 2005. *Ngā Tai Matatū: Tides of Māori endurance.* South Melbourne, AU: Oxford University Press.

Hawthorn, H.B., ed. 1966-67. *A survey of the contemporary Indians of Canada: A report of economic, political and educational needs and policies.* Ottawa: Queen's Printer.

Hunn, J.K. 1960. *Report on Department of Māori Affairs.* Wellington, NZ: Government Printer.

Maaka, R. 1994. The new tribe: Conflicts and continuities in the social organization of urban Māori. *Contemporary Pacific* 6(2): 311-36.

Meredith, P. 2000. Urban Maori as "new citizens": The quest for recognitions and resources. Paper presented to the Revisioning Citizenship in New Zealand conference, University of Waikato, 22-24 February.

Metge, J. 1964. *A new Maori migration: Rural and urban relations in northern New Zealand.* London: Athlone.

Pool, I. 1991. *Te ewe Maori: A New Zealand population past, present and projected.* Auckland, NZ: Auckland University Press.

Tremblay, J.-F., and P.-G. Forest. 1993. *Aboriginal peoples and self-determination: A few aspects of government policy in four selected countries.* Quebec City: Secrétariat aux affaires autochtones.

Walker, R. 1979. The urban Māori. In *He Matapuna: A source – Some Maori perspectives,* 32-41. Wellington, NZ: New Zealand Planning Council.

–. 1990. *Ka whawhai tonu matou: Struggle without end.* Auckland, NZ: Penguin.

Williams, H.W. 1971. A dictionary of the Maori language. 7th ed. Wellington, NZ: Government Printer.

14

The Structure of Urban Māori Identities

TAHU KUKUTAI

The rural-urban migration of New Zealand's Indigenous Māori people has frequently been described as one of the most rapid and intense of any population in the world (see Gibson 1973; Pool 1991). Before 1945, most Māori lived in rural, semi-subsistent communities, concentrated in the eastern and northern parts of the North Island. Within two decades, and for reasons that have been widely documented (Hunn 1961; McCreary 1968; Metge 1964; Pool 1966, 1977, 1991; Bedford and Pool 2004; Poulsen and Johnstone 1973), Māori underwent a massive rural exodus, reducing the rural share from three-quarters to just over one-third. Today the vast majority of Māori – 85 percent – live in statistically defined urban areas, comparable with the level recorded for non-Indigenous New Zealanders. Statistically, Māori are unequivocally an urban people. What this means substantively, however, is less certain. Though the urbanization of Māori may be near universal and no longer new, there are many dimensions of urban Māori identities and experiences that are still not well understood. Using statistical analyses of recent census data, this chapter explores the structure of contemporary identities and circumstances of Māori in urban spaces, providing a macro-level context for the more qualitative insights into urban Māori communities that follow.

In defining the parameters of urban Māori, the nuanced meanings that lie beneath this apparently neutral term require unpacking. There is no univocal, definitive meaning of what it means to be urbanized, Māori, or an urbanized Māori. Urbanization may be viewed vis-à-vis the economic and social transformations begat by spatial reorganization (often articulated in terms of "modernization") or, more narrowly, as the process by which populations become increasingly concentrated in areas that are legally or statistically defined as urban (Bedford and Pool 2004). The latter approach might appear straightforward but it involves a number of subjective, and somewhat arbitrary, distinctions. In New Zealand, the statistical definition of "urban area" ranges from small provincial towns with as few as one thousand residents (defined as minor urban areas) to cities with up to 400,000 (major urban areas). Whether living in an area designated as urban begets the label "urban Māori" is an important question. Certainly the issues, needs, and experiences of Māori living in small urban towns are likely to vary from those of their kinfolk living in densely populated metropolitan areas. To accommodate this complexity, the following analysis limits the definition of urban Māori to those residing in "cities,"[1] and it contrasts their socioeconomic, demographic, and cultural characteristics with those of Māori living beyond the city. Consideration is also given to the diversity that exists within and across cityscapes.

Who or what constitutes the Māori people is also a complex and highly contested question (Kukutai 2004; Pool 1991). Statistical representations of Indigenous peoples are constrained by official identity categories that are socially constructed and historically contingent. The concepts associated with such categories, and their usage, reflect implicit ideologies about what an "ideal" society ought to look like, how it ought to function, and who should be included within the bounds of nationhood and citizenship (Nobles 2000). Consequently, how Indigenous peoples see themselves, and how they are rendered visible in official forums such as the census, are often disconnected (see Andersen, this volume). Māori are no exception. Prior to 1986, the census and other official data collections used the concept of blood quantum to capture group membership, which is at odds with Māori conceptions of identity as centred on kinship ties. For much of the twentieth century, only those reported as "half or more" Māori were statistically counted in the Māori population.[2] The state's interest in "half-castes" was clearly linked to colonial polices of racial amalgamation, with the expectation that Māori would eventually lose their separate identity and become absorbed into what one government minister described as a "white race with a slight dash of the finest coloured race in the world" (cited in Belich 2001, 190).

Blood quantum has since been dispensed with, and, since 1991, census-based expressions of Māori identity have been expanded to include ethnic belonging, descent, and tribal identification (Kukutai 2004). However, because most census data about Māori are disseminated solely on the basis of ethnicity, the options to explore Māori identities in this chapter are limited. The following analysis is limited to Māori ethnicity data, but, where possible, a distinction is drawn between those who identified only as Māori (Māori Alone) and those reporting a complex Māori identification (Māori Plus).

I begin with a historical overview of Māori urbanization, briefly tracing key economic, social, and cultural transformations. An overview of these is vital for understanding the structures that have shaped contemporary urban Māori identities. The empirical analysis examines the spatial distribution of Māori in the 2006 census before turning to socio-economic status. The persistent disadvantage of Māori relative to the dominant European ethnic group (Blakely et al. 2005; Sporle, Pearce, and Davis 2002; Te Puni Kōkiri 2000) reflects the disadvantaged circumstances of Indigenes throughout the settler states (see, for example, Cooke et al. 2007). The complexity of ethnic inequality in New Zealand is also complicated by the considerable intra-Māori heterogeneity in class position (Chapple 2000; Durie 2005; Kukutai 2004, 2010). The following analysis thus considers intra-Māori as well as inter-ethnic diversity in educational attainment and occupational status.

The final section considers where urban-dwelling Māori fit in terms of Māori language revitalization and the political economy of retribalization. The latter has seen the emergence of *iwi* (traditional tribes) as major economic and political institutions, driven largely by government policy and financial settlements relating to the historical alienation of Māori land and resources (Barcham 1998; Hokowhitu, this volume; Rata 2000; Webster 2002). One consequence of retribalization has been the bifurcation of tribal and urban identities and interests. Much of this has been played out at the political level, involving competitive claims between tribal organizations, whose members are defined by genealogical ties, and urban authorities representing Māori communities defined by urban residence. At the symbolic level, however, urban Māori have also been discursively positioned as less tribal, less culturally endowed, and less "authentic" than their counterparts "at home" (see Coombes, this volume). This chapter examines patterns of iwi growth and identification to assess whether urban residence and tribal identification are mutually exclusive or reinforcing demographic processes.

It concludes with a brief discussion of what the foregoing themes mean for understanding contemporary Māori urban identities.

Māori Urbanization: History and Background

New Zealand is a South Pacific nation, comprised of two main islands, with an estimated population of 4.4 million in 2011 (Statistics New Zealand 2011a). A former British colony, New Zealand has a history of ethnic relations that has largely been one of two peoples: Māori, often described as a Polynesian people; and "Europeans," or "Pākehā," who are white, mostly British-descent, New Zealanders (King 1985). European exploration of New Zealand began with an offshore sighting by Dutch navigator Abel Tasman in 1642, but it was not until 1769 that extensive mapping and exploration was undertaken by English explorer Captain James Cook. The Treaty of Waitangi, 1840, signed between nearly five hundred chiefs and representatives of Queen Victoria, paved the way for rapid and expansive British colonization. By the turn of the nineteenth century, most Māori were living in abject poverty. Land alienation through *raupatu* (confiscation under the New Zealand Settlements Act, 1863), direct Crown purchase, and the dubious machinations of the Native Land Court greatly depleted the Māori estate (Williams 1999).

Prior to European settlement, Māori internal migration was extensive, reflecting factors such as changing political alliances and competition for resources. By the late nineteenth century, short-term Māori mobility was well established and included circular and seasonal migrations linked to cultivations and working in the cash economy, for example in shearing and road gangs. However, after the Second World War, the nature of Māori mobility changed dramatically in magnitude and scope. As Figure 14.1 illustrates, the urban Māori population increased from one-quarter to over three-fifths of the Māori population total in two decades, and it increased fivefold in number. Between 1961 and 1966, the number of rural Māori actually declined by about 14 percent.[3] This is remarkable given that Māori population growth in the decade from 1956 to 1966 was almost 4 percent per annum (Pool 1991, 141). Such high growth rates are now rarely seen. In 2009, for example, Liberia was the only country in the world that recorded annual growth in excess of 4 percent (World Bank 2011).

The regional distribution of Māori society also changed dramatically in the postwar period. In 1945, for example, one in five Māori lived in the Northland region; and only 6 percent lived in Auckland. By 1966, those

FIGURE 14.1 Percentage of Māori* and non-Māori† in urban and in main urban areas 1926-2006

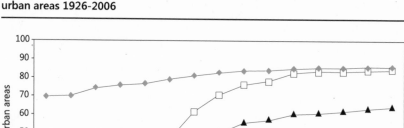

* From 1926 to 1981, persons reporting "some degree of Māori blood." In 1986, persons reporting Māori ethnic origins, either alone or in combination with some other group. From 1991 to 2006, persons reporting Māori ethnicity, either alone or in combination with some other group.
† From 1926 to 1981, persons not reporting any "degree of Māori blood." From 1986 onwards, the total NZ population.
Source: New Zealand Census of Population and Dwellings, various years.

shares had changed to 6 and 29 percent, respectively (Pool 1991, Table 7.15). The most popular destinations for migrants were neighbouring towns and small cities as well as urban areas in Auckland and Wellington. Smaller urban areas contiguous with rural areas with a high Māori concentration also grew at a tremendous rate (e.g., Hamilton and Rotorua [Bedford and Pool 2004; Pool 1991]). As Figure 14.1 shows, movement to main urban areas accounted for the majority of shifts. By 1971, half of the Māori population resided in such areas.

Apart from the rapidity of the rural Māori exodus, Figure 14.1 shows a striking spatial separation between Indigenous and non-Indigenous New Zealanders that lasted well into the twentieth century. In 1926, the vast majority of the non-Māori, mainly British settlers and their descendants, were already urbanized. By the start of the Second World War, three-quarters were living in urban-designated areas, geographically separated from the rural isolation of most Māori communities. Thus, as Pool (1991) notes, even in the absence of de jure segregation or Native reserves in the North American sense, de facto separation between Māori and Pākehā prevailed.

Economic Transformations

Prior to the Second World War, the Māori economy was largely a semi-subsistent one. Māori efforts to consolidate their residual fragmented land holdings into incorporations and to develop large-scale farming enterprises were, for many reasons, only partially successful. Nevertheless, the prevailing sentiment was that the key to Māori progress lay in rural tribal development. This position was thoroughly revised in the face of rural population pressures and the postwar manufacturing boom, both of which provided a compelling incentive for a change of tact.

One of the key legacies of urbanization was the economic incorporation of Māori into an expanding industrial economy. In 1945, just over half of the Māori male industrial labour force (twice the European share) was concentrated in the primary sector, with most of the remainder in the secondary sector. With urbanization, three shifts occurred. First a primary-secondary sectoral shift occurred that, by 1966, saw the majority of the Māori workforce located in the secondary sector (Pool 1991, Table 7.11). Over the next two decades, more Māori moved into the tertiary sector, albeit the overall level remained well below that of Pākehā. Finally, between 1986 and 2001, the country underwent major economic restructuring, which had a very negative impact upon the Māori. As occurred elsewhere in the industrialized nations, the manufacturing sector severely contracted and the financial services sector greatly expanded. The jobs in which Māori were disproportionately concentrated were either eliminated or downsized dramatically (e.g., Pool, Kukutai, and Sceats 2008). Paradoxically, as restructuring exposed the vulnerability of the Māori labour force, a growing share of Māori, especially women, entered managerial and professional jobs. These processes of intra-Māori segmentation are discussed elsewhere (Kukutai 2010) and are drawn on in subsequent analyses.

Cultural and Social Transformations

Urbanization played an important role in the imagining, and forging, of a pan-tribal collective Māori identity. Māori migrant workers and their families were assisted into urban areas through training, employment, and housing schemes, including low-interest home loans. Such policies explicitly sought to avoid the slum problem in the United States by locating Māori families in predominantly "white" suburban neighbourhoods alongside Pākehā. By the 1970s, however, the development of large, low-income housing estates in Auckland and Wellington meant that there were sizeable suburbs of Māori and Pacific Island migrants (Otara-Māngere in Auckland and Porirua in Wellington; see Bedford and Pool 2004). The government envisaged that Māori committees established by the Māori Economic and Advancement Act, 1945, under the auspices of the Department of Māori Affairs, would help ease the adjustment of Māori migrants. Such committees were intended to assist Māori to become more Westernized and, thus, assimilated; but, instead, Māori often used them for their own purposes (Hill 2005). Over time, urban-based communities of interest were established to fulfil particular needs. These included Māori community centres, churches, cultural groups, and even *marae* – meeting places traditionally linked to specific iwi and *hapū* (subtribes). Most of these urban institutions were pan-tribal or non-tribal in character, marking a significant break from tribally structured rural life. In her classic study of Māori migrants in the 1950s, Metge (1964, 58) observes that, for many, "the tribe was largely an abstract concept." Nearly thirty years later, Pool argued that transformations in demography and economy had created tension within certain cultural axes, which had remained largely poised on rural marae. He proposed that Māori social life had become "increasingly dichotomized" between urban homes and rural homelands (Pool 1991, 160).

From the 1950s, Māori migrants increasingly became the object of scholarly attention (Kawharu 1968; Metge 1964; Schwimmer 1968; Harré 1966). For a full review, see Bedford and Heenan (1987, 152-55). Some studies highlight resilience and adaptation, evident in the refashioning of old institutions and the creation of new ones to meet urban migrant needs. Others draw attention to the problems attendant upon urbanization: cultural dislocation, crime, and under-employment. New sorts of racial tensions emerged as Māori were bought into closer contact with Europeans as workmates, neighbours, and sports mates. Commentators of the day noted the existence of racial prejudice towards Māori but were conflicted about its importance. In his study of Māori-European intermarriage in Auckland, Harré (1966, 144) muses that prejudice against Māori was more "a reaction to their overall position of low socio-economic status than a device for maintaining this position." American David Ausubel (1961, 224) gives a somewhat harsher assessment, arguing that extra-legal discriminatory practices directed at Māori in employment, housing, and other key spheres of life were "not unlike those directed against Negroes in northern areas of the United States."

Indeed, the plight of racial and Indigenous minorities in the United States, and the subsequent rise of new social movements, including Black Power and Red Power, would provide a backdrop for the rise of Māori

Indigenous rights (Hokowhitu, this volume). From the late 1960s onwards, urban Māori, and urban academics in particular, played a key role in Māori grassroots activism, calling upon governments to account for recognitive (cultural), distributive (economic), and reparative (compensatory) claims. The Māori language, Te Reo Māori, was at the heart of efforts to reclaim Māori culture, identity, and political rights. Colonial policies of cultural assimilation, with various attendant sanctions, meant Māori language usage had declined sharply as the twentieth century passed. Urban Māori activists were instrumental in the movement to have Māori recognized as an official language (this occurred in 1987). Eventually, Māori was legitimized as an alternative language of instruction in Māori-run institutions and, to a lesser extent, in the mainstream. These initiatives, combined with the expansion of the tertiary education sector, mean that there are now more opportunities than at any time in the past to acquire Te Reo Māori outside of the family. These important institutional shifts mean that the "cultural" differences between urban and other Māori may not be as significant as they are typically assumed to be.

Retribalization

A more recent transformation, and one that is relevant to any discussion of urban Māori identities, is the re-emergence of tribes as key political and corporate players. Retribalization has positioned tribes as the logical beneficiaries of reparations for historical injustices and as the ideal(ized) vehicle for delivering genuine self-determination to Māori (Barcham 1998). However, critics have raised questions about the place of Māori migrants, their children, and grandchildren, who may lack a meaningful connection to, or even knowledge about, their tribal heritage. In her critique of "neo-tribal capitalism," Rata (2000) argues that new forms of tribal authority have magnified, rather than ameliorated, class and cultural divisions among Māori. Government policies, she goes on to say, have created the opportunities for reconstructed "neo-traditionalist" tribal corporate entities to receive and manage assets from settlements relating to treaty breaches and land confiscation. However, instead of providing a salve for historical injustices, tribal elites have strategically appropriated traditionalist ideologies to maintain a façade of non-exploitative relations while "concealing the underlying exploitative character of tribal capitalism" (102). Rata's arguments reflect a more general positioning of urban and tribal interests as competitive, and of urban and tribal identities as incompatible. This may be the case at the organizational level, but the fluid and subjective nature of personal identity, combined with the role of urban Māori in the so-called "Māori Renaissance," means the urban-tribal distinction is likely to be far more blurred in a demographic sense. It is to the issue of contemporary urban Māori demography that we now turn.

Contemporary Māori Urbanization: A Structural Overview

As a result of the changes outlined in the foregoing section, urban-dwelling Māori in the twenty-first century have inherited particular demographic structures. This section examines some of these, focusing on the most recent decade.

Spatial distribution

As noted earlier, the statistical meaning of "urban area" in New Zealand is broad, making it helpful to consider the distribution of Māori across areas with different population densities. Table 14.1 presents data for Māori for the period between 1986 and 2006, with figures for the total New Zealand population (which includes Māori) provided as a comparator.

TABLE 14.1

Percentage of Māori, Māori subgroups, and total New Zealand population in urban and rural areas, 1986, 1996, and 2006 Census

		Area*			
Population group	Census	Main urban	Secondary urban	Minor urban	Rural
Māori	1986	61.0	7.5	13.8	17.6
	1996	62.4	7.0	13.7	16.8
	2006	64.7	6.9	12.8	15.5
(Māori Alone)†		(61.7)	(7.1)	(14.6)	(16.6)
(Māori Plus)†		(68.0)	(6.8)	(10.8)	(14.4)
Total NZ	1986	67.5	7.1	9.2	16.2
	1996	70.2	6.5	8.7	14.6
	2006	71.8	6.0	8.1	14.0

* Main urban areas have a minimum population of 30,000; secondary urban areas have a population of between 10,000 and 29,999; minor urban areas are urbanized settlements with a population of between 1,000 and 9,999.

† Māori Alone comprises those who reported an exclusive Māori ethnic identification; Māori Plus comprises those who reported several ethnic groups, including Maori.

Source: New Zealand Census of Population and Dwellings, 1986, 1996, and 2006.

Tahu Kukutai

Table 14.1 shows that, by 1986, the Māori urban concentration closely reflected the national pattern, but with some unique features. Compared to the national pattern, Māori had a lower percentage living in main urban areas and a higher percentage living in minor urban areas. In 2006, one in eight Māori were still residing in small, non-rural towns located mostly in the northern, eastern, and central parts of the North Island.

The greater tendency for Māori to be concentrated in less densely populated and more isolated towns is more apparent if a distinction is made between people whose ethnic identification was exclusively Māori (Māori Alone) and those who recorded Māori as one of two or more ethnic groups (Māori Plus). The Māori Alone pattern is an exaggerated form of the general Māori pattern, with a higher percentage in minor urban areas. The Māori Plus pattern is closer to the national pattern, with a stronger concentration in main urban centres. The differences between the Māori categories reflect a number of factors, including the greater propensity of Māori with diverse ethnic backgrounds to live in cities, higher inter-ethnic marriage rates within more densely populated urban areas, and the greater propensity of Māori living in main urban areas to identify themselves in more complex ways.

Table 14.2 extends the analysis to inter-ethnic and intra-Māori distribution across cities and districts. A distinction is made between North Island and South Island localities and districts that contain at least one main urban area. Two sets of indicators are shown for 2006, the most recently available census. One is Māori population density within select cities and districts, the other is the distribution of Māori and non-Māori across cities and districts.

There is a significant, though not dramatic, city-district difference in Māori population density. Māori accounted for just over 10 percent of the combined population in New Zealand's sixteen cities, compared to almost 20 percent of the total district population. It should be noted that, in 2006, Māori comprised 14.6 percent of the total NZ population. There was, however, considerable variation *within* cities and districts, reflecting the effects of historical and more recent migration patterns. In the Far North District – a traditional Māori stronghold in the north of the North Island – just under half of the population was Māori, compared to less than 10 percent in the combined South Island districts. Even for city-dwelling Māori in Auckland – New Zealand's most densely concentrated and multicultural region and, since 2010, home to the country's only "supercity" – propinquity to other Māori varied considerably.[4] For example, Māori comprised just over 6 percent of the North Shore City populace, compared to 15 percent in Manukau

TABLE 14.2

Percentage of Māori and Māori subgroups in and across select cities and districts, 2006 Census

Cities and districts	Percent Māori	Distribution of Maori across cities and districts (percent)			
		Māori	Māori Alone	Māori Plus	Non-Māori
Cities					
Auckland cities	10.5	19.9	17.2	22.9	29.0
North shore	6.3	2.2	1.5	3.0	5.7
Manukau	15.3	8.4	8.4	8.3	8.0
Wellington cities	12.6	7.9	6.9	9.0	9.3
Porirua	20.9	1.7	1.5	2.0	1.1
Wellington	7.7	2.4	1.7	3.1	4.8
North Island cities	12.4	38.8	35.4	42.6	47.1
South Island cities	8.0	7.7	5.8	9.8	15.2
Total cities	11.3	46.5	41.2	52.4	62.3
Districts					
North Island districts	23.2	48.2	54.8	40.8	26.6
Urban districts*	24.4	20.7	23.6	17.4	11.0
Far North	44.0	3.9	4.9	2.8	0.9
South Island districts	7.6	5.3	4.0	6.8	11.1
Total districts	17.4	53.5	58.8	47.6	37.7
New Zealand†		14.6	7.7	6.9	85.4

* Urban district is not an official statistical term but is used here to denote a local government district that contains at least one main urban area (e.g., Whangarei District, Wanganui District). All urban districts are in the North Island
† Total NZ population that stated at least one ethnic group.
Source: Census of Population and Dwellings, 2006.

City. At their closest boundaries, the cities are only separated by about thirty-two kilometres.

Non-Indigenous New Zealanders were far more likely than were Māori to be living in cities (62 percent), and especially in Auckland's four cities (29 percent versus 20 percent for Māori). The majority of Māori lived in districts (54 percent) versus cities, though nearly half of the districts contained at least one main urban area. The latter areas have a higher concentration of

Māori (almost one-quarter) than either cities or districts as a whole. Consistent with the subgroup differences evident in Table 14.1, Table 14.2 shows significant subgroup differences across cities and districts as well as within them. More than half of those in the Māori combined category resided in cities, compared to two-fifths giving a singular Māori identification. Taken together, the foregoing shows that, while the broad Māori population is heavily urbanized, and has been for several decades, inter-ethnic and intra-Māori differences in spatial location also need to be borne in mind.

Age Structure

Major differences in the age structures of Indigenous and non-Indigenous New Zealanders are a well-known feature of the country's demography (for detailed discussions of the determinants of these differences, see Pool 1991). In 2011, the estimated median age for Māori was 23.0 years compared to 36.8 years for the total New Zealand population (Statistics New Zealand 2011a, 2011b).[5] Using data from the 2006 census, Figures 14.2 and 14.3 reveal significant, though not dramatic, city-district differences in age composition for Māori. For both men and women, a higher proportion of Māori living in cites (versus districts) were concentrated in the younger working ages (twenty-four to forty-four years), reflecting a broader national pattern. City-district differences in age composition have arisen from a number of

FIGURE 14.2 Percentage of Māori and total NZ population (males) in cities and districts, by functional age group, 2006 Census

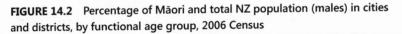
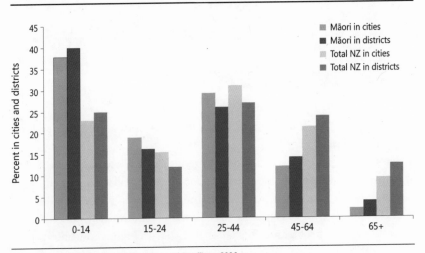

Source: New Zealand Census of Population and Dwellings, 2006.

FIGURE 14.3 Percentage of Māori and total NZ population (females) in cities and districts, by functional age group, 2006 Census

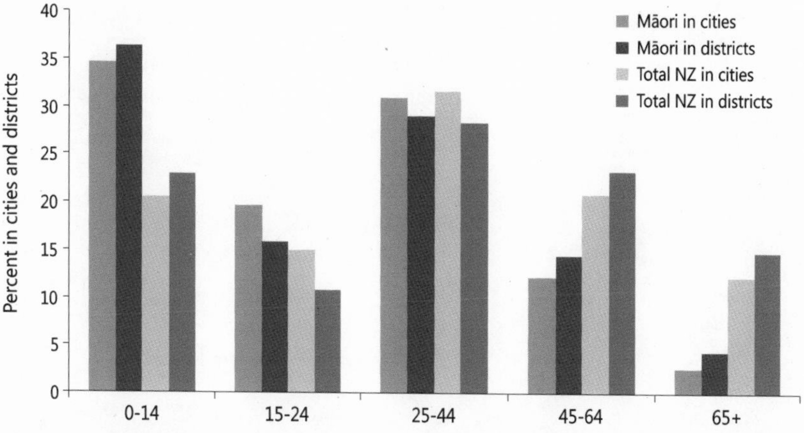

Source: New Zealand Census of Population and Dwellings, 2006.

factors, including the structure of labour markets, education/training opportunities in cities, and age-specific mobility patterns (Sin and Stillman 2005). The Māori district population had, in turn, a higher proportion at the youngest and oldest ages, similar to the pattern observed at the national level.

Socio-Economic Differences

This section considers how urban Māori experiences have been shaped by socio-economic and cultural differences between Māori. Intra-Māori heterogeneity in socio-economic status has attracted more scholarly interest in recent years, with most analysis showing a negative association between stronger ties to Māori identification and indicators of socio-economic status (Chapple 2000; Kukutai 2004, 2010). Others have shown considerable intra-regional differences in earnings for Māori, though typically of a lesser magnitude than intra-regional income inequality among Pākehā (Pool et al. 2005). Table 14.3 presents city-district data from the 2001 census for two SES indicators: (1) percentage without a formal qualification and (2) percentage in managerial and professional occupations. Analysis is limited to those in the younger working ages, 24 to 45 years.

In terms of educational profiles, a significantly higher percentage of Māori in districts lacked a formal qualification than their city-dwelling

TABLE 14.3
Percentage of Māori and total NZ population with no formal qualification
in managerial and professional occupations, men and women combined,
24-45 years, select cities and districts, 2001 Census

Cities and districts	No formal qualification		In managerial and professional occupations	
	Māori	Total NZ	Māori	Total NZ
Cities				
Auckland cities	36.7	19.7	22.6	34.1
North Shore	25.6	13.4	25.4	37.2
Manukau	45.7	29.1	16.9	25.9
Hamilton	37.3	24.1	23.1	32.3
Wellington cities	32.0	21.0	27.2	38.9
Porirua	37.3	29.2	23.3	31.0
Wellington	20.7	10.1	37.0	46.2
North Island Cities	35.9	20.1	23.4	34.7
South Island Cities	33.7	24.4	20.2	28.9
Total cities	35.5	21.1	22.8	34.9
Districts				
North Island districts	44.4	33.3	16.8	24.5
Urban districts	41.8	31.4	17.9	27.0
Far North	45.8	40.0	19.0	24.3
South Island districts	36.8	28.1	14.7	21.5
Total districts	43.7	32.0	16.6	23.7
New Zealand	39.9	25.5	19.6	30.4

Source: Census of Population and Dwellings, 2001.

counterparts (44 percent versus 36 percent). This was a more muted version of the national pattern of city-district disparities in education. Within every district and city, Māori had a higher percentage lacking a formal education than did the general population. Moving beyond city-district comparisons reveals considerable inter-city variation for Māori. In Manukau City, for example, nearly half of the population aged twenty-four to forty-five was without a formal qualification, compared to just 20 percent of Māori in Wellington City. It is important to note that the educational gap between Māori in Manukau and Wellington dwarfed the differences between Māori and the total population in either city. This reflects, in part, the unique character of Wellington, which is the nation's political capital and a beacon for educated New Zealanders, regardless of ethnicity. Overall, only one in ten Wellington City residents lacked a formal qualification, much lower than the national average of one in four.

The data on occupational structure show a similar pattern. In Wellington City, more than one-third of Māori were managers or professionals, compared to just 17 percent of Māori in Manukau City. Similar to the pattern of disparities in education, city-district differences in the percentage in managerial and professional jobs were lower for Māori (6.2 percentage points) than they were for the national population (11.2 percentage points). Unfortunately, comparable data for the Māori Alone and Māori Plus categories were not readily available, but existing research suggests such data would reveal significant differences between the categories, in addition to the intra-city and intra-district disparities already noted.

Te Reo Māori and Iwi Identification
Historical studies of urban Māori, and indeed of Aboriginal or Indigenous urbanization generally, have tended to view Indigenous urban dwellers as less culturally endowed (or less "authentic") than their counterparts living in remote or rural heartlands or on reservations. Such a view assumes that urban Natives differ from their rural kin qualitatively as well as quantitatively. Is this view empirically supported in the New Zealand context? Though the census is limited in what it can reveal about ties to cultural institutions, attitudes, and complex identities, we can assess whether urban Māori are distinctive with regard to two traditional markers of Māori identification: (1) the ability to speak Te Reo Māori and (2) iwi/tribal identification. Their usage here is not intended to essentialize Māori identity but, rather, to gauge the extent to which city-dwelling Māori have access to, and a connection with, these traditional markers of identity.

City-district differences in self-reported Māori language ability are apparent in Table 14.4 but are dwarfed by differences within cities and districts. In Hamilton City, for example, 30 percent of Māori reported Māori language proficiency, but this was the case for only 19 percent in Auckland's North Shore City. In the districts, more than one-third of Māori in the Far North could speak Māori, compared to just 16 percent in the combined South Island districts. Not surprisingly, these differences were greatly influenced by the greater propensity to speak Māori in areas with a higher Māori concentration.

Alongside Te Reo, the other symbolic lynchpin of Māori identity is *whakapapa*, or genealogical ties, often expressed in terms of ties to whānau,

TABLE 14.4
Percentage of Māori able to speak Te Reo Māori and percentage reporting
a tribe, select cities and districts, 2001 and 2006 Census

	Able to speak Māori	Report at least one iwi	
Cities and districts	2001	2001	2006
Cities			
Auckland cities	21.8	73.4	78.3
North Shore	19.0	71.9	75.9
Manukau	23.3	75.0	80.1
Hamilton	29.9	76.7	80.0
Wellington cities	25.8	77.3	81.3
Porirua	26.8	79.9	84.3
Wellington	24.6	76.7	80.9
North Island cities	24.0	74.5	79.0
South Island cities	20.4	74.2	78.7
Total cities	23.3	73.8	78.3
Districts			
North Island districts	29.2	77.3	81.6
Urban districts	28.7	77.2	81.6
Far North	35.4	82.7	88.3
South Island districts	16.2	69.1	73.3
Total districts	28.0	76.4	80.7

Source: Census of Population and Dwellings, 2001 and 2006.

hapū, and iwi. Perspectives explored earlier in this chapter suggest that urban Māori are less likely than non-urban Māori to express traditional tribal identities. However, Table 14.4 shows minor city-district differences in tribal identification. In both years, the percentage of city-dwelling Māori reporting a tribal identification was only slightly smaller than the percentage of those living outside cities (78 percent versus 81 percent in 2006). Even in North Shore City, where Māori formed a relatively small proportion of the populace, three-quarters were tribally identified. Such figures reflect the increasing popularity of tribal identification generally – up from 77 percent of the Māori descent population in 1991 to 83 percent in 2006. Because census self-identification is not explicitly connected to tribal registration status, which is typically based on whakapapa, tribal affiliation in the census may simply denote a symbolic identity rather than a meaningful engagement with tribal institutions or networks (Walling, Small-Rodriguez, and Kukutai 2009). Nevertheless, the results do not fit easily with the interpretation, widely held, that urbanization implicitly weakens tribal ties, including expressive ones.

Following this theme, Table 14.5 presents more detailed analysis for the ten largest tribes at the 2001 census, distinguishing between affiliates in cities and districts. The point is to identify whether tribes vary in their capacity to accommodate these two important processes that structure contemporary Māori society: urbanization and retribalization. The results suggest that significant intra-tribal differences do exist. Between the 2001 and 2006 censuses, the ten largest iwi experienced quite different growth patterns, from a loss of 7 percent for the Waikato iwi to an almost 50 percent gain for Te Arawa. Clearly, the growth of individual iwi has been driven by changes in self-identification rather than by the usual demographic factors of natural increase or net migration. Likely factors influencing individuals' identification choices include changes in the political environment, including treaty-related settlements, and more sustained efforts by tribes to reach potential beneficiaries (Maaka 1994; Walling, Small-Rodriguez, and Kukutai 2009).

Interestingly, for the majority of the iwi shown here, the increased propensity to report an iwi affiliation was *more marked in cities* than in districts. This growth cannot be solely attributed to the faster growth of city-dwelling populations. Between 2001 and 2006, for example, the Maori descent population in cities increased by 7.6 percent compared to 5.8 percent in districts. For some iwi, such as Tūwharetoa and Te Arawa, the influence of increasing identification within cities was especially marked. There were also large intertribal differences in the percentage of members living within the tribe's boundaries as well as the level of urbanization. For example, Ngai Tahu, Ngāpuhi, and Waikato had a relatively high percentage of city-dwelling affiliates (between 47 and 54 percent), whereas Ngāti Awa had a relatively low share (around 34 percent). Some tribes, notably Waikato and Ngai Tahu, were structurally advantaged in being able to accommodate both urbanization and retribalization. This is because their boundaries subsume several major cities. For Waikato this includes Auckland, Manukau, and Hamilton; for Ngai Tahu this includes all of the four South Island cities: Nelson, Christchurch, Dunedin, and Invercargill. Such arrangements are advantageous in that members are able to exploit the benefits that come with the infrastructure of urban living (e.g., access to specialized labour markets, tertiary education providers, hospitals, etc.) as well as to remain within reach of tribal service providers and decision-making bodies. In coming years, iwi leaders

TABLE 14.5

Indicators for ten largest iwi, 2001 and 2006 Census

Iwi	Number		Intercensal growth (%)			Percent living within tribal boundaries		Percent living in cities nationally		Characteristics of tribal regions	
	2001	2006	Total	In cities	In districts	2001	2006	2001	2006	No. of cities	% Māori
Ngāti Awa	13,050	15,258	17.0	19.3	15.8	34.6	32.0	33.1	33.8	0	51.7
Ngāti Maniapoto	27,147	33,627	23.9	25.9	22.2	17.2	19.4	42.2	42.9	0	29.9
Tūhoe	29,244	32,670	11.7	14.6	10.0	30.0	28.4	35.3	36.2	0	49.6
Tūwharetoa	29,310	34,674	18.3	24.0	15.2	16.8	17.0	36.0	37.7	0	32.2
Te Arawa*	30,321	42,159	39.1	46.3	35.4	44.6	41.4	33.5	35.2	1	28.7
Waikato	35,787	33,429	-6.6	-6.7	-6.5	56.7	57.9	46.9	46.8	3	18.2
Ngai Tahu	39,186	49,185	25.5	25.5	25.6	56.3	54.4	54.2	54.1	4	7.8
Ngāti Kahungunu*	51,555	59,946	16.2	19.0	14.0	38.8	34.5	42.2	43.4	1	23.0
Ngāti Porou	61,692	71,910	16.5	17.4	15.8	19.4	17.2	43.7	44.0	0	47.3
Ngāpuhi	102,981	122,211	18.7	18.1	19.3	19.3	19.0	50.0	49.7	0	34.5

* Figures are for iwi groupings, rather than for individual iwi. Te Arawa Includes Ngāti Pikiao (Te Arawa), Ngāti Rangiteaorere (Te Arawa), Ngāti Rangitihi (Te Arawa), Ngāti Rangiwewehi (Te Arawa), Tapuika (Te Arawa), Tarāwhai (Te Arawa), Tūhourangi (Te Arawa), Uenuku-Kōpako (Te Arawa), Waitaha (Te Arawa), Ngāti Whakaue (Te Arawa), Ngāti Tahu-Ngāti Whaoa (Te Arawa) and Te Arawa waka /confederation. Ngāti Kahungunu includes Ngāti Kahungunu ki Te Wairoa, Ngāti Kahungunu ki Heretaunga, Ngāti Kahungunu ki Wairarapa, Ngāti Kahungunu, region unspecified, Ngāti Kahungunu ki Te Whanganui-a-Orotu, Ngāti Kahungunu ki Tamatea, Ngāti Kahungunu ki Tamakinui a Rua, (and in 2006) Ngāti Pāhauwera and Ngāti Rākaipaaka.

Source: Census of Population and Dwellings, 2001 and 2006.

will need to be attuned to these structural constraints and opportunities in order to plan for and accommodate the different experiences, capabilities, and aspirations of *iwi ahi ka* (those living within the rohe) and *iwi taura here* (those resident elsewhere) (Carter 2011).

Urban Māori: Synergies and Departures

Using data from recent censuses, this chapter seeks to identify some of the key structural elements of contemporary urban Māori identities. Though the use of census data permits broader insights into arrangements at the population and subpopulation levels, it is limited in other respects. There are likely to be qualitative differences between being urban and Māori, and an urban Māori, and such meanings are beyond the scope of this chapter. It has only been possible to examine urban Māori identities within the bounds of statistical definitions, though, where possible, I have tried to provide some nuance by employing various configurations of Māori identification and urban locality.

The qualitative literature suggests that, for some, urban Māori identity may signify a break with kinship and tribal structures. Such an urban Māori identity comes from being located in place, perhaps for several generations, and may or may not be tied to specific "cultural" institutions. Work by Borrell (2005) suggests that identity construction among urban Māori youth is strongly influenced by spatial context and peer groups, and only draws loosely on traditional markers of identity. For others, being urban and Māori is not inconsistent with expressions of belonging to more traditional Māori institutions such as iwi. Indeed, as this chapter shows, the increased propensity to record a tribal identification in the census has been most pronounced among city-dwelling Māori. That urban Māori have been instrumental in the growth of tribal populations is somewhat at odds with the view that urbanization and retribalization are opposing forces. Iwi leaders would do well to bear this in mind as they grapple with where members living "away from home" fit. The challenges associated with iwi disaporas are magnified for the global diaspora, who have become an increasingly important feature of Māori demography. With more than one in six Māori identified as living abroad in 2006 (Hamer 2009), the challenge of retaining connectedness with urban diasporas may soon be superseded by issues emerging from growing Māori transnationalism.

An underlying question in this study concerns whether binaries such as urban-rural, city-district, and urban-tribal are relevant for understanding the structure of contemporary urban Māori realities. Though the rural exodus certainly begat new sources of inequality and tension, neither the gloomy scenario of a culturally dislocated, urban Māori underclass nor the vision of intractable divides across rural-urban or urban-tribal lines has been borne out here. The analysis suggests that spatial differences – whether measured as rural-urban or city-district – do exist with regard to age structure and conventional indicators of socio-economic status, Māori language use, and iwi identification. However, in most instances, these differences are outweighed or matched by differences within cities and urban spaces as well as across regions. The many permutations of Māori identity and urban locality make a general description of urban Māori realities challenging. Such variation needs to be taken into account if the richness of urban Māori realities is to be fully understood. The results caution against the use of urban-rural or urban-tribal binaries and point to the need for more nuanced frameworks in examining urban Māori structures.

Notes

1 There is no statistical definition of "city." Cities and districts are local government areas known as territorial authorities, with boundaries set by the Local Government Commission. Of the seventy-three territorial authorities existing in 2006, sixteen were city councils. Spatial analyses of urbanization typically employ the urban area statistical classification developed by Statistics New Zealand (e.g., rural to major urban area) rather than local government boundaries. However, ethnic-specific urban data were not available to the author at the time of writing. Much of the data used in this chapter were found through Statistics New Zealand's free Table Builder tool. In using a city/district distinction, one needs to be aware that some city council boundaries exclude commuting zones, while others may include sparsely populated minor urban areas within their boundaries.

2 The "half of more" rule was also embedded in many legislative definitions of Māori. For example, the Maori Land Act, 1909, defined a Native as a person "belonging to the Aboriginal race of New Zealand, and include[d] a half-caste and a person intermediate in blood between half-castes and persons of pure descent from that race." The Maori Representation Act, 1867, which provided for limited Maori enfranchisement, defined Maori as "a male Aboriginal native inhabitant of New Zealand at the age of twenty-one years and upwards and shall include half-castes." The Maori Social and Economic Advancement Act, 1945, had the more inclusive definition of "a person belonging to the aboriginal race of New Zealand, and includes any person descended from a Maori."

3 For New Zealand nationally, inter-censal urban growth consistently outpaced growth in rural areas. In several periods, rural areas suffered a numerical decline. This occurred between 1936 and 1945 through labour migration to cities (with the

expansion of manufacturing and service sectors) and the contraction of labour demand in the agricultural sector (as a result of mechanization); and again between 1961 and 1971, aided by the faster rate of fertility decline in the rural areas.

4 Almost one-third of the nation's population live in Auckland, and this over-concentration is expected to increase in coming years. In 2006, the Auckland Regional Council area comprised four city councils (Auckland, North Shore, Waitakere, and Manukau) and three district councils (Rodney, Papakura, and part of Franklin). In 2010, all of Auckland's regional, city, and district councils were merged into a "super city" council known as Auckland Council.

5 The estimated resident population is based on the census usually resident population count, with adjustments for residents missed or counted more than once (net census undercount); residents temporarily overseas on census night; and births, deaths, and net permanent and long-term migration between census night and the date.

References

Ausubel, D. 1961. The Maori: A study in resistive acculturation. *Social Forces* 39: 218-27.

Barcham, M. 1998. The challenge of urban Māori: Reconciling conceptions of Indigeneity and social change. *Asia Pacific Viewpoint* 39: 303-14.

Bedford, R., and I. Pool. 2004. Flirting with Zelinsky in Aotearoa/New Zealand: A Māori mobility transition. In *Population mobility and Indigenous peoples in Australasia and North America*, ed. J. Taylor and M. Bell, 44-74. London: Routledge.

Bedford, R., and L. Heenan. 1987. The people of New Zealand: Reflections on a revolution. In *Southern approaches: Geographies in New Zealand*, ed. P.G. Holland and W.B. Johnston, 133-77. Christchurch, NZ: New Zealand Geographical Society.

Belich, J. 2001. *Paradise reforged: A history of the New Zealanders, from the 1880s to the year 2000*. Auckland, NZ: Penguin.

Blakely, T., M. Tobias, B. Robson, S. Ajwani, M. Bonné, and A. Woodward. 2005. Widening ethnic mortality disparities in New Zealand, 1981-99. *Social Science and Medicine* 61: 2233-51.

Borell, B. 2005. Living in the city ain't so bad: Cultural identity of South Auckland rangatahi. MA thesis, Massey University.

Carter, L. 2011. The impact of changing Maori demographics on Treaty settlement governance structures. http://posttreatysettlements.org.nz/.

Chapple, S. 2000. Maori socio-economic disparity. *Political Science* 52: 101-15.

Cooke, M., F. Mitrou, D. Lawrence, E. Guimond, and D. Beavon. 2007. Indigenous well-being in four countries: An application of the UNDP's human development index to Indigenous peoples in Australia, Canada, New Zealand, and the United States. *BMC International and Human Rights* 7. http://www.biomedcentral.com/. doi: 10.1186/1472-698X-7-9.

Durie, M. 2005. *Nga tai matatu: Tides of Māori endurance*. Melbourne: Oxford University Press.

Gibson, C. 1973. Urbanization in New Zealand: A comparative analysis. *Demography* 10: 71-84.

Hamer, P. 2009. One in six? The rapid growth of the Maori population in Australia. *New Zealand Population Review* 33/34: 153-76.

Harré, J. 1966. *Maori and Pakeha: A study of mixed marriages in New Zealand.* London: Institute of Race Relations.

Hill, R. 2005. Social revolution on a small scale: Official Māori committees of the 1950s. Paper presented to the New Zealand Historical Association Conference, Auckland, 24-27 November.

Hunn, J.K. 1961. *Report on the Department of Maori Affairs.* Wellington, NZ: Government Printer.

Kawharu, I. 1968. Urban immigrants and *tangata whenua.* In *The Maori people in the nineteen-sixties,* ed. E. Schwimmer, 174-86. Auckland, NZ: Blackwood and Janet Paul.

King, M. 1985. *Being Pakeha: An encounter with New Zealand and the Maori renaissance.* Auckland, NZ: Hodder and Stoughton.

Kukutai, T. 2004. The problem of defining an ethnic group for public policy: Who is Maori and why does it matter? *Social Policy Journal of New Zealand* 23: 86-108.

—. 2010. The thin brown line: Re-indigenizing inequality in Aotearoa New Zealand. PhD diss., Stanford University.

Maaka, R. 1994. The new tribe: Conflicts and continuities in the social organization of urban Maori. *Contemporary Pacific* 6(2): 311-36.

McCreary, J. 1968. Population growth and urbanization. In *The Maori people in the nineteen-sixties,* ed. E. Schwimmer, 187-204. Auckland, NZ: Blackwood and Janet Paul.

Metge, J. 1964. *A new Maori migration.* London: Athlone Press.

Nobles, M. 2000. *Shades of citizenship: Race and the census in modern politics.* Stanford, CA: Stanford University Press.

Pool, I. 1966. The rural-urban migration of Maoris: A demographic analysis. *Pacific Viewpoint* 7(1): 88-96.

—. 1977. *The Maori population of New Zealand 1769-1971.* Auckland, NZ: Auckland University Press.

—. 1991. *Te iwi Maori: A New Zealand population past, present and projected.* Auckland, NZ: Auckland University Press.

Pool, I., S. Baxendine, W. Cochrane, and J. Lindop. 2005. *New Zealand regions, 1986-2001: Incomes.* Population Studies Centre Discussion Paper Series No. 58. Hamilton, NZ: University of Waikato.

Pool, I., T. Kukutai, and J. Sceats. 2008. *Heretaunga-Tamatea: Demographic and statistical analysis.* A Report prepared for the Crown Forestry Rental Trust. Wellington: Crown Forestry Rental Trust.

Poulson, R., and R. Johnstone. 1973. Patterns of Maori migration. In *Urbanization in New Zealand,* ed. R. Johnstone, 150-74. Wellington, NZ: Reed.

Rata, E. 2000. *A political economy of neotribal capitalism.* Lanham, MD and Oxford: Lexington Books.

Schwimmer, E., ed. 1968. *The Maori people in the nineteen-sixties*. Auckland, NZ: Blackwood and Janet Paul.

Sin, I., and S. Stillman. 2005. *The geographical mobility of Māori in New Zealand*. Motu Working Paper, 05-05. Wellington: Motu Economic and Public Policy Research.

Sporle, A., N. Pearce, and P. Davis. 2002. Social class mortality differences in Maori and non-Maori men aged 15-64 during the last two decades. *New Zealand Medical Journal* 115: 127-30.

Statistics New Zealand. 2011a. National population estimates: As at June 2011. http://www.stats.govt.nz/.

–. 2011b. Māori population estimates: As at June 2011. http://www.stats.govt.nz/.

Te Puni Kōkiri. 2000. *Progress towards closing social and economic gaps between Māori and non-Māori*. A Report to the Minister of Māori Affairs. Wellington, NZ: Te Puni Kōkiri.

Walling, J., D. Small-Rodriguez, and T. Kukutai. 2009. Tallying tribes: Waikato-Tainui in the census and Iwi register. *Social Policy Journal of New Zealand* 36: 2-15.

Webster, S. 2002. Māori retribalization and treaty rights to the New Zealand fisheries. *Contemporary Pacific* 14(2): 341-76.

Williams, D. 1999. *Te Kooti Tango Whenua: The Native Land Court, 1864-1909*. Wellington, NZ: Huia.

World Bank. 2011. http://data.worldbank.org/.

15

Māori and Environmental Justice

The Case of "Lake" Otara

BRAD COOMBES

The first generations of environmental justice research emphasized overt bias in the planning process and how that process unevenly distributes environmental goods or risks. Recently, however, geographers have focused on the plural constitution of urban environmental injustices. Just as there has been a shift from epidemiological world views to a focus on well-being in the social studies of health (Kearns and Collins 2010), so a broadening in the understanding of environmental injustices and their causation has been required. New research includes consideration of historical drivers and the subtle role of discourse in assigning values to particular landscapes, while acknowledging how disregard for local rights and self-determination produces multiple and fractured perceptions of injustice. While these shifts have opened space for specific consideration of Indigeneity alongside the conventional emphasis on race and social status, voids in conceptualizing the relationship between environmental justice and urban Indigenous communities remain. In New Zealand, for example, even though 84 percent of Māori now live in urban areas,[1] academic and policy-forming communities have been inattentive to the social status of urban Māori. They have reified *iwi* (traditional tribes) and the rural as natural domains for Māori existence, and, therefore, they have complicated the Māori pursuit of urban environmental justice.

This chapter evaluates the efforts of urban Māori to contest the environmental outcomes of a gas-fired power station in Otara, south Auckland.

Environmental agencies have been ambivalent in their responses to those efforts and to the rights of urban Māori authorities. The lack of support for such authorities seems to reflect a view that their constituencies are "out-of-place" migrants, presumably less deserving of the Treaty rights afforded to those who remain in rural areas (Rata 2006). More "traditional" Māori groups have contested the right of Māori living in Otara to speak for Otara landscapes. A cultural inquiry into how urban Māori occupy a *space of misrecognition* is required to understand how the social production of environmental injustices in Otara is connected to broader processes of identity formation.

Three Phases of Justice Research and Their Relevance to the Social Production of "Lake" Otara

The literature on environmental justice has moved through three distinct phases, reflecting concerns about distribution, procedural justice, and the cultural politics of socio-ecological change. This section combines assessment of relevant literature on those three phases with empirical detail about the evolution of environmental conflicts in Otara. The history of the Otara power station reveals the need to supplement quantitative analyses with qualitative inquiry into the discourses that normalize socio-ecological relations.

Phase One: Distributive Justice

The first generation of environmental justice research focused on allegations of maldistribution in the location of toxic facilities and on associated claims about disproportionate environmental impacts on black and Hispanic populations in major US cities. Quantitative measurement to support claims of distributive injustice – particularly, statistical correlations and GIS mapping to prove proximity to toxic facilities – preoccupied researchers during the 1980s and early 1990s (see the review by Bowen 2002). Outwardly, the Otara case might seem to fit with this emphasis on distribution. Figure 15.1 demonstrates the close proximity of a gas-fired power station, a large subdivision of social rented ("state") housing, and Ngati Otara Marae – the consecrated grounds and meeting house for Māori living in Otara. Although the subdivision was constructed for white factory workers, it has since become associated with Māori and Pacific families, along with public assumptions about welfare dependency and social deprivation (Cheer, Kearns, and Murphy 2002). With up to three-quarters of the country's electricity

Figure 15.1   Proximity of social, cultural, and economic facilities, Otara.
Source: Author

generated from renewable sources, a gas-fired facility is a unique and, therefore, a more politically sensitive feature of an urban landscape in New Zealand.

Auckland City incorporates long-standing patterns of social and cultural diversity, with Māori spread to the margins of the metropolitan area, especially towards the south.[2] Combined, Maori and Pacific peoples represent 43.6 percent of the total population of the former Manukau City – the most southern of the former "four cities" of Auckland. That compares with 20.1 percent for the former Auckland City area, 10.2 percent for North Shore, and 28.4 percent for Waitakere (see Figure 15.2; Statistics New Zealand 2006). Figure 15.2 utilizes an index of social deprivation, which is applied in New Zealand to target social policies and is comprised of census data on well-being, access to services, and employment. It also reveals the location of facilities that require an air discharge permit. Under New Zealand's Resource Management Act 1991 (RMA), standards for environmental performance are designed to be permissive, so if a facility requires a consent for its discharges to air, it is more likely to be associated with health-impairing effects (Smith and Coombes 2012). There is a strong coincidence among the distribution of socially marginalized neighbourhoods, the location of possibly toxic facilities, and the places where Māori live. Even though their combined size is greater, the less deprived meshblocks (deprivation categories 1-4) contain only 13.9 percent of the consented air discharges,

FIGURE 15.2 Coincidence of social deprivation and discharges to air that require a resource consent

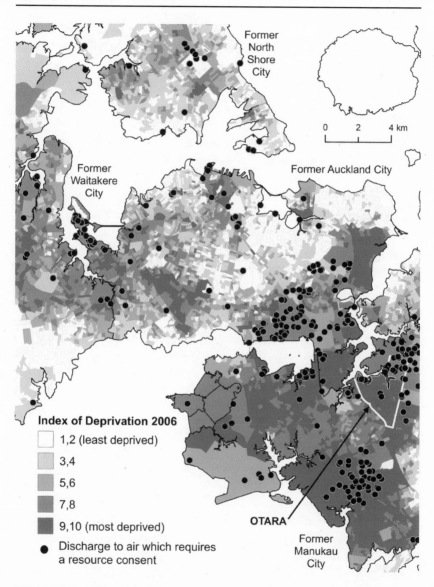

Source: Data on air discharge permits supplied by Auckland Regional Council. Index of Deprivation compiled from Salmond et al. (2007).

whereas the more deprived meshblocks (categories 7-10) contain 69.7 percent. There seems to be a continuing relevance for research that correlates the distribution of potential hazards with ethnic enclaves or poor neighbourhoods.

Nonetheless, correlations like those presented in Figure 15.2 seldom prove causation, and, because of that, this type of GIS analysis is highly contested. Empirically, there are well-known problems with ecological fallacy and modifiable aerial units; in particular, the correlations disappear at different spatial scales (Schweitzer and Stephenson 2007; Saha and Mohai 2005). Numbers cannot convey the highly contextualized experience of pollution, nor can they convey the multiple causes of its maldistribution. Likewise, the flat, Cartesian conceptions of space do not account for the effect of topology on pollution pathways, and proximity may be unrelated to magnitude of exposure (Bowen 2002). Combined, the Otahuhu B power station at Otara Creek and three other facilities in Manukau emit more SO_2 and NO_x than do the former city's 234 other facilities that require an air discharge permit (interview with air control officer, 16 March 2006). With all these grounds for contestation, it is no surprise that GIS and statistical analysis are seldom politically useful for promoting environmental change (Holifield 2004). As one interviewee confirmed: "We've tried mapping these relationships between factories and the poor, but the other side always has more experts who can cast doubt on our findings" (interview with social advocate, 20 November 2007).

Phase Two: Procedural Justice

The second phase of environmental justice research converged increasingly on the *causes* of maldistribution but, again, flawed assumptions frustrated that intent. Environmental inequalities were presumed to be "the product of isolated and intentional discriminatory acts" (Holifield, Porter, and Walker 2009, 594). According to Walker (2009, 625), researchers emphasized procedural justice, but, in doing so, they exaggerated "need, desert, and entitlement" at the expense of social recognition and other culturally specific conceptions of rights and justice. With the assumption that environmental injustices result from overt racism, there was insufficient attention to the intersection of racialization with other social relations and processes. Buckingham and Kulcur (2009) even suggest that academic contributors to these debates were themselves complicit with some types of environmental injustice. Arguing that "no society is one dimensionally exclusive," they maintain that the singular emphasis on pollution in black and

Hispanic neighbourhoods of US cities contributed to the invisibility of gender in studies about siting conflicts (660). In a similar way, I argue that the size of and preoccupation with black and Hispanic populations in US cities obscured the environmental fate of urban Indigenous populations.

Procedural fairness within processes of resource management remains important for understanding environmental injustice because it influences land allocation. Indeed, to understand the siting of the power station in Otara, it is important to interrogate contemporary planning decisions. At the time of its construction in the 1960s, residents questioned the public accessibility of decision making:

> There are many Maori and [Pacific] Islanders who don't understand the ways of the European. I am sure that if they had been made aware of the implications of the present plan, there would have been far more opposition to it. (interview with M. Freer, *New Zealand Herald* [hereafter *NZH*], 26 May 1967)

Those who did learn about the designation for the facility protested, but "locals' reservations were ignored," and, having been "told there'd be one turbine ... to be used only in peak times ... we hear there are to be four turbines used full-time" (interview with J. Anderton, *NZH*, 16 June 1967).

In retrospect, the most environmentally damaging component of the facility was the construction of a weir to raise Otara Creek, extract its waters for cooling purposes, and create a receiving environment for heated waste water. The weir now separates the creek from the Tamaki Estuary, thereby minimizing tidal flushing. Over time, other industrial discharges have been approved within the catchment of what is now, in effect, a lake, leading to the accumulation of contaminants behind the weir (Holm and Hartley 2003; see also annual engineers' reports in file BBAD 1955-79). Since that time, access to the "lake" margin has been progressively restricted because of the bacteriological, toxic, and physical dangers associated with the accumulation of sediment behind the weir. Yet, "the lake is located alongside the main sports fields in Otara, so every Saturday morning kids who have got dirty playing rugby go down there expecting a swim" (residential participant in focus group, 6 July 2005).

Officials disregarded Māori cultural values about water and associated *kaimoana* (seafood) resources, justifying the transformation of the creek with the suggestion that raising the water level would "hide a useless area of tidal mudflats" (*NZH*, 29 May 1967). Yet, many of the elders who were interviewed during my research recalled the creek as a "food basket for flat fish and eels before construction of the weir" (interview with elder, 16 May 2008). Recourse to European discourses about the inferiority of wetlands was accompanied by unrealizable promises about "turning the creek into a valuable public amenity" with "considerable recreational potential" (*NZH*, 29 May 1967). If protestors were not placated by these exaggerated claims, the minister of energy (letter to Manukau County Council, 29 March 1966, MCC 1962-2007) simply dismissed them, maintaining that siting decisions were "directed by sound engineering, not the targeting of low-income ethnic groups" and that "all classes contribute to the demand for electricity." In accordance with the logic of phase-two justice research, dispute had been managed through technocratic appeals to the capacity of experts to site facilities fairly and objectively, leading to prejudicial outcomes.

In many other respects, however, the Otara case demonstrates conceptual blind spots in second-generation research, particularly its assumption of linearity between decisions about toxic facilities and environmental outcomes. The location of communities of colour or the urban poor was assumed as a pre-existing condition; intentional bias in planning processes allegedly brought toxic facilities to those communities (Pulido 2000). Significantly, the decision to site the power station alongside Otara Creek was made in the 1930s, when the area was predominately rural or characterized by sites for the secondary processing of agricultural goods. It is relevant to the question of environmental justice that those processing firms polluted culturally important fishing resources within the creek and that Māori attachments to those resources were disregarded for many decades because it was assumed that they lapsed upon sale of land (see the petitions in ADOE 1931-42, particularly petition 3, 7 May 1936). Nonetheless, decisions about the power station preceded planning for state housing, unsettling the simplistic chronologies of environmental justice research and highlighting the need to understand the driving mechanisms of environmental change.

Official photographs of site construction during the 1960s reveal that there were few houses in Otara at the time (see folio 52, BBAD 1955-79). The "comprehensive plan" for developing Otara included provisions for a state housing subdivision of 1,600 acres (650 hectares), 4,600 housing units, and 19,000 people – a population that has doubled since that time. However, the power station was already designated, based upon that plan, as land reserved "for future Electricity Department use" (refer to labels on Figure 15.3). If limited to overt acts of racism in consent processes for the power station, any search for *causation* in relation to environmental controversies

FIGURE 15.3 Plan of the Otara subdivision, 1956

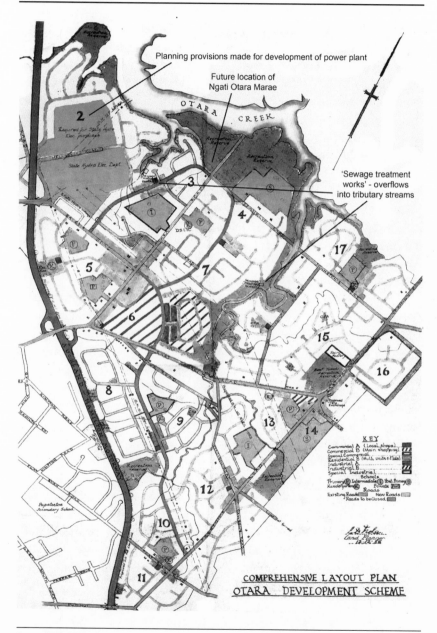

Planning provisions made for development of power plant

Future location of
Ngati Otara Marae

'Sewage treatment
works' - overflows
into tributary streams

COMPREHENSIVE LAYOUT PLAN
OTARA DEVELOPMENT SCHEME

Source: BBAD (1952-56).

at Otara would be frustrated. Bias in planning decisions did not bring hazards to the people, and, imperceptible to the conventional gaze of environmental justice research, the primary analytical need is to understand why housing policies brought people to the site of an impending hazard.

In 1950, a governmental task force defined Auckland's metropolitan urban limits (MUL) in an effort to restrict urban sprawl. Yet, the State Housing Division sought a national government exemption to the MUL so that it could bypass stricter planning regulations for subdivisions in urban areas and obtain rural land as cheaply as possible (report on proposed state housing, Otara, 16 October 1952, BBAD 1952-56). Although there were many objections to this over-ruling of planners' authority, even the mayor of Auckland conceded that the plan for Otara was to create "the greatest number of houses, in the quickest time, at the cheapest cost, on the cheapest land" (Mayor Luxford, *NZH*, 18 July 1955). The district supervisor of state housing confirmed that Otara was chosen because "development ... and basement costs would be exceptionally low" (District Supervisor, letter to Director of Housing, 10 December 1953, BBAD 1952-56).

Compounding the existing problems with industrial contaminants and lack of tidal flushing in the "lake," infrastructure for the subdivision was constructed at minimal cost. Indeed, one of the site's appeals was its "proximity to natural stormwater drainage outfalls" – that is, tributaries of Otara Creek (Memorandum, 26 January 1954, BBAD 1952-56). Stormwater and sewage pipes were provided so cheaply that they slumped and cracked within a few years, and "sewage works" and their termini were located alongside Otara Creek (sewer contract, 13 March 1957, BBAD 1952-56; refer to Figure 15.3). Although these outlets were later repurposed as emergency overflows, sewage continued to flow through them after every storm. Authorities had long-term knowledge about the mixing of waste and rain water – and, therefore, about the egress of sewage into the creek through stormwater outlets – but the problem has never been fully addressed (Holm and Hartley 2003). At the very least, therefore, an analysis of housing policies is required to comprehend the "environmental" hazard at Otara, but deeper insight requires a shift in outlook beyond policy and planning decisions regarding physical infrastructure.

Phase Three: Cultural Geographies of Inaction
The fact that the understanding of environmental injustice at Otara requires analysis of planning decisions *and* of housing policies implicates much

wider processes of place construction in the evolution of environmental injustices. Commencing with Pulido's (2000) juxtaposition of environmental injustice with suburban white privilege, a third generation of research has attained recent momentum in special issues of *Antipode* (2009) and the *International Journal of Urban and Regional Research* (2009). Along with the application of urban political ecology to justice research, two related themes have emerged. First, recent research emphasizes how the cultural politics of place-making determines which neighbourhoods are deemed worthy of rehabilitation or protection (Elliott and Pais 2006). Second, there has been significant progress in theorizing how discourses of responsibility or technocratic forms of administration normalize environmental injustices and the people who contest them as good or bad causes (Holifield 2009). Whereas the first two phases of research were obsessed with discriminatory *action* in siting decisions, the latest phase emphasizes the cultural drivers of *inaction* (Whitehead 2009).

There is insufficient space here to detail all research trajectories; however, they are united in a commitment to examining the diverse processes that drive environmental injustices (Schweitzer and Stephenson 2007). Walker and Bulkeley (2006) observe a broadening of scope in recent research, with the acceptance of plurality in the meaning of environmental injustice for different groups. Concomitantly, "far broader cross-disciplinary debate about knowledge, representation and meaning" has displaced quantitative analysis as the prime characteristic of associated research (Holifield, Porter, and Walker 2009, 593). This reinsertion of social theory into the debate about environmental justice is witnessed in Kurtz's (2009, 693) application of critical race theory to the concept of environmental racism. Whereas that was once framed as the product of racial bias in the planning process, it is now conceived as "a systemic social phenomenon." Hence, rather than the enumeration of discrete acts of racism by vested interests, the new emphasis is on the subtle, often covert, practices of racialization that extend discursively throughout cultural norms and the social formation. This shifts the objects of justice research from extra-ordinary acts and visibly polluting facilities to "more mundane and chronic forms of injustice" (Bickerstaff, Bulkeley, and Painter 2009, 594) and "the consequences of seemingly ordinary social decision making" (Whitehead 2009, 663). These *everyday* experiences shape the way people and landscapes are naturalized or prioritized in state and civil society responses to claims of injustice and are, therefore, central to understanding the geographies of inaction.

The more the concept of environmental justice has been expanded, the more it has shifted from distributive and procedural justice towards discourses of responsibility and the idea of *justice as recognition* (Schlosberg 2007). For instance, recent research has demonstrated the need to recognize the different relationships that two or more groups can have with the same space; other research has explored the different ways groups are recognized and represented in environmental controversies. Significantly, with the reconfiguration of justice as a form of recognition, it becomes easier to stake space for Indigenous peoples in theories about environmental injustice. In particular, there is considerable potential in Walker's concept of "spaces of misrecognition" for understanding the environmental dilemmas that confront urban Indigenous peoples. Walker (2009, 626) maintains that the relationships between people and place are misrecognized through "processes of disrespect, denigration, insult and stigmatisation which devalue some people in comparison to others." Revealing those processes should address the hitherto invisibility of Indigenous peoples in environmental justice research and in everyday assumptions about the normative inhabitants of urban landscapes.

Deliberate or conscious interaction between Indigenous studies and the third generation of justice research has been minimal, but there is a growing body of incidental research that attests to the promise of such interactions. O'Neill (2003) and Holifield (2009) demonstrate how the universalizing assumptions in risk management render invisible the eco-cultural values of Indigenous peoples. Others suggest that competing cultural values in the socio-natures of ecological restoration have silenced Indigenous aspirations for cultural rehabilitation (Palamar 2008). Ranco (2008) maintains that contested notions of responsibility in the doctrine of trust protection for Native land administration limit the extent to which Indigenous peoples can impose standards on use of their own land, thereby restricting their sovereignty. Likewise, several studies reveal how currently fashionable approaches to planning through deliberation or civic environmentalism overwhelm Indigenous preferences for environmental leadership (Williams and Mawdsley 2006; Lane and Williams 2008).

Individually, these are all insightful articles, but collectively they forewarn of an emerging contradiction. The appeal in applying environmental justice literature to Indigenous studies is that, historically, it has been patently urban: when applied, the former should rid the latter of its presumption that Indigenous peoples are habitually rural. Yet, it seems that research at the intersection of Indigenous studies and the third phase of research into environmental justice is mostly restricted to the non-urban reserve or to natural resource management. Third-generation research will finally, it seems, draw attention to Indigenous environmental concerns, but it dwells on tired geographies of the reservation.

Otara: People Out of Place and the Cultural Conditions for Environmental Inaction

In keeping with the intent to interrogate (mis)recognition in everyday Indigenous experiences of urban environmental injustice, it is important to account for Otara residents' understanding of their proximity to a power station. The quotations used in this section are the result of interviews with members of the public who contributed to restoration or clean-up days or who were recorded in minutes of ongoing discussion forums in which I have been involved. Initially, concerned citizens who wanted to construct a more positive profile for their place of residence established "Enterprise Otara" as a discussion forum. They were also responsible for attracting media attention to the polluted state of "Lake" Otara during the 1990s. As part of a re-source consent procedure for granting ongoing rights to Contact Energy – the new owner of the power station – those forums were later incorpor-ated into a formal consultation mechanism: the Otara Lake Working Party. Together, these multiple sources, including interviews, focus groups, residents' discussion forums, and information gleaned from participants in lake rehabilitation work, provide rich insights into why Otara residents be-lieve they have received minimal assistance in their efforts to rehabilitate Otara Creek.

Walker (2009) associates spaces of misrecognition with the *stigmatiza-tion* of peoples and places. While there are obvious cautions about label-ling Indigenous or any other community as stigmatized, Otara residents also associated their environmental condition with stigmas of place. Al-though they are intensely proud of Otara and what they have made of it, they are also troubled by the way others represent it, associating those rep-resentations with a lack of civic will to address the outcomes of historical pollution:

> *When they think of Otara, they think of all these negative things –*
> *poor, brown, graffiti, gangster rap – that's the crim image they've*
> *created for us. We are today's version of the unclean, you see. I put*
> *it to you that people who hold that image won't willingly support us*

in cleaning up the lake. (interview with former member of
Enterprise Otara, 27 November 2004)

Other residents confirmed this opinion. In explaining why an accord between government agencies and the people of Otara had not been implemented, one person recalled the statement of a regional politician at a public
meeting:

> *[He] told us that we needed to try harder. That we couldn't expect*
> *help with lake clean up if we didn't clean up our graffiti and refuse*
> *dumping problems first.* (interview with resident, 13 January 2008)

The discursive framing of Otara's physical appearance perpetuates inaction
and, therefore, associated environmental problems.

Similar discourses about the alleged uniformity of the landscape in Otara
also contribute to its lack of appropriate recognition. With the area's highly
planned state housing subdivisions based on cul-de-sacs and minimum flair
in house design (see Figure 15.3), its communities' unique needs and aspirations may be disregarded:

> *On the surface, there's a strong sense of sameness about Otara:*
> *three basic state house designs and five colours of pastel paint.*
> *I suspect that the sameness and the newness of this place counts*
> *against us. We can't make claims about ancestral connection or*
> *unique cultural association with whenua [land] because it doesn't*
> *look all historical. Those who want to dismiss our plans for the lake*
> *can easily point to the lack of anything different or special here,*
> *and they often do.* (interview with attendee, Otara Creek riparian
> planting day, 16 February 2009)

The speaker refers to the need to construct particular identities to take advantage of clauses in the RMA that can sometimes be used to implement
Māori resource rights under the Treaty of Waitangi, 1840. Otara is a palpably manufactured and relatively new place, but the act imagines the beneficiaries of treaty rights to be in a more natural, primordial state. The way
the place has been constructed – as unclean, crime-ridden, or just plain
ordinary – influences the capacity to gain access to rights that, under the
Treaty, are intended for all Māori.

From the perspective of local people, these negative influences should be associated with questions about who has control over Otara as a place. For some residents, it is impossible to disassociate pollution in Lake Otara from their cultural memories of the so-called "Dawn Raids" of the 1970s. At that time, Pacific peoples – who were initially invited to New Zealand to participate as a labour force in an industrializing economy – were reimagined as overstayers, and the police raided properties throughout south Auckland with a view to deporting surplus labour. Notably, many of the Māori interviewees connected the Dawn Raids to the fate of Lake Otara, even though they were not targeted by those raids:

> *They didn't directly affect us Māori, but we all have to consider the significance of the Dawn Raids on this place. They're a reminder that, no matter how much time we put into making Otara a community, the government has total control over us. They have the ability to evict our neighbours from the place they've made home. You need to be very confident about your standing if you want to demand justice for that creek. Who has standing and authority in the place of the Dawn Raids?* (interview with resident, 13 July 2007)

As with academics who have contributed to a third generation of justice research, so for local Māori the drivers of environmental injustice intersect with much broader social processes: "much contemporary metropolitan discontent stems from a lack of socio-ecological control and care" (Whitehead 2009, 664).

Stigmatization of place and perceived lack of control also intersect in the relationship between the marae complex and the lake. For many years after its establishment, Otara had few social facilities, even though expanding Māori and Pacific populations and their associated cultural diversity demanded spaces for cultural practice and ceremonies. The original proponents of a pan-tribal marae for Otara pursued laudable civic ideals,[3] but they had meagre funds and no land on which to site their project. To some, the shame of not having a marae is associated with the more obvious environmental injustices, as is the more recent indignity of having a marae whose upkeep they struggle to maintain:

> *Our landscape gives out cues and clues about what is possible and what isn't. In the sixties, we wanted to build a pan-iwi marae for*

our collective well-being – for us and the Island folk too – but we
were forced to beg for the land for twenty-five years or so. The
council eventually gave us part of the old landfill. Physically, that
affects the [lake] restoration because of leachate, but it's the
symbolic damage – the shame which goes with it – that counts
most. (interview with Marae Committee member, 14 May 2004)

This notion of "symbolic damage" – a form of social harm that surpasses the culturally inappropriate and somewhat coerced location of a spiritually significant facility on a former landfill – affirms the need to consider the wider cultural influences on spaces of misrecognition. The predominance of a power station in these matters may seem to replicate a phase one emphasis on "spectacular manifestations of ... injustices" resulting from larger polluting facilities (Whitehead 2009, 665), but understanding its received effects demands research into *off-site* signs and symbols of cultural repression.

The expectation that urban Māori who do not associate with a traditional tribal structure are likely to experience diminished rights dominated local discourse about the prolonged impact of the power station. Analogues for being "out of place" and its consequences were a significant undercurrent to the focus groups, public meetings, and work days. These concerns included two dimensions: first, the impacts of historical displacement on current rights; and, second, the fraught status of urban Māori authorities. A Māori political leader explained the historical complications:

Way back, Otara was Ngai Tai's land but it was sold in a pre-
Treaty [of Waitangi], illegal sale ... There's no political will to
address that type of claim, and we don't carry the clout of other iwi.
Ngai Tai has always seated itself between two great Māori empires
– Tainui to the south, Ngati Whatua to the North. We shifted about
and did things like that which aren't expected of the tangata
whenua [people of the land]. Then there's the rest of the Māori here
– migrants who shifted here for factory jobs. Everything about this
place is uncertain and unresolved – people, place and history
always somewhere in-between something else. Us Māoris here,
we're out of place and the authorities remind us of that all the time.
If we could make a case to them about the lake as tangata whenua,
that might make a difference, but that's not accepted. (interview
with runanga member, 6 June 2007)

Reflecting the extent to which urban Māori are denied the status of tangata whenua, the pan-tribal *runanga* (council) for the iwi of Otara has been forbidden access to resource management proceedings and has been excluded from the various working groups that have been established to consider options for Lake Otara. At a public meeting, one Manukau city planner stated confidently:

> *At most, the RMA says that council should consult the tangata whenua, but even a full urban Māori authority is not necessarily representative of the tangata whenua because they're for people who have lost their connection to tribe or land. It's quite deliberate that we have no working relationship with the Runanga a Iwi ki Otara.* (MCC planner, consultation meeting, 10 February 2006)

The second and third articles of the Treaty clearly state that its rights are open to all Māori; yet, councils interpret the RMA as though treaty rights are the preserve of "tangata whenua." This phrase may introduce ambiguity if it is interpreted solely to refer to a traditional tribe with a long-term connection to a particular place. The periodic displacement of less populous iwi (like Ngai Tai) or New Zealand's widespread migration of Indigenous people to urban centres unsettles any traditional reading of "tangata whenua." To complete a vicious circle of misrecognition, tangata whenua are delimited to what they might have been 170 years ago, thereby denying urban Māori with migratory forebears of their treaty rights.

These processes of disenfranchisement are applied, in particular, to the status of urban Māori authorities:

> *The marae, the restoration, Enterprise Otara, the runanga – they were all one thing really. Same people, same vision. But in the end, the success of that vision came down to the status of the runanga and if that would be recognized. If accepted, our rights may have been properly considered and resources [for lake rehabilitation] may have flowed. But it was never recognized. We considered upgrading its status by severing its ties to the Manukau UMA and applying to become an authority like that ourselves. But then we saw that they're only allowed to be service providers – in effect, few treaty rights and no meaningful [treaty] claims allowed. So we gave up on that, but it means we don't have the governance vehicle to*

push others into cleaning up the lake. (interview with elder, 17
August 2007).

The speaker makes reference to earlier events that laid bare the contradictions in New Zealand's treaty jurisprudence as it applies to urban Māori. In
1998, the Waitangi Tribunal – a permanent commission of inquiry whose
purpose is to hear Māori grievances under the Treaty – recommended that
UMAs be given the same rights as traditional tribes to receive state grants
and to deliver social services (Waitangi Tribunal 1998). Later that year, and
seemingly contradicting the tribunal's findings, the High Court determined
that UMAs did not have the same status as did traditional tribes and so
should not directly receive the financial benefits of treaty settlement
(Paterson J., *Te Waka Hi o Te Arawa and ors. v. Treaty of Waitangi Fisheries
Commission*, 4 August 1998). As is indicated by the speaker quoted above,
experience of such contradictions and continuing bias against UMAs deters
Otara Māori from pursuing environmental justice. Increasingly, they have
become "apathetic about restoring the lake because the challenges are too
great" (elder interview, 16 October 2008). Once, environmental justice research was consumed with detailing prejudicial acts *against* peoples of colour, but it must also consider how the social construction of places and
political causes generates inaction *among* those peoples.

Conclusion

*It's not what it does to us; it's what it means for us. Our people are
more likely to die from smokers' lung cancer than pollution-related
disease. It's all about what the lack of attention to the lake and the
lack of support for its restoration says about who cares and who
matters.* (interview with resident, 12 February 2008)

As this statement indicates, the discursive constitution of environmental
(in)justice requires as much, if not more, consideration than its biophysical
manifestations. The more historicized approach in this chapter reveals a
need to shift analysis away from planning decisions towards such realms of
policy making as state intervention in the housing market. However, it also
reveals a need to search beyond the policy realm and its immediate consequences to include analysis of those discourses of difference, place, and
presumed natural order that normalize socio-ecological relations. Even in
the case of such an extraordinary siting event as the location of the power

station alongside a marae and a state housing subdivision, its impact can only be understood when juxtaposed with the everyday experience of ordinary justice throughout Otara.

The new conceptualizations of third-generation research on environmental justice hold considerable promise for supporting the cause of urban Indigenes. Previously invisible both to urban planners and to environmental justice research, Indigenous migrants to cities experience cultural conditioning about where they should live, what rights to which they have access, and the quality of environments that they can expect. An understanding of how they come to occupy spaces of misrecognition and of how they both confront and perform geographies of inaction may lead to more effective research that challenges existing urban orders. As yet, however, the potential application of third-generation research to Indigenous studies is incomplete.

Notes

1 Compared with 17 percent in 1920 and 63 percent in 1956, that 84 percent of Māori now live in urban areas indicates that they represent one of the most rapidly urbanizing Indigenous populations in the world (Statistics New Zealand 2007).
2 The "four cities of Auckland" were amalgamated to become Auckland City in November 2010. Because of restrictions on space, the important interrelationships between Māori and peoples of Pacific Island descent cannot be explored fully in this chapter. The contention that experience of environmental injustice is shared mutually, albeit sometimes uncomfortably, among those populations is revealed in the fieldwork upon which this chapter is based: Māori and Pacific peoples worked alongside each other in the political and restoration campaigns from which participants were sourced.
3 At the time, the chair of the fundraising committee noted: "We do not intend that our Marae at Otara will be a retreat for Māori people or a place to fossilise old traditions. Rather it will be a firm base from which to express and evolve our culture and a facility which we wish to share, for all to use and enjoy" (appeal brochure, 1977, in BBCZ 1975-88).

References

ADOE. 1931-42. Otara Creek, Tamaki River. Discharge of waste products from dairy factories. Files of the Marine Department, Archives New Zealand, Wellington.
BBAD. 1952-56. State housing proposals for Otara and Mangere East. Files of the Auckland Branch, Ministry of Works, Archives New Zealand, Auckland.
–. 1955-79. Rivers and draingage: Otara Creek. Files of the Auckland Branch, Ministry of Works and Development, Archives New Zealand, Auckland.

BBCZ. 1975-88. Marae – Ngati Otara. Files of the Auckland Regional Office, Te Puni Kokiri, Archives New Zealand, Auckland.

Bickerstaff, K., H. Bulkeley, and J. Painter. 2009. Justice, nature and the city. *International Journal of Urban and Regional Research* 33(3): 591-600.

Bowen, W. 2002. An analytical review of environmental justice research: What do we really know? *Environmental Management* 29(1): 3-15.

Buckingham, S., and R. Kulcur. 2009. Gendered geographies of environmental injustice. *Antipode* 41(4): 659-83.

Cheer, T., R. Kearns, and L. Murphy. 2002. Housing policy, poverty, and culture: "Discounting" decisions among Pacific peoples in Auckland, New Zealand. *Environment and Planning C: Government and Policy* 20(4): 497-516.

Elliott, J.R., and J. Pais. 2006. Race, class, and Hurricane Katrina: Social differences in human responses to disaster. *Social Science Research* 35(2): 295-321.

Holifield, R. 2004. Neoliberalism and environmental justice in the United States environmental protection agency: Translating policy into managerial practice in hazardous waste remediation. *Geoforum* 35(3): 285-97.

–. 2009. Actor-network theory as a critical approach to environmental justice: A case against synthesis with urban political ecology. *Antipode* 41(4): 637-58.

Holifield, R., M. Porter, and G. Walker. 2009. Spaces of environmental justice: Frameworks for critical engagement. *Antipode* 41(4): 591-612.

Holm, P., and P. Hartley. 2003. Reconnecting the Otara community with their lake. Paper read at 3rd South Pacific Conference on Stormwater and Aquatic Resource Protection, at Auckland.

Kearns, R., and D. Collins. 2010. Health geography. In *A companion to medical and health geography*, ed. T. Brown, S. McLafferty, and G. Moon, 15-32. Oxford: Oxford University Press.

Kurtz, H.E. 2009. Acknowledging the racial state: An agenda for environmental justice research. *Antipode* 41(4): 684-704.

Lane, M.B., and L.J. Williams. 2008. Color blind: Indigenous peoples and regional environmental management. *Journal of Planning Education and Research* 28(1): 38-49.

MCC. 1962-2007. Correspondence on the Otara Power Scheme. In *Archived files of Manukau City*. Manukau: Manukau City Council.

O'Neill, C.A. 2003. Risk avoidance, cultural discrimination, and environmental justice for Indigenous peoples. *Ecology Law Quarterly* 30(1): 1-57.

Palamar, C.R. 2008. The justice of ecological restoration: Environmental history, health, ecology, and justice in the United States. *Human Ecology Review* 15(1): 82-94.

Pulido, L. 2000. Rethinking environmental racism: White privilege and urban development in southern California. *Annals of the Association of American Geographers* 90(1): 12-40.

Ranco, D.J. 2008. The trust responsibility and limited sovereignty: What can environmental justice groups learn from Indian nations? *Society and Natural Resources* 21(4): 354-62.

Rata, E. 2006. The political strategies of ethnic and Indigenous elites. In *Public policy and ethnicity: The politics of ethnic boundary-marking*, ed. E. Rata and R. Openshaw, 40-53. Houndmills: Palgrave Macmillan.

Saha, R., and P. Mohai. 2005. Historical context and hazardous waste facility siting: Understanding temporal patterns in Michigan. *Social Problems* 52(4): 618-48.

Salmond, C., P. Crampton, and J. Atkinson. 2007. *NZDep2006 Index of Deprivation.* Wellington: Ministry of Health and University of Otago.

Schlosberg, D. 2007. *Defining environmental justice: Theories, movements, and nature.* Oxford: Oxford University Press.

Schweitzer, L., and M. Stephenson. 2007. Right answers, wrong questions: Environmental justice as urban research. *Urban Studies* 44(2): 319-37.

Smith, C., and B. Coombes. 2012. Washing their hands of it? Auckland City's risk management of formerly horticultural land as neoliberal responsibilisation. In *Contradictions of neoliberal planning: Cities, policies, and politics*, ed. T. Tasan-Kok and G. Baeten, 133-50. Dordrecht: Springer.

Statistics New Zealand. 2006. *New Zealand Census of Population and Dwellings.* Wellington: Statistics New Zealand.

–. 2007. *QuickStats about Maori.* Wellington: Statistics New Zealand.

Waitangi Tribunal. 1998. Te Whanau o Waipareira report. Wellington: Waitangi Tribunal.

Walker, G. 2009. Beyond distribution and proximity: Exploring the multiple spatialities of environmental justice. *Antipode* 41(4): 614-36.

Walker, G., and H. Bulkeley. 2006. Geographies of environmental justice. *Geoforum* 37(5): 655-59.

Whitehead, M. 2009. The wood for the trees: Ordinary environmental injustice and the everyday right to urban nature. *International Journal of Urban and Regional Research* 33(3): 662-81.

Williams, G., and E. Mawdsley. 2006. Postcolonial environmental justice: Government and governance in India. *Geoforum* 37(5): 660-70.

16

Producing Indigeneity

BRENDAN HOKOWHITU

We cannot move forward unless our own backyard has been cleared and the impostors who continue to chant and make much ado over the whanau, hapu and iwi mantra as a song in itself so that few can feast in the name of the many, they also will be exposed. Let's get real. Forty-four percent of Maori households are solo-parent driven. There is no exclusive Maori way forward. Te Whanau o Waipereira and Manukau Urban Maori Authority are as legitimate in the hearts, minds and souls of young urban Maori as any iwi. (John Tamihere, maiden speech to Parliament 2000, cited in Sissons 2004, 19-20)

The continuing aspiration of the neocolonial complex is to produce an Indigenous subject concurrent with its discourses, whether through necropolitics or biopolitics: to kill or to make live, both symbolically and materially.[1] The above quote from the now ex-member of Parliament and leading advocate for the recognition of urban Māori collectives, John Tamihere, speaks to the life and death struggle of Indigenous subjectivities. In this chapter, through a relatively recent exposé of Indigenous necro- and biopolitics, I examine the production of Indigenous subjectivities and their previously unimaginable amalgamations.

In New Zealand, possibly more than in any other postcolonial society, the interstitial space occurring at the interface between the neo-formations of Indigeneity and the grid of disciplinary coercions has eventuated in a seemingly omnipresent "bicultural drama." That is, New Zealanders' postcolonial identity is a product of a bicultural imaginary (Sissons 2004), allegorically constructed and produced through the morphing notion of Indigeneity. The "Māori Problem" (i.e., 1950s to 1970s parlance for the state's desire to assimilate and modernize its Indigenous populace) has recently morphed into the "Treaty Partner," and, accordingly, the production of Indigenous subjectivities has unfolded in line with these changes in governing rhetoric. The Treaty Partner construction is narrated through the story of Māori recompense and Pākehā guilt as played out through the Treaty of Waitangi (hereafter referred to as "the Treaty") claims process.

Unsurprisingly, the authenticated, traditionalized, and reified Indigenous form of the Treaty partnership has been tribalized. What is perhaps surprising is the complicity of the neocolonial complex with this ethnic fundamentalism at the expense of other formations, such as pan-tribal urban groups. While Indigenous studies scholars, such as Kevin Bruyneel (2007), highlight the challenges to neocolonial temporal, spatial, and political models that Indigenous tribal formations have brought to bear in postcolonial politics, it seems that tribal formations are less feared in New Zealand than in other contexts. Put another way, the Indigenous subjectivities produced via the "Partnership" process, far from inherently challenging understandings of sovereignty produced by the neocolonial complex, are actually complicit with them. This "new way of doing business" flies in the face of the tacit nineteenth- and twentieth-century understandings that the most effective method of modernizing and assimilating the indigene is through detribalization: "Tribalism, in particular, was perceived to be inimical to the interests of the liberal State because it promoted historic 'we-they' attitudes and thereby militated against the liberal conception of one language, one culture, one state" (Peters 2001, 28).

In this chapter, I consciously steer away from envisaging neocolonial power hierarchically – that is, as a mere function of the state's will, as somehow possessed by individuals (i.e., the so-called "neo-tribal elite"), and/or as inherent to any one collective. Rather, and paraphrasing Foucault (1978, 93), I see the neocolonial context as "a complex strategical situation." To be an "authentic" Indigenous person, thus, is to be at one with the prevailing discourses that construct Indigeneity, which denote inclusion on the basis of exclusion, or, as Hekia Parata of Ngāti Porou (a North Island East-Coast tribe) puts it: "without tribes there is no Maori" (cited in Barcham 1998, 308). In the *Archaeology of Knowledge*, Foucault (2002) describes discourses as based on interrelated systems, processes, languages, and institutions that allow that of which they speak to emerge as "truth." Thus, rather then accepting a naturalized tribal or "*iwi* consciousness" (i.e., the authenticating and traditionalizing notion of "the tribe" as the manifest patent of Indigenous social life), I seek to uncover the constructed nature of Indigeneity; suggest that a tribal consciousness does not just occur or re-enshrine a precolonial structure but, rather, appears at the interstices of historical transformation; and ask what strategies gave corporeality to a tribal consciousness and what strategies gave rise to necropolitical sovereign power.

Moreover, in keeping with the notion that Indigenous subjectivities are produced, I am wary of falling into binaries myself: tribal/urban, traditional/modern, old guard/progressive. Academic literature is riddled with the tradition of dissent, and, therefore, I am cognizant of the desire to pit one group against another, to expose the flaws in the old guard and to valorize the new progressive, and to authenticate one and to make inauthentic the other, whereas, in reality, the production of a tribal consciousness and the subordination of other forms of Indigenous subjectivity is beyond good and evil.

Third Culture: Urban Indigeneity

In New Zealand, the official narrative of Indigenous urbanization is quite well known and roughly follows a course similar to that experienced elsewhere (see Norris, Clatworthy, and Peters, this volume; Taylor, this volume). Prior to the Second World War, 90 percent of Māori were rural (Walker 1990, 197). According to the state's principal adviser on State-Māori relationships, Te Puni Kōkiri (2007, 7) (the Ministry of Māori Development):

> Māori and Pākehā societies essentially lived and worked in separately located communities until the Māori urban migration after the Second World War ... This urban migration was stimulated by the situation for Māori in the Depression years of the 1930s. Māori were often the first to lose work, and were paid lower unemployment benefits than Pākehā ... In 1956, nearly two-thirds of Māori lived in rural areas; by 2006, 84.4 percent of Māori lived in urban areas.

Of note here are three key points. First, Māori urbanization was, in part, stimulated by the state. As Ranginui Walker outlines, during wartime, the Manpower Act directed Māori ineligible for military service towards urban areas and "essential industries," which meant "leaving the *papakainga* [original home base] and *marae* [centre of Māori social life] for towns and cities" (Walker 1990, 197). Similarly, in the 1960s, the Department of Māori Affairs formulated a relocation program that "exhorted rural families to leave the subsistence economy of the 'pipi beds' [shellfish beds] by finding them employment and accommodation in urban centres" (ibid.). Also in the 1960s, the Māori Community Development Act changed the focus of the intermediary between the Māori community and the state from "tribal committees" to "Māori committees." According to Mason Durie (1998, 55), the state "actively discouraged tribal organization," which "underline[d] the significance of a new cultural identity based less on tribe than on simply being Māori." It is apparent then that, from the state's perspective, the purpose of the urbanization of Māori was not merely to satiate labour needs in the city; rather, it was ideological. The state programs to urbanize Māori involved tactics that facilitated the ideological management of the Indigenous population. "Pepper potting," for instance, was a housing policy that encouraged assimilation by distributing Māori families within previously all-Pākehā neighbourhoods (Durie 1998, 55). As an example, by 2001 the largest tribe, Ngāpuhi (a "Far-North" North Island tribe), reported that "78% of their 103,000 members lived outside their *rohe* [district]" (Panoho and Stablein 2005, 7).

Second, the common narrative surrounding Māori urbanization has naturalized an urban/traditional tribal binary. In contrast to commonly held views, the Ngāpuhi figures above resemble the larger picture – that is, approximately one-fifth of Māori were/are not tribally conscious. In the 1991 and 1996 censuses, 22 and 19 percent of Māori, respectively, did not affiliate tribally (Durie 1998, 166). For the 1996 data at least, "living in a rural or urban setting made little difference" to tribal comprehension (Statistics New Zealand 1998, cited in Webster 2002, 360). This clearly discredits the notion that urban Māori have been detribalized to a greater extent than rural Māori. And, accordingly, there was/is no clear cultural division between urban and tribal Māori (Meredith 2000, 18). In reality, the majority of Māori who live in urban areas continue to culturally identify with their tribal heritage.

Third, and most important, while it is true that Māori and Pākehā (whites) were, in the main, discrete cultures prior to urbanization, the inter-meshing of culture Māori brought to the city, and the culture they developed once there, meant that, by Bhabha's (1994) definition at least, urbanization provided the space for the liminal negotiation of cultural identity: urbanization effected a third culture.[2] Durie (1998, 54) argues: "From 1945 urbanization became the unmarshalled force which called for fresh understandings of what it meant to be Māori." While a 1967 survey demonstrated that 90 percent of Māori families living in Otara (a suburb of Auckland) resembled the nuclear family, according to Walker (1990) the urban Māori "nuclear family" took on a different cultural form, with kinship notions such as *whanau* (family) and *hapū* (subtribes) being "transplanted, but in modified form. Whanau with siblings scattered across different suburbs meet frequently at a central place, usually the home of the kaumatua and kuia [elders] ... for mutual support in times of bereavement, or the formation of family clubs ... and the celebration of festive occasions" (Walker 1990, 200).

Regardless of the official policy of ideological assimilation, it seemed that, even in the cities, Māori and Pākehā cultures were adjacent but afar. In the 1960s, the State Advances Corporation and the Ministry of Works developed new housing estates to accommodate the increasing urban drift. In Auckland, the now infamous suburbs of Otara, Mangere, and Te Atatu – and, in Wellington, Porirua, Hutt Valley, and Wainuiomata – were formed to, in part, house an urban Indigenous and Pacific migrant working class (Walker 1990, 198). The liminal negotiation of cultural identity for the new urban Māori, thus, was decidedly working-class, largely spatially disparate from Pākehā culture, and conditioned by the culture of their rural forbearers.

On this last point, Te Puea, the first urban marae, was established in 1965 in Mangere. Significantly, although the marae was kin-based "with the tangata whenua [natal people] of Waikato in control, the marae [was] available for use to all migrants, whatever their tribal affiliation" (Walker 1990, 201). According to Walker, the lack of urban marae in the early stages meant that "the normal life-crises of birth, death and marriage had to be met with what was at hand, the family dwelling. The head of a whanau responded to death by turning the suburban State house into a 'mini-marae'" (200). Meanwhile, "community halls in the city centre served the needs of *quasi*-tribes such as Ngati Poneke in Wellington" (ibid. [emphasis added]).

Regardless, the new social formations ended up providing a sanctuary for Māori moving to the cities. Concurrently, as outlined by *kaumatua* (elder)

Tuoro, this meant an amalgamation of the tribal identities of the other most significant urban marae in Auckland, Hoani Waititi:

> You had to leave your tribalism at the door ... What we were trying to create with this Marae was a sense of family and a sense of belonging when people were no longer able to readily access their whanau [family] ties in the areas they were originally from. (cited in Meredith 2000, 6)

Of importance to the discussion that follows is the development of urban Māori authorities (UMAs), whose genesis was directly linked to the establishment of urban marae such as Hoani Waititi and Te Puea. The most well known of these are the formally incorporated Waipareira Trust and the Manukau Urban Māori Authority: "Both organizations were established by groups of first-generation urban Maori from diverse tribal backgrounds to meet the development needs of their respective communities" (Keiha and Moon 2008, 10).

In all, the state urbanization programs failed to absorb Māori into Pākehā culture, and a new cultural form was produced – one neither more nor less valid than any previous Indigenous cultural formations. One of the key points of this section, then, is the error of establishing a rural/urban, traditional/urban binary. As the following section outlines, urban forms of political resistance were fed back to Māori in rural locales, while urban Māori sought the conventions of marae culture to inform their practices in the metropolis (see also Andersen, this volume).

Third Culture: Radical Urban Indigeneity

By the 1970s, it was increasingly evident that the "Māori Problem" had not been solved via urbanization. Indeed, the threat to the nation-state that radical urban Indigeneity produced determined that the urban Māori subject needed to be reconstituted as a corrupt aberration. The Urban Māori third culture was heavily influenced by its immediate engagement with neocolonial methods of subjugation and its interaction with an increasingly politically informed, academic, metropolitan culture, which led to what became popularized as a process of "conscientization" and, later, "decolonization." To be exact, the transformative third culture produced new, radical, cutting-edge Indigenous subjectivities that drastically altered New Zealand's political landscape (a point Morgan, this volume, makes regarding urban Indigenous issues in Australia).

Significantly, urban groups came into contact with resistance, civil rights, and decolonial discourses springing from the United States and other places. In the 1970s, Walker (1990) refers to the "new wave" of Māori resisters as "Neo-Māori Activists" who formed overlapping collectives such as Ngā Tamatoa (modelled on the US Black Power movement), the Māori Organization on Human Rights (MOOHR), the Waitangi Action Committee, He Taua, the Māori People's Liberation Movement of Aotearoa, and Black Women: "The political ethos of the groups was based on the liberation struggle against racism, sexism, capitalism, and government oppression" (220). MOOHR, for instance, produced urban resistance via the newsletter *Te Hokioi* (first published in 1968), which focused on the Treaty as a vehicle for the promotion of Indigenous rights, culture, and language (209-10).

Aroha Harris (2004, 26) points out that "Ngā Tamatoa was the progenitor of a Māori movement that would eventually comprise a potent collection of Māori protest groups and individuals: politically conscious, radical, and un-waveringly committed to the pursuit of tino rangatiratanga [sovereignty]." She goes on to say: "Members were young, educated, and urbanised ... They were leaders and social commentators recently come-of-age, the new face of Māori activism" (24). At this time, Ngā Tamatoa were ensconced in the cit-ies of Auckland and Wellington, and the annual Treaty celebrations became their focus of protest. In 1971,

> Tamatoa protested by wearing black arm-bands and declaring the celebra-tion a day of mourning for the loss of 25.2 million hectares of Maori land. Embarrassed by the show of dissent the Government sought the advice of the Maori Council, which responded with a submission that cited fourteen statutes contravening Article 2 of the Treaty. (Walker 1990, 211)

The joint actions of Ngā Tamatoa and the Māori Council led to the Treaty of Waitangi Act, 1975, which subsequently established the Waitangi Tribunal, which has since functioned to assess historical grievances lodged by Māori against the state.

The actions of groups like Ngā Tamatoa, MOOHR, and WAC are import-ant to note here not only because they reflect the type of unsettling neo-formation that Bhabha had in mind but also because they expressed their resistance through the Treaty. The Treaty's promotion as the pre-eminent conduit for colonial redress was the direct result of a developing urban Indigenous subjectivity, and this should not be overlooked. Indeed, it could be said that the tribal consciousness developed since and entrenched through key strategically essentialized cornerstones of postcolonial Māori culture, such as *whakapapa* (genealogy), *reo* (language), and *tikanga* (culture), was a direct result of the urban Indigenous resistance movement (see Johnson, this volume, for a related discussion on the role of urban pow-wows). What occurred via a radical urban Māori third culture in the 1970s was a "struggle for freedom [that] does not give back to national culture its former values and shapes" (Vine Deloria, cited in Bruyneel 2007, 144). The next section examines the production of Indigeneity following the "heyday" of Indigenous urban radical resistance.

Producing Subjectivities: Juridification

> Power is not something that can be possessed, and it is not a form of might; power is never anything more than a relationship that can, and must, be studied only by looking at the interplay between the terms of that relationship. One cannot, therefore, write the history of kings or the history of peoples; one can write the history of what constitutes those opposing terms. (Foucault 2003, 168)

The concept of sovereignty is at the core of the following discussion, which traces the production of an Indigenous "Partner" capable of engaging in dialogue with the state and, concomitantly, the production of a historical binary imaginary. "Sovereignty" has various meanings, but I use the term in a Foucauldian sense: "It is the power to 'make live' and 'let' die" (Foucault 2003, 241) – that is, it is the power to produce authentic Indigenous subjectivities and to de-authenticate others. Foucault argues that,

> from the nineteenth century until the present day, we have [had] ... a legislation, a discourse, and an organization of public right articulated around the principle of the sovereignty of the social body and the delegation of individual sovereignty to the State; and we also have a tight grid of disciplinary coercions that actually guarantees the cohesion of that social body. (37)

Essentially, Foucault suggests here that Indigenous subjectivities have been "made to live and let die" via the juridification of subjectivity (i.e., via laws formalized by the state) and disciplinary coercions that, in a much less direct way, function to regulate difference via the idea of normative culture.

In the remaining part of this chapter, I argue that the modernized urban Indigenous subject has become a corrupted and inauthentic form of Indigeneity due to its devolution from traditional culture and space. Thus, it is unworthy of being a Treaty Partner. I suggest that the Māori process of claiming rights, grievances, and even the ability to call oneself Māori (or at least an authentic Māori) is attached to the development of what Robert Niezen (2009, 40) calls "ethnic formalization." Yet, rather than vilifying tribal formations, I trace a necro- and biopolitical historiography, which demonstrates that the regulation of discourse through the judicial system ushered in the range of difference within which an acceptable "Māori" subjectivity was situated. In other words, power produced an Indigenous subjectivity apposite to the context, not an Indigenous subject replete with power.

The Historical Binary Imaginary: Producing a Treaty Partner

In the New Zealand context, fundamental to bicultural sovereignty was the production of both partners in the bicultural imaginary through the Treaty of Waitangi, or what Harris (2004, 27) refers to as a "treaty consciousness." Yet, seldom has such a consciousness come under critical scrutiny to determine what it means to locate one's political liminality in a historical document, especially in terms of essentializing identity and, conversely, losing one's existentialist groundings.

The construction of sovereignty through a treaty grievance process means that political consciousness is founded in a temporarily dislocated space. A "treaty consciousness" is complicit with tribalism because, on many levels, tribalism is located in the past. It is produced in the minds of people who believe the authentic indigene became tainted at contact, who believe that biculturalism is a natural contemporary artefact of a settler/Indigenous society and, last, that tribalism is inherently rooted in genealogy. In other words, they believe that one's political genesis begins with one's biological history. Likewise, for the non-Indigenous "Partner," Jeffrey Sissons (2004, 19) suggests, "post-settler belonging absolutely requires the perpetuation of an indigeneity through which new relationships to the land may be negotiated." Sissons goes on to say: "Within this imagined political community settlers belong by virtue of a relationship between the Crown, which represents them, and Maori tribal leaders who represent *tangata whenua*" (ibid.).

While I agree with Bruyneel (2007, xi) when he says, "because a treaty is a document codifying an agreement between sovereign governments, the recognition of a tribe's treaty rights is also recognition of the tribe's sovereignty," I would also suggest that, in this "recognition" process, only certain Indigenous subjectivities prosper, while others are allowed to die. As the following section outlines, during one of the legal cases to determine the rights of urban collectives through the Treaty, the Crown counsel took the position that the urban subject should be managed through Article 3 of the Treaty, which essentially guarantees Māori "the status of British Subjects ... akin to modern-day citizenship" (Hayward 2004, 14). In other words, urban groups were not to be allocated special "Indigenous" privileges beyond normal citizenship. Article 2, however, which establishes chiefly possession and management over "their lands and Estates Forests Fisheries and other properties" (Orange 1987, 258, cited in Hayward 2004, 157-58), was pertinent only to "kin-based groups exercising customary authority over resources ... and not to non-tribal groups" (Waitangi Tribunal 1998, xxiii, cited in Levine 2001, 166).

Thus, while in some cases it may be that "indigenous tribes and nations claim a form of sovereignty that is unclear because it is not easily located inside or outside the [neocolonial state]" (Bruyneel 2007, xiii), in New Zealand tribal sovereignty is recognized *only* because this form of sovereignty is easily located within the Treaty Partnership. Indeed, because the Treaty is a historical document that has produced a grievance mentality, the "rehabilitative" approach presumes physical, spatial, spiritual, and epistemological displacement and loss, and, therefore, its discordance with the immediacy of urban groups serves to debilitate what I call Indigenous existentialism. Indigenous existentialism underscores the importance of the lived experience of Indigenous peoples; it moves beyond *ressentiment* and the focus on "decolonizing the mind" to one of choice and responsibility lost at the juncture of the primitive indigene/civilized European binary, lost when Indigenous peoples became "victims" of colonization. Indigenous existentialism implores Indigenous peoples to move beyond victimhood to reclaim choice and responsibility within their lived experiences.

Before going further, it should be restated that, while I have sympathies for the necropolitical outcomes urban Māori have suffered, I am not arguing "their case." There is no case to be argued. Biopower produced an *"iwi* [tribal] consciousness" and will continue to invent new forms of Indigeneity as power's discursiveness simultaneously wields its sword and gives life. While it may be argued that such a conception renders Indigenous agency meaningless (i.e., how can we resist if we are mere reflections of dominant discourses?), I fervently believe that to envisage new forms of resistance, self-critical awareness is key. This is especially so because Indigenous politics has become overly determined by authenticity and tradition. What this means is that the outcome of a fundamentalist Indigeneity is that there can only be one authentic culture, with all others being deemed corruptions.

The Juridical Process

> Pursuing grievances that follow from violations of rights means defining in particular terms who is the beneficiary of those rights and who is not ... It calls for clearly defined subjects attached to specific communities. (Niezen 2009, 10)

According to Manuhuia Barcham (1998, 305), for the majority of the twentieth century, "iwi [tribes] were relatively weak politically, being more a cultural institution than a political one. Then, in the mid-1980s, with the implementation of new government policies, a period of re-Iwiization began." A prominent example of how the juridical process aligns with disciplinary coercions to produce a viable Indigenous subject occurred during the distribution of a fisheries settlement awarded by the state via a Treaty of Waitangi claim. In 1989, the state awarded "pre-settlement" fisheries assets to "all Māori" through the Māori Fisheries Act, and, in 1990, Te Ohu Kai Moana, or the Māori Fisheries Commission (hereafter referred to as "the Commission"), was established to manage the allocation process. The Commission was comprised of influential Māori leaders, including Sir Tipene O'Regan, Matiu Rata, Sir Graham Latimer, and Sir Robert Mahuta. The Treaty of Waitangi (Fisheries Claims) Settlement Act, 1992, "directed the commission to allocate the pre-settlement assets to its beneficiaries ... [W]hile the act occasionally refers to these beneficiaries as 'all Māori' the role of Māori *iwi* had been given new prominence" (Webster 2002, 349-50). Although given prominence, the act did not proffer a definition of "iwi." Here it is important to understand that "iwi" can mean both "people" in the general sense of the word (and thus could relate to "all Māori") and that it can also refer to "peoples" in the sense of large genealogical formations (i.e., tribes). This ambiguity meant that "iwi" became the "focus of conflict and litigation – primarily between Māori – ever since" (350).

Without juridical definition, the Commission took it upon itself to determine Indigenous contemporary rights via postcolonial imaginings of precolonial "traditional" culture. The Commission decreed that "iwi" referred to tribes as the original social formations under the Treaty and that settlements could be divvied out accordingly. It defines "iwi" as a composite of: "(i) shared descent from *tipuna* [ancestors]; (ii) *hapü*; (iii) *marae*; (iv) belong[ing] historically to a *takiwa* [geographical district]; and (v) [having] an existence traditionally acknowledged by other *iwi*" (cited in Webster 2002, 350). For all intents and purposes, the Commission outlined what has become commonly understood as a "traditional" tribal conglomerate. Under this decree it was argued that "all Māori" would gain advantage from the allocation as derivatives of original iwi (ibid.). Soon afterwards, urban Māori collectives strongly voiced their dissatisfaction with being excised from the Treaty process, centring their protests around the idea that the fundamental purpose of the settlement was to benefit "all Māori," yet, via the hierarchy of tribal structures, it would only benefit an elite few, while the majority of Māori who resided in urban spaces would gain little.[3]

The battle lines were drawn. What ensued over more than a decade was a series of proceedings and appeals: "two initial sets of High Court judicial review proceedings, consolidated appeals and cross-appeals in the Court of Appeal, an appeal to the Privy Council, a further hearing in the High Court, another appeal to the Court of Appeal, and a further appeal to the Privy Council" (Gover and Baird 2002, 61-62). I do not have the space to delve into all the iterations of each case, yet it should be highlighted that, through the years, the Commission's original definition of "iwi" was fundamentally upheld, even though in 1996, for example, the Court of Appeal found that "iwi referred to the people of a tribe, not the representatives of the tribal leaders ... including those who did not have or were unable to establish specific tribal affiliations" (Durie 1998, 166).

Following the 1996 decision, it was expected that the National Party-led government would effectively support the resolution through to the impending Privy Council hearing. However, the government backed away from lending its weight to the decision and effectively aided the tribal groups. In London, Tamihere suggested the government had been influenced by a Māori old-boys network: "the old guard who control and hold all the Māori money now – the Sir Tipene O'Regans, the Sir Graham Latimers ... National has caved in to political pressure" (cited in Durie 1998, 167). Eventually, in January 1997, while the Privy Council made no recommendation of what constituted an iwi, essentially it reinforced the Commission's original definition by quashing the Court of Appeal judgment, arguing that it had gone too far in defining what an iwi was on the evidence given.

Following the Privy Council ruling, in April 1997 the Commission moved quickly to devise a plan to allocate fisheries assets between $250 and $350 million, omitting any reference to UMA (Durie 1998, 167-9). Subsequent hearings continued to reinforce the initial definition and stymied any further challenges by urban groups. In August 1998, for instance, the Court of Appeal concluded:

> The implementation of the settlement accords with Maori traditional values, although it will necessarily utilize modern-day mechanisms ... The settlement was of the historical grievances of a tribal people. It ought to be implemented in a manner consistent with that fact. With all due respect to UMA, who are formed on the basis of kaupapa not whakapapa, they cannot fulfil such a role. (cited in Meredith 2000, 11)

Unfortunately, the fundamental lines of reasoning taken by both sides were lamentable because they attempted to invalidate each other's definition of Indigenous subjectivity. While iwi groups endeavoured to position urban groups as unworthy of historical recognition, urban groups were forced into discrediting the use of "iwi" to mean "tribe." For instance, a primary argument that emerged suggested that the Treaty referred to "hapü," not "iwi," based on the idea that "traditional iwi were intermittent and non-territorial formations ... [I]wi tended to be arbitrarily defined by those in power with regard to current political and economic opportunities rather than merely by kinship or descent" (Webster 2002, 366).

Such lobbying required a degree of self-conscious manipulation, as was evident following the 1996 Privy Council decision, when both sides attempted to influence the depiction of reality. The UMA collectives set about recruiting non-iwi affiliated members, succeeding in enlisting "over 10,000 Māori who accepted their mandate to demand a share of the fisheries allocations regardless of iwi affiliation" (Webster 2002, 360). At the same time, the Commission initiated an "iwi helpline," which helped Māori gain assistance in "discovering" their iwi affiliation(s). Over six months, the helpline received twenty-nine hundred enquiries (360-61). Durie (1998, 169) concludes: "The Commission was keen to render Māori urban authorities unnecessary by boosting iwi registers."

Interestingly, in his summation of the 1998 Court of Appeal decision, Judge Paterson clearly outlines the development of an iwi partnership ideal though the juridical process: "The government has encouraged the iwi concept over the last 20 to 30 years ... [D]ecision making is now more from the top down rather than from the bottom up" (cited in Webster 2002, 367). The implication is clear here that, in formulating the best procedure to manage the Māori problem, the state concluded that a hierarchical model was most "re-cognizable," with iwi leadership at the apex of the triangle – a hierarchical structure that would facilitate the funnelling of power and resources downwards and outwards via hapü, whanau, and eventually to the Indigenous citizen. Such a construction is commonly thought to be the constituent scaffold of "Māori society." Actually, the structure reflects a patriarchal social assembly, an "old-boys' network," able to work with the upper echelons of state power – a configuration that merely reinforces the general conception of Indigenous cultures as patriarchal, sexist, and patrilineal.

The individual Indigenous leader produced was thus gendered, classed, and, in some cases, deemed "chivalrous" (many of the original Commission members were knighted by the Queen of England, including Sirs Tipene O'Regan, Robert Mahuta, and Graham Latimer). O'Regan was also named by the right-wing *National Business Review* as one of the "New Zealanders of the Year." In all, this led Tamihere to talk of the Commission's "new corporates, the Knights of the Brown Table – and their new weapon – money" (cited in Webster 2002, 365). Hence, while it was often poor urban Māori women and men who originally championed Indigenous rights via the Treaty, two decades later the Treaty Partner was male and wealthy.

The production of male leadership at the expense of women leaders, who were at the vanguard of the 1970s political conscientization movement, eventually led to a claim's being brought to the Waitangi Tribunal. The submission stated:

> These actions and policies have resulted in an undermining of Māori women so that their status as rangatira [chiefs] has been expropriated due to the Crown's failure to accord Māori women status and power within the political, social and economic structures it has created. (cited in Mikaere 1994, 144)

Unfortunately, the laying of responsibility solely at the feet of "the Crown" diminished the complicity of Māori male leadership in this process. Regarding class, although framing power hegemonically, Evan Poata-Smith (2004, 61) succinctly shows that the settlements process contributed to, rather than diminished, the gap between the Māori elite and a typically urban Māori underclass, resulting in "a substantial shift in resources and compensation to those sections of Māori society already wealthy and powerful."

Most important, in attempts to authenticate and manipulate one version of identity over another, both urban and tribal groups enabled the debate to be framed by a single-truth-seeking ideology. During one of the High Court cases, for example, the chairperson of a tribal coalition admonished the urban collectives by asking: "Who are they!? Will they be here in another hundred years? *Nga Puhi* will!" (cited in Webster 2002, 136). Such framing was detrimental to the broader vision of Indigeneity as it permitted the regulation of difference within the space of an "authentic reality." Thus, both sides relinquished the right to self-define by enabling the halls of colonial power in "Mother" England and one of its satellites to determine "Indigeneity." Overall, the process reinforced the reification of "Māori culture" at the expense of the *possibility* of culture. As articulated by Steven Webster (2002, 368), the juridical process "entrenched in the law a rigidified sense of iwi" in both senses of the word's meanings. The juridical process described in this section further highlights the Nietzschean concept of morality, which is that there is neither good nor evil. In other words, neither side possessed an inherent morality that profited a "truthful" outcome; rather, subjectivities were produced via power's discursive nature.

Disciplinary Coercion: Biopolitics and Necropolitics

This contestation and political struggle is partly one of who is a Maori citizen and what constitutes Maori citizenship. (Meredith 2000, 12)

In this section I focus on what, as previously mentioned, Foucault refers to as the "tight grid of disciplinary coercions that guarantees the cohesion of a social body." The production of an "iwi consciousness" as a unitary form of Indigenous subjectivity is legitimized and thus animated by the series of discourses. Iwi consciousness is like Foucault's (2002, 39) "organism with its own needs, its own internal force and its own capacity for survival." Central to this organism are the notions of "tradition" and "authenticity" and how they, in combination with Indigeneity, serve to produce and exclude. Here I align with Paul Meredith (2000, 16), who suggests that "tradition" within the context of ethnic formalization "is not only utilised as a normative guide but also to establish and sustain a citizenship which is structured around subordinate/dominant power relations and inclusive/exclusive membership."

As the juridical conflict over the definition of "iwi" raged, the discourse produced by tribal fundamentalists attempted to institutionalize a tribal consciousness. As Robin Hapi argues: "tribes have always been here and are here to stay" (cited in Barcham 1998, 309). Thus, part of the disciplinary grid involved "formally articulating ... boundaries of culture and citizenship" (Niezen 2009, 10). According to Niezen, a simple logic underpins such "ethnic formalization":

> The more human groups are displaced, removed from familiar relationships and strategies of power-accumulation and peacemaking, the more they will attach themselves to leaders, organizations, and social movements that offer stability and self-esteem through the reinventions of their past, often making social belonging more exclusive and sharply defined. (176)

Along similar lines, Sissons (2004, 29) argues: "Whereas settler nationhood required Maori to become Pakeha [i.e., New Zealanders of settler genealogy], post-settler nationhood requires Maori to become Maori." Of note here is the attendant "iwification" of the New Zealand census at about this time. While the identification label "Māori" had been offered as an ethnicity for many years previously, following the 1991 census those who ascribed to being Māori were subsequently offered the ability to "identify one or more iwi affiliations" (Webster 2002, 359; see Kukutai, this volume, for the impact of these categorical changes on Maori population dynamics).

According to Arjun Appadurai (1996), such ethnic formalization defines culture as a noun, as opposed to an adjective – that is, as a quantifiable object as opposed to a dynamic idea. Such cultural sanctification has led to Māori publishing a number of "Māoriness" scales that closely relate to the earlier anthropological scales produced by James Ritchie (1963) and Joan Metge (1976). Interestingly, Hana O'Regan (2001, 91), Sir Tipene O'Regan's daughter, outlines the quantification of "Māoriness" as an enabler of social reality: "By accepting that people may possess varying levels or degrees of identity we engage in a process of redefining and revaluing the criteria of cultural identity in order to accommodate the social and cultural reality."

Similarly, Durie (1998, 58) suggests, "the concept of a secure identity rests on definite self-identification as Māori together with quantifiable involvement in, and/or knowledge of, whakapapa, marae participation, whānau, whenua tipu (ancestral land), contacts with Māori people, and Māori language." In relation to these, Durie goes on to list "secure," "positive," "notional," and "compromised" identity profiles as descending categories. For both O'Regan and Durie, and many others, culture becomes an essentialized noun, a quantifiable thing, a constituent model that allows for qualitative analyses on an "authentic/corrupt" scale. Of central importance to this chapter, then, is how the definition of Indigenous subjectivity is related to the processes of "ethnic formalization" and, subsequently, to the rights to postcolonial grieving, treaty claims, and privilege.

With particular regard to the corrupt urban Māori subject, from their inception until now, discourses surrounding Māori urbanization have mutated to support radically different tactics. As outlined above, urbanization was initially closely affiliated with assimilation and modernization. The derogatory "pipi beds" notion to which Walker (1990) makes reference, for instance, is a thinly veiled allusion to premodernity underpinned by the logic that modernization was the answer to "the Māori Problem." Those Māori who moved to the cities beginning in the 1950s, on the other hand, were the new "brown skinned citizens" that Pākehā New Zealand desired (at least in their working class form). From the late 1970s to the 1980s, the "Māori Problem" became the corrupted nature of the assimilated urban Māori subject. Gangs, domestic violence, and urban Māori violence in general became (and remain) the focus of media reportage on Māori. Yet, recently, in the search for an amicable Treaty Partner, the discourse has further morphed so that primitive culture is now regarded as the essential make-up of an Indigenous citizen. One contemptible aspect of this short genealogy is that Māori were compelled to move to the city and, consequently, could not but help to reconstruct their identity: yet, today, changes to identity construction are deliberated as inauthentic. Thus, in the temporal, spatial, and political identity formations, or what Bruyneel (2007) refers to as "politics on the boundaries," Indigenous subjectivities are much more produced and conditioned through disciplinary coercions than Bruyneel and others imagine.

Also in this genealogy we see a reversal of the civilization logic that has pervaded much of colonization and postcolonization. Today, the more assimilated Māori are afforded fewer rights than are the tribally based groups. Essentially, for an Indigenous group to be recognized, it must display premodern configurations. Modern configurations, on the other hand, are inauthentic and thus unworthy. Within the logic of "traditional" Indigeneity, the key questions become: After what temporal point are neo-formations of Indigenous groupings no longer considered Indigenous? At what spatial point do new Indigenous cultural formations become corrupt? Clearly, within this logic, the temporally and spatially defined "urban drift" is that point.

In the above process, it is apparent that, via the juridical process, urban groups were written out of a "Partner" formation. More important than the actual exclusion from access to colonial coffers is what urban groups potentiate and, thus, what their exclusion represents symbolically. What is crucial here is the traditional/progressive binary that tribal/urban groups supposedly and respectively represent. Via the Treaty, the temporal location of Indigenous subjectivity as historical and archaic displaced Indigenous existentialism. It disabled the immediacy of Indigenous politics; it dislocated Indigenous identity into the past and, thus, the social problems Māori face in both urban and rural areas are resignified as dependent upon the incapacities of a premodern culture. The necropolitics enabled by this process symbolically determined neo-Indigenous formations as corrupted, and, thus, rather than accepting the "Māori problem" as a production of colonization, Māori social decline continues to be met with doubt, suspicion, and recrimination.

The logic of tradition clearly located urban Māori "at a loose end," as Indigenous vagabonds unable to be moored within the neocolonial complex, unable to be helped because they could not help themselves. At the *Hui Ara Ahu Whakamua* conference in 1994, whose purpose was to examine Māori diversity, Māori language expert Timoti Kāretu argued that contemporary Māori were often "iho ngaro" (without a base), "many of these children look Māori and are identified as such by their peers, but that is where their Māoriness ends" (cited in Durie 1998, 94). In a similar vein, Sir Tipene O'Regan argued that, because it was possible for any Māori to discover and lay claim to a precolonial ancestor, if Māori forewent this opportunity "they were in effect giving up their claim to be Māori at all" (Webster 2002, 358).

In reality, what iwi fundamentalists forewent in their complicit exclusion of urban groups was the unsettling nature these collectives represented to the state. Urban groups posed the greatest threat to the neocolonial state, spatially, politically, and temporally. In other words, urban groups represented what state conceptions of Indigeneity feared the most: *immediacy*. The possibility of politically robust Indigenous groups located in the city, as opposed to on distant rural marae, signalled the threat of *physical immediacy*; the neo-Indigenous collectives represent a conception of Indigeniety not located in the historical, authentic, or traditional imaginary but possessing *temporal immediacy* and thus demanding immediate dialogue regarding Māori social dissoluteness; neo-Indigenous collectives represent *political immediacy* because they demand that the state enter into an unsettling dialogue associated with Indigenous rights – a dialogue that goes beyond the historical grievance mentality and through the immediacy of Indigenous facticity. Both physical and temporal immediacy require a paradigmatic shift to view Indigeneity in life as opposed to *buried in state*.

Conclusion: Fourth Space and Indigenous Existentialism

It is perfectly true, as philosophers say, that life must be understood backwards. But they forget the other proposition, that it must be lived forwards.
And if one thinks over that proposition it becomes more and more evident
that life can never really be understood in time simply because at no particular moment can I find the necessary resting-place from which to understand it backwards. (Søren Kierkegaard, cited in Flynn 2006, 101)

When one thinks of Bhabha's conception of "third culture" it is easy to ro-
mantically imagine neo-Indigenous cultural formations unsettling the national narrative to the point that these cultural expansions gain a foothold
and disrupt the entrenched binary. Yet, Indigenous scholarship has located
itself within the colonizer/colonized binary for so long that, even as we set
about to "decolonize," we tend to romanticize the forms of resistance
taken and the resultant postcolonial social formations. In doing so, we fore-
go Indigenous responsibility within the neocolonial complex: we forget to
hold Indigenous people accountable for their choices, for the complicity of
Indigenous identity formations, and for the necropolitics such complicity
enables.

It is, therefore, inauthentic to appropriate the idea of a third space without also understanding how the discursive nature of power works within
this space to produce subjectivities. Simply being Indigenous or adhering to
"traditional" cultural practices or even resisting the neocolonial state does
not naturalize a sovereign space located beyond the neocolonial complex. If
we look at the genealogy of urban Māori resistance, for instance, the original
cultural essentialism first promoted eventually came to exclude some of the
original cohort it was designed to embolden. Significantly, the subjectivities
excluded were those unsettling political formations that indeed challenged
binary notions.

It is with the above in mind that I critique some of the tacit understandings offered by Bruyneel (2007). In his work, there is a tendency to uncompli-
catedly accept that Indigenous forms of resistance inherently challenge
neocolonial structures. For instance:

In resistance to this colonial rule, indigenous political actors work across
American spatial and temporal boundaries, demanding rights and resources from the liberal democratic settler-state while also challenging the imposition of colonial rule on their lives. This resistance engenders a "third

space of sovereignty" that resides neither simply inside nor outside the American political system but rather exists on these very boundaries exposing both the practices and the contingencies of American colonial rule. (xvii)

Too often in Indigenous studies we fall into a colonizer/colonized binary, which debilitates our ability to see the density of the neocolonial complex. Too often, Indigenous studies scholars envisage Indigenous acts as inherently sovereign acts against an omnipresent hegemonic colonial state and, in so doing, valorize the reactionary productions of Indigenous subjectivities that binary creates. Lost in this battle of good and evil is the idea that the neocolonial complex produces both non-Indigenous and Indigenous citizens, while other subjectivities are excluded.

In a radical critique of the innate unsettling qualities of simply "being" Indigenous, which is evident in both Bhabha's and Bruyneel's conceptions of third space, I would argue that the neocolonial complex, through a force field of discursive strategies, produces forms of Indigeneity complicit with its agenda, which, indeed, are produced by the mere fact that they are more recognizable to the neocolonial state and are very much "inside" that state and complicit with neocolonial liberalization. While acknowledging that neo-cultures are an implicit production of colonization, it is imperative that notions of self-critique and responsibility underpin these new cultural spaces, along with a will to investigate what is being included and thus excluded under the name of "Indigeneity" – typically, the exclusion involves those who have been most displaced by colonial rule.

Hence, I propose a concomitant fourth space of necro-sovereignty, a dead space or a void of possibility where those excluded subjectivities are encouraged to die yet, simultaneously, are freed from the will to be recognized. I argue that, for Indigenous scholars, this space is as important to analyze as is the biopolitical third space of sovereignty. As I see it, any analysis of third and fourth spaces of Indigenous sovereignty must be underpinned by the notion of Indigenous existentialism. Primarily, Indigenous existentialism focuses our historical remembrances along the paths of political resistance and on forms of third culture that have been produced. The result of this is that we understand the production of Indigenous identities as a matter of Indigenous responsibility, as the outcomes of the choices Indigenous people have made. In the case at hand, many Māori have chosen to undertake political resistance through the formation of a Treaty relationship with the state and, accordingly, have been produced as the Treaty

Partner, have handed the ability to self-define back to "Mother Britain," and have fought among each other tooth and nail to exclude one another's right to procure subjectivity.

Thus, Indigenous political intelligence requires Indigenous people to foresee the outcomes of paths of political recognition. In relation to this chapter, one could question what narratives the iwi fundamentalist formations serve to unsettle, or, rather, does their complicity as the Treaty Partner reside within or without the neocolonial political imaginary? And, subsequently, what benefits have their recent paths of political recognition led to with regard to their constituents? One could also question the urban collectives, for instance, for their obsession to be recognized by the state as legitimate Indigenous collectives. What is the cost of recognition? In the act of desiring recognition, what choices do we lose? Or do we simply lose choice? What freedoms are enabled via the necropolitics outlined above? Is a fourth sovereign space determined by necropolitics actually a space of *possibility?* Will choices of political recognition through state bodies (which inherently relocate Indigenous groups within the colonizer/colonized binary) lead to outcomes of self-definition, choice, and responsibility?

While other Māori signed the Treaty of Waitangi in 1840, Iwikau Te Heuheu Tukino III, leader of Ngāti Tūwharetoa o Taupō, made a different choice:

> I will not agree to the mana of a strange people being placed over this land. Though every chief in the island consent to it, yet I will not. I will consent to neither your act nor your goods. As for these blankets, burn them. (cited in Walker 1990, 97)

Notes

1 Both "necropolitics" and "biopolitics" centre on the notion of "sovereignty" – that is, "the power and the capacity to dictate who may live and who must die" (Mbembe 2003, 11). Achille Mbembe builds (as do I in this chapter) on Foucault's (2003) critique of sovereignty, particularly in *Society Must Be Defended.* I define "biopolitics" crudely, and in relation to Foucault's classic notion of "biopower," to be a "productive" concept: it describes how citizens, through both discursive and non-discursive methods, become subjects of the state. I take "necropolitics" to be the negative assumption that biopolitcs allows for – meaning that, if subjects are produced, then, conversely, many subjectivities are left to die. Necro-subjectivities need not be an ethereal concept. Foucault, for instance, suggests that the proposed extermination of the Jews by the Nazis reflected an extreme (modern) account of the sovereign right

to kill via the technologies of biopower that every modern state possesses. In relation to the contemporary postcolonial, the biopolitical can be defined as the production of indigenous subjectivities that enable the liberal pluralist state to accommodate recourses to indigeneity. In the New Zealand context, this would be the production of what I go on to describe as the "Treaty Partner." Conversely, necropolitics is the conscious or unconscious, wilful or discursive, "letting die" of indigenous subjectivities that inherently occurs at the production site of indigenous subjectivities.

2 For a similar discussion in a Canadian context, see Andersen (this volume). For the intergenerational effects of urbanization in an American context, see Lucero (this volume).

3 This lack of positioning of urban "tribes" as authentic Māori spaces seems at odds with juridical findings in a Canadian context (see Belanger, this volume, for a contrasting discussion).

References

Appadurai, A. 1996. *Modernity at large: Cultural dimensions of globalization.* Minneapolis: University of Minnesota Press.

Barcham, M. 1998. The challenge of urban Maori: Reconciling conceptions of Indigeneity and social change. *Asia Pacific Viewpoint* 39: 303-14.

Bhabha, H. 1994. *The location of culture.* London: Routledge.

Bruyneel, K. 2007. *The third space of sovereignty.* Minneapolis: University of Minnesota Press.

Durie, M. 1998. *Te mana, te kāwanatanga: The politics of Māori self-determination.* Auckland, NZ: Oxford University Press.

Flynn, T. 2006. *Existentialism.* Oxford: Oxford University Press.

Foucault, M. 1978. *The history of sexuality: An introduction.* Harmondsworth, UK: Penguin.

–. 2002. *The archaeology of knowledge.* London: Routledge.

–. 2003. *Society must be defended: Lectures at the Collège de France, 1975-1976.* New York: Picador.

Gover, K., and N. Baird. 2002. Identifying the Māori treaty partner. *University of Toronto Law Journal* 52: 39-68.

Harris, A. 2004. *Hīkoi: Forty years of Māori protest.* Wellington, NZ: Huia.

Hayward, J. 2004. Te Tiriti o Waitangi: The Treaty of Waitangi. In *Ki te whaiao: An introduction to Māori culture and society,* ed. T. Ka'ai, J. Moorfield, M. Reilly, and S. Mosley, 151-62. Auckland, NZ: Pearson.

Keiha, P., and P. Moon. 2008. The emergence and evolution of urban Maori authorities: A response to Maori urbanization. *Te Kaharoa* 1: 1-17.

Levine, H. 2001. Can a voluntary organization be a treaty partner? The case of Te Whānau o Waipareira Trust. *Social Policy Journal of New Zealand* 17: 161-70.

Mbembe, A. 2003. Necropolitics. *Public Culture* 15: 11-40.

Meredith, P. 2000. Urban Maori as "new citizens." Paper presented at the Revisioning Citizenship in New Zealand conference, Hamilton, New Zealand.

Metge, J. 1976. *The Maoris of New Zealand.* London: Routledge and Kegan Paul.

Mikaere, A. 1994. Maori women: Caught in the contradictions of a colonised reality. *Waikato Law Review* 2: 125-49.

Niezen, R. 2009. *The rediscovered self: Indigenous identity and cultural justice.* Montreal and Kingston: McGill-Queen's University Press.

O'Regan, H. 2001. *Ko Tahu, ko au: Kai Tahu – tribal identity.* Christchurch, NZ: Horomaka.

Panoho, J., and R. Stablein. 2005. A postcolonial perspective on organizational governance in New Zealand. Paper presented at the Critical Management Studies 4 conference, Cambridge, UK.

Peters, M. 2001. Cultural studies and the future of "culture." *New Zealand Sociology* 16: 26-47.

Poata-Smith, E. 2004. Ka tika a muri, ka tika a mua? In *Tangata tangata: The changing ethnic contours of New Zealand,* ed. P. Spoonley, C. Macpherson, and D. Pearson, 59-88. Southbank Victoria, NZ: Thomson/Dunmore.

Ritchie, J. 1963. *The making of a Maori: A case study of a changing community.* Wellington, NZ: A.H. and A.W. Reed.

Sissons, J. 2004. Maori tribalism and post-settler nationhood in New Zealand. *Oceania* 75: 19-31.

Te Puni Kōkiri. 2007. Historical influences: Māori and the economy. Wellington, NZ: Government Printer.

Walker, R. 1990. *Ka whawhai tonu matou: Struggle without end.* Auckland, NZ: Penguin.

Webster, S. 2002. Māori retribalization and treaty rights to the New Zealand fisheries. *Contemporary Pacific* 14: 341-76.

Conclusion

Indigenizing Modernity or Modernizing Indigeneity?

CHRIS ANDERSEN AND EVELYN PETERS

The chapters in this volume have sought to explore the implications of urbanization on the production of distinctive Indigenous identities: the culture and lived experiences of the communities in which they are embedded (and their connections to non-urban locales) as well as how these manifest themselves in distinctive demographic characteristics. We position these as elements of the current complexity of Indigenous experiences produced in the wake of Western colonialisms and their attendant processes of modernity as well as Indigenous resistances to, and incorporation of, such processes into their social relations.

More specifically, we are interested not only in examining how particular urban areas exert influence over the struggles for meaning of Indigenous identities specific to those locales but also in the ways in which Indigenous communities produce their own forms of endogamous identification – sometimes in conflict with the broader community, sometimes in concert. What forms of resilience and innovation mark these spaces? What continuities continue to shape the complex relations between urban and non-urban Indigenous spaces? In what ways are Western institutions and practices reformulated to support the production of Indigenous identities and practices?

Despite the geographical distance between the cities researched in this volume and the disciplinary differences of its contributors, several broad trends emerge from the complex social relations that embed Indigenous and settler societies. This conclusion briefly summarizes these trends with an eye to what they can tell us about the meanings and manifestations of Indigeneity as they express themselves in these urban locales; the trends are divided into four broad categories: (1) broad socio-demographic similarities; (2) the "out of place"-ness of urban Indigenous communities; (3) the deep complexity of the interculturality that manifests itself in urban centres; and (4) the continuities between urban and non-urban Indigenous locales.

Broad Socio-Demographic Similarities

This volume explores urban Indigeneity in four countries: Canada, the United States, Australia, and New Zealand. While these countries possess distinctive policy histories (which, in turn, have shaped contemporary policy concerns), it is nonetheless instructive to note the similarities of the urban Indigenous populations. For example, although for different reasons, the demographic analyses provided for each country demonstrate the broad movement of Indigenous people from a primarily rural to an increasingly urban population. So much so, in fact, that, while in Canada the proportion of Indigenous people residing in urban areas is roughly 50 percent (due to Indian Act regulations that produced and maintain reserves), in New Zealand it is well over 80 percent, in Australia (when including peri-urban locales) it is over 80 percent, and in the United States, roughly two-thirds of American Indians live in urban areas.

Contributors to this volume note myriad reasons for this migration from rural to urban areas – not the least of these includes a plethora of government interventions that sought, in various ways and for various reasons, to move Indigenous individuals and families from rural to urban locations. For example, with respect to the American situation, Snipp notes a number of factors, including the impact of the Second World War and the ensuing GI bill as well as a formal relocation program and the destabilization of traditional economies that steadily increased the hardship of everyday life in traditional, often rural territories while also increasing the apparent attractiveness of city life. The volume's Australian contributors similarly note that affordable housing programs were offered for those Indigenous individuals and families who were thought capable of the evident "civilizing" opportunities such programs offered, and Hokowhitu emphasizes the impact of Māori labour on urban "public works" employment in New Zealand (also stimulated by relocation programs). While in a Canadian context the specific auspices of the Indian Act functioned as a damper on the movement of those legally positioned as "Indians" to urban areas, the Canadian government nonetheless provided relocation programs similar to those offered in the United States, with similar effects (see Peters 2002). Likewise, various authors (Taylor, Morgan, Snipp) note the impact of "chain migration," the process of family members following kin to various regions and cities.

A second socio-demographic issue has muddied the statistical ability to position urban Indigenous populations and communities in each of the countries in similar ways: namely, changes in the categories used to measure Indigeneity as well as the increasing tendency towards what demographers refer to as "ethnic mobility." Canada, for example, has undergone a host of changes in terminology over the twentieth century (as well as in the standards used to measure them), and, as Norris, Clatworthy, and Peters (Chapter 1) note, the lack of a category for "Métis" in the period from 1951 to 1971 seriously affected population counts, as did moving from "ancestry" to "identity" when measuring Indigeneity in the early 1980s. Similarly, Taylor (Chapter 11) notes the impact that changes in census classifications had with regard to statistically determining population levels throughout the twentieth century in Australia, and Snipp (Chapter 8) discusses similar issues in a US context. Finally, Kukutai (Chapter 14) notes that neither "Māori" nor "urban" has a particularly stable meaning in a New Zealand census context, rendering statistical determinations fraught in similar ways.

Third, in addition to changes in official categorization, the demographic contributors to this volume note the problems raised by the growth of "ethnic mobility." Broadly speaking, the term refers to the phenomenon by which individuals "switch" their ethnic identity choices from one census to the next (a trend normally determined by scrutinizing otherwise implausible changes in a population over time). While this phenomenon appears more often in Canada, the United States, and Australia than it does in New Zealand, in the latter context, Kukutai nevertheless notes the interplay between individual self-identification and official categorization in the construction and analysis of Māori population changes over time. As we explain later, this ethnic mobility is strongly affiliated with powerful processes of interculturality that mark urban Indigenous social relations.

The "Out of Place"-ness of Urban Indigenous Communities

Perhaps more than any other issue, contributors to this volume explore how urban Indigenous communities do not "fit" into dominant, whitestream (Denis 1997) imaginings about where Indigenous people *really* belong (i.e., in rural areas). And they assess how these elementally powerful – and largely unconscious – perceptions affect governing strategies with respect to these communities. Authorities either presuppose the illegitimacy of these communities or attempt to find in them stereotypical elements deemed sufficiently "different" for governing purposes. With respect to rural reserve communities, bureaucratic constructions of "authentic" Indigeneity are deeply rooted in stereotypes that tether such definitions not to the pristine, precontact existence often discussed in legal discourse, but rather, to definitions and reserve locations constructed by the Indian Act. Whether bureaucrats are aware of it or not, the policies they enact and enforce continue to trade in such currency. This has manifested itself in powerful and largely unacknowledged ways in urban areas.

In a Canadian context, Belanger (Chapter 3) documents how this presupposition of illegitimacy manifests itself in various strategies employed by government agencies in attempts to prevent urban Aboriginal communities from attaining formal, political standing. Although, in the case Belanger discusses, these attempts failed and the judges found that urban Aboriginal communities did constitute a political community for the purposes of attaining and dispensing funding (a decision, Belanger notes, that lacked the teeth it might have had), this case is nonetheless instructive for the extent to which policy makers and service deliverers expressed discomfort with it. This speaks to a broader unease about the tangled legal identities that play out in an urban context (also discussed in Andersen's chapter).

In a New Zealand context, Hokowhitu (Chapter 16) powerfully documents the enormous impact of deeply rooted stereotypes on determinations about the political salience of urban Māori communities. In particular, he explores what he terms the "necropolitical" discourses animating the governance strategies situated around the apparent inability of urban Māori communities to constitute adequate "Treaty Partners." Similarly, Coombes (Chapter 15) explores the ways in which the assumed "out of placeness" of urban Māori in the Otara region of the North Island of New Zealand shaped their (in)ability to resist and to produce recognized forms of self-government in the local context of preventing environmental degradation being caused by regional industrialization. Specific to the New Zealand context, Coombes explains how the particular politics around the inability of local Māori to position themselves as *tangata whenua* (people of the land) resulted in their being denied a place in local and regional resource management policy formation and delivery. As explained further below, interculturality is assumed in a context in which an urban community is unable to demonstrate *tangata whenua*.

In addition to the myriad legal issues that emanate from these stereotypes and the entrenched policy tracks they anchor, other contributors note the various impacts of dominant expectations about the "truth" of Indigeneity. Morgan (Chapter 13), in particular, explores the subtle ways in which, in an urban context, governing authorities tie stereotypes about the (supposed) fundamental *difference* of Indigenous culture to neoliberal discourses about self-sufficiency and an entrepreneurial spirit in the context of encouraging Indigenous youth to emphasize the exotic part of their "selves" to bring in tourist dollars. He argues that such programs assume both an entrepreneurial spirit among Indigenous youth *and* that the pre-packaged and largely de-contextualized notions of culture tied to such tourist economies square with the youths' own understandings of Indigenous culture. Both of these are problematic for obvious reasons, but of particular interest here is the strategic (if largely unconscious) reversal of authenticity: instead of attempting to position these Indigenous youth as "out of place," government efforts are dedicated to attempting to make these Indigenous subjects "fit" such de-contextualized and (thus) reconstituted notions of Indigenous authenticity.

The Distinct Interculturality of Urban Indigenous Life
A third broad similarity between the contributions to this volume is their emphasis on the interculturality of urban Indigenous life. Indeed, they note that part of what renders constructions of urban Indigenous authenticity problematic is an emphasis on its supposed interculturality. The point is that, since urban Indigenous residents are always already positioned as less authentic than their rural counterparts, many (including Indigenous people) look for – and thus find – interculturality in urban spaces when, given a more critical lens, it might be equally apparent in rural places.

Having said that, even critical evaluations of dominant constructions of Indigenous authenticity are necessarily tethered to the processes of modernity that cities are thought to typify. In this context, various contributors note the "pitch" of this interculturality and the discursive and material pre-suppositions it is forced to straddle – a pitch that retains a startling familiarity regardless of the temporal or geographical diversity of empirical subject matter. In other words, specific features of the city, and of particular cities (whether physical or otherwise), take on cultural meanings derived from urban Indigenous relationships.

One of the more obvious manifestations of interculturality is found in the migration of individuals and families from a diversity of Indigenous backgrounds into "new" geographical and cultural spaces. Unlike their home communities (whether reserves/reservations, small towns, or rural locales), urban Indigenous communities are constituted by a mélange of Indigenous customs, traditions, conventions, and languages. Given that the governments of each nation-state whose policies we explore engaged in similar policies and planning regarding the value of urbanizing Indigenous people(s), this should come as no surprise. As Morgan (2008) argues, urban Indigenous communities mimic precisely neither the expectations of formal government policy – the settlement patterns and adaptive strategies of other "othered" communities (like those of immigrants) – nor, least of all, the culture of largely white communities that preceded their urban presence.

Nearly all the contributors emphasize this interculturality. In a Canadian context, Andersen (Chapter 2) explores the features of urban Aboriginal identities that distinguish them from their rural or reserve counterparts, including (but not limited to) the interculturality of legal status, national/ cultural background, socio-demographic characteristics, and the particular policy relations history distinctive to specific cities. Walker (Chapter 7) and Ouart (Chapter 6) similarly point out the city-specific distinctiveness of urban Aboriginal policy relations, a point that broadly mirrors previous literature that explores the city-distinctiveness of urban Indigenous policy making (while this literature does not make this precise point, it is nonetheless extractable from its discussions of the city studied [i.e., Saskatoon]). Belanger (Chapter 3) explores the extent to which the Canadian courts attempted to come to grips with a conception of Aboriginal community that did not seem to fit the pre-existing mould to which they had become accustomed. In this context, various policy actors attempted to utilize the apparent interculturality of the urban Aboriginal community as a marker of its *in*authenticity (while First Nations people living on reserves are arguably every bit as intercultural as those living in urban communities, such discussions are rarely raised since their juridical – and policy – legitimacy is largely taken for granted).

In an American context, Johnson (Chapter 10) discusses the role that urban powwows play in building and maintaining a sense of community among urban Indigenous residents. Like rural powwows, urban powwows represent a distinct amalgamation of various Indigenous nations and, like much of urban Indigenous culture, are more than the sum of their parts.

Like Johnson, Lucero (Chapter 9) is attuned to the interculturality of her research informants' experiences, particularly with regard to their "urban-ness" intergenerationally in the changing milieu of Denver, Colorado. What is particularly interesting about Lucero's discussion is her careful explora-tion of the intergenerational differences in the context and meaning of an urban American Indian community as well as of the powerful ways in which migration to (rather than being raised in) an urban community shapes per-ceptions about what it means to be an American Indian (whether tribally specific or not, and particularly in the context of "internal" rather than "ex-ternal" validation).

In Australia, all of the contributors (Morgan, Taylor, and Greenop and Memmott) note both the problems and the promise of the interculturality of urban Indigenous life. As noted earlier, Morgan explores the gap be-tween the lived realities for many Indigenous youth (produced in the specific, intercultural "gravitational pull" of the community of Redfern) and the pre-packaged and (thus) highly processed strands of Indigenous cul-ture favoured by neoliberal employment programs. Similarly, while Taylor's (Chapter 11) demographic depiction of Indigenous migration in Australia points out that not only are urban Indigenous populations similar to those of their jurisdictional "country areas" but they also, in many cases, consist of the same people (who move back in forth over the course of their lives). Such a finding ironically bolsters the claim that urban Indigenous life is dis-tinctive from that found in smaller towns and rural areas. After all, motiva-tion to move from one location to another is conventionally said to be shaped by a series of complex push-pull factors (kinship connections, em-ployment, education opportunities, etc.). This is really just another word for "culture": as people move from one geographical and cultural space to an-other, they become immersed in the specific culture of that space.

Greenop and Memmott (Chapter 12) carefully trace the rise of an urban Indigenous presence in the City of Brisbane. More specifically, they explore the "mutually constitutive" nature of Indigenous and non-Indigenous rela-tions in the city, the interculturality produced in the wake of such relations (a point raised, in a Canadian context, in Walker's and Ouart's discussion of a normatively co-productive ethos), and the persistence of kinship taxono-mies and feelings of responsibility to those so classified. These have mani-fested themselves in ways distinctive to the Brisbane urban Indigenous community, as have various ceremonial processes for expressing relationship to land and territory that can be either tribally specific or pan-Indigenous, depending on the context.

Finally, the New Zealand contributions present a specific – and fairly distinctive – context for understanding interculturality. Each of the contributors (Hokowhitu, Coombs, and Kukutai) highlight the power of invoking the concept of *tengata whenua* (people of the land), and the ways in which this evocation has functioned as a double-edged sword for those who, while Māori, are not from a local *iwi* (tribe). The concept is double edged in the sense that, for those who are able to demonstrate their *tengata whenua* status, certain political privileges accrue according to whitestream governing authorities. Conversely, an inability to demonstrate such status is often utilized to delegitimize one's struggles. In any case, Kukutai (Chapter 14) notes the powerful role played by urbanization in the creation of a distinctive (i.e., intercultural) *pan-tribal* collective Māori identity (a similar point is made in Lucero's and Johnson's chapters). This pan-Māori identity was harnessed in the context of grassroots activism in pursuit of Māori Indigenous rights. Kukutai notes the central role urban activists played in the creation of Māori as an officially recognized language and the creation of Māori language-based tertiary education. Perhaps most extensively, she documents the extent to which such intercultural differences are manifested in the socio-demographic characteristics of the urban Māori population.

Like Kukutai, Hokowhitu (Chapter 16) explores the rise of distinctively urban forms of Māori identity. Unlike Kukutai, however, Hokowhitu's major challenge is to understand the persistence of urban Māori communities (which, by their very definition, are intercultural) in light of the conflicting dynamics of what he terms "bio-" and "necro-politics." For Hokowhitu, what is important in this dynamic is the ways in which retribalized entities have risen to the crest as political actors in the larger New Zealand political scene. Hokowhitu explores the extent to which the interculturalty of urban Māori identity (manifested in its pan-identity and non-*tengata whenua*-based politics) limits its ability to be understood as a major political player – not only by the whitestream "powers that be" but also by other Māori tribal actors. His purpose is not to vilify one side and valorize the other but, rather, to trace the larger optics within which these protracted debates play out. For Hokowhitu, a critical self-awareness about the ultimate arbitrariness of *either* account is central to producing a compassionate agonism that will produce a politics sensitive to both. In a similar way, Coombes (Chapter 15) traces the ways in which interculturality (again, tacitly, as something other than *tengata fenua*) is positioned as a harbinger of inauthenticity in the context of "socio-ecological relations." And, while he holds out hope for how future relations might better account for the voices of urban Māori/

"mixed" communities in this context, current relations do little to foster such a relationship.

Continuity between Urban/Non-Urban Locales

Perhaps one of the most direct ways that contributors to this volume speak to the larger question of indigenizing modernity, most recently inaugurated by Sahlins, is through their emphasis on the fact that, ironically, part of the distinctiveness of urban Indigenous communities lies in the connections they retain to non-urban spaces (connections that, of course, are closely linked to the interculturality we just discussed). The bulk of the contributors emphasize, in one way or another, the continued connections between urban and non-urban Indigenous kin and community. In a New Zealand context, for example, through a demographic analysis, Kukutai challenges whether simplistic rural/urban binaries adequately capture the flavour and richness of "urban Māori realities." Both Hokowhitu and Coombes similarly challenge governing authorities' attempts to delegitimize Māori political power by creating a binary between "authentic" communities (*tengata whenua*) and "inauthentic" communities (urban communities), as though the former were a natural entity rather than something produced in the interstices of centuries of colonialism.

The Australian contributors in particular seek to demonstrate the continued links between urban Indigenous communities in Australia's cities and those of many of their kin still living in less urban (i.e., smaller towns) and more rural areas. In particular, Taylor, Greenop and Memmot, and Morgan speak to the importance of "chain migration" as an Indigenous strategy for moving into Australia's cities. Significantly, however, the discussions of chain migration are not offered as a critique of the legitimacy of urban Indigenous communities in Australia (Greenop and Memmot, in particular, note the subtle ways in which an Indigenous sense of place – of home – is mediated in and by the realities of urban life) but, rather, to show the complexity of Indigenous kinship and to offer a cultural/political, rather than a merely geographical, understanding of community. Indeed, as we noted earlier, Taylor goes so far as to suggest that the urban and non-urban communities are not simply similar: in some cases they are the same people/families.

In an American context, Johnson explains how – and the extent to which – American Indians moved into urban spaces, bringing cultural elements with them. For Johnson, the physical and cultural space of the powwow allows him (as it does others) to "express identity" and to "create meeting

places far from home." His phrasing obviously speaks not to a physical representation of home (since urban American Indians have being living in cities for decades) but, rather, to the extent to which powwows allow him to
"carry home" with him. In a similar way, Lucero notes the challenges to
American Indian identity faced by third- and fourth-generation American
Indians living in Denver – challenges they felt were not faced by those who
grew up on a reservation, even if they eventually moved to a city. Lucero also
shows that, given the limited extent to which third- and fourth-generation
urban American Indians are likely to have first-hand knowledge about reservations, their understandings of "real" Indians are shaped by powerful
forms of *nostalgia*.

In a Canadian context, Andersen notes that an important element in
understanding the complexity of urban Aboriginal communities is the extent to which attachments to non-urban communities continue to shape the
context through which everyday life is negotiated. Demographically, Norris,
Clatworthy, and Peters speak of the "hypermobility" (the phenomenon of
Aboriginal residents' moving more quickly than census enumeration can
capture) of urban Aboriginal residents. Certainly, some of this mobility is
contained within or even between urban areas. But much of it also takes
place between urban and non-urban locales (like smaller towns and reserves). Similarly, in his analysis of urban Métis identity in Saskatoon,
Saskatchewan, Laliberte anecdotally notes the extent to which Métis differ-
entiated between their urban residence and their community of origin. Even
Walker, in his discussion of policy making in Winnipeg, notes the political
power of Aboriginal organizations whose constituencies are not just urban
Aboriginals but also those from non-urban areas and reserves.

We conclude by restating what we hope is by now an obvious point: while
complex in their local idiosyncrasies, urban Indigenous identities are part of
broader global processes that have produced a number of broadly similar
patterns. These include the difficulties their complexity poses to measurement; the powerful stereotypes that anchor official designations of Indigenous identity and the limitations these stereotypes impose on urban
Indigenous aspirations; the ways in which urban Indigenous communities
serve as an engine of Indigenous cultural production (and the intercultural-
ities within which it is nested); and, finally, the undeniable attachments between urban and non-urban Indigenous locales that continue to shape, in a
mutually (though unequally) constitutive manner, the institutional structures and lived experiences of both communities.

Ultimately, the power of urban Indigenous identities lies in their ability to transgress the classic rural/urban binaries that underlie much of the last two hundred-plus years of research on or about (though rarely with) Indigenous communities. While research relating to urban Indigenous identities has probably been no less immune to these gaps, fissures, and limitations, it has nonetheless forged ahead as a distinctive object of research related to, but not defined or limited by, previous research on non-urban communities. The chapters in this book provide – in rich, idiosyncratic, empirical detail – a novel and theoretically sophisticated analysis of the complex phenomenon of urban Indigenous identity. What they collectively demonstrate is that much more research on this phenomenon needs to be undertaken.

References

Denis, C. 1997. *We are not you: First Nations and Canadian modernity.* Peterborough, ON: Broadview Press.

Morgan, G. 2008. Aboriginal migration to Sydney since World War II. *Sydney Journal* 1(3): 75-82.

Peters, E.J. 2002. "Our City Indians": Negotiating the meaning of First Nations urbanization in Canada, 1945-1975. *Historical Geography* 30: 75-92.

Contributors

Chris Andersen (PhD) is Michif (Métis) and an associate professor in the Faculty of Native Studies at the University of Alberta. From a research perspective, he is interested in the ways in which the Canadian nation-state has created "identity" categories relating to Aboriginal communities and, in particular, the term "Métis." He has been on a number of national academic award adjudication committees, is a member of Statistics Canada's Advisory Committee on Social Conditions, a member of the Office of the Federal Interlocutor for Métis and Non-Status Indians Research Advisory Circle, the co-chair of the Urban Aboriginal Strategy's Wicihitowin Research Action Circle, and, most recently, the editor of the new journal *Aboriginal Policy Studies.*

Yale D. Belanger (PhD) is an associate professor of Native American Studies and an adjunct associate professor with the Faculty of Health Sciences at the University of Lethbridge. He is a member of the Alberta Homelessness Research Consortium (AHRC), a member of the Canadian Homelessness Research Network (CHRN), and an editorial board member of the Australia Housing and Urban Research Institute (AHURI).

Stewart J. Clatworthy is the owner and principal researcher of Four Directions Project Consultants, a Winnipeg-based consulting firm specializing in demographic and socio-economic research, information systems development, and program evaluation. Since 1980, he has been active in Aboriginal research and has completed numerous studies on demography and migration, population, membership and student enrolment projections, and socio-economic, housing, and employment conditions. Through this research, he has gained a national reputation as a leading scholar of Canadian Aboriginal socio-economic and demographic circumstances.

Brad Coombes (Kati Mamoe, Ngati Kahungunu) is a senior lecturer in the School of Environment, University of Auckland, New Zealand. His research explores the intersections among environmental justice, postcolonial politics, and Indigenous rights. He is currently the co-director of Te Whare Kura: Indigenous Knowledges, Peoples, and Identities, a thematic research initiative that brings together 180 Maori and Pacific faculty of his university in collaborative research projects. He is also the chair of the Indigenous Knowledges, Peoples, and Rights Commission of the International Geographical Union.

Kelly Greenop completed a bachelor of architecture degree at the University of Queensland in 1996, with a major theme of her studies being Indigenous place and architecture in Australia. She is nearing completion of her PhD at the Aboriginal Environments Research Centre in the School of Architecture at the University of Queensland; her research examines the relationship between Indigenous people and place in urban Brisbane through a case study of Inala, an Indigenous "centre" in Brisbane's southwestern suburbs. She has undertaken fieldwork with Indigenous people in urban areas of South East Queensland since 2005.

Brendan Hokowhitu is of Ngāti Pukenga descent, an iwi (people) from Aotearoa/New Zealand. He is the dean of and a professor in the Faculty of Native Studies at the University of Alberta in Edmonton. His research interests include Indigenous critical theory, masculinity, media, and sport.

Jay T. Johnson is an assistant professor of geography and Indigenous studies at the University of Kansas. His research interests concern the broad area of Indigenous peoples' cultural survival, with specific regard to the areas of resource management, political activism at national and international levels, and the philosophies and politics of place that underpin the drive for cultural survival. Much of his work is comparative but has focused on New Zealand and North America.

Tahu Kukutai (Waikato-Tainui, Ngāti Maniapoto, Te Aupōuri) is a senior research fellow at the National Institute of Demographic and Economic Analysis at the University of Waikato. Tahu specializes in Māori and Indigenous population research and has written extensively on issues of Māori identity, inequality, and population change for New Zealand and international audiences. Tahu serves on the Statistics New Zealand Māori Statistics Advisory Committee, the Population Association of New Zealand Council, and the Māori Association of Social Science Executive.

Carol Lafond is a member of the Muskeg Lake Cree Nations, where she is the director of health and social development. She received her BEd from the University of Saskatchewan and has held positions with the Saskatoon Tribal Council and the Federation of Saskatchewan Indian Nations. In her present position, she focuses on encouraging community members to be miyo-mah-chi-ho-win – living well.

Ron Laliberte (PhD) is Métis and was born in Prince Albert, Saskatchewan. He is an assistant professor in the Department of Native Studies at the University of Saskatchewan. His research interests include Métis issues and history, Aboriginal labour in western Canada, the history of the sugar beet industry in southern Alberta, and theoretical perspectives on migrant labour forces.

Nancy M. Lucero (PhD, LCSW, Mississippi Choctaw) is an assistant professor of social work at Colorado State University – Pueblo and is an affiliated researcher with the Butler Institute for Families at the University of Denver Graduate School of Social Work. Her research examines cultural identity and cultural connectedness among urban-based American Indians, urban Indian Child Welfare (ICW) interventions and service delivery systems, and the treatment of caregiver trauma to improve ICW case outcomes.

Paul Memmott is a multidisciplinary researcher (architect/anthropologist) and the director of the Aboriginal Environments Research Centre (AERC) at the University of Queensland, Brisbane. He has half-time positions in both the School of Architecture and the Institute for Social Science Research (ISSR). The AERC field of research encompasses the cross-cultural study of the people-environment relations of Indigenous peoples with their natural and built environments. His research interests encompass Aboriginal housing and settlement design, Aboriginal access to institutional architecture,

Indigenous constructs of place and cultural heritage, vernacular architecture and Native title, social planning in Indigenous communities, and sustainable remote area buildings and villages.

George Morgan is a researcher at the Institute for Culture and Society at the University of Western Sydney. His books include (as sole author) *Unsettled Places: Aboriginal People and Urbanisation in New South Wales* (Wakefield Press, 2006) and (as editor with Scott Poynting) *Outrageous: Moral Panics in Australia* (ACYS Press, 2007) and *Global Islamophobia* (Ashgate, 2012).

Mary Jane Norris is a demographer and consultant who has specialized in Aboriginal research over the past thirty-five years and has held a number of senior research positions within the federal government of Canada, including Indian and Northern Affairs Canada, Statistics Canada, and Canadian Heritage. Her areas of research and publication include Aboriginal languages and demography, including mobility and migration, urbanization, population projections, and the demographics of languages. Of mixed Aboriginal and non-Aboriginal ancestry, she is an off-reserve Registered Indian member of the Algonquins of Pikwákanagán (Golden Lake) in the Ottawa Valley. She holds a master's degree in sociology and a BA Honours degree in sociology and economics from Carleton University.

Pam Ouart is a PhD student at Trent University in the Indigenous Studies Department. The research presented in this volume was part of her master's degree from the University of Saskatchewan. She would like to thank the Saskatoon Indian and Métis Friendship Centre for all of the time and knowledge that they shared.

Evelyn Peters is a professor and Canada Research Chair in urban and inner-city studies at the University of Winnipeg. Her research has focused on working with a variety of urban Aboriginal and government organizations on issues facing First Nations and Métis people in cities.

C. Matthew Snipp is the Burnet C. and Mildred Finley Wohlford professor of humanities and sciences in the Department of Sociology at Stanford University. He is also the chair of Native American Studies and the deputy director of the Institute for Research in the Social Sciences. His tribal heritage is Oklahoma Cherokee and Choctaw.

John Taylor is a professor in and the director of the Centre for Aboriginal Economic Policy Research at the Australian National University. For the past twenty-five years, he has conducted research on demographic, social, and economic change among Indigenous Australians and has published widely on these issues in Australian and international books and journals. He is a member of the Australian Bureau of Statistics Advisory Group on Aboriginal and Torres Strait Islander Statistics, a member of the Expert Group on Aboriginal and Torres Strait Islander Statistics, and a board member of the Australian government's Closing the Gap Clearinghouse. He has been prominent in demonstrating the application of demographic analysis to Indigenous policy.

Ryan Walker is an associate professor in the Department of Geography and Planning at the University of Saskatchewan. He is director of the Prairie Research Centre in the Urban Aboriginal Knowledge Network and past chair of the university's Regional and Urban Planning Program.

Index

Foucault, Michel: on disciplinary coercions to guarantee cohesion of social body, 368; on neocolonial context for Indigenous people, 355; on power as relationship, 361; on "truth" in *Archaeology of Knowledge*, 356
Fredericks, Bronwyn, 113
Fresno (US), 185

Gabriel Dumont Institute (Canada), 124
Gadigal people (Australia), 298
George, Pamela, 53
Gerbasi, Jenny, 153, 154
Ghost Dance, 222
GI Bill (US), 176
Giorgi, Amadeo, 198-99
Goldie, Terry, 5
Goodale, Ralph, 158
Grass Dance, 222
Growing Together: Youth Helping Youth Mentorship Program (Canada), 159
Gull Bay First Nation (Ontario), 75

Hall, Stuart, 48-51
Hamer, David, 4
Hamilton (New Zealand), 327
Hanselmann, Calvin, 56
Hapi, Robin, 368-69
Harris, Aroha, 360
Harvard Project on American Indian Economic Development (US), 84
Haskell Indian Nations University (US), 222
Haudenosaunee. *See* Iroquois Confederacy (Canada)
Hawthorn Report (Canada, 1966-67), 24, 307
He Taua (New Zealand), 360
Heartbeat of the People: Music and Dance of the Northern Pow-Wow (Browner), 221
Hickey, TJ, 235, 285
homelands, Indigenous: as access to culturally specific services, 25;

Australia, circular mobility, from city to homelands and back, 235, 245, 262, 291-92; and circular migration of some urban Indigenous residents, 7; as larger territories which include contemporary urban settlements, 7-8; New Zealand, and urban Māori Aboriginal rights, 71; preoccupation with relationship to, as deflecting from Indigenous identity expression in contemporary urban settlements, 9. *See also* authenticity, of Indigenous cultures; migration, Indigenous
Honolulu (US), 183, 185
Honolulu Intertribal powwow, 217
hooks, bell, 104-5
housing, Indigenous: Australia, choices based on kinship and community, 258, 260, 261, 269, 273, 274, 276, 283, 284; Australia, discrimination against Aboriginal tenants, 270; Australia, migration and housing programs, 5, 233, 234, 240, 245, 246, 247, 259; Australia, organizations providing, 284-85; Canada, discrimination against Aboriginal tenants, 53, 93, 107; Canada, Métis struggle for, 126, 128; Canada, organizations providing, 62, 141, 142, 153; Canada, poverty and marginalization, 112; New Zealand, and power station siting plans, 335, 340-42, 346, 350-51; New Zealand, as vehicle for assimilation policies, 316. 357, 358, 378; New Zealand, discrimination against Aboriginal tenants, 317; US, as vehicle for assimilation policies, 170, 177
Houston (US), 185
Howard, Heather, 9
Hudson's Bay Company (HBC), 115
Hui Ara Ahu Whakamua conference (New Zealand, 1994), 371
Human Resources and Skills Development Canada (HRSDC): and *Canada v. Misquadis* ruling, on access to

Printed and bound in Canada by Friesens

Set in Segoe and Warnock by Artegraphica Design Co. Ltd.

Copy editor: Joanne Richardson

Proofreader: Dianne Tiefensee

Indexer: Annette Lorek